THE DEATH OF ENDLESS DAMNATION

The Death of Endless Damnation

Terry Lee Miller, Sr.

DISCLAIMER:

LET THE READER BE AWARE THAT THIS ASSOCIATION FIRMLY HOLDS THAT THE SCRIPTURES ARE ABUNDANTLY CLEAR THAT THERE IS NO SALVATION OUTSIDE OF THE NEW BIRTH INTO THE FAMILY OF GOD BY REPENTANCE AND FAITH IN GOD OUR SAVIOR THE LORD JESUS CHRIST. THIS ASSOCIATION ALSO HOLDS THAT THE SCRIPTURES TEACH EVENTUAL UNIVERSAL SALVATION FOR ALL MEN, "...AND EVERY KNEE SHALL BOW AND EVERY TONGUE SHALL CONFESS THAT JESUS CHRIST IS LORD TO THE GLORY OF GOD THE FATHER." WHILE IT IS NOT CLAIMED THAT THESE PAPERS ANSWER ALL QUESTIONS REGARDING POST MORTEM PUNISHMENT AND EVENTUAL UNIVERSAL SALVATION FOR ALL (AFTER THE WHITE THRONE JUDGMENT REV.21:4), THE FACT REMAINS THAT THEY CLEARLY SHOW THAT GOD IS THE ULTIMATE VICTOR OVER DEATH SIN HELL AND THE GRAVE. FURTHERMORE IT MUST BE REMEMBERED THAT THERE IS TERRIBLE SUFFERING IN PARTS OF HELL IN WHICH THE DESERVING UNSAVED DEAD CONSCIOUSLY SUFFER FOR THEIR SINS, AND AS WELL A REAL LITERAL HEAVEN INTO WHICH ONLY THEY THAT ARE TRULY BORN AGAIN CAN ENTER THEREIN. LASTLY, WE HOLD ABSOLUTELY NO ILL WILL TOWARDS THOSE WE TERM AS 'FUNDAMENTALIST DAMNATIONISTS,' BUT RATHER SEE THOSE WHO ARE DEDICATED TO THIS POSITION AS GOOD AND GODLY PEOPLE, BUT PEOPLE WHO ARE DECEIVED AND MISLED BY AUGUSTINIAN SO CALLED SCHOLARS. IT CAN TRULY BE SAID THAT THE STRONGEST AND MOST DEDICATED FUNDAMENTALIST DAMNATIONISTS CHURCHES USUALLY ARE THE STRONGEST AND BEST SOULWINNING CHURCHES, WITH THE MOST WONDERFUL DEDICATED PARISHONERS. THEY ARE USUALLY THE INDEPENDENT/BIBLE/BAPTIST/SOUTHERN BAPTIST PERSUASION. HOW MUCH MORE COULD THEY ACCOMPLISH FOR THE LORD, IF THEY WERE ONLY TO COME TO SEE THE TRUTH OF EVENTUAL UNIVERSAL RECONCILLIATION AND SALVATION FOR ALL MANKIND. ONE LAST WORD OF WARNING. THOSE WHO HAVE BEEN FIRMLY ENTRENCHED IN DAMNATIONISM AND READING THIS BOOK WILL FIND THEMSELVES GREIVED AND AGITATED, FROM HAVING THEIR UNDERSTANDING OF ENDLESS DAMNATION BEING CHALLANGED AND SCRIPTURALLY OVERTHROWN. WE INVITE THOSE WHO DISAGREE WITH THESE BIBLICAL FACTS TO SCRIPTURALLY REFUTE THEM, BUT THAT CANNOT BE DONE. WE ARE HONOR BOUND TO STAND ON TRUTH, NOT ON NEARLY 1500 YEARS OF AUGUSTINIAN CORRUPTION OF GOD'S WORD. OUR MOTTO PROUDLY STANDS, "TRUTH WILL STAND EXAMINATION

Copyright © 2015, 2025. All rights reserved. Rev. Terry Lee Miller Sr. D.MIN.
Christian Universal Redemption Baptist Association • C.U.R.B.A.

Published by Eternity Publications, 1252 Sessions Rd. Elgin, S.C. 29045. U.S.A.

Paperback ISBN 978-0-692-48808-9

THIS DOCUMENT MAY NOT BE REPRODUCED IN ANY MANNER WITHOUT EXPRESS PERMISSION FROM TERRY LEE MILLER SR. OR HEIR.

This book was printed in the United States of America.

Monstrous Betrayal of the Centuries Exposed!

Within these pages the Fundamentalist Damnationist Movement is shown to betray the New Testament Church and the Biblical Doctrine of Universal Christian Redemption to promote the Augustinian/Romish false doctrine of hideous merciless and endless punishment in the Lake of Fire for All of Eternity.

Terry Lee Miller Sr.

George Hawtin has so aptly written: "Is it any wonder that in the face of such sadistic humbug there has been a wholesale manufacture of infidels? All these statements (by eternal Hell-fire preachers) may be a show of oratorical eloquence, but they are nothing more. They hold no part of truth. They deny every attribute of God. They make wisdom foolishness, turn eternal love into exasperated hate, make omnipotence helplessness, and make the justice of God the grossest injustice in the universe. To say that I believe in such repugnance would be a lie of the first order. I do not believe it because it is contrary to the nature of God. It is contrary to the love of God. It is contrary to the justice of God. It is contrary to the power of God. It is contrary to the Word of God and it puts God in the ridiculous position of being the almighty King of kings and Lord of lords yet having dominion a vast pocket of hate and resistance that even He cannot overcome. Further than this it makes the mighty sacrifice of Christ that was made for all the world to be almost impotent in its power and scope. Worst of all, it frustrates the purpose of God laid down in the beginning when He said, 'Let us make man in our image and after our likeness.' Some will immediately ask me whether I do not believe in Hell. My answer is very definite on this point. I most certainly DO BELIEVE in Hell, but the Hell of the Bible and the Hell of human tradition is not the same thing at all. The Hell of tradition is hopeless and eternal, while the Hell of the Scripture like every judgment of God is corrective, remedial, and restorative." -end quote. If only one truth can be learned from this book it will be worth it all and that is, 'continuous is not endless, and endless is not continuous.

DEDICATION

This book is dedicated to those early Christians who held to universal Christian redemption for the first five hundred years or so of church history. Unfortunately Augustinianism came to overthrow this truth held by these early saints, those who often gave their lives to protect and promote New Testament Biblical truth. May the Lord use this humble book to reestablish the truth that God is not willing that any should perish but that all men should come to repentance. It must be remembered that true justice always works hand in hand with mercy. Justice cannot be administered for eternity without mercy!

Continuous is not endless and endless is not continuous!

Aionios is not aidios and aidios is not aionios

Truth will stand examination!

IN GOOD CONSCIENCE

Having been an 'endless damnationist' for over 50 years, this author felt it imperative to have men with much more highly earned theological credentials to at least examine this book if in but nothing more than a quick review to evaluate this theological position as to Biblical soundness. Having studied and writing on this subject for over five years, and carefully using the Greek word studies of Greek scholar J.W. Hanson, etc., I wanted to get feedback to find any possible doctrinal error this work may be involved in. We electronically sent out dozens and dozens of these books to institutions such as Liberty Baptist College, Lynchburg Va., Dallas Theological Seminary etc., asking these men to give us a brief theological review, and that if this book "The Death of Endless Damnation," (quoting Dr. J.W. Hanson Greek scholar chapter 8) could not be shown to be in error that it would be printed. To my utter amazement absolutely not one review was returned, not even a single paragraph. The only one to respond was (an endless damnationist) Dr.William P. Welty Ph.D. executive director of ISV Foundation. His only concern was whether or not I had sufficient training in the original languages. He said as follows:

"Would you mind responding by informing me what training you have had in biblical languages that leads you to this conclusion? Knowing the degree of your proficiency in these languages will help me respond to your inquiry. Absent you sending an answer to the above question, I'm limited in how I can respond cogently to your inquiry." *As well without even reading the booklet, or skimming it he said, "…. She (a Mrs. Harris) is* as biblically wrong and misinformed on the subject of her presentation as are those who hold to the 'death of endless damnation' (your term, not mine) view." End of quote. *(Interesting that he disagreed with the book without even reading it. To this author at least, it seems Dr. Welty is more interested in exalting education levels over doctrinal soundness!)*

Once I answered him, plainly explaining my education (which admittedly is inferior to his), that I was not a Greek scholar but a student of the Word of God for over 50 years and a theological school grad, he refused to answer in any fashion. It well appears that he as most others have taken the position, "Don't confuse me with the facts, I have already made up my mind." Sadly, it is evident that the body of Christ has been mentally enslaved to Augustinianism's endless damnationism and blinded to Universal Christian Redemption by corrupted Greek/Hebrew word studies, and a misunderstanding of some old English terms in the K.J.V. versions (which terms are *not* clearly translated from the original languages). May God deliver us is our prayer.

PREFACE

Universal Christian redemption teaches all will be saved between birth and death in this life and none will go to Hell/Lake of Fire???

The above statement is absolutely false! The above statement reflects the gross ignorance of nearly all who hold to the 'Endless Damnation/Hell Fire Brimstone' false theology. The doctrine of Universal Christian Redemption as clearly taught in the Word of God teaches no such thing. U.C.R. teaches after death all lost souls will go to Hell then later to the Lake of Fire to be thoroughly punished and humiliated for their wickedness and sins. U.C.R. does *not* teach that there is salvation available after death, while in Hell/Lake of Fire. It does however teach that there is salvation for the wicked after having received newly resurrected bodies, and then after being punished in the L.O.F bending their knees and confessing unto salvation.

Yes, they will have bodies which will live for eternity in the grace and favor of God after having been 'punished according to their works in the Lake of Fire and Brimstone and then becoming born again. Remember, *'Every knee shall bow, and every tongue shall confess that Jesus Christ is Lord to the glory of God the Father!'* (Phil. 2:10-11). Revelation 21 plainly teaches that 'the former things will pass away' that *there will be no more sin, death, sorrow or suffering proving the Lake of Fire, the old Heaven and Earth will pass away, and there will be a new Heaven and Earth.* We challenge any reader of God's word to refute and disprove the following: (Quoting pg. 23 point 10)

"We would challenge any one, to show one verse in Revelation 20 which indicates that those who are cast into the Lake of Fire, are sent there forever/endlessly for eternity! Quite on the contrary. It must be noted that the unsaved dead are judged *according to their works!* Their works were only temporal, during their lifetime, and justice cannot be served to punish someone for endless eternity for temporal works. Their punishment will be proportional to their works, forever and forever, "aionios ton aionios" *(the original Greek, means continuous/unknown duration NOT 'aidios' or 'endless')* with no indication of length of suffering since sentences will vary according to wickedness. Chapter 21 gives the plain and simple truth that once the Lake of Fire has fulfilled its purpose; it will be obsolete and done away with, being part of the first heaven and the first earth. Eternal justice cannot exist without eternal mercy!"

Rev. 21:1-4

"Now I saw a new heaven and a new earth, for the first heaven and the first earth had passed away. Also there was no more sea… And I heard a loud voice from heaven saying, Behold the tabernacle of God is with men, and He will dwell with them, and they shall be His people. God Himself will be with them and he their God, and God shall wipe away every tear from their eyes, *there shall be no more death, nor sorrow, nor crying. There shall be no more pain, for the former things have passed away."*

(Damnationists say there will be death and pain for endless eternity for a majority of humanity which clearly contradicts vs.4.)"

Christendom today is so polluted with the sadist doctrine of endless torment and damnation at the hands of a defeated god, that books such as this are easily scorned and relegated to being placed on the 'book burning list.' We challenge theologians or laymen, to refute the contents of this book, carefully and thoughtfully, but that will not be, nor can be done. Truth will reign supreme, and truth will stand examination. The false doctrine of endless damnation in Hell-fire and brimstone at the hands of a sadist dysfunctional god must be defeated. When will the fundamental church begin to stand on the Word of God, rather than on false Augustinian theology saying, "Don't confuse me with the facts, I have already made up my mind!"

At the outset it is important to state some incontrovertible facts concerning this subject:

1. If it can be proven that "Aionios" has indeed been mistranslated/misunderstood then that will once and for all prove the character of the Lord has been impugned and maligned by extremely serious misunderstanding of the 1611 K.J.V. and other translations as they relate to punishment of the unsaved after death and as well their salvation. A serious misunderstanding in translation/language usage.

2. That the punishment which the wicked/unsaved will be subjected to, due to misunderstanding in translation, is *not* endless/eternal in duration, but rather *limited*. The torment, anguish, pain and suffering in Hell, leaving an eternal/everlasting imprint of remembrance on the soul however, still honorably stands.

3. That "Aionios" and "Aidios" in the Greek are *not* two identical words, as the translation has not helped the issue, (no doubt under the tutelage of mislead theologians of the 1600's), but rather are "two" separate and distinct Greek words meaning two entirely different things. That "Aionios" in itself and by itself cannot have four five or six different meanings (as nearly all Greek concordances and lexicons falsely claim) such as, "world, age, eternal, endless, everlasting, eternity, forever, never ending etc.

4. That death is *not* the final chapter in man's decision concerning salvation.

5. That the Holy Scriptures, as written and read in the common Greek of Jesus' day do in fact teach the eventual universal salvation of all men, and Christians in the first centuries after Christ commonly held to the same view.

6. That the pagans, and some groups of Jews during the time of Christ did indeed hold to the doctrine of "Aidios" endless punishment of the lost,

7. That Jesus NEVER used the term "Aidios" (endless) for the duration of the punishment of the wicked/lost. Rather He carefully used the term "Aionios" which rightly translated means "ages," or an indefinite/indeterminate/limited period of time.

8. That the 1611 K.J.V. despite its beauty and popularity, is *not* a 100% perfect translation of the originals, but sometimes does need clarification in a small number of places. (Only the Lord can convince the Ruckmanites of this, and that will no doubt be after their demise. Their attitude is, "Don't confuse me with the facts; I've already made up my mind). The K.J.V. is merely "another" translation, one of many which as a vehicle has brought us the Words of God. It is nothing more, or nothing less. It needs to be said here that the "King James Only Version Crowd" are dishonest in their claim to be using the 1611 K.J.V.

Absolutely no one today uses the 1611 K.J.V. Those who do claim so, in reality are using "versions" of the 1611 translation, since it has gone thru a number of "updates and revisions" since that time. Merely looking at an original copy of the 1611 translation shows it is barely understandable in today's English, and as well uses many many antiquated and obsolete old English words, letters and phrases. While the modern 1611 version surely brings us the truth of God and this author uses it constantly, it cannot equal in purity copies of copies of the original Greek and Hebrew manuscripts. The K.J.V. needs to be clarified in some places by the original languages.

Claiming differently is grossly ignorant. (For anyone, such as the Ruckmanites, to say the need for clarification in some places of the K.J.V. is saying that there are errors in the Word of God is grossly ignorant. Anything that is translated from one language to another brings word/word tense problems as well as certain words that have changed in meanings over the centuries or have become obsolete etc. If this author understands the issue, then the Ruckmanites and those following their skewed logic are the ones who are attacking the Word of God since they claim the Greek and Hebrew MS. which are extant are corrupt and not worthy of being called the Word of God.

Though there are small differences in these manuscripts, those differences which arise from copyist errors and errors in translation etc., can be and are resolved by comparison with other reliable texts, so thus establishing a truly valid text, and as well outstanding/reliable English translations thereof. Ruckmanism denies this and always will, and that system of thinking must be avoided at all costs).

9. That wicked men must indeed suffer punishment for their sins, and that being "conscious suffering" in the next life, only stands to common sense/reasoning and of course is supported by the Word of God.

10. That the scriptures absolutely do not teach "eternal/endless death" which of course is the teaching of annihilation, or that the wicked simply "cease to exist" after being cast into the Lake of Fire.

11. That the suffering in Hell is not "sadistically inflicted suffering." No the suffering there is "punishment" to the wicked for their sins, **not** purgation/or cleansing, but yea rather "pay back" to everlastingly teach the wicked that sin cannot be endorsed or tolerated by our Creator, and they must not, nor should have been involved in it.

12. That those who hold the false view that there is no possibility of post-mortem salvation must come to only one of two conclusions. A. That of endless punishment for the unsaved, or B. That of the total annihilation of the wicked/unsaved. No other conclusions are possible.

Common sense, logic, (and of course scripture) cannot be abandoned in considering eternal/endless damnation suffering in Hell fire as do the

Calvinists in saying non-elect babies go to Hell forever, and as well God's sovereignty decides who He will save and who He will damn forever/eternally. As well can we really conceive a God who will one day tell the unsaved the following? "You have been deceived by Satan and false religious leaders, you were raised in ignorance and heathendom and died unsaved in your sins, and even though perhaps no one ever was able to reach you with the truth of the gospel I am consigning you to be tormented in fire and brimstone for endless eternity." Who but those who hold to endless damnation in Hell fire and brimstone could embrace such a concept of God!! As well who else but those who hold the K.J.V. English and misunderstood words as superior to the Greek/Hebrew text?

Reader note: The 1611 K.J.V. 'only' crowd has strained in vain to prove that the version they have exalted to the position of an idol is identical to the original manuscripts in every sense. They are quick to attack anyone who attempts to expose their positions as someone who denies the preservation of the scriptures. Remember, a version/translation of the original languages is never equal in purity to those manuscripts but certainly can preserve and bring to us the perfect truth of the word of God. The false positions of this group have been fully exposed by examining the following web. http://www.bible.ca/b-kjv-only.htm#proof authored by Mr. Steve Rudd.

Reader note: J.W. Hanson wrote: "And let us pause a moment on the brink of our investigation to speak of the utter absurdity of the idea that God has hung the great topic of the immortal welfare of millions of souls on the meaning of a single equivocal word. Had he intended to teach endless punishment by one word, that word would have been so explicit and uniform and frequent that no mortal could mistake its meaning. It would have stood unique and peculiar among words. It would no more be found conveying a limited meaning than is the sacred name of Jehovah applied to any finite being. Instead of denoting every degree of duration, as it does, it never would have meant less than eternity. The thought that God has suspended the question of man's final destiny on such a word (as "Aionios/aion" ed.) would seem too preposterous to be entertained by any reflecting mind, did we not know that such an idea is held by Christians. Endless duration is never expressed or implied in the new/Old Testament by Aión or any of its derivatives. (Ed. to be exactly accurate, the K.J.V.'S terms "everlasting-eternal-forever" Greek aionios/aion, all need to be correctly retranslated as 'continuous' or 'ages and ages with no indication of duration or length' but certainly not 'endless' Greek aidios!)

Disagreeing with Romish/Augustinian Doctrine of Endless Damnation is Uncharitable?

We are now living in an era of extreme pacifist mentality among many Christians. 'Live and let live,' is their basic motto. They want to ignore doctrinal soundness in favor of settling back in the pew to flowery non-confrontational type sermons. Sermons which indicate that all people have a right to their own particular theology and that God is pleased with that and so should we. Now no doubt everyone should have religious freedom, but everyone does not have the right *before God*, and in the light of the firm doctrinal positions of the Bible to believe anything they want about the doctrines of the Word of God. Paul plainly told us the "…time would come when they would not endure *sound doctrine* but heap to themselves teachers having itching ears…" II Tim. 4:3.

Paul also told us he delivered Hymaneaus and Phyletus over to Satan for the destruction of the flesh that they may learn not to blaspheme. I Tim. 1:20 and II Tim. 2:17. These two men had erred and were teaching heresy about the resurrection saying it was past. These pacifists are those who falsely claim that exposing doctrinal differences with Rome is showing hatred and an unchristian attitude. This anti-Christian attitude *they carry* is no doubt demonic, and Paul as well said that even in his day, some were giving heed to '…seducing spirits and doctrines of devils.' I Tim. 4:1. Heresy must therefore be exposed out of love for the truth and love for our Savior.

To say the Augustinian/Roman doctrine of endless damnation really doesn't matter is to endorse the hideous false notion that our blessed Savior the Lord Jesus Christ is a sadist who torments people He is unable to reach in this life with fire and brimstone for eternity. No, absolutely not! He as God the Son will continue with His unlimited resources to woo and win all men to gladly embrace the blood of the cross. Exposing heresy therefore is really glorifying to our Lord in promoting His unconditional love for all of mankind, to the exception of none.

Last Serious Question For The Eternal Damnationist Who Say God Is Going To Burn Lost Souls In Hellfire/Lake of Fire For Eternity

Say our Lord Jesus were hired by you to be warden over Rikers Island (were He still here in bodily form)...the penitentiary for the worst of the worst, the death row cell block. I ask you just what do you as a damnationist say would be the living conditions there in as allowed by Jesus under His watch? Hmmmmm?

* No or little food and water for days and days at a time??

* Unmerciful whippings and beatings for hours and weeks upon weeks??

* Cell temperatures in to the hundreds of degrees constantly??

* Deprivation of sleep and medical treatment??

* Coals of fire over his floors him barefoot and firery brimstone splashed on him at times??

* Never visitation by loved ones but only surrounded by his kind day and night?? Endless suffering??

You Damnationists paint that kind of Jesus over hell and the Lake of fire for eternity, what a blasphemous insult to our Lord Jesus Christ who in love lay down His life a ransom for all!

Jude 3-4

> **Beloved when I gave all diligence to write to you concerning the common salvation, it was needful for me to write to you and exhort you that ye should earnestly contend for the faith, which was once delivered to the saints. For certain men have crept in unawares, who were of old ordained to this condemnation, ungodly men, turning the grace of our God into lasciviousness and denying the only Lord God and our Lord Jesus Christ.**

The bottom line in the debate on "endless punishment" or not, is that if the Hebrew/Greek scriptures do teach "endless punishment" then "eventual universal salvation" cannot stand as true. If indeed the scriptures do or should translate differently than from what they have been, then "endless punishment" falls, and "eventual universal salvation" becomes a reality! Herein lays the real war....a war of who is translating the scriptures correctly! Truth will stand examination! Then lastly the following thoughts must be considered. It is in the light of Golgotha that we see sin as exceedingly sinful, so sinful that nothing less than the death of Jesus, God incarnate, could pay for it.

Let us be careful, lest in thinking we are honoring the atonement, but are actually dishonoring it, by limiting its power to save by teaching that Jesus will fail in His mission as Savior of the world to save all! This makes Him a liar, because He never said, "If I am lifted up I will draw SOME men to myself," or (Jn. 12:32) "I will TRY to draw all men to myself," but, "I WILL draw ALL MEN to myself!" As God He cannot fail! It is imperative to remember that, 'endless is not continuous' and 'continuous is not endless.'

Serious Problems Fundamentalist Damnationists Raise if Eventual Universal Salvation is Indeed False

1. Are we to believe that over the past 6000 years or so of human history, millions upon billions have died having never heard the saving gospel, have never had a chance to reject it and are now going to be tormented in fire and brimstone for eternity? Damnationists say yes!

2. Are we to believe that God has the power to perfectly bring the gospel message to all souls who have ever lived, but has failed/will fail to do so? Damnationists infer yes!

3. Are we to believe that Satan has more inflluence than God, by winning billions upon billions to himself in and by deception (God winning only a sparse few), and causing them to be damned endlessly for eternity in fire and brimstone? Damnationists say yes!

4. Are we to believe the church has the commission to preach the gospel to "every creature" but having failed to do so, now God is going to ignore His own commission and allow those who have never heard to die and be tormented endlessly in fire and brimstone for eternity? Damnationists say yes!

5. Are we to believe that Satan will be able to circumvent the will of God,(which will is that "God is not willing that any should perish, but that all should come to repentance") and make his will reign supreme over God's will for endless eternity by endlessly damning the majority of humanity to torment in fire and brimstone? Damnationists infer such!

6. Does not God's supposed failure to win all of mankind to Himself, and Satan's supposed victory in winning billions upon billions more to himself, make God's will subject to Satan's? Damnationists infer such!

7. If the possibility of 'post mortem' salvation is false, and eternal/endless destiny is determined at death, then God failed in offering salvation to all men since billions have died over the centuries having never heard the true gospel. Damnationists say yes!

8. So an Omnipotent, Omnipresent, Omniscient God is defeated in the end by one of His fallen angelic subjects named Satan, in the deception and eternal endless damnation of billions of souls in Hell-fire for eternity, souls God could have won, but couldn't, wouldn't or didn't. Damnationists say yes!

9. Are we to believe that God refuses to use his Omnipotence to bring the gospel to billions, and thereby forces them to be endlessly consigned to burn in Hell-fire for endless eternity due to satanic delusions and deception? Damnationists say yes!

10. Do not all of the above show a Creator who has failed (will fail) in winning all souls to himself, and has failed to overcome the powers and influence of Satan in the endless damnation of countless precious souls? And does it not show a God who is defeated in the end by Satan? Damnationists infer such!

11. Does not God have enough wisdom to convince the wicked/lost souls who would not, or will not be convinced of the truth in this life so they are totally abandoned beyond hope to burn in Hell fire endlessly for eternity? Does not this contradict Jude 15 which plainly states Jesus will come to "convict/convince" them of the truth? Is He to convict/convince them of the truth only to consign them to endless torment in Hell/the Lake of Fire? Damnationists infer such!

Scriptural Universalism does not violate the doctrine of punishment in Hell or the Lake of Fire, nor does it violate the doctrine of salvation only through God and Savior, the Lord Jesus Christ.

Dangers of "Mainstream" Universalist Theology

In studying the doctrines of "Main Stream Universalists" it soon became apparent that most of them have seriously erred in understanding the reality of a literal burning Hell, and also have "shelved" the most important, or at least a most important aspect of Biblical Christianity, that of personal soul winning and evangelism. This author came up in the atmosphere of the doctrines of eternal/endless damnation for all who were not saved, that coupled with strong evangelistic soul winning services in the local church gave me the utmost concern for lost perishing souls.

To think that a soul could perish at any given moment, and be sent to an endless burning Hell/Lake of Fire gave me a huge burden for lost souls. To think that I could do something to stumble a poor lost soul into such a Hell was a great incentive for holiness of living, and as well for my reaching out with tracts, daily/weekly visitation soul winning and evangelism for all those I could possibly come into contact with. (No matter though, welfare of lost souls must always be of top priority).

It seems that most of the "these Universalists" we have been reading, maybe with the exception of a small few, deny the reality of a literal burning Hell/Lake of Fire, and if they do believe it is literal, they believe it to be some sort of "purifying cleansing" action involving the lost sinner, and not a literal place of pain and suffering in fire affliction and torment. Now to accept the fact that the Bible does indeed teach the eventual universal salvation of all men must not dampen the evangelistic zeal of any dedicated servant of the Lord.

We have aptly proven in this booklet, namely in the section dealing with Luke chap. 16 that Jesus did not intend for the story of the rich man and Lazarus to be taken figuratively or as a parable. No indeed, even though eventual universal salvation is plainly taught in the Word of God, this account should give us that much more incentive to reach the lost with the gospel err it be too late. Remember, that lost and damned soul will surely suffer on and on after death for an indefinite (not endless) period in terrible pain, anguish and isolation!

If we see a poor helpless soul in a burning building, in a sinking vessel, or being attacked and viciously beaten, does not rise in our bosom the utmost desire to reach out and save that soul from pain and suffering? Certainly it does and well it should. But to the Universalist who denies a literal Hell, and holds that his only mission, or his main mission is to spread the doctrine of universal salvation, and the false idea that a literal burning Hell does not really exist except as a parable etc, he has breached the sacred truths in the Word of God, and misunderstood his calling. The pain and suffering lost souls will experience in the next life if they die unsaved is absolutely unfathomable. How heartless and cruel must one be who has no real interest in winning that soul from the wrath of Almighty God in this life, to prevent his suffering in the next.

John tells us, "...Whosoever believeth not the Son shall not see life but the wrath of God abides on him." On the same token, it was sad, upon reading the testimony of a Universalist who used to believe in eternal/endless damnation, and at that time was a dynamic soul winner, passing out tracts and constantly daily preaching and teaching the way of salvation, every day winning or attempting to win the lost. But then, somehow he came upon the doctrine of Universal Salvation, and upon embracing it proceeded to stop his wonderful evangelistic efforts, only to begin to widely promote the doctrine of Universal Salvation!

Is it not plain to see that our Savior came to save mankind from first their sins and secondly the pain, suffering, anguish, isolation and separation from God not only in this life but in the next as well!?

There is a huge difference between Biblical Christian Universal Reconciliation and Unitarian Universalism. The false doctrine of Unitarian Universalism has severely crippled most true evangelical Christians from even remotely considering the possibility of Christian Universal Reconciliation. Unitarianism usually rejects the possibility of a literal Hell, and to embrace the doctrine of Universalism without a literal Hell is a big step down for anyone which can open the door to embrace the false doctrines of Unitarianism/Universalism. If all are going to be saved eventually, without the pain of a literal Hell, then it may not matter what you believe in this life since in the next surely one will find out what the truth really is and be saved.

Unitarian doctrine is just that, believe anything you want, as long as you believe in something, and as well any concept of God you may have is fine. They say all will eventually be saved in the next life regardless of what they believe, and that there is no pain or suffering to fear from punishment for sins in Hell/Lake of Fire. Now that is gross heresy! Interesting it is, that the majority of evangelical Christians look upon U.C.R. (universal Christian redemption) with much disdain and repulse. This author believes the reason for such is that Unitarianism or Universal Unitarianism that deadly heresy has been mistaken as U.C.R. and vice versa.

The primary thought which comes to mind in the average parishioner when someone promotes U.C.R. is that they are teaching everyone is going to be saved and no one needs to worry about going to Hell. Of course that is false. Most shocking is that evangelical Christians, from pastors to seminaries, and from Christian publishers to churches readily accept and promote Calvinism. (Example is Erwin Lutzer pastor of Moody church who is a five point Calvinist, see 'Calvinism the Trojan Horse Within' page 15) and their unscriptural books which promote the horrific idea that God predetermines just who will and who will not be saved according to His own will, and consigns all others (who He could have chosen to be saved but didn't) to be tormented in Hell-fire and brimstone for eternity. (I.e. forced salvation and forced damnation!) So now we have four gods presented to evangelical Christianity, and all four vastly differ one from the other, and only one can be the one and only true God!

1. The god of Calvinism, again the one who sovereignly decides who will be saved and who will not be, giving no regard to the choice man could make. Then he sadistically torments those who he didn't want to save in fire and brimstone for endless eternity.

2. The god of Unitarianism, which saves everyone regardless of their theological belief, as long as they believe in some supreme being,

even those who deny the Deity of Christ. Hell/Lake of Fire to them is only figurative or symbolic and not literal.

3. The god of most evangelical Christians, the god who is only able to win a small minority of souls to himself, and gives up in utter defeat and frustration with those who refuse to accept Christ, and therefore sadistically consigns them to be tortured in endless fire and brimstone. (Torturing them endlessly forever because he couldn't reach them?).

4. The God of U.C.R., the one who cannot be, nor will be defeated by the will of man demon or angel. The all compassionate God who deals justly with *all* of mankind, and finally woos and wins all to saving knowledge of Christ. This God, creator of the type of Hell/Lake of Fire which is curative of rebellion, disciplinary and corrective unto eventual humbling, bending of the knee and new birth unto salvation. As well the God of U.C.R. is the God who in total victory defeats sin, pain, Hell, death and the grave unto a perfected universe where only righteousness reigns, having won all souls to endless salvation.

Here the shocking truth is seen, that evangelical Christians will more readily accept gods 1 and 3 than the true God of 4, which clearly shows the extent of corrupt theological brainwashing! The following question is revealing of the same stupor the modern church is steeped in. Say for instance someone raised in total ignorance of theology is shown the above 4 concepts of God. He is asked which of the four concepts of God he would believe would be the most reasonable concept to define the Creator as according to his God given conscience.

Could he conceivably choose a sadist god, who elects/selects only a small minority for Jesus to save and force them into salvation, consigning the rest of billions and billions to burn endlessly/eternally in torture in Hell-fire? Or would he conceivably choose the god who is all powerful but gives up in frustration and anger on those who are self willed wicked and rebellious, and thereby consigns them to be sadistically tormented endlessly/eternally in Hell-fire and brimstone? The answer should be obvious; he no doubt would choose the all powerful, compassionate Savior Jesus under '4' as the most desirable and reasonable. The one who defeats the final enemy of death, pain suffering and alienation from God by sin, winning all unto Himself, and using every means including the corrective, disciplinary influence of a literal (temporal) Hell/Lake of Fire! Truth must prevail!

Endlessly Damned for Violation of Conscience?

Romans chapters 1-2, as well as many other references, make it perfectly clear that while heathen may not have the Word of God, they none the less *are* responsible for their actions, and *do* become guilty before God for their sins. Naturally the question arises that if they do die in such condition, without having ever heard the gospel, and if "…faith cometh by hearing, and hearing by the Word of God," and as well "…how shall they hear without a preacher and how shall they preach except they be sent," then is it true justice to consign them to burn endlessly/eternally in Hell's fires and the Lake of Fire for NOT rejecting the Gospel, a Gospel they have never had the opportunity/occasion to reject? (Now this author is not saying by any stretch that anyone can enter heaven or the kingdom of God without being saved or born again, the scripture is too clear on that point!)

The point begging to be answered though is if death is the point eternal destiny is determined, and eternal salvation is "only" determined by hearing and believing the Gospel, then how can eternal/endless damnation be determined by NOT hearing and NOT having the occasion to accept or reject the saving Gospel? I.e. when have these lost souls had the opportunity to reject the Gospel to be damned endlessly/eternally? Should we believe that God agreeably consigns someone to burn in Hell fire endlessly/eternally for that which they have never had the occasion to reject? Augustinian theology certainly teaches such.

Our fundamentalist churches today are saturated with such aberrant theology. The fact is, one cannot reject that which he has had no occasion to reject! Thus a man to knowingly and willingly violate his God given conscience (which all men are born with) and all will violate at some point in their lives of course except for babies and those not reaching the age of reason/accountability, *is not hearing and rejecting the gospel! By no stretch can it be made to be such!* No man can be endlessly/eternally damned for sinning against his conscience! Did Jesus tell the heathen who never heard the Gospel "I never knew you, depart into everlasting fire prepared for the Devil and his angels..."? No! He did not tell the heathen that! He told those who *"had heard, those who did believe the gospel, those who preached falsely in His name* (but were still unconverted) "...depart into everlasting fire... "I never knew you!"

Again, all this speaks plainly to the Biblical fact that those who have never heard the gospel and have perished, (while of course they cannot enter into heaven without being born again) cannot be justifiably endlessly/eternally damned for that which they have not had the occasion to reject! The Word of God states unequivocally of the Gospel message and its rejection, that "...he that believeth not...shall be damned," not "...he that has never heard and believeth not shall be endlessly/eternally damned." Endless/eternal damnation for those who have died because they have never heard? Absolutely not. On the same token, those died having never heard will go to heaven and not to Hell? Absolutely not, they will go to that spirit world called Sheol/Hades the place of suffering for their sins, but not endlessly so.

At the end of that time of suffering and pain, after the final judgment (duration/punishment according to works at the Great White Throne), "Every knee shall bow and every tongue shall confess that Jesus Christ is Lord to the Glory of God the Father." Truly eventual universal salvation for all Men! Consider precious children who are raised thinking that God is one who will force the unsaved into a fiery Hell/Lake of Fire to be endlessly tortured/tormented with pain and suffering! No doubt when the invitation is given to be saved from such suffering, little children cannot help but attempt to 'come to Jesus' to escape such a terrible fate. Now that is a real problem, since 'escaping such a fate' is not the reason Jesus came to save us, He came to save us from our sins and to reconcile us to God, not to save us from going to Hell 'endlessly forever!'

The bottom line therefore is no doubt that many many children are raised with a false profession of faith in Christ by seeking to be delivered from Hell, rather than to be convicted of their sins and seek deliverance and salvation from the same! This author wonders how many precious children are raised with a false profession of faith, thinking they are saved because they went to the altar, then have gone through life, died and were lost anyway!?

Then also there are children who no doubt sit under the 'endless damnation of Hell-fire brimstone preaching and become paralyzed with fear of such a God. My aunt was one such person. She died unsaved as far as I know. My great grandfather preached endless Hell-fire damnation as she sat traumatized under his ministry (when just a little girl), and as a result totally rejected God and Christ. I often witnessed to her, but her fear with such a concept of God was so predominate that she closed her mind to any idea of coming to Christ. Eventually she became senile and died in a nursing home in her 90's no doubt to all appearances, unsaved having never been born again.

Amazing, that the fundamentalists (damnationists) who teach endless damnation/Hell fire on one hand, present Jesus as the all loving, kind compassionate caring Savior, who willingly and unselfishly laid down His life for ALL, but then on the other hand teach that this same Jesus will fail in reaching ALL of humanity. They believe He will torment those He couldn't wouldn't reach (without compassion) for endless eternity, in fire and brimstone, but believe He as God had the power to reach ALL with the gospel, but couldn't wouldn't or didn't! This is a huge insult to the integrity and justice of God.

The message then becomes Jesus as saying, "Come to me and I will give you free salvation, and if you don't accept me I will be vindictive to the utmost in my dealings with you by putting you in eternal endless torment in a lake of Hell-fire and brimstone!" This is the Jesus of the Bible?

Absolutely not! Then what about those who have never heard, or those who have been deceived by Satan in a false religion and have perished? Are we to believe that Jesus lines them up on the other side of death, reads them the endless damnation act and sends them screaming into the endless fires of eternal damnation? I think not. There is no doubt that these will go to Sheol/Hades, to suffer in a place there, <u>to whatever degree they deserve</u>. But rest assured immediately after death, they will instantly see the irrefutable revelation of just who Jesus Christ really is and how much He loved them!

The Jesus of the Bible shows infinite love and concern to the lost and dying by promising never to give over to losing one soul to sin's degradation, even though that soul has died unrepentant. No doubt after death, and being sent to a place of suffering in Hell under the wrath of God, that lost and damned (judged) soul finds so many lessons by suffering in the regions of the damned, that one day he is truly able willingly and sincerely to bend those knees to Jesus and thank Him for such terrible chastisement/punishment!

Yes, punishment under the wrath and anger of Almighty God on the one hand, but on the other, punishment done in love with the goal of true sorrow and repentance unto the new birth, which brings free endless salvation! Now THAT is the Jesus of John 3:16, one who gives Himself for our salvation, that we would not perish, or as dying unsaved we would not remain in an endless Hell but certainly and eventually come to endless salvation. (It has well been said that Divine judgment is reformative, not vindictive. The word used in the original Greek New Testament is *kolasis*, which means a beneficial chastening such as a gardener prunes a vine to remove dead vegetation and make it grow more fruitfully.)

So which God is yours? One who designed an endless place of torment to inflict unimaginable pain for endless eternity as payback for not accepting Jesus, or one who designed a place to measure out remedial correction and punishment to bring one to redemption and repentance in

Christ Jesus? Truly the 'damnationist' (those who believe in endless torment in Hell-fire the Lake of Fire) must answer for teaching and preaching such false doctrine! A closing though here simply is that while eventual universal salvation for all is Biblical, for we who hold this scriptural view to be called 'universalists' is an egregious insult! The reason being is they (traditional universalists) teach the only prerequisite for being saved is a belief in a Supreme Being, which of course makes belief in the deity of Christ optional, which emphatically it is not.

Readers note: There is a Christian (?) - universalist fellowship/organization found at christianuniversalist.org which is not of the same theological persuasion as this book is of. This author finds their view of salvation to be foreign to the New Testament. As well they seem to have quite a garden variety of churches, some which are not quite sound doctrinally. They say and we quote as follows: "We see salvation as more of a process of growth and transformation of the soul to become one with the Christ Spirit, rather than being saved from God's anger and the threat of punishment. This concept, called "theosis" (Greek for divinization) is the original teaching of the Bible and most of the early church fathers about human nature and destiny, which was mostly lost in the Western churches (Catholic and Protestant) but has been retained to some limited degree in the Eastern Orthodox churches." (End quote).These doctrines are very contradictory to New Testament conversion and salvation by the new birth into the family of God. It is doubtful that these churches are aggressively soul winning/evangelical with this "…growth and transformation" type salvation, rather than repentance/faith and instant conversion into the family of God. Also: "In the first five or six centuries of Christianity there were six theological schools, of which four (Alexandria, Antioch, Caesarea, and Edessa, or Nisibis) were Universalist, one (Ephesus) accepted conditional immortality; one (Carthage or Rome) taught endless punishment of the wicked. <u>Other theological schools are mentioned as founded by Universalists, but their actual doctrine on this subject is not known.</u>" "The Encyclopedia of Religious Knowledge" by Schaff-Herzog, 1908, volume 12, page96.

INTRODUCTION

Little Billy and His Wicked Dog

Little Billy being raised in Sunday school, adored the precious songs about the love of Jesus, "Jesus Loves the Little Children," the John 3:16 song, "For God So Loved the World" and "Jesus Loves Me This I Know." He would clap his small hands in delight that Jesus loved him so much to die for him. He had given his heart to the Lord. Being raised in children's church he had not been able to listen to his father's sermons, so this Sunday would be different. He was so happy he had 'graduated' into the adult congregation. Billy enjoyed the sermon, the love of God so aptly presented, the choir singing magnificent praise/ worship songs.

Then came the end of the service and invitation. His father, the fundamentalist (damnationist) pastor thundered from the pulpit, "If you are not willing to bend your knee and embrace Jesus as your personal Savior, God will torment you endlessly in fire and brimstone for time and eternity. Jesus has prepared a place for you called Hell/Lake of Fire. You will gnaw your tongue in pain, you will scream out in agony and pain for only a single drop of water to cool your tongue, you will beg for mercy, but there will be no mercy and never forgiveness, and yea no escape from that terrible place called Hell/Lake of Fire!!" The pastor's small son, taking this all in was shocked but nodded in agreement.

Several months later, the small boy after saving a considerable sum purchased a young dog and began a regimen of strict training to teach it obedience and loyalty. To his chagrin and disappointment the dog simply had an unbreakable stubborn streak of rebellion and an absolute refusal to learn from his master. Day after day, week after week, the boy worked and worked with the animal to teach it obedience and after months of failure he gave up in despair. Life went on as usual; faithful church attendance, Sunday school, and one day the pastor noticed that the dog was missing.

"Son," he said, "Just what happened to your new dog, why I haven't seen it in weeks?" To which his son said, "Well dad, that dog was so rebellious and impossible to tame I put it in Hell fire, I just gave up with it!" Visibly stunned, Billy's father said, "Now just what do you mean you put it in Hell fire, I certainly hope you didn't kill it did you?!" "Oh no!" exclaimed the son, "I wouldn't do that, but I did put him somewhere that I could pay him back for all the trouble he caused me, he even bit me a lot and refused to obey me." His son continued, "I put him in the back barn in the tack room since we don't use it anymore, he cannot get out, and I am never letting him out anyway."

Now the father with a sinking feeling in the pit of his stomach said, "Well let's go and check on him, to see how he's doing, and by the way, what do you mean you are 'paying him back,' what does that mean?" "Why, I am giving to him exactly what Jesus my Lord is going to give all who won't obey and bow to Him... I made a place I call Hell for that wicked dog just as Jesus did for the wicked people that won't obey Him. Just like Jesus torments the wicked forever I am tormenting that wicked dog forever. I am proud to say I put pain and suffering on that dog every day, day and night and I can say he sure doesn't like it!" By now they reached the barn and coming up to the tack room the father was shocked to hear pitiful moans and whines and as well smelling a horrible stench coming from the room. His son had painted in huge red letters on the door "This is Hell."

Introduction

Upon opening the door the pastor nearly fainted at the sight and putrid smell coming from the room. There, chained to the floor in the thick darkness was such a pitiful creature as he had ever seen. The dog was nearly skin and bones from malnutrition, feces and waste covered the floor, the dog had burnt patches all over his body with oozing scabs forming everywhere. Nearby lay a can of lighter fluid and matches which were used to burn the dog to create the utmost pain and suffering possible. The dogs eyes were nearly swollen shut from the burnings, and it could hardly stand while staggering and continually falling

It was evident a sharp stick lying close by was used to stab the dog repeatedly to inflict more pain and suffering. The pastor was aghast and covering his nose staggered back out of the room tightly holding his son's hand. Seeing his dad's obvious horror and displeasure, his son said, "But dad, you said that Jesus was going to burn the wicked in Hellfire and brimstone forever because they wouldn't obey Him, and I am just following His example and putting the dog in a same place. Besides I give him bread and water every several days, and people in the real Hell don't get that!" "Son," the father now in tears said, "We are going to have to put this dog out of his misery, this is simply inhumane to treat any creature like this!" "No father," the child said, "You said that this is the way Jesus is going to punish the wicked forever, you said that Jesus is God so this cannot be wrong to do to the dog!"

Suddenly the fundamentalist pastor saw the apparent insanity of such a charge against God and still trembling at the horrific sight said, "No son, I now come to see I have misunderstood the Word of God. God is not a sadist, He is not the sadist I have been preaching that He is, and I am going to have to revisit the Word of God to learn where I have been wrong."

Perverted Concepts of Hell and Endless Torment…

…do nothing but impugn the justice and integrity of All Mighty God, making our Savior to be vicious and vindictive to those who die without accepting Him. As well, He thereby becomes a sadist who delights in tormenting those who oppose Him and His plan of redemption by supposedly burning them endlessly in fire and brimstone. This concept of God/Christ further does nothing but to breed atheism, and contempt for the Word of God, and Fundamental Christianity. It makes Jesus to be one who is ultimately defeated in winning the majority of humanity to Himself, and He therefore supposedly responds in final frustration and anger by consigning them to burn helplessly in Hell fire and brimstone endlessly for eternity!

Only a God who ultimately wins all to Himself, and only inflicts remedial punishment to bring repentance and sorrow for sin to all men who fail to accept Him can truly be said to be our God and Savior the Lord Jesus Christ, King of kings, and Lord of lords!

Do What I Say or I'll Burn You with Fire and Brimstone for Eternty!

Away with the doctrine of endless damnation. The Biblical Hell/Lake of Fire *is* literally real, and certainly a place of controlled/remedial/correction (no not a purgatory) unto future salvation. On the other hand the traditional Hell/Lake of Fire is an imaginative eternal torture chamber created by a defeated sadistic god, unable with his unlimited power and resources to woo and win all of mankind to himself, thus allowing Satan to win and eternally damn the majority of humanity.(The Bible teaches this? Not hardly).

Now consider this. Any reasonable unsaved person who reflects upon the laws of God as given in the Bible, (and his own conscience) can understand that when God's laws are broken, the offender must and should be punished. When such a person is witnessed to concerning his need of salvation and told how much Jesus loves him, he can only have one of two responses depending on if the person doing the witnessing is a damnationist or not. If he is a damnationist then Jesus is made to be a loving caring Savior only on this side of the grave, but on the other side after death Jesus becomes a sadist who delights in torturing and endlessly burning lost souls in fire and brimstone because they reject Him and His redemption. In other words he sees Jesus as saying, "I love you and want to give you free salvation for eternity, but if you do not accept me I will torment and burn you with fire in the pit of Hell and later the Lake of Fire for endless eternity."

Now pray tell dear friend, just what kind of love is shown by someone who tells people he will burn them with fire forever if they don't do what he wants them to do??!! Just what kind of god would tell someone he loves them, but if they refuse to obey his commands he will burn them endlessly forever in fire and brimstone??!! Certainly not the Jesus or Jehovah of the Bible! On the other hand, the true God and Redeemer the Lord Jesus Christ weeps over lost souls, has no pleasure in the death of the wicked, and no doubt sorrows deeply that lost souls must suffer for their sins after death in Hell and later the Lake of Fire. Ultimately however this wonderful Savior will rejoice in seeing all lost souls being brought to total submission, bended knee and eternal redemption at the end of time and the beginning of eternity.

Damnationists are Brainwashed with the Following False Ideas

1. That the English words commonly used in the K.J.V, 'eternal, everlasting/forever,' have always been part of the English language.

2. That these words only or can only mean 'endless or permanent forever' and were correctly translated from the original languages of the scriptures.

3. That these English words are faithful/true translations of the underlying Greek words 'aionios/aion.'

4. That the universal Christian redemption/restoration view *(which is scriptural and was commonly held by the early church of the first century's ed.)* equates with or to Unitarian Universalism *(a deadly heresy.ed)*.

5. That Christian Universal Redemption theology teaches there is not a literal Hell/Lake of Fire in which the lost are punished.

6. That since the leaders with PhD's and D.D's in the damnationist movement are such highly educated 'men of the cloth' then those endless damnationists doctrines must be true and any doctrine which contradicts the same must be ignored. (*Thus highly educated men holding PhD's and Doctorates supposedly proficient in the original languages, are able to keep the masses of 'commoners' in the church in mental slavery to the false endless damnationist heresy. i.e. who would dare to contradict men of such high learning.ed*).

7. That since the average Christian is ignorant of the original languages, then only those who hold degrees are proficient enough to speak on these issues. (*During the dark ages, common people who did not know Latin were held in bondage to false interpretations by the Roman Catholic Church. As well when the scriptures were finally translated into the common languages of the day, the Roman Catholic people were adamantly told by the church that while they could read the Bible they were not to attempt to understand it unless the priest did so for them. Today is much the same with the proper understanding and rightly dividing of the Word of God, as leaders in most evangelical circles are thoroughly saturated with Augustinian damnationist heresies These 'leaders' will have much to answer for in the day of judgment. Ed.*)

The Doctrine of Universal Christian Redemption Vastly Expands Our Evangelistic Vision

Remember this: To believe that all will eventually be saved, means that anyone can be saved now, not that some people are totally incorrigible and without hope or possibility of redemption. This should broaden our evangelistic zeal and love for all men everywhere. This simple Biblical truth tells us that anyone, anywhere, no matter how wicked, or perverse can possibly be won to a saving knowledge of Christ, yea if only enough time and effort is expended towards that end. Yes it may take years and years of work to win them, but it can be done. The only exception to

Introduction

this is of course if they have grievously and violently sinned against the Holy Spirit. In such case they would not be saved in this 'age or the age' to come, simply meaning 'this life/age or the millennium age to come.

Yea they would have to await the Great White Throne Judgment and the Lake of Fire to be humbled to submission bended knee and confession unto salvation. (Remember the K.J.V. incorrectly says "this world or the world to come" seeming to make them to have committed a so called 'unpardonable sin,' when it should say, "…this age or the age to come."

Recently in talking to a traveling evangelist, I asked him about the death of the many who have never heard the gospel, yea those who were/are steeped in heathenism such as Buddhism, Islam, Hinduism, etc. I asked him if it were really justice to consign such to burn in Hell-fire for eternity for *not rejecting a gospel they have never had the opportunity to reject*. His first answer was that God is able to send a Christian messenger to anyone at any time. Of course I had to agree. Then I pressed the issue that many have never ever had an opportunity to be approached with the gospel even one time. To this he simply answered that they wouldn't listen even if someone was sent to share the gospel message to them, and that God could not be under indictment. Of course many times this is the case but is it true justice to send someone to burn in Hell-fire for eternity that was such as these?

There are many in this life who are so steeped in their false theology that only death (and the perfect revelation brought them when standing before Jesus Christ the God of the universe after death), will perfectly enlighten them. Even this though would not be true justice for these people to be consigned to endless damnation, those who died being completely deceived by false theology. Yea rather here again, God shows His infinite love and mercy to these seemingly incorrigibles by giving them irrefutable revelation of Himself and His true plan of salvation after death. Yes, even though they are sent to Sheol/Hades, they one day on bended knee make that wonderful humbled confession unto salvation after being thoroughly punished according to their works in the Lake of Fire after resurrection. "Every knee shall bow, and every tongue shall confess..." Phil. 2:10-11, Rom. 14:11.

Readers note: The shocking fact is that Augustine defaced Biblical Christianity or Christian universalism with the false doctrine of "infinite/endless punishment" which infers that the powers of darkness finally defeat the Lord God Almighty in his desire that all men be saved and come to knowledge of the truth. So the question arises. In the day of judgment, just how well will the damnationists fare due to their preaching and teaching such aberrant false theology, propagating a sadist god who delights in tormenting poor lost deceived souls in Hell-fire/brimstone for endless eternity? No doubt the 'commoner' will point fingers at their highly educated blind leaders, leaders who climbed theological ladders to bask in economic security, acclamation in their theological circles and cushy positions in colleges and seminaries while passing on the heresies they learned from other Augustinian damnationist theologians! So damnationist leaders are locked in, and locked away from ever remotely considering the universal Christian redemption doctrines as a possibility. Lastly, by the time damnationists leaders have reached the 'top' so often they are polluted with Calvinism, a very deadly heresy as well.

TABLE OF CONTENTS

Chapter One	The Biblical Hell	 1
Chapter Two	Dare to Insult Jehovah!?	 41
Chapter Three	Endless Punishment and the Greek	 77
Chapter Four	Matthew 25:46 Correction	 107
Chapter Five	The Christian, the Jew and Eternal Damnation	 149
Chapter Six	Thank God for Hell? Yes!	 167
Chapter Seven	Limited...The God of the Damnationists	 187
Chapter Eight	J.W. Hanson Greek Scholar	 223
Chapter Nine	So Who Wins the Game?	 275
Chapter Ten	Conclusion	 325
	Epilogue	 353
	The 'Christian Church' in Disarray – 2018	 367
	Closing Thought	 389
	Lastly	 391
	An Infallibly Perfect Translation?	 395

FOREWORD

Having written more than a dozen books on the subject of Christ's all-inclusive redemption vs. the common notion of eternal damnation for the vast majority of mankind, and having read many other volumes on this theme, I was especially pleased and uniquely blessed when brother Terry Lee Miller Sr. forwarded a copy of his yet unpublished manuscript to me requesting me to critique it. Although I had never met this brother I was moved to accommodate his request and began what turned out to be a fascinating journey through the fields of biblical evidence, divine logic, and revelatory quickening. I really thought I had just about exhausted these issues-I had heard it all! But Brother Miller led me into beautiful and captivating insights I had not before heard or considered. I am happy to commend this work unto all who are hungry for the *truth* about the limitless love of God, the measureless grace of God, and the universality of the atoning, reconciling, and transforming work of our Lord Jesus the Christ.

-J. Preston Eby

In a Nutshell ... 7 Reasons Endless Damnation Fails Biblical Examination

1. Neither Jesus our Lord nor His disciples ever taught endless/permanent punishment for the unsaved wicked, by using said terms to denote such in the language of their day. 'Continuous' yes, 'Indefinite duration' yes, 'Ages and Ages' yes. 'Endless, forever/endlessly, permanent, eternal/endlessly' absolutely not! That is a fact.

2. The Greek terms for permanent/endless are not the same words for 'indefinite' or 'undetermined' length/duration for punishment of the wicked in the final Lake of Fire. That is a fact.

3. The English terms (which denote endless in the English language) everlasting, eternal, eternity came into use in the 1300's and are an incorrect translation of the underlying Greek. That is a fact.

4. Indeed the wicked/unsaved are punished in Hell/Lake of Fire for their sins/works, but the punishment is, a. Of indefinite limited duration, not endless and to degree according to their works. b. Remedial, restorative and corrective leading to sorrow, remorse and ultimately a bowing of the knee unto confession unto salvation. That is a fact.

5. Nowhere in the N.T. can it be shown that Jesus the creator of Hell and the Lake of Fire could possibly be a sadist or one who derives pleasure from seeing the suffering of others. Jesus our Lord is rather the Savior of ALL men, and one who ultimately woos and wins all to Himself, and will never give up until that last soul is saved and born again. That is a fact.

6. The last enemy Jesus destroys is death *for all* unconditionally. That is a fact.

7. The Lake of Fire is part of *the old heavens and earth (Revelation 21)* and passes away forever when God generates the new heaven and earth. That is a fact.

CHAPTER ONE

THE BIBLICAL HELL

Perverted concepts of Hell

How interesting it is that some have come forward claiming to have had some type of journey to Hell in the spirit, or in some sort of trance at night. Naturally, they precipitate much interest from the Christian community, write and sell many books etc., and often travel to churches far and wide to appear on mostly Pentecostal/Fullness type television programs. (Pentecostalist Mary K. Baxter had a very wild [very unscriptural] so-called journey thru Hell, by which she has no doubt gained considerable notoriety, attention and probably financial gain.) Unfortunately though, what they have to say certainly does not fit the Biblical description of that Biblical place of pain and suffering. I have heard them speak of skeletons with rotting flesh and clothing playing pianos (see Baxter's so called 'revelation' on the internet), maggots and worms abundant, huge snakes slithering here and there, big horrible beasts which attack them and devour chunks of flesh torn from their bodies, falling endlessly through space, on and on myriads of horrors totally unknown to mankind, and revealed to them (?) for us to tremble at.

Bill Weise has written on the subject, a book entitled, "23 Minutes in Hell." While this author has no doubt that his heart is set on winning lost souls, and warning the wicked of the perils of Hell, Mr. Wiese's description of Hell, and his supposed out of the body experience, in this author's estimation, is indeed faulty. First, any man can claim anything, but that does not indicate the claim is completely legitimate.

We have no doubt that Mr. Wiese probably did have some sort of dream, but not a literal out of the body experience. Saying so does not make it so. Secondly, that he claimed to see spiders, snakes, 13 foot tall scaly demonic creatures with foot long claws which were used to rip his chest open, things which are all totally foreign to God's word. Nowhere in God's word does it say that anything other than fire and isolation are used to afflict the wicked lost. He says that there were demons around the edge of the fiery pit, pushing the ascending lost souls screaming back into the fire and brimstone. Demons, satanic spirits and the Devil himself are not in Hell yet, and when they are sent there, they will not be there to help God punish the wicked, but will be there to suffer for their rebellion against the All Mighty.

To put credibility in what he says he saw would be to be able to say anything was there, even bicycles and roller skates. No doubt the saved are relieved that they will never have to go to such a place (and of course don't question these visions), and the unsaved rightly scoff at such revelations as being to grotesque and deranged to reflect a merciful creator, especially the man Jesus who had love and compassion for lost souls while here, and who wept over their lost estate.

The unsaved have a valid point here, namely that if Hell is endless and the horrors there are as previously stated, then these hideous sufferings can serve to do nothing but to make God out to be a sadist, or one who delights in inflicting terrible sufferings and anguish on the souls of the damned, and that being for no other reason than to sadistically terrify the lost for endless eternity. (Wikipedia defines sadism: "Sadism is the derivation of pleasure as a result of inflicting pain, cruelty, degradation, or humiliation, or, watching such behaviors inflicted on others.") I think not. The Bible is clear that Jesus warned, and warned the lost about the judgment of being placed in Hell-fire, and *those warnings were with great sorrow and compassion*! If one is warning another about some terrible consequence 'to their actions, it certainly shows love and concern to that one being warned. The scripture is clear that "...His mercy endureth forever..." Ps. 106:7, and that God has "...no pleasure in the death of the wicked Ez. 38:11.

Plainly then God has no pleasure that the wicked must undergo sufferings of the damned in the next life. On the other hand, since it is clear that Hell or the Lake of Fire (Rev. 20) is a place of punishment, that the wicked were "...judged according to their works..." then it is only reasonable to believe that the unsaved will be suffering a period for their sins, i.e. learning that sin is against God and all He stands for, and that they must suffer for what they have done in the flesh.

No doubt when they have fully suffered for their evil works, the lesson having been learned, they will gladly bend their knee (Phil. 2:10 & Rom. 10:9-10-13) and embrace salvation and the new birth into the family of God. Getting back to a true description of Hell, it certainly is a place of confinement, and is inescapable, the temperature in some levels thereof is extremely hot, but no doubt it is not unbearable. If it were 'unbearable' then the pain could not be borne, and God puts on no man what he cannot bear.

While the pain is horrible, and the suffering is great it will not be 'unbearable.' No doubt that damned (judged) sinful soul will suffer terrific hunger and thirst, having no rest day or night, extreme exhaustion, no sleep, and as well the total isolation from all family/friends, life's blessings, and of all good on the earth will certainly be added torment (affliction) in itself. As far as scorpions, spiders, snakes, skeletons playing pianos, rotting flesh continually falling away, and other myriad mind bending terrors in Hell, absolutely not. Jesus the creator of all things in the heavens, earth and under the earth has no interest in 'terrorizing' or sadistically ridiculing the lost in Sheol/Hades, but yea only to bring punishment and suffering as a lesson against giving one's self over to wickedness and neglecting God's free gift of salvation!

God's great love and compassion is shown for the all powerful God of the universe to put the lost in such a place as Sheol, (the place of everlasting 'continuous' but not 'endless' punishment which will ultimately bring that judged soul to bended knee, and fully humbled to repent and embrace the new birth in Christ Jesus). What greater love could be than for God to channel the wicked unsaved in a direction that will ultimately lead to their salvation and redemption? With that view of Hell, who including the wicked could fault God for sending anyone to suffer in Hell?

An Endless Hell 'Filled' with Fire and Brimstone?

Another very important consideration is to examine the Damnationists purported accurate (?) description of Hell/Sheol in its entirety. While it is true that there is fire and suffering *in parts/sections* of this place, they portray it as one which is totally filled with fire, smoke and brimstone etc. Now, where in the Word of God does such a complete description come from? The answer is 'nowhere!' Nowhere in the Word of God does it give such a description as that. While there are levels/areas or places in Sheol/Hell that such fire and suffering do exist, as clearly shown from the account in Luke chapter 16 for the wicked, no doubt there are areas there which will be as the 'suffering in outer darkness' where there will be weeping wailing and gnashing of teeth. (See Matthew chapters, 18, 13, 22, 24, 25 and Luke chapter 13).

No doubt this/these areas of Hell are in the upper sections/levels thereof. As well no doubt, some places in this 'spirit underworld' will be more or less neutral in so far as pain and suffering goes, for those who perhaps have reached the age of accountability/reason with some minor sin and have had an untimely death, such as younger persons etc. Who knows? A compassionate loving God executing justice, certainly will not plunge them into the lowest Hell to suffer endless fire and brimstone along with the incorrigible wicked. We dare not go beyond these above lines due to lack of fuller revelation.

Universal Salvation Plainly Taught in Romans 5

For years this author read, and re-read Romans chapter 5 and yet failed to see that universal salvation is plainly taught there. In simply allowing this important chapter to speak to us and not trying to "interpret" these verses no other conclusion can be reached other than eventually all souls will ultimately experience salvation and the new birth in Christ Jesus. Following we will quote verses starting with vs.6, and go on thru to the end of the chapter, giving simple comments as we go.

Vs. 6. 'For when we were yet without strength, in due time Christ died for the ungodly."

1. "All" of those outside of Christ are easily termed "Ungodly." Now the question therefore arises "Have not there been millions and millions of souls over the past six thousand years whether Catholic, Muslim, Jehovah Witness, Mormons, Buddhists, Moabites, Sodomites, Hittites, Philistines, Egyptians, etc, etc, who have lived and died without ever coming to a saving knowledge of Christ? How many heathen nations there have been who were or are steeped in false worship and idolatry, and those souls are dying every day without Christ!" And NO, the church is not reaching but only a small minority of these souls!

   To simply say they have their conscience to judge them (which it will do is true) is still to avoid the plain fact in this verse that Christ Jesus died FOR THEM! Jesus loved and died for these lost souls. If He did indeed die for them then to say that they died in ignorance with a soiled conscience and must be eternally damned due to violation of their conscience with never hearing the gospel, is to say that they were "locked away from" His death for them. Many and even most of these souls have barely (if ever) even heard of the name of Jesus, and certainly did die mostly in ignorance of the fullness of the gospels claims!

   The only way these lost souls could have been saved while alive was for them to be fully educated and evangelized in the simple gospel message under the conviction of the Spirit of God. To respond to the gospel message, these souls would have to have access to its message under the conviction of the Holy Spirit. When the Holy Spirit uses the Word of God, which is the 'sword of the Spirit,' no person can for too long resist that call to be saved. The fact Jesus died for them, the ungodly, then at some point they must have intelligent access to the truth of the gospel if not in this life then certainly the next. If such does not come in this life it will in the next. See section entitled, "Deaths Improvement of the Wicked." If God does not give ALL of the 'ungodly' access to the gospel of free salvation at some point, then it cannot truly be said that Christ 'died for them.'

Vs. 8-11. "But God commendeth His love toward us, in that while we were yet sinners, Christ died for us…"

2. Plain here that 'sinners' and 'ungodly' are synonymous; all are sinners, so all are ungodly. All means all. Remember, in Adam the entire human race was tested. When Adam fell, the entire human race fell. Now some have trouble with our having been found guilty in Adam, saying that it is not fair for someone else to be charged with the sins of another. The truth is, while we all are each accountable to God for our own personal sins and transgressions, and will be judged accordingly, we still have received the sentence of death, which was placed upon the first man and woman.

Someone says, "But that is unjust, for God to sentence us to death for what another (Adam) did. To which we answer as follows. Let us use a hypothetical illustration. Say an automobile manufacturer mass produces a brand new line of cars, with 100% of the parts used are manufactured and built by different shops in the plant. Let's say there are 10,000 new cars ready for shipment. Proudly, the company president looks over the cars ready for delivery and shipping, when suddenly one of his R&D men comes breathlessly to him with the bad news that all cars will fail due to a common mechanical defect built into all of them. His department just finished testing one car under road conditions and the motor failed. It seems that all of the engine castings mass-produced have one faulty cylinder water jacket, which was due to a defective mold in the foundry.

What is the solution? Well all engines must be scrapped and new ones installed, what was a defect in one automatically is a defect in all. Now Adam was created a perfect man, with no defects, none at all. Had the afore mentioned automobiles been built with no defect in them, it could not be said that all should be scrapped. Now the Biblical truth being driven at here is simply that we, the entire human race, all persons of all nations and of all centuries up to the last one to ever be born, were tested in Adam.

When Adam fell, we all fell. It must be remembered that Adam was created a perfect man, fully educated, and with perfect faculties, perfect mentally and physically. No man since Adam had that honor, Eve, the same. All who have ever been born since must develop, grow and be educated, must learn, and learning presents many problems since that learning can be, and often is, faulty. Therefore all born into this world are weak, uneducated, subject to being powered by the desires of the fleshly nature, which if followed as it desires to lead us, will inevitably lead us to sin and ruin. That is why the Apostle Paul said in Romans 7:9, "... For I was alive without the law once, but when the commandment came, sin revived and I died, and the commandment which was ordained unto life, I found to be unto death."

This verse simply shows that as a baby and small child we are alive spiritually until the age of reason, at which age we have learned enough to understand right from wrong, hear the commandment "Thou shalt not," act opposite of that command, and die a spiritual death. It is at the age of reason, or some call it the age of accountability that from that point on, the soul is lost to God and needs regeneration and salvation to cleanse away those sins. James 1:15 as well says, "... lust when it is conceived bringeth forth sin, and sin when it is finished bringeth forth death." Clearly then, it is just and proper that all humans are born into the race of Adam with that defect, some call it the "sinful nature" or "fleshly nature," and become guilt before God in Adam.

The question arises, "Just how does universal salvation fit in here?" To which the answer is simple. Adam and Eve 'died spiritually' the day they sinned, and did not God slay the animal and clothe them with the skins thereof picturing the sacrifice of the innocent for the guilty? Did not Adam and Eve gladly and willingly receive this sacrifice for their sins and save themselves from condemnation of God? Absolutely so! Adam had never seen the 'sacrifice' of an animal with its blood being spilt which of course was a foreshadowing of the coming sacrifice Jesus made on the cross for our sins.

The fact that our first parents did not reject this sacrifice clearly indicates that 'in Adam' we will all, all without exception, universally and eventually accept the same salvation in Christ Jesus. All will be saved eventually, whether it is now or 'post mortem.' This author believes that if Adam had not been a 'fully educated' man, which he was, and as well had not God personally confronted him giving him a complete and perfect revelation of salvation thru the blood of the sacrifice, he could well have been lost and gone to Hell.

The fact that God did indeed see fit to 'personally appear' and bring the revelation of salvation to the first man and woman, ones who were perfectly educated, then to be fair Jehovah would need to do the same for everyone who ever live after that. No doubt then, those who have died having never heard, ones who have died in ignorance, are therefore promised to receive such revelation unto salvation in the next life.

Vs. 12, 15, 18-19. Wherefore as by one man sin entered into the world, and death by sin, and so death passed upon *all* men for that all have sinned, But not as the offence, so also is the free gift. For if through the offence of one *many* be dead, much more the grace of God and the gift by grace which is by one man, Jesus Christ, hath abounded unto *many*. Therefore as by the offence of one judgment came upon *all* men to condemnation even so by the righteousness of one the free gift came upon *all* men unto justification of life. For as by one man's disobedience *many* were made sinners, so by the obedience of one shall *many* be made righteous.

3. How much plainer does the scripture need to be? In these verses the "all" and the "many" are synonymous! Death passes upon ALL men for ALL have sinned. Yes "ALL" have sinned IN Adam. He was tested as a perfect representative for everyone who ever lives, and since he sinned and died ALL of mankind following Adam are charged with sin and die as well. Then the term "many" is used to mean "all" without exception.

   The "many" be dead has already been clarified by the word "ALL." How many have sinned in Adam? ALL! How many have (or will) die in Adam? ALL! Then the blessing of salvation comes to how many? "ALL" since "ALL" and "MANY" are used equally. Notice again, by the "offence" of one judgment came upon "ALL" men to die, then by the obedience of one shall "MANY" (ALL) be made righteous. Endless damnation for the majority of the human race for eternity? Is that what these verses teach? Absolutely not! "All" die in Adam, and "ALL" are saved in Christ!! Universal salvation taught here, irrefutably so! Now that "ALL" and "MANY" are synonymous in these verses, lets read verses 18-19 in that light: (Paraphrased)

THEREFORE AS BY THE OFFENCE OF ONE JUDGMENT CAME UPON <u>ALL</u> MEN TO CONDEMNATION, EVEN SO BY THE RIGHTEOUSNESS OF ONE THE FREE GIFT CAME UPON <u>ALL</u> MEN UNTO JUSTIFICATION OF LIFE. FOR AS BY ONE MAN <u>ALL</u> WERE MADE SINNERS, SO BY THE OBEDIENCE OF ONE SHALL <u>ALL</u> BE MADE RIGHTEOUS.

Now how many times does the Lord have to say something before He means it? This last verse plainly states that "...BY THE OBEDIENCE OF ONE SHALL ALL BE MADE RIGHTEOUS. "ALL" does not mean that the majority of people will burn in Hell endlessly for eternity and only a small minority will be saved to walk the streets of gold! Our Savior died for "ALL" and is offering salvation to "ALL" and is *not willing that any should perish* but that "ALL" should come to repentance! Lastly, let no one even dare to say, "Yes of course, all who come to Christ will be saved, but many don't." To which we say, "Wrong, the scripture is plain that 'all' die in Adam so 'all' will be made alive (saved) in Christ." We therefore should agree that ALL will one day taste of the water of life, the water which springs up into everlasting life.

Hell/Hades/Sheol and the Original Languages

In examining the Biblical doctrine of Hell some very important things come to light from the original languages. The watchtower and others who deny the reality of a literal burning Hell in the afterlife, and unsaved souls suffering there, use the shallow argument that "Sheol" (Hebrew), or the Greek "Hades" (same word in different languages which indicate the underworld/abode of the departed spirits) is translated three different ways, first, Hell, secondly, Grave, thirdly, Pit. Now there is no objection to this as a historical fact at all, for this is the way the scriptures were translated into the English. BUT, it must also be remembered that those translating these two words, did so giving them English words, which have very different meanings. A "grave" has one meaning, a "pit" has another meaning, two totally different words with two different English meanings.

The equalivent meaning in the Greek for 'Pit' from the English translation is "phrear" pn. "frehar" Strongs 5421. This word is used for "hole in the ground" and as well for "...the beast which ascended out of the bottomless pit" instances such as these. Then the word "grave" has an equalivent in the Greek as well which is "mnemeion" pn. Mnay'-mion Strongs 3419 which literally means tomb, grave, sepulcher.

Chapter One | The Biblical Hell

Herein lies the problem. The weakness of the K.J.V. translation in properly representing the Greek and Hebrew in some few places such as this, has failed to clearly translate such as it should be. "Hades" Strong's 86, should never have been translated as "pit" nor should it have been translated as "grave." These are three separate and distinct words with three different meanings. True the "bottomless pit" can mean the "bottomless pit/abode of the departed spirits" metaphorically speaking, but 'pit' in the Greek can never actually mean 'Sheol in Hebrew, or Hades" in the Greek. The same with "grave" which can never mean "Sheol" in the Hebrew, or "Hades" in the Greek.

Why the translators determined to mis-translate as they did remains to be dealt with elsewhere not here. The simple fact now can be stated, that nowhere in scripture is it said that a physical body was ever placed in "Sheol" or "Hades." This simple fact, defuses once and for all the false idea that all three words are equal in the Hebrew and in the Greek. They are not, nor ever will be! "Mnay'-mion" (Greek for 'grave') is not "Phrear" (Greek for 'pit') and neither one is "Hades." Three separate and distinct words, with three separate and distinct meanings! Luke chap. 16 gives an accurate picture of life in the realms of the damned. Mistranslations such as these and as well in other few places certainly cannot be called the "inspired Word of God!" For anyone to claim that the 1611 K.J.V. as a translation is 100% equal to the original autographs is totally false. To say the translation does clearly bring us the message of salvation and redemption, though, is without dispute.

Now having established clearly, that Sheol-Hades is not a "grave or pit" (except where erroneously translated in English versions) it leaves only one conclusion which of course is fully supported by scripture, that being that these words (Sheol/Hades) identify the abode of departed spirits, the "spirit world/underworld."

Never in scripture is it said, (at least as this author has found), that a physical body was put into "Sheol or Hades." Of course the case of Jonah is raised in answer to this latter statement. The scripture quotes Jonah as saying, "…out of the belly of Hell cried I and thou heard my voice." Jonah 2:2.

There are some Bible teachers who teach that Jonah actually did die, and descend into Sheol for three days and nights. Matthew 12:40 tells us, "For as Jonas was three days and three nights in the whales belly; so shall the Son of man be three days and three nights in the heart of the earth." Jonah did indeed indicate that his "…life was brought up from corruption," which no doubt indicates a physical resurrection from deterioration and decay which does spell death and the departure of the soul.

Some may argue that this indicates that he actually did not die, but nearly did, and that when the whale vomited him out he was spared from an untimely death. I suppose if this were the only reference to his state of existence in the whale, possibly so. (The Watchtower etc. do use this account to teach that "Sheol" equals the "grave.") But, since Jesus used Jonah's experience to mirror His own descent into the heart of the earth, it seems probable, yea even likely that Jonah did die and was raised back to life and subsequently vomited back on the beach.

The fact that Jonah did emphatically say "…out of the belly of Hell (Sheol) cried I and thou heard my voice," is clear that he did indeed physically die, and descend into the underworld. He said, "…I went down to the bottoms of the mountains: the earth with her bars was about me forever: yet hast thou brought up my life from corruption O lord my God." Vs. 6. Not only that, but the fact that for Jonah to be a true type of Christ in being three days and nights in the heart of the earth as Jesus said He would be, then he did no doubt die and descend into Sheol the abode of the spirits, the underworld/spirit world.

I suppose at this point it is important to re-explain to the reader why when Jesus went to Sheol/Hades after death for three days and nights that He actually did not enter into the fires of such place as did the rich man in Luke. 16. The reason being that there were two compartments in Hades for all departed spirits (at that time), the lost souls going into fire torment and affliction of one side, the righteous going into the place of paradise and peace of the other side as Lazarus did, (with a great gulf fixed between the two, so that they could not go back and forth from one to the other). After the death of Jesus and His descent into Sheol/Hades the scriptures indicate that paradise with the righteous, was moved from there to heaven and into the very presence of God.

Reason? Before the perfect sacrifice Jesus made on the cross, no soul could enter into the very presence of God due to the fact his sin was only covered (atoned for) and not removed. Once Jesus made that perfect offering for sin as Hebrews teaches, and those sins were removed, then He moved paradise into heaven and into the very presence of God. This is indicated where the scripture says that He (Eph. 4:8) "…led captivity captive." So simply put, after death Jesus descended into the paradise side of Sheol/Hades.

The Fires of Gehennah

Another Greek word which needs to be looked at is "Gehennah." Strongs 1067. Strong's definition is given as, "Valley of the son of Hinnon. A valley Jesus used figurative as a name for the place (or state) of everlasting punishment. Hell." Now outside of Jerusalem was a garbage dump where fires continued to consume garbage day after day, on and on. Jesus told the wicked "How can you escape the damnation of Hell. (Gehenna)" Matt. 23:15. He also said, to fear him which could…."… destroy both body and soul in Hell (Gehenna)." Matt. 10:28. Mk. 9:43-46. "And if thy hand offend thee, cut it off, it is better for thee to enter into life maimed, than having two hands to go into Hell (Gehenna) into the fire that never shall be quenched where the worm dieth not and the fire is not quenched. And if thy foot offend thee cut it off, it is better for thee to enter halt into life, than having two feet to be cast into Hell into the fire that never shall be quenched where their worm dieth not and the fire is not quenched."

Now the Watchtower, and many others use this (garbage dump) fact to try to prove that all Jesus meant concerning Gehenna was that the final judgment was to be like being cast into the garbage dump, i.e. being burned up or annihilated. We quote from a Watchtower publication:

"...Gehenna ... Valley of Hinnom ... Greek form of the Hebrew Ge'i-Hin·om'. ... This valley lay to the west and south of ancient Jerusalem. ... it was used for the idolatrous worship of the pagan god Molech, to which god human sacrifices were offered by fire. ... it came to be the dumping place and incinerator for the filth of Jerusalem. ... the bodies of dead animals were thrown to be consumed in the fires to which sulphur or brimstone was added .... Occasionally the bodies of executed criminals were thrown in .... No living animals or human creatures were pitched into Gehenna to be burned alive or tormented.

Hence the place could never symbolize an invisible region where human souls are tormented in literal fire ... forever and ever. (Here the Watchtower forgets that Jesus said the difference in the coming "Gehenna" would be the place where **the worm dieth not, and the fire is not quenched.** Ed.) ... Gehenna was used by Jesus and his disciples to symbolize everlasting destruction, annihilation from God's universe, or `second death', an eternal punishment. .... From the literal Gehenna and from its significance the symbol of the `lake burning with fire and sulphur' was drawn ..." (WB&TS, 1950, "**New World Translation of the Christian Greek Scriptures**," pp.766-767). End.

This word occurs twelve times in the New Testament, and is always translated "Hell." But as the Evangelists repeat the same discourses, the Savior did not really use it more than six or seven times in His recorded ministry. The following are the texts: Matt. 5:22, 29, 30, 10:28, 18:9, 23:15, 33; Mark 9:43, 45, 47; Luke 12:5; James 3:6. By consulting these passages the reader will see how many of them are simply repetitions, and how very few times this word is used, on which, nevertheless, more reliance is placed than on all others, to prove that "Hell" is a place of endless torment The following from Schleusner, a distinguished lexicographer and critic, will show the origin of the word, and indicate its scriptural usage: "Gehenna, originally a Hebrew word, which signifies valley of Hinnom. Here the Jews placed that brazen image of Moloch.

It is said, on the authority of the ancient Rabbis, which to this image the idolatrous Jews were wont not only to sacrifice doves, pigeons, lambs, but even to offer their own children. In the prophecies of Jeremiah (7:31), this valley is called Tophet, from Toph, a drum; because they beat a drum during these horrible rites, lest the cries and shrieks of the infants who were burned should be heard by the assembly. At length these nefarious practices were abolished by Josiah, and the Jews brought back to the pure worship of God, 2 Kings 23. After this they held the place in such abomination that they cast into it all kinds of filth, and the carcasses of beasts, and the unburied bodies of criminals who had been executed. Continual fires were necessary in order to consume these, lest the putrefaction should infect the air; and there were always worms feeding on the remaining relics. Hence it came, that any severe punishment, especially an infamous kind of death, was described by the word Gehenna, or Hell."

Now from the statements Jesus made it is evident that He was deeply concerned that these unrepentant persons would go to the real "Gehenna" or place of torment/affliction. That this garbage dump no doubt in His mind, was a parallel future type of Hell in a literal sense and cannot be doubted. The differing opinion simply is that such as the Watchtower believe that the final "Gehenna" will be a place of annihilation, while many universalists only view it as symbolic of trouble and affliction in this life etc. That Jesus had a very different view of the final judgment however is evident when the following facts are reviewed.

1. That Jesus was referring to a "future" judgment is evident from His statement about the coming future judgment in which the living person having been raised from the dead and after being judged unworthy/unsaved, is cast into fire for destruction/punishment.

2. Interesting is that while Watchtower/Mormons etc, use the "red hot coals in the eyes of a dog" idea to ridicule the idea that God would put someone into a lake of fire forever and ever to suffer on and on since Jesus does indeed say that living persons would be cast there.

Now would not those who are cast into the fire feel at least for a few seconds excruciating pain and suffering before death if they were indeed to die and be annihilated? Our Savior could 'delight' in that? The same could be said of a cruel boy in slowly burning a lowly worm or frog to death with fire, in glee watching as they die squirming in agony. Now is this the God of the Bible? Of course not! Now for anyone about to be cast into a lake of fire would raise the utmost terror/fear in their hearts.

Are we to believe that if souls are to be annihilated in the last judgment that God is going to have one last bit of pleasure in seeing them scream and writhe in agony as they are being physically consumed by liquid fire and brimstone Also would they not be screaming, begging and pleading for mercy upon hearing God sentence them to be annihilated in the burning brimstone and fire? The Watchtower say that it would be cruel for God to allow someone to consciously suffer on and on endlessly in fire and brimstone (which is true), but then they turn around and contradict themselves by saying God is going to "burn them up and thus annihilate them." Either way the lost would suffer unimaginable horror, terror and fear under the hand of Almighty God, whether it be for several seconds or hours while being judged before being 'annihilated,' or being sentenced to suffer on and on, indeterminately.

The Watchtower cannot have it their way if it cannot be the other way as well! If the lost souls are not to suffer on and on (indeterminately) saying that would make God "cruel," then they cannot suffer even a few seconds, as would be the case if the Watchtower theory is correct. (If any contact with the Lake of Fire would be cruel then God would have to 'speak the wicked souls out of existence.') The word 'torment' in the English language has come to mean 'unjustified pain and suffering,' which I suppose it can mean, but in the Greek it merely means 'affliction' or 'punishment.' In that regards, then it certainly can be said that God 'torments people in Hell fire!' He 'afflicts, punishes them in Hell fire,' but does not unjustifiably do so endlessly. Certainly if He did so, then such would be unjustified 'torment pain and affliction,' and we would have to agree with the Watchtower. God could surely "speak them out of existence" if He needed to, just after totally condemning them being lost. Now that would keep God from being 'cruel' for a few seconds or hours as He would be, if the Watchtower theory were correct.

Surely this last fact does point to the truth that (due to God creating it) the fires of Hell/Lake of Fire are indeed curative by allowing man to feel the pain of his sins on and on, an eternal everlasting lesson, and no of course not redemptive. In other words, why would God use His creative powers to make such a Lake of Fire/Hell just to "to cruelly burn someone up forever," when He could just as easily "speak them out of existence?"

3. That Jesus did indeed endorse suffering on and on, "aionios and aionios" is evident since He said that the coming judgment unto damnation was to be a "garbage dump for the lost souls" or a "Gehennah for lost souls," in the which the difference being that the "fire in this final judgment was unquenchable (Gehennah in Jerusalem burns no more and the worms in Gehennah did die but die no more as it is no more used) <u>and the worm</u> (which is a lowly debased creature i.e. a picture of the lost soul) <u>dieth not</u>!

What did Jesus say again? What did He say? He plainly said that in the final judgment which was a parallel to the "garbage dump Gehennah," that the fire <u>there</u> is (in the final judgment) "Not quenched and where the worm <u>dieth not</u>." End of parallel? No not quite. Since the fires in the Valley of Hinnon burnt on and on or "aionios and aionios, at that time (until the end of their usefulness), and now they do not, then that future judgment will burn on and on, or "aionios and aionios" as well, but not "aidios and aidios!"

One day that punishment will end as well. Remember that "inflicted pain" can be a curative remedy, and yea an eternal forever, endless reminder that sin must be totally abandoned. Thus those cast into the lake of fire, the final "Gehenna," will be "judged according to their works." Different lengths of curative pain for differing degrees for their sin and wickedness. Then at the end of that indeterminate period of suffering for souls so unfortunate to enter therein, they will be released to willingly and gladly embrace the only way of salvation thru the new birth, repentance and faith in Jesus Christ.

4. That Jesus did indeed look upon the fires of the final judgment or Hell/the Lake of Fire as continuous, on and on, is plain here. There is no annihilation here at all, and the fact that Jesus clarified the true differences between the garbage dump Gehenna and the last Gehenna as a final place of judgment shows He did indeed consider the place to be "aionios and aionios" or on and on of indefinite duration, but of course not "aidios" or endless.

5. One interesting point of consideration is that if the "Gehenna" judgment is to be a time of annihilation for the wicked, then why should Jesus call them from the realms of the dead, to awake from 'soul sleep.' (The Watchtower teach that the wicked are merely 'asleep' in the grave with no consciousness after death, i.e. if they are 'asleep' then why not let them continue as such?) After 'awakening' then the wicked supposedly faces a judgment, which by Watchtower doctrine will cause the wicked to cease to exist (annihilation) for all eternity!

So, supposedly the wicked no matter how wicked, upon death, simply go into a deep sleep for a long period of time until the second resurrection, then are brought back to life, stood before God, listen to their sentence of 'annihilation' being read, and are cast into a lake of fire to be "burned up" forever. Thus they would 'know nothing' after death until the resurrection, no doubt be 'quite comfortable' standing before God while hearing this judgment, and only suffer for a few seconds before they 'cease to exist' for eternity!

Now does that make sense that someone as wicked as Hitler or Stalin should 'sleep,' be awakened for a few moments, and then (the same as being put back to sleep) be annihilated for eternity? That is all the punishment they will receive for slaughtering millions of innocent men, women, and children? I guess it is plain the Watchtower say so. The wrath and justice of God upon the wicked only lasts for a few seconds of their consciousness at the white throne judgment when they are thrown alive into the Lake of Fire to be annihilated?

Following are scriptures, which show the severity of punishment (conscious punishment after death at that) and the warnings for all to avoid such a place at all costs. Jesus could not have been using only figurative speech for a symbolic place since His warnings had to have been actual and literally true. If not actual and literally true, then He did not mean anything!

> Matthew 5:29 And if thy right eye offend thee, pluck it out, and cast it from thee: for it is profitable for thee that one of thy members should perish, and not that thy whole body should be cast into Hell.

> Matthew 5:30 And if thy right hand offend thee, cut it off, and cast it from thee: for it is profitable for thee that one of thy members should perish, and not that thy whole body should be cast into Hell.

> Matthew 10:28 And fear not them which kill the body, but are not able to kill the soul: but rather fear him which is able to destroy both soul and body in Hell.

> Matthew 18:9 And if thine eye offend thee, pluck it out, and cast it from thee: it is better for thee to enter into life with one eye, rather than having two eyes to be cast into Hell fire.

> Matthew 23:15 Woe unto you, scribes and Pharisees, hypocrites! for ye compass sea and land to make one proselyte, and when he is made, ye make him twofold more the child of Hell than yourselves.

> Matthew 23:33 Ye serpents, ye generation of vipers, how can ye escape the damnation of Hell?

> Mark 9:43 And if thy hand offend thee, cut it off: it is better for thee to enter into life maimed, than having two hands to go into Hell, into the fire that never shall be quenched:

Mark 9:45 And if thy foot offend thee, cut it off: it is better for thee to enter halt into life, than having two feet to be cast into Hell, into the fire that never shall be quenched:

Mark 9:47 And if thine eye offend thee, pluck it out: it is better for thee to enter into the kingdom of God with one eye, than having two eyes to be cast into Hell fire:

Luke 12:5 But I will forewarn you whom ye shall fear: Fear him, which after he hath killed hath power to cast into Hell; yea, I say unto you, Fear him.

Tartarus

"Tartarus in Greek" a place in the underworld — even lower than Hades. This word only occurs once (in 2 Peter 2:4) where it is translated "Hell." Strongs Concord.

> "for if God spared not the angels that sinned, but cast them down to Hell, and delivered them into chains of darkness, to be reserved unto JUDGMENT...."

There are no Biblical references to people going to Tartarus, which seems to be a separate place from Hades and reserved for fallen angels.

The Final Lake of Fire Rev. 20

The following facts are clearly drawn from this chapter and the account of judgment at the Great White throne and Lake of Fire.

1. The totality of lost humanity, no doubt an innumerable number of souls are at this final of all final judgments and are brought to stand before God at the Great White Throne.

2. Every dead body in the grave from the earth and the sea is resurrected their souls taken out of Sheol/Hades having been reunited with their bodies. These 'bodies' are raised eternal bodies, not sub-

ject to death/disease etc but will be subject to pain and suffering according to their sentence in the Lake of Fire.

3. These resurrected persons are those who have not been saved while alive, and as well of course did not meet the Lord in the air at His second coming thus remaining in Sheol/Hades the abode of those in the spirit world.

4. The fact that the grave whether it be earth or sea, and as well as Sheol/Hades is emptied of all bodies and souls contained therein voids the need for both places (the grave and Sheol/Hades) since they will die (physically) no more. Those places thus will permanently cease to exist. Physical death separation of body and spirit as we know it today) will be abolished. No more will anyone 'die' since they will be in an eternal body fit to exist for eternity.

5. The 'books of God' are opened, i.e. the records containing all of the works of all the unsaved and their punishment is set according to their works, punishment to be meted out in the Lake of Fire. The book of life is as well opened, and this is the fate of those not found in the book. Some falsely say that only the lost are at this judgment and no saved will be there. However it must be remembered that during the 1000 year millennial reign of Christ that though life span is greatly increased people will still be born and die as they do today! Therefore those who died saved (during the millennium), will enter heaven during that time, and those dying lost will go to abode of the damned.

Remember, the saved 144,000 Jews of the twelve tribes of Israel will repopulate the earth after Daniel's 70th week and their children and grandchildren, etc, will need to hopefully find salvation as we do today. Thus those saints who die during the 1000 year millennium must have a resurrection, which will take place at the White Throne Judgment. We, who were raptured before the millennium, will be here in glorified perfect bodies ruling with Christ over those 144,000 and their offspring for 1,000 years.

6. That 'death' is destroyed in the Lake of Fire is factual. The idea that some say 'the Lake of Fire is the second death' and so it just as well can be said that 'the second death is the Lake of Fire' appears valid. It is further stated that 'death' is destroyed in the Lake of Fire. That there will be no more death I Cor. 15:55, that the last enemy to be destroyed is death itself and that is the purpose of the Lake of Fire. It appears to fit perfectly. To say that the Lake of Fire is 'eternal/endless death is to violate God's intended understanding that 'death will be no more.' But to say that the Lake of Fire is the 'destruction' of death, and the 'end' of death and that death will be no more is certainly true to God's Word.

   The 'second death' plainly therefore is not endless 'death' for the wicked unsaved but the 'end' of death and separation from God forever. Plainly the Lake of Fire will 'end forever' separation of the wicked from their God as soon as their sentence is completed 'according to their works' in that Lake of Fire! Then and only then "Every knee shall bow and every tongue shall confess…" The Lake of Fire is the second death, the end of death.

7. This 'Lake of Fire' already contains the anti-christ, the beast and the false prophet, all who were plainly 'men' driven by Satan to oppose God. They enter the Lake of Fire in Rev. 19 at their defeat at the battle of Armageddon. The armies of the anti-christ (slain at Armageddon) will not be cast into the Lake until the second resurrection after the millennium. Their abode will of course be Sheol/Hades until then.

   For whatever reason the false trinity is housed separately in the Lake of Fire until then. To say that when one is cast into the Lake of Fire he is annihilated is clearly shown to be false by Rev. 19. This is where the beast and false prophet were cast, and are clearly still alive when after the 1,000 years Satan is cast there. Rev20. The scripture plainly says they will be tormented (afflicted/punished) day and night forever and forever *(Greek for 'continuously' not 'endlessly' ed.).* Certainly not annihilated when cast there.

8. The fact that all unsaved souls enter the realm of the damned as having been 'deceived' by lies and Satan and his emissaries' gives weight to the truth that God does not give infinite punishment for finite sins. It gives weight to the fact that the punishment Jesus described as coming for the lost was to be "Aionios" and not "Aidios." No not 'endless punishment' but punishment of indefinite duration as 'Aionios' indicates. The Lake of Fire is to 'punish' the lost, 'according to their works' and that can only be by degree, or punishment deserved according to wickedness.

   Once that punishment has reached its climax in its effects on that lost souls say 'restoration to agreement with God's will and experiencing suffering because of violating it,' then it will of necessity have to cease, and there will be no more need for such painful suffering ever again. If punishment were to be endless, then only Hell would exist and no need for the Lake of Fire/ judgment. How much weight these facts must come to bear upon us as Christians to win the lost who are deceived by Satan. God has given us that commission, and laid upon us that responsibility to do our best to win them to Jesus! If we fail, the Lake of Fire will not!

9. No, while the Lake of Fire is indeed the last and final judgment in the universe, it is not the endless final state of the unsaved. It is clearly a place of punishment, retribution, and yes/yea an 'improvement' and a move to eventual repentance and forgiveness in experiencing the new birth in Jesus Christ. There is much the scripture does not tell us about the future in Heaven, but one thing certain God will be the ultimate victor and ruler of the universe over sin Hell and the grave and all will be ultimately saved after much pain sorrow and suffering.

10. We would challenge any one, to show one verse in Chapter 20 which indicates that those who are cast into the Lake of Fire, are sent there

forever/endlessly for eternity! Quite the contrary. It must be noted that the unsaved dead are judged *according to their works*! Their works were only temporal, during their lifetime, and justice cannot be served to punish someone for endless eternity for temporal works. Their punishment will be proportional to their works, forever and forever, "aionios ton aionios" or on and on continuously (not endlessly) with no indication of how long since sentences will vary according to wickedness. Chapter 21 gives the plain and simple truth that once the Lake of Fire has fulfilled its purpose; it will be obsolete and done away with, being part of the first heaven and the first earth. Eternal justice cannot exist without eternal mercy!

Rev. 21:1-4

"Now I saw a new heaven and a new earth, for the first heaven and the first earth had passed away. Also there was no more sea... And I heard a loud voice from heaven saying, Behold the tabernacle of God is with men, and He will dwell with them, and they shall be His people. God Himself will be with them and he their God, and God shall wipe away every tear from their eyes, *there shall be no more death, nor sorrow, nor crying. There shall be no more pain, for the former things have passed away.*"

(Damnationists say there will be death and pain for endless eternity contradicting vs.4.)

Here as well no doubt the tears of sorrow and emotional pain in the hearts of mothers and fathers (who have lost children or relatives due to their lost condition and being sent to the Lake of Fire) will finally be healed once the sentence of their loved one is fulfilled, and conversion completed. Note that though verses 5-8 were written *in* chapter 21 (the prophetical scene of the new heaven and earth), they are none the less *historical* at the future fulfillment of verses 1-4 (*not prophetical* especially noting verse 8).

Rev. 21:8
But the fearful and unbelieving and the abominable and murderers and lewd men, and sorcerers, and idolaters and all liars shall have their part in the lake which burneth with fire and brimstone which is the second death. (*This 'second death' was historically and previously fulfilled in Rev. 20:15*).

Verse 5 makes this very plain, "…I make all things new, and he said unto me, **write**: for these words are true and faithful." This word "write" was spoken in about A.D. 90 when John was on the Isle of Patmos receiving the Revelation from the Lord as He sat on His throne in glory. One last point, the damnationist sees chapter 21 *immediately* taking place after the White Throne Judgment. No! This period of time could be fifty or one thousand years, etc, who knows, but certainly long enough for the sentences in the Lake of Fire to be carried out. Long enough for punishment, humiliation and subjection of the lost, and finally seeing them bend their knees in full conversion to Jesus Christ King of kings and Lord of lords! At the end of this period, "…every knee shall bow" and all be converted!

Eventual universal salvation? Absolutely yes. "And every knee shall bow, and every tongue shall confess that Jesus Christ is Lord to the glory of God the Father." As stated, and restated here, these confessions will not be cynical but true heartfelt confessions which will lead to repentance and the new birth in Christ. It can be no other way. The Lake of Fire, the ultimate punishment leading to the eventual confession/conversion of all sinners, no matter how wicked or depraved.

Destruction of the Lake of Fire And Brimstone
Damnationists adamantly declare that sinners will be tormented day and night for eternity in the Lake of Fire and Brimstone when the Word of God actually teaches no such thing. Yes, absolutely there will be a

Lake of Fire, a place of controlled limited punishment, but that final place of punishment will one day be destroyed once its purpose is fulfilled. A careful and honest reading of Revelation 19 and 20 proves beyond reasonable doubt that such will be the case. To claim differently, as the damnationists do, is a flagrant and serious addition to the Word of God! First notice the scriptures mentioning this Lake of Fire.

Revelation 19:20

And the beast was taken, and with him the false prophet that wrought miracles before him, with which he deceived them that had received the mark of the beast, and them that worshipped his image. These both were cast alive into a lake of fire burning with brimstone.

Revelation 20:14

And death and Hell were cast into the lake of fire. This is the second death.

Revelation 20:15

And whosoever was not found written in the book of life was cast into the lake of fire.

Revelation 14:10

the same shall drink of the wine of the wrath of God, which is poured out without mixture into the cup of his indignation; and he shall be tormented with fire and brimstone in the presence of the Holy angels, and in the presence of the Lamb:

Revelation 20:10

And the devil that deceived them was cast into the lake of fire and brimstone, where the beast and the false prophet are, and shall be tormented day and night forever and ever.

Revelation 21:8

Chapter One | The Biblical Hell

But the fearful, and unbelieving, and the abominable, and murderers, and whoremongers, and sorcerers, and idolaters, and all liars, shall have their part in the lake which burneth with fire and brimstone: which is the second death.

1. The Lake of Fire is first seen where? In Revelation 19:20.

2. Now *where* is the Lake of Fire (exact location) mentioned in these verses, and just *when* does this event take place? The facts are the Lake of Fire is **on the** earth into which the beast and false prophet are cast into at the end of their hideous reign **upon the** earth. Someone asks where did the Lake of Fire come from? To which the only logical answer possible is that God created it somewhere on earth during the period of time called 'The Day of the Lord.' (Remember the 'Day of the Lord' begins with the opening of the sixth seal of the seven sealed book by the angel in Revelation, and lasts on to the end of the millennium).

    Remember that during the vial judgment the angel pours out (Rev. 15:8) upon the sun, that it scorches the earth with great heat. Maybe the heat is so immense that it evaporates a large enough body of water to make room for the Lake of Fire, but who knows since with God all things are possible.

3. The Lake of Fire is the place of final punishment for the unsaved, in which they are judged and punished *'according to their works.'* Rev. 20:12. There is absolutely no mention of 'endless or eternal/forever (aidios) never ending punishment' anywhere in these chapters. Yes, (aionios) continuous temporal indefinite length punishment for temporal evil works, but not endless punishment for temporal works. God does not give infinite punishment for finite sins.

4. Now notice carefully, that the beast and false prophet are held in the Lake of Fire under punishment, 'on the earth' during the 1000 year earthly reign of Christ. They are still there, (Rev. 20:10) at the end of the 1000 years when Satan is loosed from his prison, the bottom-

less pit (in the earth), and goes throughout the earth to deceive the nations, again '*on the* earth' this is where the Lake of Fire will be.

5. Simply spoken, the scriptures do not place the Lake of Fire anywhere in outer space, or somewhere on another planet such as the sun, but rather 'on the earth' in which will be the residence of the beast and the false prophet for 1000 years until the end of the millennium. It is clear *only they* will inhabit this place until the final judgment at the end of the millennium, the great White Throne Judgment, and then they'll be cast into the Lake of Fire. Clearly the Lake of fire is a part of the old original heavens and earth.

6. Having dealt sufficiently with the terms 'forever and forever' or 'aionios ton aionios' which is not 'endless' but only 'continuous,' in other parts of this book, now the question begs to be answered, 'When will the Lake of Fire be destroyed?' The answer to this is quite simple. It is destroyed when the new heavens and new earth take the place of the old heavens and earth, when they are renovated by fire and pass away. Clearly since the Lake of Fire is a part of the old earth, it as well ceases to be and passes away. It is an indisputable fact then that the Lake of Fire is a part of the old heavens and earth and is destroyed! Notice:

Revelation 21:1
And I saw a new heaven and a new earth for the first heaven and the first earth were passed away and there was no more sea.

2 Peter 3:9-10
The Lord is not slack concerning His promise as some men count slackness but is long suffering to us-ward, not willing that any should perish, but that all should come to repentance. But the day of the Lord will come as a thief in the night, in the which the heavens shall pass away with fervent heat, the earth also and the works that are therein shall be burned up.

To claim that Revelation 21:8 (one verse which describes the depravity of the people who will be consigned to the Lake of Fire in chapter 20), belongs chronologically in order in chapter 21 is false. Reading the book of Revelation, it is clearly apparent that many places are not meant to be chronologically in sequence, but are diversions to previous events, times and places. Take chapter 12, which clearly is a diversion from the sounding of the seventh trumpet in chapter 11. Chapter 12 refers back to the birth and incarnation of our Savior and as well to His ascension and later rule over the earth with a rod of iron. Events which take place over thousands of years. Verse four of chapter 21 clearly proves that verse 8 literally should be placed back in chapter 20 chronologically at least. Verse four proves beyond doubt that all pain and suffering, all separation from God, all crying/sorrow for lost loved ones etc. will be finished forever/endlessly!

Revelation 21:4
> ...and God shall wipe away all tears from their eyes, and there shall be no more death, neither sorrow, nor crying, neither shall there be any more pain for the former things are passed away.

Clearly then, the Lake of Fire being a creation '**on** the original earth' passes away/is destroyed when the new heavens and earth are created. *"The former things are passed away."* Praise God! Pain and suffering in the Lake of Fire, separation from God and loved ones, no more death for endless eternity as those things shall pass away with the creation of a new heaven and earth! Universal Christian Redemption stands as a Biblical fact which these verses clearly prove. The wicked were punished 'according to their works' and the Lake of Fire finds it culmination of usefulness at the end of such punishment which results in every knee bowing, and every tongue confessing (unto the new birth and salvation for all Romans 10:13) that Jesus Christ is Lord to the glory of God the Father. To deny this is to deny the plain Word of God.

Hell and the Road to Damascus

Paul's experience on the road to Damascus teaches us an important lesson concerning God given revelation and it's relation to salvation. There is no doubt that the apostle Paul would not have been saved/converted had he not had the supernatural revelation on the road to Damascus. While on the road, he was staunchly a Pharisee of the Pharisees, bent on continuing persecuting and putting to death Christians by the thousands, and then suddenly the heavenly vision and voice which brought about his solid conversion.

The simple truth here is that once an unsaved soul is exposed to an irrefutable revelation of truth, that soul then submits to that revelation. Once Saul of Tarsus had the Damascus revelation, he was forced to concede that Jesus was indeed the true and Mighty God whom he was persecuting. Was he saved on the road to Damascus? No absolutely not. The scripture is clear, that "... if any man have not the Spirit of God, he is none of His." Paul was not saved until Ananias entered the house where he was blind, and laid his hands on him. Acts 9 tells us that he was filled with the Holy Spirit (converted/born again) and regained his sight at that time. From the time Jesus appeared to him on the road to Damascus, until Ananias entered the house where he was, Paul was 'digesting' the following facts, which of course he found to be incontrovertible:

1. That Jesus was indeed God, God the Son, and that He indeed had been raised from the dead.

2. That God/Jesus was judging him a wicked man who was totally contrary to His will.

3. That God was highly displeased with him, taking his sight away.

4. That God being highly displeased with him meant he must repent and accept Jesus as his Savior or face dire consequences.

Now this certainly was a very 'mild' revelation when compared with the revelation an unsaved man has when he dies and finds himself in Hell-fire. Whether the 'revelation' is a revelation in this life or the next matters not. The fact is that when any man has such irrefutable revelation if he is lost, he will give ascent to it and submit. The only difference is that some men are so wicked and hardened in their sins, that any simple revelation given to them in this life would be rejected; they simply are not 'open to receive it.' In the next life however, dying and finding themselves in the literal revelation of Hell's torment/affliction, they are forced to accept the same 4 conclusions Paul was.

The sad difference then is though, that they must consciously suffer for their sins aionios and aionios, on and on, until such a time as God sees fit to 'lay His hands on them.' An interesting thought is that we should praise God for His love and concern in giving irrefutable revelations even if it means a man going to Hell to receive it. God placing a man in Hell, and He is certainly the one who does it, does indeed bring wrath and punishment upon the lost by placing him in there, but at the same time, it is His love which allows Him to do it. The ultimate end of anyone suffering in Hell is to experience such a revelation that he cannot deny, and as well bring him one day to bended knee and salvation. Hell/Lake of Fire therefore becomes a tool of God's everlasting mercy to force a man to see/accept the truth and be saved!

'Hell' in the English

The Hebrew word Sheol occurs sixty-five times in the Old Testament. The KJV translates Sheol into into 'pit' three times and 'Hell' 31 times. Sheol is translated as grave, a total of 31 times. It is obvious that if "Sheol" means "Hell," it should not be translated "grave/pit." Here is a prime example of a weakness of the K.J.V. translation into English by the King James translators. It is needful at this point to remind the reader of some very important facts concerning the K.J.V. translation.

1. The 1611 K.J.V is just that, another translation among many others by fallible men.
2. To say this version is equal to the original Greek/Hebrew in purity is to say that the translators of this version acted under divine inspiration. The Word of God plainly says that "All scripture is given by

inspiration of God..." which can only be said of the Greek and Hebrew (original autographs). Now "scripture" is not given to anyone today, nor has been since it was solely given to the writers of the 66 books of the Bible. The 1611 '*version*' was not "God breathed" as was the original autographs.

3. To teach as the Ruckmanites do that the 1611 version is superior to the Greek/Hebrew from which it was taken is to insult the scriptures as they are contained in the original languages (with only miniscule differences), which are readily accessible today.

4. To say that all Greek/Hebrew MSS are corrupt, or have been corrupted and are unworthy of notice is to say the world has not had the Word of God from the destruction of the original autographs, until the 1611 version came to be. That assumption is the only conclusion one can reach if Ruckmanism is true and thank God it is not. I don't think that the 'gates of Hell' prevailed against the church for all those centuries.

Jesus said they would not. The simple fact is, that while the 'received text' also known as the 'Byzantine Text' or 'Textus Receptus' does indeed have some variations. (The 'Textus Receptus' was originally compiled by Roman Catholic Priest and Christian humanist Desiderius Erasmus, [1469?-1536] from seven manuscripts none of them dated before the 11th Century. These manuscripts are listed in point 10 of this section. Over 5000 manuscripts are available to scholars today). Those variations are irrelevant to important doctrine, and when compared with other Greek/Hebrew texts, do indeed correct each other.

To those who love the KJV, the fact is there were three editions of the KJV in 1611 and not one entirely agrees with the other! Nearly all AV's in current use are the Benjamin Blayney revision of 1769, and none of them are the 1611. At the time he produced the revision, Blayney was, and remained a respected member of the Oxford faculty. Virtually no one today uses a 1611 AV, nor would any reasonable person wish to do so; there are simply too many irregularities. The 1769 Blayney revision is far closer to the intentions of the KJV translators than any of the publications that emerged in 1611, but even that version contains some inaccuracies.

Certainly a translation cannot be superior to that from which it was translated as Ruckmanism falsely claims. Nothing done by fallible man can be equal or superior to the Greek/Hebrew. The tenants of Ruckmanism are akin to 'doctrines of devils.' Those following Ruckmanism often quote "The words of the Lord are pure words: as silver tried in a furnace of earth, purified seven times. Thou shalt keep them O Lord, thou shalt preserve them from this generation forever." Ps. 12:6-7. They claim that proves that the K.J.V. must be perfect in every regards else it could not be said that we have the Word of God today.

It must be remembered that of the thousands of Biblical manuscripts not one is identical to another in every miniscule detail. Indeed though the precious Word of God can be reestablished with complete accuracy by comparing scripture with scripture.

5. What can be said of the 1611 version is that it is a wonderful and beautiful translation of God's Word, and indeed God has blessed the usage of it over the centuries. It must also be said that any weakness in any part of its translation no matter how small or large, does not and cannot affect any major/important doctrines.

The argument that the K.J.V. is the Word of God in the English language, and if it has errors in it, then it can be said the Word of God is impure and has errors in it, and riddled with errors is false! First, the A.V. is for a fact a _translation_ of the Word of God from the Greek/Hebrew. Therefore it cannot be said to be more than a translation, no more than the many other translation over the centuries. The Greek plainly states that, "… All scripture is given by inspiration of God…" it does not say that "… All translations of scripture are given by inspiration of God…!" 'Translation' of scripture cannot be said to be 'inspiration' of scripture so no <u>translation</u> done by fallible man can be said to be error free.

The only correct thing that can be said is that the K.J.V. gives us the exact, perfect, Word of God in the English in so far as it is translated correctly. To say it perfectly mirrors the Word of God in the Greek is totally false. There is no doubt though, that we can know exactly what God wants us to know from studying it, along with the Greek and Hebrew. The final word here is that the K.J.V. is a beautiful translation of the Word of God from the Greek/Hebrew, and nothing more can be said.

6. To say the K.J.V. 'contains' the Word of God is not correct. That statement infers that it 'contains' along with, the uninspired writings of men, the Word of God. That is totally false and unacceptable.

7. To say the K.J.V. is the infallible, inspired Word of God, inerrant, and without flaw, and in need of no correction (Ruckmanism teaches this), definitely is in serious error. Any translation (including the 1611 version) of the extant MSS Heb/Gk. is subject to flaw. ANY translation is open to correction/evaluation and fuller explanation, and as well those few difficult words/passages can be illuminated as to meaning by examining the original languages.

8. If indeed the previous false claim were true, then extant Greek/Hebrew MSS must be relegated to the waste basket, and totally ignored. As well then, any translations done in any other languages must use only the 1611 version as its base. If that is to be the case, then the new translation done by Dr. John Doe, or professor whoever, will be subject to being in error and therefore not 100% guaranteed to fully be the exact Word of God.

9. The only truly correct statement which can be made concerning the K.J.V. (or any translation) is that; The 1611 version brings to us the infallible, perfect Word of God, (insofar as it is correctly translated), and the A.V. has been greatly blessed by God over the centu-

ries in doing just that. (Quoting from Theodore H. Mann Translation Problems... "No translation lasts forever, and this is as true for the KJV as it was for the Wycliff Version, the Bishops' Bible, or the Geneva Bible.

It will also be true for the reputable contemporary translations if their editors cease to periodically revise them. Language eventually changes, and it becomes necessary to produce translations that reflect that change. Older and better ancient biblical manuscripts are discovered. Techniques for examining and assessing the relative reliability of the manuscripts improve, providing biblical-language scholars with improved means of making accurate text-critical decisions. Remember the original biblical documents no longer exist. The A.V. long ago became antiquated, but due to outcries against change by those who felt that new translations were somehow offensive to God, public acceptance of new and better versions was long delayed. That is to say, new translations were produced, but they usually failed to gain a foothold.")

10. The manuscripts used by Erasmus were minuscules: (1) Codex 1eap (the entire NT except for Revelation—12th Century); (2) Codex 1r (the book of Revelation except for the last six verses—12th Century); (3) Codex 2e (the Gospels—12th Century); (4) Codex 2ap (Acts and the Epistles—12th Century or later); (5) Codex 4ap (Acts and the Epistles—15th); (6) Codex 7p (Pauline Epistles—11th); (7) Codex 817 (Gospels—15th). [Key: e=Gospels; a=Acts and Catholic letters; p=Pauline letters, including Hebrews; r=Revelation] (From Translation Problems in the KJV New Testament by Theodore H. Mann).

(Getting back to the translators and their translation of 'Hell' into the English.) It is evident the translators were trying to say something in English that is totally unsupported by the Greek. 'Sheol' does not, nor can it mean 'grave or pit.' As plainly stated earlier, 'pit and grave' have two entirely different Greek words to represent them. There are some who try to go back to the original meaning of 'Hell' in the old English common word usage, such as a place to hide, or some sort of covering or even such as a common potato cellar, or even tiles of a roof which 'cover or hide,' in order to claim that was or is the actual meaning of the word 'Hades,' and that it therefore cannot mean a place of conscious suffering on and on in the afterlife.

A simple answer to that is the English cannot determine what any Greek or Hebrew word means, nor can it void what Jesus taught Sheol/Hades was all about. Even though the word Hell may have had the afore mentioned meanings at some point in the distant past, many words metamorphose from their original meanings to mean something entirely different. Take the word in our lifetime "gay." Fifty years ago, if someone was said to be "gay" it simply meant he was "happy." Now though it has come to mean that someone is homosexual/lesbian etc. The fact is, it makes absolutely no difference what the old English word 'Hell' originally meant, or whence it was derived, the underlying Greek/Hebrew words 'Sheol/Hades' denote the place of departed spirits in the underworld!

As well that old English word took upon a new meaning denoting the underworld the place of departed unsaved/wicked spirits. The Greek must be honored, and take precedence over the English. To say that 'Hell' as it is understood today must be understood as it was hundreds of years ago therefore is false since words do metamorphose as did the word 'gay.' The word 'Hell' today (in English) means the same thing as the words 'Sheol/Hades,' the underworld, the place of departed spirits. J.W. Hanson brings some interesting facts to the table concerning the origin of the doctrine of "endless/eternal punishment" as follows"

Origin of Endless Punishment

When our Lord spoke, the doctrine of unending torment was believed by many of those who listened to his words, and they stated it in terms and employed others, entirely differently, in describing the duration of punishment, from the terms afterward used by those who taught universal salvation and annihilation, and so gave to the terms in question the sense of unlimited duration. For example, the Pharisees, according to Josephus, regarded the penalty of sin as torment without end, and they stated the doctrine in unambiguous terms. They called it eirgmos aidios (eternal imprisonment) and timorion adialeipton (endless torment), while our Lord called the punishment of sin aionion kolasin (age-long chastisement).

Meaning of Scriptural Terms

The language of Josephus is used by the profane Greeks, but is never found in the New Testament connected with punishment. Josephus, writing in Greek to Jews, frequently employs the word that our Lord used to define the duration of punishment (aionios), but he applies it to things that had ended or that will end. Can it be doubted that our Lord placed his ban on the doctrine that the Jews had derived from the heathen by never using their terms describing it, and that he taught a limited punishment by employing words to define it that only meant limited duration in contemporaneous literature? Josephus used the word aionos with its current meaning of limited duration. He applies it to the imprisonment of John the Tyrant; to Herod's reputation; to the glory acquired by soldiers; to the fame of an army as a "happy life and aionian glory." He used the words as do the Scriptures to denote limited duration, but when he would describe endless duration he uses different terms. Of the doctrine of the Pharisees he says: They believe that wicked spirits are to be kept in an eternal imprisonment (eirgmon aidion). The Pharisees say all souls are incorruptible, but while those of good men are removed into other bodies those of bad men are subject to eternal punishment" (aidios timoria). Elsewhere he says that the Essenes, "allot to bad souls a dark, tempestuous place, full of never-ceasing torment (timoria adialeipton), where they suffer a deathless torment" (athanaton timorion). Aidion and athanaton are his favorite terms for duration, and timoria (torment) for punishment.

Let the reader be fully aware that the author of this booklet in no way endorses all of Hanson's doctrinal positions, in particular his view that Hell is merely figurative, or not a place of punishment in the next world in the Word of God. It is indeed amazing that he has written such a brilliant expose' on the perversion of translating "aionios" as endless, but misses the true punishment aspect of Sheol/Hades. He is quoted in tentmaker.org, a site which also holds such an unscriptural view as follows: We deny that inspiration has named Hell as a place or condition of punishment in the spirit world. It seems a philosophical conclusion and there are Scriptures that appear to many Universalists to teach that the future life is affected to a greater or less extent, by human conduct here; but that Hell is a place or condition of suffering after death is not believed by any and as we trust we have shown, the Scriptures never so designate it *(as such. Ed.)*.

So we are to believe that God's patience finally runs out for the incorrigibly wicked, and that He in utter disgust, anger, wrath and frustration simply forever/eternally turns His back on them, consigning them to be tormented in Hell-fire and brimstone in the Lake of Fire for eternity? This is what the scriptures teach? Not hardly! We know the scriptures teach that His mercy endures forever. See Psalm 106:1 and 107:1. It certainly cannot be said that His mercy is only reserved for the saints, the people of God. The scripture is clear that God does not give up, but 'teaches' sinners in the way of righteousness. Notice the following:

Psalm 25:8

Good and upright is the Lord, therefore He will teach sinners in the way.

Now what 'way' is it that the Lord teaches the wicked? Why simply the way of righteousness!

1. The fact is that all sinners need to be taught.

2. The wicked will not therefore be abandoned to ignorance for eternity.

3. Hell and the Lake of Fire therefore become ultimate tools in instruction of the need for righteousness and holiness, but certainly not a tool of sadistic punishment for all of eternity! The terrible suffering for some in these places certainly will bring punishment for evil and as well will burn away the dross of unbelief, and pave the way to repentance unto salvation.

CHAPTER TWO

DARE TO INSULT JEHOVAH!?

God the "Inventor" of Endless Suffering in the Lake of Fire?

Absolutely everything that God plans He plans and executes for a justified reason and purpose. God cannot be the author of sin (as the Calvinists falsely claim), nor can He design, plan and purpose to do anything, which contradicts His holy and righteous character. No one can deny that! If, and we say IF, endless/never ending torment/affliction in the Lake of Fire/Hell and as well endless/eternal conscious existence and suffering there for the damned were true, then God Himself designed it that way. No one can deny that.

Readers note: Recently, a pastor was proudly proclaiming that years ago, his fundamentalist church voted to come out of the Southern Baptist Convention to become independent, due to some tendencies toward modernism/compromise in the convention. No doubt this good pastor is totally ignorant of the gross insult against Christ his own church is embroiled in under his leadership, by standing firmly on the false doctrine of endless/eternal torment of lost souls in the Lake of Fire. That gross insult of course is the false claim that our blessed Savior is going to soak His enemies in liquid fire and brimstone, and torment them endlessly/eternally. "For God so loved the world…"??? Now a relevant question arises, 'Just how can God/Christ, so love the unsaved world, if they are worthy of endless/eternal never ending torment in the Lake of Fire?' if their sinful actions are truly worthy of such endless torment, then why save them at all, or even why love them at all? The fact is that if anyone is worthy of eternal/endless torment in fire and brimstone, then we all are worthy of the same! The truth is, that we all without exception deserve punishment for our sins, and that according to our sins, but certainly not merciless eternal/endless torment in liquid fire and brimstone for eternity.

Now think, say in the next life you the reader or I were given the responsibility to monitor the pain and suffering of those in torments, and say even to be responsible to "add" occasional suffering and pain to their bodies in the Lake of Fire endlessly/forever. That would mean simply that what we were doing would be at the plan/design of God for His purpose whatever. Can there be "unbearable pain in Hell and the Lake of Fire?" Certainly it could not be that since the wicked supposedly would have to bear it for endless eternity.

In this life when pain is termed "unbearable" there is usually always an escape by sedative, pain killer, or even the sinful act of suicide. The doctrine of "endless suffering in Hell and later the Lake of Fire," simply teaches that God, the designer and creator of the universe spoke these terrible places of torment/affliction into existence with a designed purpose and goal. Now I ask you the reader, what conceivable purpose/purposes with what goals could that possibly be?

1. The first could be that God wants them to suffer for what they "did" or for the sins they committed while alive on earth and also for dying in an unsaved/unregenerate state. Now for them to "suffer" for the sins they committed is righteous indeed. How many wicked people in this life live out their lives in wantonness and lawlessness, and that being sometimes very short lives, seeming to enjoy luxury and depravity, with very little suffering, and then die in that state. (Recently a very popular Democratic senator died, [Teddy Kennedy, and to all appearances unrepentant] after having been very immoral. When asked about all of the millions he had to pay to cover up his sexual flings or hush money to quiet an angry husband, or pay for a divorce he caused, he proudly answered, "It was worth every nickel of it."

Now the Word of God is plain, he will face the judgment and punishment of Almighty God after death!) The very suffering they would endure, since it is "conscious suffering," *would speak invaluable words of a lesson to the unsaved.* The lesson? First, simply that he the lost soul should not have lived and died in sin. Secondly, that he must be punished for his sins since they are against the will and counsel of Almighty God and His laws.

Break the law of God, and suffer the consequences. Thirdly, that it was not worth doing whatever sins the wicked committed since the pain and suffering endured by him far outweighs any *supposed* benefits the sin brought him. Fourthly, that sin cannot be gotten by with, as God's word plainly says, "Be sure your sin will find you out." Fifthly, the lesson that the unsaved cannot escape punishment for his sins. Sixth, that God is justified in punishing the wicked for their sins. They are His creation, living in His universe, under His laws, and therefore owe their allegiance and obedience to Him, not Satan.

Now what person (except an atheist,) could possibly deny that all of these listed reasons have full credibility and teach lessons to the lost? Seventh, remember that when the white throne judgment takes place, the wicked are "judged according to their works" which plainly indicates that there will be degrees of suffering in the place called the Lake of Fire. Lessons, lessons, lessons no doubt.

2. Secondly, would be that God simply enjoys seeing a lost soul writhing in anguish suffering and pain, for being counter to His will for the universe and laws. Since in this case no "lessons" are sought to "instruct" the wicked in torments (the suffering supposedly being endless), then the suffering would/could only give "sadistic" pleasure to God. Now who, who in heaven or earth could possibly believe that God enjoys seeing pain and suffering where there are no lessons to be learned by those suffering?

If suffering in Hell and later the Lake of Fire is to be endless, then there could be no "lessons" for the unsaved, except that God is sadistically inflicting pain and suffering on them forever/endlessly because they disobeyed Him. The "endless torment doctrine" is what some use as a spring board to try to teach that Hell cannot be endless due to the cruelty incurred, and they are right that far, but then go too far by saying therefore Hell or the Lake of Fire is merely symbolic etc., and not literal.

Now these two above points in this authors opinion, are the only two possible reasons for Hell to exist, and of course the first must stand as the truth. God has the best of intentions in everything He does, the best intentions for all of mankind. "God is not willing that any should perish, but that *all* should come unto repentance." Sad it is, that when considering the false doctrine of never ending punishment in torment, is to realize that this aberration of the scriptural truth of justified but temporary suffering for the unsaved in the afterlife, no doubt has been a breeding ground for unbelief and atheism, and ridicule of God and His Word! Endless punishment paints no different picture than unjust suffering at the hands of an unjust god! One writer put it thusly,

"The Hell of tradition is hopeless and eternal, while the Hell of the Scripture like every judgment of God is corrective, remedial, and restorative."

Infinite punishment for finite sins, endless torment which does not "teach" or bring a sinner to an understanding that the punishment he is enduring in Hell/the Lake of Fire is retribution and suffering for the sins he personally committed!? How sad the truth, as one writer so aptly stated it, "...I do not say that all of the definitions by Strong are correct, as Strong based his work on the sometimes erroneous work of the K.J.V. translators, but it (*Strong's concordance-ed.*) is at least consistent with the present Christian misunderstandings of Biblical texts." (*i.e. Strong does not necessarily give definitions of Greek words consistent with the original Greek etc. but rather he gives definitions which are consistent with present Christian understandings or 'interpretations' of original Greek terms.Ed*) J.W. Hanson who has written on Universal salvation gives a simple explanation of the origin of "endless woe and punishment." Note as follows:

"...the doctrine of universal redemption was first made prominent by those to whom Greek was their native tongue, and that they declared that they derived it from the Greek Scriptures, while endless punishment was first taught by Africans and Latins, who derived it from a foreign tongue of which the great teacher of it confesses he was ignorant. *("Augustine" discussed later. Ed.)* Let the reader give to these considerations their full and proper weight, and it will be impossible to believe that the fathers regarded the impenitent as consigned at death to hopeless and endless woe." (Ed. While Hanson's view of Hell is in error [that it is not literal], still his works are right on target in regards to the duration of Hell and the Lake of Fire.)

God Presides Over the Endless/Eternal Ruination of Man?

Man's sin ruined God's perfect creation in the Garden of Eden. There is continued ruination in this present world because of sin and its consequences. For a man to be endlessly damned in Hell/the Lake of Fire would indicate not only did he ruin his life by neglecting free salvation, but after death God continues man's ruination and alienation from salvation confining him in the pit of the damned for endless eternity. Are we to believe this? As well are we to believe that God allows the sinner's will to reign above His for endless eternity. Are we to believe this? Are we to believe that Jesus' will is that the unsaved are to be ruined for eternity, and that He has prepared a place to continue that ruination for time and eternity? Not hardly.

No man can cause the will of God to fail, whether in his life or another. God is not willing that any should perish, but that all should come to repentance! Interesting it is, that some universalists will be quick to deny a literal Hell and punishment therein, but then will agree with the 'eternal/everlasting' (not endless) aspect thereof only to end up with the total destruction/annihilation of the wicked for eternity! While this author does not agree with the following web site http://Hellbusters.8m.com, he finds the following quote from them of particular and telling interest.

"The early writers of the church frequently speak of "everlasting" or "eternal punishment." But these expressions are used just as freely by those who are known to believe in the annihilation of the wicked, and by those who are acknowledged on all hands as believers in universal redemption; so that these phrases are no evidence of a belief in endless punishment.   There is a great difference, as the Scriptures show, between "eternal" or "everlasting," and "endless."

For example: Justin Martyr and Irenaeus say the wicked will be condemned to everlasting punishment, and after this will be annihilated. So the author of the Sibylline Oracles, Clement of Alexandria, Origen, Titus, Bishop of Bostra, Gregory, use the phrase "everlasting" or "eternal punishment" without reserve, though they were acknowledged Universalists. It is plain, therefore, that aionios or "eternal" was not employed by them in the sense of endless; and that the use of this phraseology among the early Christians is no evidence of their belief in endless torments.

Augustine, who flourished about A.D. 400 to 430, was the first to argue that aionios signified strictly endless. He attempted a criticism on the original word, maintaining at first that it always meant endless; but this being so bold and palpable a blunder, he was compelled to abandon it, admitting that it did not always mean endless, but did sometimes; and he brings Matt. 25:46, as proof, arguing that if the "everlasting punishment" was not endless, the "eternal life" was not. And this criticism has been handed down from his time to the present, and is still employed with great confidence, notwithstanding it forces into the spiritual world a judgment which the Savior expressly declared should take place in that generation, before some ('them' ed.) then living should die. Matt. 24:30-34; 16:28; Luke 9:26, 27." (End of quote.)

Now the Watchtower, and other groups etc, hold the doctrine that when the wicked are cast into the Lake of Fire, they are "destroyed" but in this regard they claim that they are "burnt up" and no longer exist in any state, and simply cease to exist. They say that man was made a "living soul," and that man has no inner distinctly separate soul and spirit. Therefore they say that the "soul" of man is really his physical body. On the other hand, the scripture (1 Thess. 5:23) surely teaches as Paul plainly stated, that we are made up of "body, soul, and spirit," as a triune being made in the likeness and image of Almighty God as Genesis 1-2 plainly teaches.

When the body dies and is consumed by decay destruction by fire, or just goes back to dust of the earth, the soul/spirit lives on in another dimension. This is plainly seen in many portions of scripture. Samuel appearing to King Saul (I Sam. 28:13-15) before the witch of Endor in spirit form, Moses and Elijah appearing to Jesus on the mount of transfiguration in spirit form Mk.9, and especially the "souls under the altar in Revelation 6:9 who were martyred under the reign of the coming antichrist the 'son of perdition.'

There are those who falsely teach that Revelation is not to be literally believed, but is only to be interpreted as symbolic with spiritual applications. To this we heartily disagree. If that is the case, then one could interpret Revelation to mean anything that he wanted it to mean, or to mean nothing at all. That would mean there could be an infinite number of possibilities as to the meaning of that wonderful God inspired book penned by John.

No, a simple rule of thumb is that the book of Revelation must be interpreted as literal, unless a figurative/symbolic interpretation is demanded by terms, "such as," "likened unto," etc. To say as the Watchtower that since the scriptures says that man became "a living soul," that when his body dies his soul dies as well is incorrect. Man's soul/spirit does indeed live on as did Lazarus and the rich man in Luke. 16. To spiritualize this chapter is to say that it can mean anything one wants it to mean. As well Jesus never did "interpret" this story to mean something else, or to spiritualize it as he did all parables. He never called this a parable so He meant it to be taken as literally true. Even if it were a parable, all parables without exception were "true stories in themselves" drawn from real life but were used to convey a parallel spiritual truth etc.!

"Everlasting destruction" can easily mean "on and on, continuing punishment and change." When applied to the unsaved dwelling in that terrible place Hell/the Lake of Fire it shows that the "continued punishment and change" the unsaved are having is "corrective pain and suffering" administered to them which will certainly be 'everlasting,' or everlasting in its effects on permanently changing their attitudes, perceptions and proclivity to wickedness! After being released from Hell/Lake of Fire, as they will be one day, how could they not be 'everlastingly changed?' Saved? Certainly not! But that they will be brought to a place of bended knee, and as well to total humiliation and shame being then forced to admit their guilt and blame. "Every knee shall bow, and every tongue shall confess that Jesus Christ is Lord to the glory of God the Father."

The confession which will come from their lips will not be cynical or facieses (tongue in cheek). When upon bended knee, when all those loquacious tongues are finally and permanently silenced, and when those same tongues are humbled sufficiently to admit and declare that they now know and admit the truth they were wrong and need Jesus Christ to be their Savior as well, then they are candidates for the new birth and redemption.

Then they will be willingly, born again! Someone may say such is 'forced salvation' or 'salvation being forced upon the lost. To that claim it is simply the fact that a truth is a truth and all men without exception will finally one day see and fully understand the truth of salvation etc. When one is forced to finally see the error of their way and as well finally willingly and gladly agree as to God's only way of salvation they will be glad to be saved. No forced salvation here. No one can be forced to be saved against his will that is not salvation.

The Augustinian Jesus
Tormenting Lost Souls Forever/Endlessly

Hell and the Lake of Fire were designed and created by none other than our Blessed Savior. Colossians (1:16) tells us that "…by Him were all things created…" That terrible place was not 'made for man' but for the devil and his angels (Matt.25:41), but man has certainly earned his place there by choosing evil rather than good starting in the Garden of Eden and on. The scriptures are absolutely clear on that point when taken literally as they should be. Those therefore who are cleansed of their sins before death escape it, those who are not go there. Now if we are to use today's English and its ***basically accepted definitions***, then we find the popular English translations would teach the following: (Note, yes points 1 and 2 are scripturally sound)

1. Jesus created Hell fire the Lake of Fire for fallen angels (and of course man follows later).

2. Jesus designed the fires in Hell/the Lake of Fire that man and angels would be grievously tormented and punished for their sins. (*Remember, Webster/English definition of 'torment' is "... extreme pain or anguish of body or mind : agony: a source of vexation or pain ..." Sadly the common idea most people have today with the usage of this word, is that it conveys 'unjust, undeserved pain and suffering,' which of course goes against the usage of it in the scriptures*).

3. Jesus desires and does indeed fulfill that desire to torment/afflict in fire and brimstone the lost damned souls endlessly for eternity for not accepting Him as Savior and God. I.E. 'Payback' for rejecting Him and His way of salvation eternally and endlessly. 'Payback' (and *not* punishment with a view of correction and improvement) for those lost souls is what Jesus taught.

Yes certainly the 'English' translation does seem to teach point three of the above, but the authoritative Greek/Hebrew does not! Every word given to the original writers of the Old and New Testaments, every jot and tittle, were given under Divine inspiration of God, and are authoritative over all translations regardless. Having examined the true meanings of 'aionios' and 'aidios' concerning suffering in Hell etc, the scriptures certainly do teach points one and two above, but certainly not point three!

Further, the K.J./Authorized version seems to teach that Jesus' compassion for lost souls ends at their death because they die unsaved and later are resurrected after being tormented in Hell fire for their sins. Then they on bended knee <u>willingly and gladly</u> confess the truth that Jesus Christ is Lord and God, but Jesus standing triumphantly with His foot on their necks, unmercifully sends them screaming into an endless burning Lake of Fire for eternity. Are we to believe this??? Our Savior who with the greatest compassion wept over wicked Jerusalem, who rejected Him, our Savior who loved and called little children to come unto Him, He 'desires' to torment those who are blinded by sin, fear and prejudice in Hell fire for endless eternity?

If this were true, then the fact He created and designed Hell-fire, would naturally show that He desired to torment them for eternity. The scriptures certainly do not teach so in the original languages. No indeed, His will is that 'none shall perish but that *all* should come to a knowledge of the truth' and that desire does not end with the death of the wicked since they immediately after death begin to improve. What about the many many saints in Heaven who have a lost loved one, maybe a son or daughter, maybe a husband or wife who died unsaved and went to Hell. Are we to believe that for endless eternity that lost loved one in Hell/Lake of Fire suffers on and on never ceasing and his/her loved ones in heaven can ignore their terrible suffering?

Are we to believe that those loved ones in Heaven suddenly stop loving and caring about the suffering of those they loved on earth? That loving precious mother who prayed for her wayward son for years and years, only to see him die from an overdose of drugs and wind up in Hell-fire endlessly. She doesn't care anymore? She doesn't care for eternity? She somehow stops loving her son who died in sin and ignorance? Jesus asks her to forget her son and commands her to stop loving him that she will not be unhappy in Heaven? That will be Heaven? Millions in heaven (knowing that millions are in Hell-fire endlessly and in vain are forever pleading for mercy) who have loved ones in Hell-fire pleading with God to end the suffering of their loved ones only to have their pleas fall on God's deaf ears?

Are we to believe that God commands/endorses the spurning of love for lost loved ones being tormented in Hell-fire by those in heaven? As a matter of fact, the only way for one in heaven to cease being broken hearted over their loved one in Hell is for them to stop loving them! Certainly not! Rather they will rejoice that their loved one in Hell-fire is in a place of correction and punishment which when that punishment produces the needed effects on that lost soul, they will be released to bow their knee and embrace their Savior, fulfilling the scripture, ("And every knee shall bow and every tongue shall confess that Jesus Christ is Lord…") and will be happily reunited with them in Heaven/the new earth for eternity!

It needs to be added here also that when one soul repents and is saved there is "…rejoicing in the presence of angels over one sinner which repenteth," So plainly saints in Heaven do not lose their love for their lost loved ones, nor do they when that lost loved one dies and enters the purifying flames of Hells fires. Sorrow on one hand yes, at their lost loved one entering Hell, but on the other gladness that the end of that soul's rebellion against God is going to be forever done away with.

The Christian Universal Commission Shows the So Called 'Non Elect' Don't Exist!

Calvinists claims that the 'elect' were soverignly chosen as such before or at the foundation of the world and of course, that would mean anyone who was 'not pre-elect' from that point on, would have no possibility of salvation, and that the 'elect' were chosen to 'ferret' out the 'pre-elect' from out of the masses of non elect humanity (in the future once they themselves find salvation according to their 'pre-elect' blessing unto salvation). Now that is the basic false heresy promoted by the Calvinist. The real truth is, there is no such thing as 'non elect' persons. Astonishing it is that 'all of mankind' are elect or pre-elect (in Christ)!

Plain it is then, that no man can be said to be a sole 'soverignly' elected person to the exclusion of any others! In fact one does not become one of the 'elect' until he becomes born-again (much to the Augustinian/

Calvinists chagrin). The word 'elect' is no different in the Word of God than the words, saints, Christians, sons of God, chosen. So saying non-elect is the same as saying non-saint?! It just doesn't make sense!

Considering the fact of eventual universal salvation for all men, it comes to light that the so called 'non elect' really can and will be saved. Again as well, the elect can and are to win the so called non elect to Christ! Since all men are eventually to come to Christ and be saved, then it only stands to reason that the elect have the commission to win the so called non elect to Christ! This in turn raises the question for the Calvinist, "Just where in the Word of God does it say that the unsaved are called the "non elect?" Certainly the saved are called the 'elect' but never are the unsaved or wicked lost ever called the 'non elect.' Scripture and verse please?!

The only thing that can be said of the lost soul is that it is 'awaiting election' by accepting Jesus as Savior. One last point here is that this being the case, then 'all men' were chosen/elected unto salvation from the foundation of the world, and gradually their names *are* added to the Lambs book of life as they come to Christ over the coming centuries. Remember Romans 5:18 tells us, "Therefore as by the offence of one judgment came upon *all men* to condemnation even so by the righteousness of one the free gift came upon *all men* unto justification of life." Naturally the question is raised about…

Revelation 13:8

"And all that dwell upon the earth shall worship him, whose names are not written in the book of life of the Lamb, slain from the foundation of the foundation of the world."

The only thing that can be said at the time of this event, is that no unsaved person here is written in the book of life of the Lamb, and that those who do worship the beast during this last seventieth week of Daniel simply were not saved/written in said book of life (*'yet' or at the time this event takes place. ed*). When these unsaved people do believe (future) on Jesus then and only then are their names written down! Then there is the question about…

Revelation 17:8

"The beast that thou saw was, and is not, and shall ascend out of the bottomless pit, and go into perdition and they that dwell on the earth shall wonder whose names were not written in the book of life *('which dates' ed)* from the foundation of the world, when they behold the beast that was and is not, and yet is."

The emphasis here is that (first) the book of life simply dates from the foundation of the earth. In this book (secondly) only the names of the redeemed are found, and (thirdly and again) only the unsaved or those not yet in the book of life when this event finally does take place (future) are the only ones who will worship the beast. (Sorry all you Calvinists, no pre-elect damned here.) Then the question about…

Ephesians 1:4

"According as he hath chosen us in Him before the foundation of the world that we should be holy and without blame before Him in love."

Here it is plain that before the world was founded, God designed our salvation to be founded ('in Him') on the righteousness of Jesus Christ, thus eliminating our works of righteousness as a basis or a condition of our salvation. Simply stated, when we stand before God after death, we have the holiness and blamelessness of our Savior which Jesus imputed to us, which is the sole basis of our salvation. Our works are as 'filthy rags.'

I Peter 1:18-20

"Forasmuch as ye know that ye were not redeemed with incorruptible things as silver and gold, from your vain course of life received from tradition of your fathers, but with the precious blood of Christ as a lamb without blemish and spot, who was verily foreordained before the foundation of the world, but was manifested in these last times for you."

This verse, and the preceding verses all point not to predetermined election to salvation, and non election to damnation, but rather predetermined salvation (for all who come to Christ in the ages to come) to be based on the precious sinless blood of our Savior the Lord Jesus Christ, giving us His holiness and righteousness. Nothing more, nothing less.

Thus the so called 'non elect' simply do not, nor ever have existed, except in the deranged perverted theology of Augustinian Calvinism.

Jesus Our Blessed Savior, Creator, Designer, and Engineer of a Place of Eternal Suffering, Damnation and Pain?

J. Preston Eby has written a very informative article which we reproduce here. It certainly does reveal the hideous thinking which so many have come to endorse maligning our blessed compassionate Savior with the false idea that He torments the unsaved in Hell/Lake of Fire for all eternity. While the author of this book does not necessarily agree with J. Preston Eby, Pentecostal (The Latter Rain Movement), author and preacher on some issues (what two ministers do agree on everything), we still are glad to see the light 'turned on here.' Years ago I heard Dr. Bob Jones Sr. say that while he may not fully agree doctrinally with one who turns the light switch on, he still is thankful the switch was turned on. Note as follows:

Will Jesus Torture Billions Forever?
By J. Preston Eby

Our Lord Jesus Christ is the Creator and Sustainer of ALL things and ALL people. He either does or allows everything that is done in heaven or on earth. If one hundred billion helpless human beings are being tortured, then Jesus is doing it. Satan has brought suffering and death to the whole human race. However, if eternal torment IS TRUE, then Jesus Christ will torture forever the whole human race, except the small handful who will be saved. In one hour, in a hot searing Hell, our Lord will inflict more pain and agony on each person than Satan inflicted on that person during his entire life.

If this torture lasts throughout eternity, then each unsaved person will suffer more than all the suffering of all the people that ever lived on earth. Think of it! Billions have suffered horrible pain for hours, days, weeks, months, and years, during the time they were alive. And yet, after they die, EVERY unsaved person will suffer more agony than all the suffering of the whole race PUT TOGETHER from Adam until now. This is so horrible, so frightful, that it is difficult for our minds to grasp. Except Satan himself, Pharaoh, Nero, and Hitler were among the most horrible killers of men this world has ever known. Yet, the doctrine of eternal torture makes Jesus a million times more vicious and vindictive than these three put together. You see, these brutal murderers killed their victims. Death brought sweet relief in a moment of time. However, that Man of Galilee, that Man whom we love, praise, and worship, that Man who taught that we should forgive four hundred and ninety times a day, that Man who told us that we should love our enemies and bless them that curse us, that Man who died for all men, will never, never forgive ANYONE who has rejected Him in this frail life, or, worse yet, who merely failed to believe on Him during this brief time. Instead of torturing them for a season and then ending their suffering with death, He will torture them through all eternity.

Even the hardest, cruelest, most brutal men cannot torture their fellow men for more than two or three hours without growing weak, faint, and sick (see Fox Book of Martyrs). However, Christian leaders teach that our Lord will torture His victims through endless ages. The Scripture reveals that Christ Jesus is the kindest, the most tender-hearted and merciful Person this world has ever known. His mercy endures forever, or to all generations of time. The doctrine of eternal torment pictures Him to be the most horrible monster, the most beastly, brutal, cruel, vicious Person this world has ever known. The governments of this world, ruled by unregenerate men, put their rebels in prisons, and the very worst offenders they put to death. But our Lord Jesus Christ, the Creator and

Redeemer of the world, will mercilessly torture those who offend Him to the most hideous and incomprehensible degree. Surely, this pagan and Romish doctrine of eternal torture does NOT glorify HIM!

One of the theologians of the Church of England (Jeremy Taylor) speaks of the fate of the wicked in the following terms: "In Hell every sense and organ shall be assailed forever with its own appropriate and most exquisite sufferings. We are amazed at the inhumanity of Phalaris who roasted men in his brazen bull, but THAT WAS A JOY IN COMPARISON WITH HELL." And here is what the renowned evangelist, C. H. Spurgeon, said on the same subject: "There is real fire in Hell. The body shall be suffused with agony; your head tormented with racking pains; your eyes starting from their sockets; your ears tortured with horrid sounds; your pulse rattling with anguish; your limbs crackling in the flame; every vein a pathway for the fire to tread; every nerve a string on which the devil shall forever play the diabolical tune of Hell's unutterable lament."

If it were true, it is so awful that it should never be spoken without tears and a broken heart. How does the mother of a murderer speak of the coming execution of her boy? Yet the prospect to her is only one of time, and in the limits of the physical. If the people believe it, then their attitude about the whole thing reveals that they could care less if the creation burns forever. The fact is, NO ONE really believes in an eternal burning Hell if we are to judge by their actions. If they saw a person in a burning building, they would put forth every effort to save them; they would cry and scream for help; they would be late for work; they would not rest until the victims were rescued. Yet, those who teach eternal torment can spend their hours relaxing in front of the television screen, visiting and feasting upon rich dainties with their friends, and whole days in camping, vacationing, fishing, and playing, and then lay their heads upon a pillow every night and sleep soundly, while, according to their own teaching, countless millions are going to a place a million times worse than a burning building!

If they believed what they teach, they would never cease, day and night until they dropped, and others came to take their places, in their efforts to save men from such a place! They excuse themselves by saying, "All we can do is warn." But if they were standing before a burning building would they preach a thirty-minute sermon, then turn and walk away, saying, "All we can do is warn!" And how many do they meet day after day, and never mention their danger? Ah, precious friend of mine, if my concept of Hell were what modern Christendom's is, then it is my conviction that I would not be able to wait for God to send me to preach the Gospel! I would have to spend my every wakened hour pleading, working, struggling, fighting to save men from such a fate. I would be compelled to spend hours upon hours in the chronic wards of hospitals, in rest homes, with the elderly and those working on dangerous jobs, begging men to repent and turn to Jesus before they die. And I am convinced that anyone with the love of God in his heart would do the same IF HE REALLY BELIEVED the fables that are being taught today about Hell. I will say this, either those who teach eternal torture are EXTREMELY CALLOUSED or they do not believe what they teach!

George Hawtin has so aptly written: "Is it any wonder that in the face of such sadistic humbug there has been a wholesale manufacture of infidels? All these statements (by eternal Hell-fire preachers) may be a show of oratorical eloquence, but they are nothing more. They hold no part of truth. They deny every attribute of God. They make wisdom foolishness, turn eternal love into exasperated hate, make omnipotence helplessness, and make the justice of God the grossest injustice in the universe. To say that I believe in such repugnance would be a lie of the first order. I do not believe it because it is contrary to the nature of God. It is contrary to the love of God. It is contrary to the justice of God. It is contrary to the power of God. It is contrary to the Word of God and it puts God in the ridiculous position of being the almighty King of kings and Lord of lords yet having dominion a vast pocket of hate and resistance that even He cannot overcome. Further than this it makes the mighty sacrifice of Christ that was made for all the world to be almost impotent in its power and scope. Worst of all, it frustrates the purpose of God laid down in the beginning when He said, 'Let us make man in our image and after our likeness.' Some will immediately ask me whether I do not believe in Hell. My answer is very definite on this point. I most certainly DO BELIEVE in Hell, but the Hell of the Bible and the Hell of human tradition are not the same thing at all. The Hell of tradition is hopeless and eternal, while the Hell of the Scripture like every judgment of God is corrective, remedial, and restorative." -end quote.

I do not like to differ, even in minor things, from those whom I esteem for their devotion to Christ and their valuable service in the cause of His Kingdom. But in the immortal words of the great Martin Luther, "Here I stand - I can do no other. So help me God!" Long centuries ago the faithful apostle Peter penned these inspired words, "Who by the power of God are kept through faith unto a salvation ready to be revealed in the last time" (I Pet. 1:5). My conviction before God is that the extent of the salvation of Jesus, the Christ, our Lord, is to be known only in the last time. Jesus Himself said to His disciples, "I have yet many things to say unto you, but you cannot bear them now." But He said when the Holy Spirit should come, He would lead his people step by step - patiently lead them into the way of All Truth; so that when the last time (end of the age) came, the full revelation of that salvation would be made. I believe that I am writing in the last time. Writings of this kind do not endear the hearts of many people. I fear that enemies are made instead. Every time a truth is spoken, many become offended and many are filled with wrath. People always astonish me. It is never possible to know what attitude they will take under any given circumstance. They will believe and trust you and feed from your table, and for many years, only to become suddenly offended because of some point upon which they disagree, and often become hostile and sometimes even vicious, calling you a heretic and a false prophet, cutting you off from an fellowship and spiritual communication, and warning other saints near and far not to have anything to do with you.

I am also perfectly aware that these profound truths will be misapplied by another class, and some will twist and wrest them to their own destruction in their carnal and wicked endeavor to set aside all repentance of sin and annul all holiness of life, as some men in their zeal to display the grace of God have done, ridiculously living in sin and turning the grace of God into lasciviousness (Jude 4). These beautiful truths are not now written to men of corrupt minds who have no desire to walk in the Spirit, but to all who walk in the whole counsel of God, serving God because they love and know Him and not in fear of some dreadful judgment that hangs like a horrible terror before their eyes. I do not address those who would pervert the right ways of the Lord, using God's gracious plan and His great mercy as an excuse for careless living or unconcern for lost men, but to those children of the Most High God who, seeing their infinite identity in Christ, are consumed with the holy passion of becoming the very instrument of God to fight the good fight of faith, destroying sin and death and Hell, and bringing all men back into the loving embrace of their God and Redeemer. So be it!

I recognize that there will be some still unanswered questions in some minds, but there is neither time to write nor finances to print a treatise dealing with every small point. How can we put the ocean of eternal truth into the limited pages of one small book? If God will have all men to be saved, and the Scripture is very clear on this point, then there must be a way by which this truth falls into perfect harmony with every other Scripture which seems to teach otherwise. We do ourselves much injury when we seize upon every Scripture which proclaims the salvation of all men, but carefully avoid all Scripture which speaks of the fearful judgment of the wicked. Yet even greater harm is done when people insist upon taking the other point of view, as almost the entire Church system has done for centuries, emphasizing only those Scriptures which seem to teach the unending doom of those unfortunate creatures who never once heard that God had a Son and skillfully avoiding every direct statement of Scripture which indicates that God has reconciled all things to Himself, and that every knee shall bow and every tongue shall confess to God of things in heaven and things in earth and under the earth. There is always a place of harmony if we look for it, and it is not usually difficult to find. Otherwise we will be forced onto that untenable ground of having to say that the Bible contradicts itself - which, of course, it never does. Whenever you find two Scriptures that seem to set forth conflicting views, there is always a simple explanation, and, if we will diligently inquire of the Lord, He will give us a definite answer. Human understanding is almost always prone to seize upon one side of a statement and will cling to that with the grip of death, refusing to even investigate or seek the wisdom of God to harmonize the truth. Worldly wise men are forever saying that the Bible contradicts itself.

I have never believed that by teaching the ultimate salvation of all men we were pitting one group of Scriptures against another, for it is my conviction that the solution can only be found in the correct HARMONIZATION of all the Scriptures, not ignoring one group while advancing the other. I believe I speak by the Spirit of God when I assert that the only sensible harmonization of all the Scriptures lies in the fact that Jesus is indeed THE SAVIOUR OF ALL MEN, that He is in very fact THE SAVIOUR OF THE WORLD, and that HE WILL HAVE ALL MEN TO BE SAVED and come to the knowledge of the truth, DRAWING ALL MEN UNTO HIMSELF. To me this is a most glorious and wonderful fact! I find all the judgments of God to be correctional and disciplinary rather than vindictive and final. Therein lies the harmonization of which I speak. This leaves us free to believe ALL of God's Word. It magnifies the cross. It glorifies God. It honors the atonement. It gives meaning to the ministry of the Sons of God. It gives purpose to the ages yet to come, all planned and arranged beforehand by our wonderful Creator. Sin, judgment, and death are temporary, all to be dealt with by the mighty power of God invested in His saints. The entire universe will be reconciled to God through the blood of Christ's cross. God will become All-in-All. Here is a God worthy of your worship and adoration!

Several brethren have written or discussed this subject with me through the years, adamant against the truth I see. But their arguments are shallow and twisted and their spirits generally harsh against men whom God loves and for whom the Christ died, as though they wanted to make CERTAIN that everybody gets every thing they "deserve." Their theology is lopsided, distorted, out of balance, and it will be smashed in the end! Those who walk in that attitude know but little of the love of Him who is at the same time the JUDGE OF ALL and the SAVIOUR OF ALL. He is not the Judge of some and the Saviour of some, but both Judge and Saviour of ALL! If "Judge of ALL" means that He judges all, then "Saviour of ALL" must mean that He saves all, for the Scriptures plainly make both statements. Within that one fact again can be seen the HARMONIZATION of the justice and the love of God - His judgment leading to repentance and a knowledge of His mercy. Praise His wonderful name!

How Men are Saved

It is estimated that about one hundred and sixty billions of human beings have lived on the earth in the six thousand years since Adam departed from Eden. Of these, the very broadest estimate that could be made with reason would be that less than five billion were saints of God. This broad estimate would leave the immense aggregate of one hundred and fifty-five billions (155,000,000,000) who went down into death without faith and hope in the only name given under heaven or among men whereby we must be saved. Indeed, the vast majority of these never knew or heard of Jesus, and could not believe in Him of whom they had not heard. What, I ask, has become of this vast multitude, of which figures give a wholly inadequate idea? What is, and is to be, their condition? Did God make no provision for these, whose condition and circumstances He must have foreseen? Or did He, from the foundation of the world, make a wretched and merciless provision for their hopeless, eternal torment, as many of His children claim? To these questions, which every thinking Christian asks himself, and yearns to see answered truthfully, and in harmony with the character of God, comes a variety of answers:

CALVINISM ANSWERS: God is all-wise; He knew the end from the beginning; and as all His purposes shall be accomplished, He never could have intended to save any but a few, the Church. These He elected and fore-ordained to be eternally saved; all others were equally fore-ordained and elected to be lost - to go to eternal torment; and they are there now, writhing in indescribable agony, where they will ever remain, without hope.

ARMINIANISM ANSWERS: Yes, God is love; and in bringing humanity into the world He meant them no harm - only good. But Satan succeeded in tempting the first pair, and thus sin entered into the world, and death by sin. And ever since, God has been doing all He can to deliver man from his enemy, even to the giving of His Son. And though now, six thousand years after, the Gospel has reached only a very small proportion of mankind, yet we do hope and trust that within six thousand years more, through the energy and liberality of the Church, God will so far have remedied the evil introduced by Satan that all then living may at least know of His love, and have an opportunity to believe and be saved. We believe that God excuses many of them on account of ignorance. Those who did the best they knew how will be sure of being a part of the saved, even though they never heard of Jesus.

FUNDAMENTALISM ANSWERS: Only those who here and now, during the fleeting years of this life, truly repent and receive the Lord Jesus as Savior are saved. All others have been and are and shall be eternally lost without retrieve and go to a merciless, hopeless, Hell-fire and damnation.

There is one beautiful and undeniable truth in the Word of God. The Scriptures clearly show that there is only one ground of salvation and that is FAITH IN JESUS CHRIST as our Redeemer and Lord. "By grace are you saved, through faith" (Eph. 2:8). Justification by faith is the underlying principle of the whole system of New Testament revelation. When asked, "What must I do to be saved?" the apostles answered, "Believe on the Lord Jesus Christ and you shall be saved" (Acts 16:31). "There is none other name under heaven given among men whereby we must be saved" (Acts 4:12). "Whosoever shall call upon the name of the Lord shall be saved" (Rom. 10:13).

The apostle Paul warned of those who would depart from the utter simplicity of this truth to preach ANOTHER WAY, and ANOTHER GOSPEL. "I fear lest by any means, as the serpent beguiled Eve through his subtlety, so your minds should be corrupted from the simplicity that is in Christ. For if he that comes preaching ANOTHER Jesus, whom we have not preached, or if yea receive ANOTHER Spirit, which yea have not received, or ANOTHER Gospel, which yea have not accepted, yea might well bear with him" (11 OCR. 11:3-4). ANOTHER JESUS, ANOTHER SPIRIT, ANOTHER GOSPEL - ANOTHER W-A-Y!

Many today who claim to be "Bible believing," "Evangelical" or "Fundamental" preach ANOTHER GOSPEL and ANOTHER W-A-Y OF SALVATION. There are some who feel the burden of the awful doctrine of eternal torture which they embrace, and unconsciously their souls revolt at the ghastly conclusions to which it leads. Such ones have resorted to various makeshifts to escape the inevitable conclusions. I will mention two or three of these. It is said that although it is true that the great mass of the race have thus far died in their sins, yet it does not follow that they have been lost; for if those who are unavoidably ignorant live up to the light they have, they will be saved. These claim that Paul teaches that IGNORANCE will save men, when he says that "The Gentiles, which have not the law, are a law unto themselves" (Rom. 2:14). They gather from this that the law which their conscience furnishes is sufficient to justify them. But such persons misunderstand Paul. His argument is that the whole world is guilty before God (Rom. 3:19); that the Gentiles, who had not the written law, were condemned, not justified, by the light of conscience, which, whether it excused them or accused them proved that they were unworthy sinners and thus estranged from the life of God, even as Israel who had the written law were condemned by it; "For by the law is the knowledge of sin" (Rom. 3:20). The law given to the Israelite revealed his weakness, and was intended to show him that he was unable to justify himself before God; for "By the deeds of the law there shall no flesh be justified in His sight." The written law condemned the Israelite, and the Gentiles had light enough in their conscience to condemn them; and thus every mouth is stopped from claiming any inherent life, and all the world stands guilty before God.

Remembering the statement of James (2:10), that whosoever shall keep the whole law, except to offend in one point, is guilty of all, and cannot claim any blessing promised by the Law Covenant, we realize that indeed "there is none righteous; no, not one" (Rom. 3:10). And thus the Scriptures close every door of hope save one, showing that not one of the condemned is able to secure eternal life by meritorious works, and that it is equally useless to plead ignorance as a ground of salvation. Ignorance cannot entitle anyone to the REWARD of faith and obedience! Salvation by IGNORANCE! Indeed! ANOTHER GOSPEL! ANOTHER WAY! "For there is none other name under heaven, given among men, whereby we M-U-S-T be saved!" (Acts 4:12).

Many Christians, unwilling to believe that so many billions of ignorant heathen will be eternally lost (which they have been taught means to be sent to a place of eternal and hopeless torment), insist, notwithstanding these Bible statements, that God will not condemn the ignorant. I admire their liberality of heart and their appreciation of God's goodness, but urge them not to be too hasty about discarding or ignoring the words of Scripture. God has a blessing for all, IN A BETTER WAY THAN THROUGH IGNORANCE!

But do these erring ones act in accordance with their stated belief? NO! Though they profess to believe that the ignorant will be saved on account of their ignorance, they continue to send missionaries to the heathen at the cost of thousands of valuable lives and untold millions of dollars. If they all, or even half of them, would be saved through ignorance, it is doing them a positive injury to send missionaries to teach them of Christ; for only about one in a thousand believes when the missionaries go to them. If this idea be correct, it would be much better to let them remain in ignorance; for then a much larger proportion would be saved. Continuing the same line of argument, might we not reason that if God had left ALL MEN in ignorance, ALL would have been saved? If so, the coming and death of Jesus were useless, the preaching and suffering of apostles and saints were vain, and the so-called Gospel, instead of being good news, is very bad news. Leave the heathen alone in their darkness and ignorance and the majority will be saved by living up to the light they have. Send them the Gospel and we know from past experience that the majority of them will reject it and be lost. These conclusions are inevitable. You cannot escape them while you entertain the notion of the majority of the heathen being saved by living up to the light they have. Such reasoning is a hideous affront to the atoning sacrifice of Jesus, and a wicked blasphemy against God and His plan of redemption. ANOTHER GOSPEL! ANOTHER W-A-Y!

Others, craftily seeking to evade these conclusions, invent the silly myth that in some unexplained way ALL MEN HAVE BEEN DEALT WITH BY GOD. These conniving souls presume that in some mysterious way God reveals Himself to each and every son of Adam sometime during his life. Perhaps through the conscience — or one dark night while the heathen is standing under the canopy of the heavens observing the majesty of the star-studded sky - there suddenly comes that burst of inner revelation there is a GOD! And if, in that instant, we are told, that man will seek after God he will find Him. To which I answer: Tommyrot! Rubbish! ANOTHER GOSPEL! ANOTHER W-A-Y! And those who teach the lie are deceivers. Why, bless your heart, if God habitually and consistently reveals Himself sovereignly and independently to every man who lives upon this earth, then what need is there to print Bibles, or send missionaries, or intercede in prayer, or preach the Gospel? You will have to tear the Bible all to pieces if you teach such nonsense. It is blasphemy. The Word of God asks the burning question: "HOW THEN SHALL they call on Him in whom they have not believed? and HOW SHALL they believe on Him of whom they HAVE NOT HEARD? and HOW SHALL they hear WITHOUT A PREACHER? and HOW SHALL they preach, EXCEPT THEY BE SENT?" (Rom. 10: 14-15). And these poor deluded souls pretend to answer all these "HOW SHALLS" of Scripture by creating a method by which it CAN BE DONE! They have invented a system by which men can believe without hearing and hear without a preacher, and under this system no preacher need be sent.

But, I ask, how are the heathen, or any lost men, to be justified by faith by this method since "faith comes BY HEARING and hearing by the Word of God," and "it pleased God BY THE FOOLISHNESS OF PREACHING to save them that believe" (Rom. 10: 17; 1 Cor. 1:21). Nowhere in all the pages of God's blessed Book does it state that God sometime, somewhere, somehow, reveals himself to every man during his brief life in the flesh. Show me! Here is God's estimation of the condition of the heathen: "Wherefore remember, that you being in time past Gentiles in the flesh, who are called Uncircumcision by that which is called Circumcision in the flesh made by hands; that at that time you were without Christ, being aliens from the commonwealth of Israel, and strangers from the covenants of promise, having NO HOPE, and without God in the world..." (Eph. 2:11-12).

If God independently and sovereignly reveals Himself to every man then the "Great Commission" is a monstrous farce and should be torn out of the Bible and deposited on the garbage heap. No need to "go into ALL THE WORLD and preach the Gospel to EVERY CREATURE" if the Spirit deals with EVERY MAN sometime, somewhere, somehow during his life APART FROM THE MINISTRY OF THE BODY OF CHRIST. Ah! The argument is really the great "cop out," a silly invention of conniving deceivers who are unwilling to face the fact that God would permit billions of men to pass through this life without any chance of salvation, and equally unwilling to concede that God has any plan for the salvation of those billions in the future. So - in order to consign them an to eternal damnation they concoct this outrageous lie that God really DID give these billions a chance, apart from the preaching of the Gospel of God's grace in Jesus Christ, that these rejected His dealing, and have of their own free wills been damned. Such a teaching contradicts the Word of God, making a travesty of the fact that "God has committed unto US the word of reconciliation" and has "given to US the ministry of reconciliation" (II Cor. 5:18-19). The fundamental flaw in the theory is that even if a heathen looked up at the stars one beautiful night and became deeply impressed that there must be a great God out there somewhere, such understanding in no way reveals to his darkened heart the wonderful truth that this God HAS A SON, that His Son's name is JESUS, that JESUS DIED FOR HIS SINS, and that ONLY BY FAITH IN JESUS CHRIST CAN A MAN BE SAVED. I challenge anyone to prove that the vast multitudes of heathen die having REJECTED JESUS CHRIST WHO DIED FOR THEM who was revealed to their hearts by the Holy Spirit apart from the preaching of the Gospel. How foolish can men be! Let someone answer - if they can! Ah, it is but ANOTHER GOSPEL! ANOTHER W-A-Y!

End of Eby quote.

Damnationists Seriously Immersed in Doctrinal Sin

Damnationism, the doctrine of endless damnation for poor lost souls, has immersed, baptized the Body of Christ into a monstrously depraved concept of God! No doubt, God, Christ, the Holy Spirit are grieved, offended, quenched and viciously insulted to the highest degree with the false doctrine of endless sadistic torment of lost sinners in Hell/the Lake of Fire.

To say God is a God of love and compassion (as exemplified in and through the incarnation of Jesus) only on this side of the grave, but then after death He becomes a God of sadism, who endlessly torments the wicked after their death for eternity, certainly paints a picture of a God of sadistic pleasure embroiled in infinite torment on myriads of ignorant, unlearned, and/or wicked rebellious people. Then, since Jesus our Lord created all things (Col. 1:16) which necessarily includes Hell/the Lake of Fire He is made to be the creator of sadism and vicious torture.

No! Rather, Jesus is the initiator of remedial suffering, (which is what Hell/the Lake of Fire are all about) which being done in true love and concern will win those precious lost souls to Himself. "Every knee shall bow, every tongue shall confess." In that day, no soul will be left lost and undone for eternity. Romans 10:9&10 are God's spoken Word which will prevail forever. In that day, all will bow before Jesus and make confession to Him unto salvation and the new birth into the family of God

The Doctrine of Endless Punishment Unwittingly Endorsing the Horrors of the Inquisition?

Supposing that the doctrine of "endless torment/punishment" in Hell/Lake of Fire were true, then it would only stand to reason that no matter what method is needed to convince a man (thus his posterity as well) to convert to Christianity, including physical/mental torture, super aggressive threats etc, could be justified. Is not the doctrine of "endless torment/damnation" a primary motive for aggressive evangelism for those who hold to that position in present day churches and missionary work?

If someone is not saved then they supposedly face death and endless torment in Hell/Lake of Fire for eternity! Mothers and fathers who desperately love their children and relatives certainly would not want them to be tormented endlessly in fire and brimstone for eternity! As believing parents, they would/should be willing to do whatever it would take to win them to Christ. Thus no doubt, the inquisitions could be justified as they were by the Roman Catholic Church to root out heresy and heretics to keep the church "pure (?)!" During the dark ages, since the state and church were "married" under Constantine (and Augustinian theology) people could be held in check and in subjection through fear of ex-communication, torture, and threat of eternal/endless damnation.

What better way to subject the parishioner to obey the Church and fatten the coffers, than the threat of endless torture in the Lake of Fire. "Torturing" someone into subjection to the claims of, and obedience to the Church therefore would be far better than to allow that poor soul to go to endless torment in Hell/Lake of Fire taking his wife and children with him IF that goal could be reached. Interestingly when the U.S. defeated Japan in WWII, General Douglas MacArthur begged the U.S. to send 3-4000 missionaries there to win the Japanese from their heathen type systems of worship. Many churches that held to the doctrines of endless damnation however did not respond, but rather continued to hold deep-rooted anger and hatred toward the Japanese.

If Christians are to "Love their neighbor as themselves," then why pray tell, are thousands and yea millions dying every day around the world who have never had a fair opportunity and exposure to the claims of the gospel? If these millions are dying in every century without Biblical salvation, then the doctrine of endless damnation/torment in Hell/Lake of Fire, should force Christians to do everything humanly possible to get the gospel to them. One unsaved man said that if he believed eternal never ending Hell awaited the non-Christians he would crawl over broken glass on hands and knees if need be, to get the gospel message out.

It seems to this author that Christians (damnationist type) do not really "love their neighbors as themselves" as they say they do, since worldwide evangelism certainly does fall short in every generation. Just think, if endless damnation is true, then using torture, the rack, and other hideous means as they did in the inquisition could conceivably force everyone after several generations, to convert to Christianity. So who could fault such means if it achieved worldwide acceptance of Christianity? Certainly those holding to E.D. believe God will torment someone for eternity for not embracing Christianity. But no! Thankfully endless damnation is not a Biblical truth, but an all knowing, all sufficient, and all caring Savior will eventually bring the truth of salvation to all, whether in this life or the next!

Remember that Jesus descended into Hell to empty paradise, and no doubt spoke the message of His conquering death Hell and the grave to all those who were imprisoned on both sides. Are we to believe when He did such that only the saints of all ages who were in the Paradise side of Hades were aware of this glorious victory? Not hardly! No doubt those who had been suffering in the other side of the gulf were forced to witness this revelation, and when faced with such incontrovertible truth what else could they do than to totally surrender to the truth?

If an unsaved person were asked, "Which would you rather choose, to spend endless eternity burning in Hell-fire, or rather in this life be forced to come to salvation, no matter what it took, even for God allowing extreme torture/affliction/punishment to come into your life to thus spare you of such a horrible destiny?" Now (no doubt) any unsaved person, who really believes the Word of God, will choose the second scenario. Who wouldn't?

Consider this. Death is only incidental to our existence. We were created in the image of God, and in that image we will continue to exist for all of eternity future, having of course no previous pre-existence. There will never be a time when we simply cease to be, but will dwell forever in a resurrected body... saved and unsaved alike will receive an eternal body. We Christians will receive our new glorified bodies at the coming of Christ for his saints, and the unsaved will receive their eternal bodies at the second resurrection at the white throne judgment in Rev. chap. 20. Our judgment will be at the bema seat of Christ the rapture, the unsaved will be judged at the white throne. There is a strong indication that some or many who are raised in that last judgment will not face the second death, having already bent their knee and confessed unto salvation (during the millennial age). The scripture plainly says:"And whosoever was not found written in the book of life was cast into the Lake of Fire." Rev. 20.

Reader note: It is well to comment here that while Eby does see the salvation of children who perish, he does not accept the biblical doctrine of the "age of accountability" as plainly taught in Romans and James, and claims that fundamentalists view children as "saved" when entering into this world which is not generally true. Usually the fundamentalists teach that they are "safe" which goes without dispute.

Revelation 20 Does Not Say
"All who were resurrected at this white throne judgment were not written in the book of life."

To say it does say that is to plainly change the meaning of this verse, and as well add to the Word of God. To say it infers such is an untruth as well and totally changes the meaning of this verse.

To Reword This Verse and Still Keep the Same Meaning is Much More Clear as Follows: (Paraphrased)
"And the book of life was examined for names of these resurrected souls at the White Throne Judgment, and those whose names were not found therein were cast into the Lake of Fire, while those names that were found therein were delivered from the second death."

No doubt these who were indeed written in the book of life, died after the rapture and had (while living during the millennial reign of Christ) come to terms with their sins, and had sought pardon, cleansing and salvation by embracing the Lord Jesus Christ in the new birth. To say there is no "post-mortem learning" has previously been shown to be false in these papers, and so it becomes plain that 'post mortem salvation' for all unsaved, must occur at the end of punishment inflicted at the white throne judgment. Remember the rich man in Hell etc. Certainly a true thorough humbling, a genuine sorrow for sins, a thorough scourging for wickedness, and as well a true recognition/acceptance of Jesus as Savior as Lord of Lords and King of Kings will beyond doubt bring salvation and the new birth!

The Old Testament simply does not give any teaching as to the duration of suffering of those in Sheol. Jesus certainly did not as we have already shown. Certainly if the duration of suffering in Sheol during O.T. times was to be endless and eternally so, the O.T. scriptures would have plainly indicated such, but are silent on the matter. Some are quick to quote Jesus where He said... "And if thy eye offends thee... pluck it out, and if thy hand offend thee cut it off.... etc.

Jesus endorsed self-mutilation? He certainly did not endorse the government to do such! Rather He gave the clear message that punishment in Hell is so terrible that if a member of your body could not be controlled and was endlessly leading one to be enslaved to sin leading to the loss of one's soul to that terrible place, then it would be better for you to remove that offending member and be saved. If endless damnation were indeed a fact, then no doubt it could be wise for the church to enact the horrors of the inquisitions to force all to subjection to Christ.

The doctrine of E.D. "if" preached is counterproductive to bring a man to true repentance and salvation! Why so? Which produces the most fear in people? Teaching them that their sins are offensive to God and are a violation of His Holy Word, or that God is angry at them for their sins and is going to torment them in fire and brimstone for endless eternity whether they have true remorse of not. Teaching E.D. will therefore no doubt, (and has) bred many false conversions!

The real truth is that man will either have Holy Ghost conviction for his wickedness and be saved, or have a repentance based on fear of E.D. rather than godly sorrow for his sin! The scripture is clear on that issue, "Godly sorrow worketh repentance unto salvation which is not repented of, but the sorrow of the world worketh death." II Cor. 7:10. Notice here, that 'godly sorrow' works true repentance unto true salvation. Repentance of what? Of sin we answer. The Holy Spirit convicts a man of his wickedness and sin, bringing him to true and complete repentance and salvation. The 'sorrow of the world' which well could be sorrow based on fear of endless damnation or of 'getting caught' and suffering for it, which works what? Death we answer and not aionios life in Christ.

The Fundamentalist Damnationists love to hear children sing 'Jesus Loves the Little Children," but then tell these precious children that Jesus will burn them with fire and brimstone for eternity if they do not 'come to Him.' How many countless children have been wrongly prompted to 'come to Jesus' to be saved (with no real conviction of *guilt and sin* which conviction would or could bring conversion and Biblical salvation), so that Jesus will not burn them with fire and brimstone for eternity?

Now that is not the Jesus of the Bible, nor is it salvation! Think about it this way. A child (or anyone else for that matter), who is caught doing wrong etc. always has one of two responses. First, they no doubt are sorry they are caught and exposed, or secondly they may truly be sorry for what they have done. Here plainly the first 'sorrow' is not godly sorrow unto repentance, and the next time the child/person will be more careful not to be caught and will no doubt re-offend. The second is result of true conviction of the Spirit of God unto repentance and salvation. There is a world of difference.

Perverted Concepts of Hell and Endless Torment...

...do nothing but impugn the justice and integrity of All Mighty God, making our Savior to be vicious and vindictive to those who die without accepting Him. As well, He thereby becomes a sadist who delights in tormenting those who oppose Him and His plan of redemption by supposedly burning them endlessly in fire and brimstone.

This concept of God/Christ further does nothing but to breed atheism, and contempt for the Word of God, and Fundamental Christianity. It makes Jesus to be one who is ultimately defeated in winning the majority of humanity to Himself, and He responds in final frustration and anger by consigning them to burn helplessly in Hell fire and brimstone endlessly for eternity! Only a God who ultimately wins all to Himself, and only inflicts remedial punishment to bring repentance and sorrow for sin to all men who fail to accept Him can truly be said to be our God and Savior the Lord Jesus Christ, King of kings, and Lord of lords!

Hell-God's Dungeon/Torture Chamber?
Created and Run by Creator and Lord Jesus Christ?

Pain and suffering are natural to this present life. Pain and suffering can come from a number of sources, such as physical injuries, sickness and disease, or pain related to aging, or remedial surgeries and hospital care. Then there is justified pain and suffering from physical punishment upon the guilty or unjustified pain and suffering inflicted upon an innocent person by someone. Interesting it is that God endorses physical pain and suffering upon a child from the hand of a loving parent that the child might 'learn' from such painful experience, and hopefully be spared from the pain of Hell/Sheol/Hades.

If Hell/Lake of Fire were an endless dungeon torture chamber would not such a place lower Jesus our all loving, compassionate God and Savior to the same level as religious fanatical terrorists who over the centuries have at point of sword, at threat of physical suffering and death threatened all who opposed the spread of their doctrines? Someone who does this in today's society plainly in simple terms is a **terrorist!**

We as Christians cringe when we imagine a radical religious zealot telling us that if we do not bow to, adhere to, and practice their particular religious views they will torture, kill or behead us. So, the question looms, does the Jesus of the Bible act as a terrorist and tell the unsaved if they do not accept Him that He will put them in a dungeon of fire and brimstone for eternity? (Is that the love of Christ?) Or does the Jesus of the Bible weep over lost souls (yes the wrath of God still abiding on the wicked as John 3:36 says) and tell them He loves them with an eternal unconditional love, and that if they do not accept Him he will use whatever means necessary whether in this life or the next to convince them of the truth of endless eternal salvation.

As well He in love and compassion will woo and win them to Himself and His free salvation no matter what it takes. And that would include *all* of mankind. This author for one knows his Savior is not a terrorist type redeemer.

Notice the following scriptures.

Proverbs 13:24; 22:15; 23:13, 14

"He that spareth his rod hateth his son but he that loveth him chasteneth him betimes. Foolishness is bound in the heart of a child, but the rod of correction shall drive it far from him. Withhold not correction from the child, for if thou beatest him with the rod he shall not die. Thou shalt beat him with the rod and shalt deliver his soul from Hell *(Sheol! No not the grave or the pit, which two English words have their own Hebrew/Greek equivalents. i.e. So the Hebrew word Sheol does not mean grave or pit as the Watchtower would have everyone believe! Besides, spanking delivering from the grave?).*

These verses bring some very interesting points to light concerning the parent inflicting physical pain on his disobedient child. Parentally inflicted pain to a disobedient son or daughter, plainly is corrective, remedial, restorative when done in love, (and certainly must not be done sadistically or to inflict permanent injuries on the child). The most important point to note here is that this pain is 'preventative' as well to keep the child from eventually being consigned to Hell/Sheol, which plainly infers that Hell/Sheol is the ultimate place of correction, or a place of infinitely valued punishment to bring a soul to complete repentance and obedience *(but not a place to be tortured endlessly forever)*!

Should a child be spanked endlessly hour after hour, day after day etc? The scripture does not give indication of whether the child is born again or not, saved or lost who is to be punished. Surely the child has reached the age of accountability else it would be unwise or unjust to punish it with physical pain, such as a small baby. So there you have it. Either Hell/Sheol (or the Lake of Fire) is a place of correction unto repentance, and total submission leading eventually to the new birth in Christ, or it is a place of unjustified torture endlessly/forever with horrific pain and suffering for refusing to accept Jesus. By punishing a child with limited brief justified physical pain, he is more likely to find Christ and be spared from being punished in Hell.

The parallel between a wayward child being punished (like spanked) now for correction, discipline and restoration, or being placed in Hell later after death due to a lack of such punishment shows that this is just what Hell/Sheol/Lake of Fire is all about, the ultimate place of correction, discipline and restoration! And of course that is restoration unto eventual repentance and the new birth in Christ Jesus, without which no man can be saved.

Is it any wonder that so many young people have gone wayward, into sin, profligacy and degradation, when being raised by 'politically correct' parents who have been corrupted with the idea that physically punishing a child with pain and suffering by such as paddling, is a crime which should be punished by the law or the state!? Far better is it to obey the wisdom of the Scriptures and have your child properly corrected and disciplined (eventually leading to salvation) to become a decent honorable productive person, making right choices (and the choice to be saved), than to allow it to eventually die and go to Hell to receive such severe correction.   So, Hell/Lake of fire is not an "endless torture chamber" for not accepting Jesus!

If an unsaved young person who has reached the age of accountability should be punished in Hell for not accepting Jesus, then punish him now for the same thing!? Absolutely not, nor will Jesus so the same. Hell/Lake of Fire is not a place to punish people eternally/endlessly for not accepting Jesus as damnationists teach, but rather a place of punishment unto humiliation, sorrow and repentance unto eventual salvation and the new birth!

CHAPTER THREE

"ENDLESS PUNISHMENT" AND THE GREEK

Aionios Olethros

Another word which needs to be closely examined is the Greek word "Olethros" Stong's 3639, which means to destroy or ruin, punish or death.

II Thess. 1:8-9 In flaming fire taking vengeance on them that know not God, and that obey not the gospel of our Lord Jesus Christ: Who shall be punished with everlasting destruction from the presence of the Lord, and from the glory of his power.

"Aionios Olethros" simply means 'everlasting destruction.' 'Destruction' can easily be said to be 'punishment' as was the destruction of Sodom and Gomorrah. Now the point here needs to be made that 'everlasting (physical) destruction (punishment or ruination) was exactly

---

Readers note: Someone says, "Well, if all men eventually will be saved, then Satan and his angels will be as well?!" To which all we can say at this point is that scriptures don't speak as to their restoration to holiness, and indeed God could simply speak them out of existence. That however is speculation and a thousand suppositions prove nothing. 'Hypotheticals,' it is said are a fools playground. For sure we'll know the answer when we get to heaven. Such cannot be answered in this life.

what God brought upon these cities and will bring upon the wicked at His coming.

No doubt these wicked souls are sent to suffer in Hell, but Hell is not a place of *endless* ruination under the hand of Almighty God! If something is destroyed, it is simply changed from one form or state to another.

If a piece of wood is destroyed by fire, it simply is changed from one state to another, i.e. from solid to gaseous state. In a strict sense freezing water can be said to destroy the water by changing it into another state called ice. The 'destruction' the wicked experience is a change from the physical world to the spirit world, entering into the place called Hell and the punishment therein, punishment at least in the lower levels thereof.

Aidios/Adialeipton Timoria

"Aidios" defined by Strong's (126) as "Forward and backward or forward only, eternal or everlasting." *(Here without doubt, Strong plainly means "Aidios" means "endless/never ending).*

The above Greek simply says "Endless" punishment or torment. Now it stands as an irrefutable fact that never did our Savior, or his disciples, or any scripture in the Old or New Testaments teach such a doctrine as "endless torment or punishment." Universal salvation stands or falls with the usage of "Aionios" which again means on and on, ages and ages with indefinite duration, or "Aidios" which plainly means only endless. Jesus and His disciples called punishment "Kolasis Aionios" punishment, chastisement, or indefinite limited duration.

If indeed eternal/endless damnation were a truth, certainly the Lord would have been clearer in warning of such. It would then be of paramount importance to spread such a message to the entire world. Clement says that "…punishment no matter how severe is purification *(No not the cleansing of sin. Ed)*, and the torments of the damned are curative." It is a simple fact that during the time of Christ, many pagans, and Jews did indeed believe in "Aidios or Adialeipton Timora" (endless punishment.) Jesus was very careful therefore not to speak any words which would give the impression that He believed such a doctrine. Indeed a cruel hurtful and yea a slanderous doctrine against the love and compassion of Christ and Jehovah!

Confusion in Translation—Aionios Not Aidios Punishment

Is the doctrine of "everlasting (on and on) punishment, eternal (continuous on and on) punishment, aionios punishment" (ages and ages punishment, or on and on of indefinite duration punishment), taught in the Holy Scriptures? Absolutely yes, the *Word of God teaches it*. Is the doctrine of "infinite punishment," or punishment which is infinite (forever <u>without end</u>) in its *duration* taught in the Holy Scriptures? Absolutely not!

Is the doctrine of "infinite punishment" defined as punishment, which has an *infinite impact* on the unsaved (but not infinite in duration), and as well an *infinite impact* on his infinite relationship to the Almighty (all souls have infinite/never ending existence starting from their creation at conception and on and on without end) taught in the Scriptures? Absolutely, yes. Is the doctrine of eternal punishment meaning never ending punishment, with the pain and punishment on the sinner never ending taught in the Scriptures? Absolutely, not.

Of course to say that the doctrine of eternal/everlasting punishment is true but the doctrine of infinite/never ending punishment is not, seems to be contradictory. On the surface it is, but the simple irrefutable fact is that according to a simple study of the Greek/English words used in those cases the seeming contradiction is easily solved. First though it is well to say that the scriptures are abundantly clear that God is not willing that any should perish, but that all should come to repentance. Does not all mean all? Is not Jesus the light that lighteth every man that comes into the world Jn.1: 9? Of course He is.

That simple fact alone, coupled with the fact that many do indeed die without ever hearing the name of Jesus, and that millions and millions for centuries have thusly died and will continue to die, exposes the lie that they go to torment in an infinite burning Hell, on and on forever time without end, and infinitely never ceasing in that pain.

Herein lays the problem which has unwittingly, by false doctrine, painted a picture of a defeated Jehovah, and a victorious Satan in the fight for the salvation or damnation of the majority of souls for eternity! This must be the conclusion if the doctrine of infinite punishment in its *duration* if it is taught in the Scriptures. Jehovah then ultimately becomes defeated by the loss of the majority of the masses of unregenerate humanity to a supposed infinite burning Hell, because His power in seeking to win them to Christ through His church was successfully thwarted by a lesser power!

That power, the power of Satan, and the power of the rebellious will of man thus successful against the Almighty! In that scenario God was unable to reach them, and Satan thus gained the victory against their salvation making God the looser in not winning them! Satan then becomes the victor ruling and reigning over the infinite/endless damnation of the majority of humanity though he himself is there as well? We are to believe this? (Even though in Hell, he is shown to have permanently won their undying allegiance and worship?) Herein it is clearly shown that God cannot be the ultimate looser, and that unregenerate man and Satan cannot be the victor in their rebellion against Almighty God.

Plain and simple, the perfect plan of God for man, is that man be in perfect harmony, happiness, and relationship with him for eternity. That God no doubt has that plan for man is clearly revealed in the Scriptures from Gen.1:1 to Rev. 22:21. Are we to believe, that Satan in his warfare against the Almighty, and his full strength being exercised in this world to delude and deceive mankind, or as many as he can, was finally able in the end ages of ages, for time and eternity to cause the majority of humanity, men, women, boys and girls, to be lost and be tormented in

Chapter Three | "Endless Punishment" and the Greek

Hell fire and brimstone forever and ever/endlessly? Satan won?? Not hardly. Holy Scripture does not teach such!

Does not the scripture plainly teach in Revelation that... "…. And the devil that deceived them, was cast into the lake of fire and brimstone, and shall be tormented day and night forever and ever." Does it not also say in those same related passages that those deceived will receive the same fate? Absolutely so! Yes they will be cast into the Lake of Fire and be tormented with fire and brimstone forever and forever. Why are these people cast into the Lake of Fire? Why? They were DECEIVED into rejecting Jesus Christ so would it be just for God to punish them for eternity/endlessly when they were "deceived" into doing so?

This class of unsaved persons were not damned because they believed in the truth of Jesus but merely neglected it and put off salvation (of course those who do so will be damned as well) but were sent to the Lake of Fire because of "deception" from Satan! How many millions and millions over the centuries have died in their sins as Muslims, Buddhists, true Roman Catholics, Mormons, Watchtower etc, etc. being deceived as to who Jesus really was, and as to the true way of salvation! Upon their demise from this life, dying in an unrepentant unregenerate state, they will find themselves in Hell/the Lake of Fire to "experience" the lesson of the truth of who the Lord Jesus Christ really was and is.

THEN they will become convinced they were wrong and be tormented/afflicted forever and ever however long as God intends, and that "according to their works" they are judged. Duration/degree of affliction according to just that, the Holy Scriptures clearly indicate so. Remember, forever and ever, or ages and ages, or Aionios and Aionios, certainly irrefutably does not mean for "infinity."

On the other hand, a simple study of the Greek word "Aionios" plainly and irrefutably shows that Aionios ***can*** mean "infinity," ***if*** used with an accompanying modifying word. Aionios simply portrays, "on and on, forever, or ages upon ages upon ages," with NO indication of the duration of time/length of time. Naturally, with casual usage making the

English words "eternal, everlasting," to mean "infinity" in the English sense "never ending" or "forever and ever time without end," the above scriptural definition of Aionios and related reasoning is contradictory to the general thinking in the fundamental church and rejected by it. This author holds to the firm saying that "Truth will stand examination."

The word "eternal" or "everlasting" is used in several ways. It is used of God, to denote that His existence is not measurable by man and cannot be defined except to say He exists "on and on and on." Then it is used of an unknown period of time, such as ages upon ages. We commonly use the words eternal and eternity in a casual manner when we tell someone we haven't seen for a long long time, "I haven't seen you forever," or "It's been an eternity since I saw you last," or "My shoulder is forever hurting." In the Bible it is used of the "eternal mountains," but then we all know that the mountains in the new heaven and new earth will no longer exist, simply put, the mountains *will* exist for ages and ages or of an unknown period of time, but certainly not for never ending eternity or infinity.

The Old Testament Hebrew "Ad Olam" which is the counterpart of the N.T. "Aionios," also can mean "Forever" in a limited sense. The servant in Ex. 21:5-6, was to have his ear pierced through with an awl, and was to serve his master "forever." Certainly he was not to serve his master throughout eternity! In Jn.3:16 the word "everlasting life" is used to counter the word "perish" in the same verse. Here it is simply saying that our existence in the presence of God as saved and redeemed people will go on and on and on with no indication of length in time and that we are promised not to perish or be separated from God, thus making "aionios" in this case since modified by "God" to mean "endlessly."

Consider the message of our Savior. Just suppose our present day English language as it is spoken today had been used by our Savior during His life time. Just suppose that when he was speaking of the duration of suffering in Hell/the lake of fire He had said (in our present English), "The wicked shall be cast into Hell and later the Lake of Fire to be tormented day and night forever and forever endlessly."

To be sure then, the matter would be forever settled, irrefutably so, that the suffering of the unsaved/wicked in torments would be endless with "forever" being defined by "endless." On the other hand, suppose He said in the English, "The wicked/unsaved shall be punished in Hell/the Lake of Fire for ages and ages and ages." Then, no doubt the conclusion would arise and be plain that "endless" was not to be the duration of their suffering. Plain and simple

Now take the Greek word "Akatalutos" Strongs 179, which plainly means "indisoluable, endless, or permanent." Pray tell, where in Jesus' teachings concerning Hell/the Lake of Fire, did He use this term to define punishment therein? Where? It cannot be found! Then take the term "Adialeiptos," Strongs 88-89 which again means "permanent, without ceasing i.e. endless" The same applies to the word "Aidios" Strongs (126) "Everduring, forward or backward or forward only." The same applies to the word "Aidios" Strongs (126) "Everduring, forward or backward or forward only." Where did our Savior use these terms concerning the punishment for the unsaved in the Greek? Nowhere!

Our Savior Never Said in Greek
"Adialeipton/Akatalutos (or Aidios) Timoria" or "Endless Torment/punishment" for the wicked unsaved.

But Our Savior Did Use The Terms In Greek
"Kolasis Aionios or "Indefinite (duration) Punishment.

The "Strong" Problem
Before examining the 'Strong' problem, one seeming problem needs to be addressed. That problem: Since the Word of God was originally given in the Masoretic Hebrew, and Koine/Hellenistic Greek which was the common Greek of that century, many Christians experience a feeling of being held hostage to those who have studied and are fluent in the original languages, i.e. the scholars and theologians of the day. One scholar

claims such and such concerning word meanings, and another just the opposite, which gives the impression that "who can know for sure?"

Certainly it is true that the Church of Rome was able to keep millions of souls enslaved to false doctrines for centuries, by forbidding parishioners to learn and study for themselves. For years and years the Roman Church used the Latin in their services, telling parishioners that yes they could read the English translation, but that they were forbidden to try to understand what they were reading on their own. Following are simple steps for anyone to take in resolving doctrines that are debatable, and for doctrinal positions one may be unsure of.

1. Understand that every word in the Bible has a primary meaning and if it is not used in an allegorical (figurative sense) it must hold true to its given meaning. Take the word 'forever' which can indeed mean endless *if modified*, but certainly means an 'indeterminate period or unknown period of time' certainly not endless in and by itself! Since there are several distinct Greek words meaning 'endless' with no need for modification then forever in the Greek/Aionios cannot possibly mean 'endless' by itself.

2. Do not simply bow to any theological position unless it is plainly taught in the Word of God. The Deity of Christ, His bodily resurrection, the virgin birth, the verbal plenary inspiration of the Holy Scriptures etc, are all plainly revealed in the Word of God, too plain and clear to consider compromise or question.

3. Pray fervently for the Lord to open the eyes of your understanding when confronted by theological issues you may be unclear on, and continue to study until you reach a certain irrefutable conclusion.

4. Remember when serious theological differences arise, there is no doubt that Satan is behind the difference to cause certain damage to the cause of Christ.

5. The scripture plainly teaches that the Holy Spirit will guide His people into all truth. Jn. 16:13. While we can certainly learn from

one to whom the Spirit has revealed much truth, it is still important we do not put our full and total confidence in the teaching of any theologian, but be ready to examine what we are being taught. Truth will stand examination.

In any language, a word can only have one primary meaning, but then can as well have a figurative meaning when determined such need by the context of how it is used. Take the Greek word "Aion." Strong defined this Greek word, or perhaps it should be said he "explained" that this word was <u>translated</u> with the following meanings.

First though it must be understood that "aionios" is an adjective which modifies (explains) the noun from which it comes. To say He is a man, "man" being a noun, is one thing, but to say he is a "cruel man" makes the word "cruel" an adjective which describes the man and nothing else. That the two words are only for each other and nothing else is the same as "Aion" the noun, and "Aionios" the adjective which modifies the word "Aion." How does the Greek/Hebrew scholar Strong (parroting the translators) define "Aion?" Notice as follows:

"Aion"

Strong's (165) Concordance states as follows: "(1) forever, an unbroken age, perpetuity of time, eternity. (2) the worlds, universe. (3) period of time, age.

Now the exact meaning of this Greek word is "Age or Ages (in the plural)." It plainly and irrefutably does not give an exact length of time, it gives an indeterminate or an undetermined period of time, nor does it mean "infinite or endless, or world, eternity or universe, nor forever in the literal endless sense." (Unfortunately the translators did translate it in these ways, ways that have distorted the true meaning of the word, and as well have opened the door to continue propagating the false Augustinian doctrine of endless punishment.) As a noun it has a firm, exact meaning, and when Aionios (166) is used as the adjective it is, then the term simply means "on and on of non-determinate length."

Nothing more, and nothing less, and certainly not "endless." So let's see, (Strong says) the Greek word "Aion" means "forever, and forever means endless, and forever and endless mean an unbroken age, err no it means the universe, or maybe better yet the worlds, oh well maybe it means a period of time probably an age….oh well, we'll just make it mean whatever we want and ignore the firm Greek meaning "Period of Time/Age or Ages!?" So can you the reader really claim that Strong properly defined the meaning of "Aion." Or did he explain the different ways it was translated? Endless damnationism cannot stand without the perversion of Aionios to mean what it does not!

The Greek noun "Aion" literally means "an age" or "an indeterminate period of time." Hebrews 1:2 "…hath spoken unto us by His son…...by whom He made the worlds (Here a plain error in translation, "world" should be Aion or ages). Now if something has a beginning and an ending, then it cannot be endless or unending! Another mis-translation in 1Cor. 2:7, "…which God ordained before the world (Aion or ages) unto our glory." If "Aion" does mean "eternal" then how could God ordain something before eternity? It appears here very plain that Augustus Strong was wrong about the definition of Aion. There is no doubt that he was simply stating exactly how the *translators* translated "Aion" in different scriptures, but that *does not* make the translation correct. According to the just mentioned scriptures it cannot mean both eternity and an indefinite period of time! Eternal never-ending torment? Notice the mistranslation of the following scripture.

Unclear Translation in the 1611 K.J.V. of Rev. 14:10-11

"The same shall drink of the wine of the wrath of God, which is poured out without mixture into the cup of his indignation; and he shall be tormented with fire and brimstone in the presence of the holy angels, and in the presence of the Lamb.

And the smoke of their torment ascendeth up forever and ever: and they have no rest day nor night, who worship the beast and his image and whosoever receiveth the mark of his name."

Both the KJV and the NIV say that they will be "tormented" day and night forever and ever. Here we see both translations producing contradictions, which would not occur had they translated "aion" correctly. The words "forever and ever" are in Greek, "aionas ton aionon." The Zondervan Parallel New Testament in Greek and English, which has the KJV, NIV, the Nestle's Greek text with a literal rendering beneath the Greek, reveals on page 771 that "aionas ton aionon" literally reads "ages of the ages." This makes much more sense since this passage also refers to "day and night." Technically, if "aion" means eternity, then this would be rendered "eternities of eternities" which is absurd and contradictory.

Then the terms neither "day nor night" are used. The Lord created the sun moon and stars for times and seasons. "Time" is only for the ages, not for eternity. Here a clear indication that the word "aion" should not be translated as eternal/eternity. It needs to be added here, that the Bible was not originally written in English, and as well "inspiration of the Holy Spirit" only applies to the original M.S. To those who follow the false teachings of Peter S. Ruckman, also known as "Ruckmanites", (sorry not as "RuckmanKnights" as they like to be called) for this author or any other writer to correct the K.J.V. (to them) is tantamount to tampering with Divine Inspiration, which is absolute foolishness. To say as they do that the K.J.V. was translated under a special "superintendence" of God equal to Divine Inspiration, opens the door for other books to be falsely claimed to be "inspired by God" such as the Book of Mormon etc. Only one book in this world was given by direct inspiration of Almighty God, the Old and New Testaments, and that being in their original languages!

Now take the Greek word "Akatalutos" Strongs 179, which plainly means "indisoluable, endless, or permanent." Pray tell, where in Jesus' teachings concerning Hell/the Lake of Fire, did He use this term to define punishment therein? Where? It cannot be found! Then take the term "Adialeiptos," Strongs 88-89 which again means "permanent, without ceasing i.e. endless" The same applies to the word "Aidios" Strongs (126) "Everduring, forward or backward or forward only." Where did our Savior use these terms concerning the punishment for the unsaved in the Greek? Nowhere! Writer Ken Eckerty concludes the following observations about 'Aionios.'

"Aionios"

The adjective "aionios" comes from the noun "aion" and means "age-abiding" or "age-lasting." It is a common rule of language that an adjective can have no more force than the noun from which it is derived. For example, if I say that my grandfather is my <u>elder</u>, I mean to say that he is older than myself, and therefore, is to be respected. However, if I change this noun to its adjective form, this, in no way, changes the meaning of the word. By using the word <u>elderly</u>, I am still saying that my grandfather is old. It's the same meaning—all that has changed is the form. The same is true with "aionios." If "aion" (the noun) means "an indeterminate period of time" then it goes to follow that "aionios" (the adjective) will also have the same basic meaning.

This adjective is never found until the writings of Plato (427 BC - 347 BC) who only used the word five times, and while he did use this word in the context of eternity, he never used it by itself to mean such. Why? Because the word, in and of itself does not mean "eternity." Whenever he wanted to convey the idea of eternity, he always combined a stronger forced word with it (such as "aidios"), but not once did he ever use "aionios" by itself to mean "endless." However, both Plato and Aristotle did use the word "aionios" by itself to mean temporary. Here is an excerpt by J. W. Hanson from his book <u>Bible Threatenings Explained</u>:

> Plato, referring to certain souls in Hades, describes them as being in "aionian" intoxication. But that he does not use the word in the sense of endless is evident from the Phaedon, where he says, "It is a very ancient opinion that souls quitting the world, repair to the infernal regions, and return after that, to live in this world." After the "aionian" intoxication is over, they return to earth, which demonstrates that the word was not used by him as meaning endless.

Aristotle uses the word in the same sense. He says of the earth, "All these things seem to be done for her good, in order to maintain safety during her aionos," duration, or life. And still more to the purpose is this quotation concerning God's existence: "Life and an aion continuous and eternal, zoe kai aion sunekes kai aidios.'" Here the word aidios, (eternal) is employed to qualify aion and impart to it what it had not of itself, the sense of eternal. (End of quote.)

The real problem now becomes clear. Augustine and Constantine cleared the way for the overthrow of the Biblical teaching of eventual universal salvation for all. Augustinian theology of endless punishment in torments became a permanent fixture in the church especially since Constantine had previously married the church and the state. It is common knowledge that when that marriage happened, that Biblical doctrine of regeneration unto salvation by the new birth became obscured, and along with the false doctrines of Calvinism, i.e. double predestination,

Unregenerate unspiritual men, yea even wicked men, flooded into the "church state offices" by appointment, thus rising to power and political influence bringing in the terrible "dark ages."

The doctrine of "endless punishment" became a useful tool to intimidate and bring fearful leaders and parishioners in the Roman Church to subjection. *The fact also that Augustine was not a Greek scholar, and knew very little of the subject is important to remember.* He confessed that he "hated Greek" and the "grammar learning of the Greeks." Amazing that generations of scholars should take the opinion of one who had "learned almost nothing of Greek" and was "not competent to read and understand" the language over those who were born Greeks!

Readers note: Please note especially in Chapter 8 under 'THE NEW TESTAMENT USAGE AION THE SAME IN BOTH TESTAMENTS' point number six on 'Applied to God'.

That such a man should contradict and subvert the teachings of such men as Clement, Origen, the Gregories *(Ed. This booklet is in no means endorsing some of the unusual doctrines of these men, only their proper Greek word usage)* and others whose mother tongue was Greek, is passing strange. But his powerful influence, aided by civil arm, established his doctrine till it came to rule the centuries. Augustine always quotes the New Testament from the old Latin version, the Itala, from which the Vulgate was formed, instead of the original Greek. (See preface to "Confessions.") Note that Jerome's translation of Origen's book "Principas" had circulated with good effect and Augustine, to counteract the influence of Origen's book wrote in 415 a small work, "Against the Priscillianists and Origenists."

From this time the efforts of Augustine and his followers subsequently changed the character of Christian theology. ***With Origen, God triumphs in final unity and universal salvation for all, with Augustine man continues in endless rebellion and God is defeated and eternal dualism prevails (endless torment for the majority, and endless heaven for a select few.)*** The bottom line is, which should be held superior, the true definitions and understanding of Greek from the first centuries, or those from the fourth century onward, skewed by Augustine and weak translator definitions?

Then there is the matter of truth. Truth must reign supreme throughout eternity/infinity! There can be no point in eternity future, after the final put down of sin, Hell, and the grave that it could or will be said that truth was finally and ultimately defeated in the eternal purpose of God for all living souls whether saved or lost. To say that precious souls for whom Christ died were ultimately and finally subjected to a lie and falsehood, which falsehood caused their final and infinite damnation, is to plainly say that error finally gained the upper hand and infinitely, permanently and irretrievably caused them to be lost forever without end.

The will of Almighty God, may well be resisted, spurned, laughed at, ignored etc., but eventually at some point in time or eternity, God's will shall finally lovingly seduce and bring to complete subjection and perfect obedience, all souls, regardless of how long it takes. The fact that man is able to continue to learn new ideas, concepts, and truth about God simply does not end at the grave. If you the reader believe the Bible speaks infallibly, then the rich man in Lk. 16 was learning many new things after death that he was totally unaware of or willingly ignorant of while alive and in the body! What things did he *learn*? Let the Word of God speak!

Luke 16:22-31

And it came to pass, that the beggar died, and was carried by the angels into Abraham's bosom: the rich man also died and was buried; and in Hell he lift up his eyes being in torments and seeth Abraham afar off and Lazarus in his bosom. And he cried and said father Abraham have mercy on me and send Lazarus that he may dip the tip of his finger in water, and cool my tongue for I am tormented in this flame. But Abraham said, Son remember that thou in thy lifetime receivedst thy good things and likewise Lazarus evil things: but now he is comforted and thou art tormented. And beside all this between us and you there is a great gulf fixed so that they which would pass from hence to you cannot: neither can they pass to us that would come from thence. Then he said, I pray thee therefore father, that thou wouldest send him to my father's house: For I have five brethren that he may testify unto them lest they also come into this place of torment. Abraham saith unto him, They have Moses and the prophets, let them hear them. And he said, Nay father Abraham: but if one went unto them from the dead they will repent. And he said unto him, If they hear not Moses and the prophets, neither will they be persuaded though one rose from the dead.

1. He learned that there is no comfort or freedom from pain in Hell. (While alive he did not know nor believe that). He also learned (continue)…

2. That no one could leave that place in the underworld to warn others of the pain and suffering in Hell. (It is evident that while alive he did not believe in such pain and suffering after death).

3. That those on earth could only be reached by the Word of God. (While on earth he rejected the authority of the Word of God).

4. That those in paradise could not come to visit him and comfort him. (While alive he knew nothing of this coming peril).

5. That he was in a prison with no immediate escape. (While alive with a hardened conscience he rejected/ignored the teaching of suffering and pain after death).

6. That even a resurrected person from Hell could not convince sinners of their fate if they would not hear the scriptures. (It is evident that while alive he felt the "gods" were pleased with him).

7. That the doctrine of "soul sleep" or "no conscious existence after death" was false. The term "death" in the scriptures never means "cease to exist" or "annihilation." It means "separation." When the body "dies" there is a separation of the life or spirit of man, from the body and its return to God as Ecclesiastes plainly teaches. At the "second death" the souls of the lost are "separated" from God a second time.

   If "death" did mean "annihilation" then would the following make sense? "Verily verily I say unto you, he that heareth my word, and believeth on him that sent me, hath everlasting life and shall not come into condemnation but is passed from *non-existence* into life." Jn. 5:24. Or what about the scripture in Revelation, which says… "…and whosoever was not found written in the book of life was cast into the Lake of Fire this is the second *non existence*." Does that make sense? Absolutely not. This story our Savior told was indeed true, and painted a perfect picture of understanding about the conditions of the damned after death. This cannot be refuted!

8. Since he knew Abraham and recognized him, no doubt he lived during the same time period as Abraham. His recognition of Abraham and Lazarus was made when he "lifted up his eyes (being in torments)" which shows that there is facial recognition in the next world. He knew Abraham and Abraham knew him.

9. He, the rich man learned quickly, that there were two kinds of people, the righteous and the unrighteous, of course he being the unrighteous deserving of punishment/torment/affliction. Sad the English word "torment" has come to mean "unjustified suffering" which it does not mean in the Bible. The fact he called him "father Abraham" shows he no doubt was a Hebrew as well.

10. He further quickly learned that his suffering was for a specific reason, and not some "sadistically inflicted torment." Simply put the rich man traded the salvation of his soul for material comfort and gain, as do so many in this life. Being rich sends no one to Hell, but trading the salvation of one's soul for material wealth will.

Unfortunately there are those who categorize Lk.16 as a parable, and thus try to play down its literally true meaning saying that this is merely a parable designed to tell another truth, but certainly not to teach a real burning Hell where people suffer. The Watchtower Society commonly called the "Jehovah Witnesses" embrace that error. Such error is easy to answer as follows:

1. Jesus did not "interpret" this story as He did all other parables, without exception, showing Lk.16 was a truth in itself.

2. Even if it were a parable, all parables without exception were true stories, drawn from real life occurrences, and that would make it as well a truth in itself.

3. If Lk.16 were not a truth in itself that would make Jesus telling a lie, or a falsehood to teach a truth. The sinless spotless Son of God would never do that!

4. Proper names were used in these passages, Lazarus and Abraham, and never are they used in any parable in the Bible. That shows this is a true account of conditions in the underworld. This plainly was not a parable but a true story.

Now can any reader of this booklet, claim that "learning" ends with death and the grave for anyone? Certainly not! In fact we will go on learning for eternity after death. The simple fact about truth, is that truth may well be learned as a doctrine in this life, but *not experienced* until the next life. Take the atheist for example. Many many men and women, have lived out their lives denying and ridiculing the belief in the existence of Almighty God, and then have died with those beliefs. That the truth of Hell was taught over and over again to these people while alive, but rejected and laughed at goes without saying.

Once that atheist passes away, and steps into eternity, suddenly He meets the God he has denied, judged and is sent to that place of torment in Hell to "experience" that truth he so boldly denounced. Does he not "learn" new things after death that he did not know? Absolutely yes. Now he is being "forced" to ascent to the truth which truth he so boldly denied. Now he is "experiencing truth."

Now he is forced to believe the truth of God's Word and immediately changes his mind about the existence of God. Along with that, he also suddenly and immediately, upon being placed in the torments of Hell, is forced to accept the punishment and pain of his unwise and foolish rejection of God's Word, and God's son! In other words, he forever, and that being for eternity for certain, changes his theological position about God, Heaven, and Hell and is forced to finally admit how wrong he was!

Not only that but now he is forced to admit that his sentence in being tormented (the same Greek word "afflicted") and punished in a burning Hell is well deserved! How many people reared in false religions have there been over the short span of man's history? Those raised and having perished while embracing such heresies, suddenly and instantly know, after dying, that they were deceived by what they were taught. That they immediately face God in judgment, and instantly learn that indeed Jesus Christ was the only Way, the Truth and the Life!!

Does not God then instantly "win" in His revelation to them? Do they not then suddenly realize that they deserve the pain and suffering they are in, by foolishly denying the Savior who died for them and offered them a simple and paid for salvation? Absolutely! Are they not in Hell forever and forever? Absolutely they are. But that they are not in Hell for infinity is a fact that cannot be denied. Yes they are there for ages upon ages, and while there they are "*learning by experience*" those truths they rejected while alive.

The idea that God is somehow able to "throw away" millions of lost souls for them to suffer screaming and writhing in insufferable pain and anguish in the halls of the damned burning in torment/fire and brimstone for infinity/eternity certainly is a repulsive doctrine when it is carefully considered. The fact that man was God's crowning creation, one who He meant to fellowship with, to love, and be loved by, to work with in His creation yea for eternity/infinity is clearly an indication of an intention that cannot ever be voided. What man/devil can void the intention of the Almighty? To say as the Calvinists say that "God intended for man to sin" and thus set him up for a fall is to make God the author of sin. God's intention for man was for man to love and serve Him and fellowship with Him in His creation.

Man, not God (as the Calvinists make it), was the one responsible for sin entering the human race. To say that God cannot ultimately reach man, to convince him of his error, is to limit the abilities of an Almighty God. Now who can do that? Is not man in his rebellion and rejection of the ways of God, infantile in his thinking? Is he not like the small somewhat rebellious child who has been repeatedly warned about the dangers of the hot stove, the busy street, or yea the older teenager about the dangers of sex, drugs, and then they for whatever reason "touch the forbidden" and are scarred and sometimes maimed for life? Is not that wicked sinner soon caught up in those wicked enjoyable pleasures of sin "for a season" and easy enslaving sinful life style, though his conscience troubles him day and night? Are we to believe that God's resources are limited in their ability to reach that man with the truth in this life and the next?

"Aidios-Endless"

Strong (126), "Aidios"-everduring, (forward and backward, or forward only): eternal, everlasting.

Clearly this is a proper term for "endless" or "never ending," and yea- even more noteworthy the true "endless, eternal everlasting never ending" Greek word chosen by the Almighty Himself! Interesting enough it is that this term is *never* used in the original languages in conjunction with Hell and the Lake of fire! To say that Hell and the Lake of Fire is for "endless punishment" simply not supported in Holy Scripture. To say Hell and the Lake of Fire is a place of Aionios, on and on, forever and forever i.e. - ages and ages punishment is indeed scriptural, but certainly not "endless." Notice as follows the usage of this term "aidios" in Romans.

Romans 1:20. For the invisible things of Him from the creation of the world are clearly seen, being understood by the things that are made, even His *eternal* (Aidios) power and Godhead: so they are without excuse.

Romans 2:7. To them who by patient continuance in well doing seek for glory and honor and immortality, *eternal* (Aidios) life.

Correct Translation of Titus 1:2 in K.J.V.

1) "In hope of eternal (aionios) life which God that cannot lie, promised before the world (aionios) began. *(See the Greek/English interlinear to verify this irrefutable fact.)*

   Now to translate this verse with the "eternal" word in both places would not make sense, were it translated that way, therefore the translators had to change the second "Aionios" to mean something differently. Notice as follows what it would have been had they not done so: (second case)

2) "In hope of eternal life, which God that cannot lie, promised before the eternity began."

Chapter Three | "Endless Punishment" and the Greek

Now it stands to reason that *nothing can happen before eternity began*! So this verse should have been translated as follows:

"In hope of ages (and ages of) life, which God that cannot lie, promised before the ages began."

Carefully notice, the K.J.V. *translators* erroneously used two totally different words to represent "Aionios." The word "eternal in the first case, and the word "world" in the second. Why? Simply because the verse would not make sense were it translated as shown in the above "second case." There is a separate and distinct word for "world" and that is the Greek noun "Kosmos." The irrefutable fact is that the Greek word "Kosmos" was **NOT** used in the original text. Plainly a translation error.

The fact is, the translation is faulty and represents a Greek word for something it is not! That fact cannot be disputed! We can now hear the cry from the Ruckmanite or the K.J.V. "only" crowd, that this author is saying that … '*the Bible is not the Word of God'* since he is correcting it, because if it is the Word of God it can need no correction. To which it must be answered as follows:

1. The K.J.V. is a "translation" of the precious Old and New Testament M.S. nothing more and nothing less. While it is a beautiful and blessed translation, it is none the less *not* a 100% flawless translation, as it never claimed to be by the translators. While countless have been saved and blessed through its usage, it does need Hebrew/Greek clarification in some places. Anyone who says it is a flawless translation is ignorant of the facts.

2. The translators never claimed to be under direct Divine supernatural inspiration while doing their translating.

3. Had the translators been "inspired of God" in the same way the original autographed manuscripts were "God Breathed" and every word, jot and title was translated exactly as God wanted, then there would not have needed to be over 40 men working on it, translating and comparing each other's work. There would have only needed

to be one, or 66, one for each book of the Bible. That they had to wrestle over differences of opinion goes without saying.

4. The K.J.V. did not exist for 1600+ years of church history. Are we to believe that for over 1600 years the world was without the Word of God and the gates of Hell did indeed prevail against it? Did not Jesus say in the first century that the gates of Hell would not ever prevail against the church?

5. Are we to believe that the only two things we need are a K.J.V. 1600 version and an English dictionary? (The K.J.V is long overdue correction regarding 'aionios/aidios etc).

6. Is the K.J.V. exactly the same today as it was in 1611, with no revisions or updates in wording or spellings, or in word definitions? The fact is it has been revised a number of times. If it were translated under Divine inspiration then certainly it could not have been revised in any text/spelling etc., without "changing the Words of God!!"

7. Which is more accurate; a film about a book, or the book itself? The K.J.V is a type of "film" about "The Book." "The Book" is the God breathed original manuscripts which are still available to us contained in the Masoretic Hebrew and Koine Greek Received Text. For anyone to say that the K.J.V. 1611 is superior to those manuscripts from which it was translated, is to clearly belittle and malign the precious Word of God in its original tongues.

8. For those who look upon King James as a Godly man, one needs only to search out the plain historical facts concerning his morality. Many deny that he was an immoral king, but a simple on line historical search into his character and morals reveals the "smoking gun" to say the least. While the K.J.V. 1611 translation is indeed a beautiful Christian translation/version, it certainly does *not* reflect his well documented character and morals.

Two further examples of "world" erroneously being translated in the English in place of "aionios" –"ages" is as follows:

Romans 16:25. "…according to the revelation of the mystery, which was kept secret since the <u>world</u> ("ages"- Aionios) began." (Not since "eternity" began).

IITim. 1:9. "…but according to His own purpose and grace, which was given us in Christ Jesus before the <u>world</u> ("ages"-Aionios) began." (Again, not since "eternity" began.)

Here are two perfect examples of the mistranslation of Aionios as eternal/everlasting (and world) and in other places as well. Here a wrong translation of a Greek word into English, which English word was *not in the original text.* Someone asks, "But does not the English in these above verses make sense in this case." To which we answer of course it does, and no doubt these verses are true and convey truth which God can honor, but the fact remains that the English translation does not correctly convey the true meaning of the Greek in these verses.

No Unpardonable Sin!

J.W. Hanson (1875) has written the following very scriptural explanation why there is no such thing as an unpardonable sin. The Authorized Version has failed to convey the proper Greek words into the English, and thusly has clouded the issues surrounding the so called "unpardonable sin." The simple fact is there is no such thing as an unpardonable sin! How many people have lived and died believing they have done such a thing.No doubt for one to believe such is possible, he or she could well fall into the doctrinal error that "Now there is no hope for me to ever be saved, so I may as well totally ignore the claims of Christ." No! Nothing could be further from the truth.The fact is, the Greek term "Aion" has/was improperly translated as 'world' rather than 'age.' As a result, many many over the centuries accepting this unclear translation, have in their own view (and in many pastors etc. estimation) done such, and have thus totally given up on God and gone away into irretrievable apostasy/sin. Very sad indeed.

J.W. Hanson on the 'Unpardonable Sin' (1875)

No! There is no eternal/endless unpardonable sin. But yes, It is unpardonable for two ages, the church and millennial ages.

> "Matt. 12:32. Whosoever speaketh against the Holy Ghost, it shall not be forgiven him, neither in this *world*, neither in the world to come." Parallel passages: Mark 3:29. "But he that shall blaspheme against the Holy Ghost hath never (*aióna*) forgiveness, but is in danger of eternal (*aiónion*) damnation." Luke 12:10. "And whosoever shall Speak a word against the Son of man, it shall be forgiven him; but unto him that blasphemeth against the Holy Ghost it shall not be forgiven." Literally, "neither in this age nor the coming," that is, neither in the Mosaic, nor the Christian age or dispensation. but then, these ages will both end, and in the dispensation of the fullness of times, or ages, all are to be redeemed, (Eph. 1:10.) Mark 3:29 is the same as Matt. 12:32. The Greek differs slightly, and is rendered literally, "has not forgiveness to the age, but is liable to age-lasting judgment." The thought of the Savior is, that those who should attribute his good deeds to an evil spirit would be so hardened that his religion would have difficulty in affecting them. Endless damnation is not thought of, and cannot be extorted from the language. In the New Testament the "end of the age," and "ages" is a common expression, referring to what has now passed. See Col. 1:26, Heb. 9:26, Matt. 13:39, 40, 49, 24:3. Says Locke "The nation of the Jews were the kingdom and people God whilst the law stood. And this kingdom of God, under the Mosaic constitution was called *aión outos*, this age, or as it is commonly translated, this world.

But the kingdom of God was to be under the Messiah, wherein the economy and constitution of the Jewish church, and the nation itself, that in opposition to Christ adhered to it, was to be laid aside, is in the New Testament called *aión mellon*, the world or age to come." In the New Testament the "end of the age," and "ages" is a common expression, referring to what has now passed. See Col. 1:26, Heb. 9:26, Matt. 13:39, 40, 49, 24:3. *(End of Hanson quote).*

Readers note: If the K.J. 1611 version is the only "Word of God" and that being only in the English in the world, then that would make all other translations to be imposters, no matter what the language be, whether Spanish, French, Dutch, German etc, etc. Also that would mean that God could not honor the preaching from any of those stated languages, and as well then no one else could be saved unless he was saved by direct influence in and through the English language K.J.V. These points easily show the irrationality of Ruckmanism.

A Twist On "No Post Mortem Salvation"

There is an interesting twist on the adamant conclusion of the fundamentalist damnationists that there is no possibility of post mortem salvation for the wicked. They contend if one dies unrepentant/unregenerate, then that lost soul would be in the spirit world of Sheol/Hades, having lost their bodies, and of course would not be 'in the flesh' to entertain the message of salvation. To this we can heartily agree, and do as well agree that there will be no salvation after death in Sheol/Hades. But, the scripture is very clear that there will be salvation 'in the flesh' for the lost, *after* these lost souls are raised from the dead, reunited with their bodies, and then have finished their punishment in the Lake of Fire!

The scriptures are clear that all lost souls who have ever lived, having served their time in Sheol/Hades, will be resurrected and be stood before Jesus at the Great White Throne Judgment Revelation chapter 20. Then while 'in the flesh' in resurrected bodies, they will be punished 'according to their works' (but not endlessly eternally) and once that punishment is completed, they, 'in the flesh' will bend their knee before the throne of Jesus to gladly, gloriously, and thankfully embrace His glorious salvation (every knee shall bow and every tongue shall confess... and also Romans 10:9-10&13) becoming born again believers 'in the flesh' in glorified bodies, to spend eternity in the new heaven and earth.

An Imperfect Revelation and Eternal Damnation?

This heading clearly shows the damnationists preach that God will consign ignorant, unlearned, and heathen type people to be tormented in fire and brimstone for eternity without giving these unfortunate souls a full revelation of Himself (and the true plan of salvation) until after death. Now is that justice? Is not hind sight 20/20?? If all of these mentioned souls have perished in ignorance and false religion, etc, then are we to believe that when they stand before God and seeing a complete irrefutable revelation of who God really is, and what He really is all about, we are to believe that God will endlessly damn them due to the ignorance and lack of revelation they had when alive?

Did not the rich man in Luke 16 after death and having a full revelation of the afterlife have a complete turnabout in his attitude towards the realities of the afterlife? No doubt this hindsight will plague all and every lost soul who dies without Christ, however to consign them to be tormented eternally/endlessly in the Lake of Fire for not having a full revelation of God and the true plan of salvation is too much to believe. True justice is therefore to give all men everywhere, at sometime either in this life or the next a full and perfect revelation of just who God really is and just what the true plan of salvation really is. God is not willing that any should perish but that all should come to repentance. God's perfect revelation will come to all men either in this life or the next.

Watchtower and Others Teach that Death Means Annihilation but the Facts Are...

Chapter Three | "Endless Punishment" and the Greek

Watchtower (falsely named the Jehovah Witnesses) teach (the false doctrine) that eternal death for the wicked will be eternal annihilation. Quoting here:

"God provided through Christ a redemptive price whereby those of men who have faith in God's provision may come into harmony with him and, serving him faithfully, they may receive the gift of life, being freed from inherited sin and from eternal death as a result of sin" (Let God Be True, page 113). It should be noted at this point, that according to Watchtower, the penalty for Adam's sin was physical death which was to be followed by annihilation (of the body), thus the purpose of Christ's death was to rescue men from physical annihilation in which they would otherwise have remained after death (Watchtower deny the existence of an immortal soul inside man's body which after death goes either to Heaven or to Hell).

Now the scriptures plainly teach that in Adam all *die*, that Jesus tasted *death* for every man, and that *death* passed upon all men for all have sinned! Further examination of scriptures concerning 'death' and its supposed meaning of 'annihilation, brings the following facts to light:

1. Question: The scripture teaches that we are passed from 'death into life by our faith in Christ. John 5:24. "... hath everlasting life and shall not come into condemnation but is passed from death unto life." Now if death means 'annihilation' and annihilation means one ceases to exist, then are we to believe that we are 'passed from non-existence into life?' (I.e. that we don't 'exist' before our faith in Christ being 'dead' in trespasses and sins as Eph. 2:1 says? "And you hath He quickened who were dead [*non existent?*] in trespasses and sins...").

No! Plainly death means simply 'separation' of life, when the body dies life is separated from it, when the soul dies it is separated from God. Remember in Revelation 20 when the wicked dead are cast into the Lake of Fire (after physical resurrection) nowhere does it say they cease to exist, or are 'burned up' as the Watchtower teaches, but rather are said to experience a second death which is a second separation from God to be punished for their sins.

2. Question: The scripture teaches that our Lord tasted 'death' for every man. Hebrews 2:9. "But we see Jesus, who was made a little lower than the angels for the suffering of 'annihilation' (?), crowned with glory and honor, that he by the grace of God should taste 'annihilation' (?) for every man. It makes sense to say that death means annihilation? Again it ought to be plain that the true meaning of 'death' in the scriptures is not annihilation but rather *'separation from God.'*

3. Question: The scripture teaches that the last enemy to be destroyed is 'death.' I Cor. 15:25-26. "For He must reign till He hath put all enemies under His feet. The last enemy that shall be destroyed is death." Revelation 21:4. "…there shall be no more death neither sorrow…" For the sake of arguing, even if death meant 'annihilation' we see from these verses that there will be no more 'annihilation' that Jesus vanquishes and totally defeats it clearly meaning that no one will experience it ever in the new heaven and earth! No! Death means simply 'separation' from God, and absolutely no one will ever be separated from God again.

Why would He taste death for every man if every man is not going to be saved? The Lake of Fire which will contain the wicked/lost souls is simply a place of punishment *according to their works* (no not endlessly/eternally as the damnationists read in) and will cease to exist in the new heavens and earth. Its purpose will have been fulfilled when those who were physically resurrected in eternal bodies, are justly and thoroughly punished therein. Then at the end of their punishment they will bow their knee and confess unto salvation. Damnationists falsely read in that the Lake of Fire will exist for eternity tormenting lost souls, but Revelation plainly tells us that in the new heavens and earth those former things (which include the Lake of Fire) will pass away or be no more!

4. Question: Revelation tells us that the Lake of Fire is the 'second death.' Rev. 20:14. "And death and Hell were cast into the Lake of Fire, this is the second death." Now would it make sense to say that "...and annihilation and Hell were cast into the Lake of Fire, this is the second annihilation." (?) So if they were already 'annihilated' the first time and 'ceased to exist' then how could they cease not to exist only to 'cease to exist' a second time when cast into the Lake of Fire? Does that make sense? Are we to say God contradicts His supposed 'cease to exist plan?'

5. Question: Now if the wicked dead are raised from supposed 'soul sleep' as the Watchtower teach, and then are judged according to their works and cast into the Lake of Fire to be instantly 'burned up or totally incinerated forever, just what purpose would this serve? Watchtower teaches that man has no spirit/soul living in his body, but rather his body is his only entity. They say man has no body soul and spirit as the scriptures plainly teach. I Thess. 5:23: "...I pray God your whole spirit and soul and body be preserved blameless unto the coming of our Lord Jesus Christ."

Notice the Mount of Transfiguration where Moses and Elijah appeared to Peter, James and John in spirit bodies, the witch of Endor and Samuel appearing in spirit body, as well as the souls under the altar in heaven in Revelation 6, and the white robed multitude of disembodied spirits, in the next chapter 7. The simple fact is that those raised from the dead to be judged according to their works, and then cast into the Lake of Fire, are raised with new bodies that will indeed be indestructible, but still subject to pain and suffering in that terrible place as God deems necessary. It should be plain that the Lake of Fire is a place of punishment for the evil done by these people while in the flesh, and certainly not a place of annihilation as Watchtower falsely teaches.

These people, subsequent to their severe punishment according to their works, will come to true remorse, sorrow and confession on bended knee unto salvation and thereafter live forever with Christ in the new Heaven and Earth. The Watchtower plainly and unashamedly teaches that when cast into the Lake of Fire they are consumed and burnt up, to which we say "Nowhere in scripture does it say that!" To say such is plainly to add to the scriptures and bring a curse upon one's self.

6. Question: "Is it not plain to see that the last enemy our Savior defeats is 'death.' Now if He is successful in doing that, and IF death were annihilation, then all those supposedly 'annihilated' in the Lake of Fire would have their condition reversed! Thus they would live again forever to be with Christ and praise Him for bringing them back to be with their loved ones, and rule and reign with Christ for eternity! I Cor. 15: 24-26. "Then cometh the end when He shall have delivered up the kingdom to God, even the Father when He shall have put down all rule and all authority and power. For He must reign till He hath put all enemies under His feet. The last enemy that shall be destroyed is death."

Wonderful it is then, that Jesus our Lord and Savior totally defeats death, and so even if death meant 'annihilation' then it will be reversed as well and absolutely no one would enter such a state for all of eternity! A real doctrinal defeat for Watchtower and Seventh Day Adventists and others!

CHAPTER FOUR

TRANSLATION CORRECTION OF MATTHEW 25:46

Jesus Teaching the Resurrection Not "Eternal Punishment"!

In the following verse, Matt. 25:46, proponents of "eternal never ending punishment" claim this verse validates their point using "eternal/ everlasting" being translated from the Greek word "Aionios" into the

---

Readers note: Augustine, Bishop of Hippo, 354-430 a.d. no doubt laid the theological breeding ground which finally gave birth to Calvinism in the 1500's, which subverted and violated the Biblical doctrine of eventual universal salvation for all men. Wikipedia states as follows: "Many **Protestants**, especially **Calvinists**, consider him to be one of the theological fathers of the **Protestant Reformation** due to his teachings on **salvation** and **divine grace**." No doubt Calvinism, readily recognized in its infancy that not all are saved, nor have the opportunity to do so before death, that coupled with the fact that God cannot be unjust in consigning any one to eternity in Hell/Lake of Fire, therefore came to the erroneous conclusion that since death supposedly ends all possibilities for salvation that God must choose some to be damned forever. True it is that one heresy gives rise and birth to heresy after heresy. This author believes that Calvinism could not have possibly risen, had not the simple doctrine of eventual universal reconciliation for all men become corrupted by Augustine and his followers.

English. (It must be remembered that in the original language "Aionios" cannot mean eternal/endless/everlasting since it cannot be consistently translated that way in all places, examples as shown above in Romans and II Tim. Also, our Savior was very careful *never* to use the word "Aidios" (endless in reference to duration of the punishment of the unsaved/lost)

Matthew 25:46

"And these shall go away into everlasting (Aionios) punishment, but the righteous into life (Aionios) eternal."

The Greek word aionios, accordingly was translated by the KJV translators in several different ways, and cannot possibly mean "eternal/never ending." The King James translation being in plain error here has definitely affected other translations as well and grievously so. Other popular Bibles have followed the tradition of the "Authorized Version" in perpetuating this error. The early revisionists of the KJV received (and still do) great persecution for correcting this error in dozens of places. There is much available research proving that the Greek word "aion" when properly translated is a *time word* with a beginning and an end. The word "eternal" in this verse is the adjective of the word "aion."

An adjective cannot have a greater meaning than the noun from which it is derived. The adjective "hourly" must pertain to the "hour," it cannot mean "weekly," "monthly," or "eternally." The Greek word "aion" means "age." It would be improper grammar to give the adjective "aionios" a greater meaning than its noun. Aions (ages) are made (Heb. 1:2), there is before the aions (1 Cor. 2:7, 2 Tim. 1:9), the end of the aions (ages) (Heb. 9:26, 1 Cor. 10:11, Matt. 24:3). There are at least five ages mentioned in the Bible: ages past (Col. 1:26), present age (Luke 20:34), and at least two more in the future (Eph. 2:7). Reader, please note below that Mark 10:30 illustrates the fact as well that the 'eternal life' should not be translated as 'eternal' but rather as 'continuous,' for the same following reason. In doing justice to the inspired words of Jehovah in the original text, verse (46) should be translated as follows:

Chapter Four | Translation Correction of Matthew 25:46

"And these shall go away into ages of *(continuous)* **punishment** *(the wicked are resurrected and a resurrection will happen contrary to what the Sadducees teach),* **while the righteous will go away** *(with rewards),* **into ages and ages** *(the kingdom ages and ages equaling 1000 years.)* **of life**.

Professor Tayler Lewis gives us another fair translation of this seemingly difficult verse:

These shall go into the pain of the *Olam* (*aión*) (the world to come), and these to the life of the *Olam* (*aión*) (the world to come)

Professor A. T. Robertson in his Word Pictures in the N.T. and A.B. Bruce, in the Expositors Greek Testament agree that the "kolasis aionion" the "everlasting punishment" of the KJV has a literal meaning of "age-lasting correction."

An argument was introduced by Augustine, and since his day incessantly repeated, that if "aionios kolasis" does not mean "endless punishment" then there is no security for the believer that "aionios zoe" means "endless life," or that he will possibly not enjoy the promise of endless happiness. However it must be pointed out that Matt. 25:46 shows the "eonian chastisement" and the "eonion life" are of exactly the same duration lasting through the "eons," and when the "eons" *(ages)* do end as the Scripture states that they will, then plainly the ages of time will be permanently end! Now remember, what happens when the 'ages' end? The great White Throne Judgment, where death finally comes to an end in the Lake of Fire. Truly the 'death of death.'

Dr. G. Campbell Morgan, preacher, teacher, evangelist and author; sometimes called the "prince of expositors," wrote in his Studies of the Four Gospels concerning Matt. 25: 31-46, "Then, moreover, we must be careful not to read into this section of prophecies things which it does not contain; for while it has been interpreted as though it were a description of the final judgment, the Great White Throne-These shall go away into age-abiding punishment, but the righteous into age-abiding life-the terms are co-equal in value, and whatever one means the other means. Only remember that here Christ is not dealing with the subject of the soul's destiny either in Heaven or Hell. They are terms that have to do wholly with the setting up of the kingdom here in this world…"

In Dr. Morgan's, "God's Methods with Men," he says, (pp.185-186) "Let me say to Bible students that we must be very careful how we use the word 'eternity.' We have fallen into great error in our constant usage of that word. There is no word in the whole Book of God corresponding with our 'eternal,' which as commonly used among us, means "absolutely without end." In his book The Corinthian Letters of Paul, the same author states concerning 1 Cor. 15:22, "For as in Adam all die, even so in Christ shall all be made alive." (p. 191):

"The word Adam is used here in the sense of headship of a race, the one from whom the race springs. But God's second Man was the last Adam. If we say second Adam, we presuppose the possibility of a third Adam, another whom a race shall spring. There will be no such though. It is 'first Adam' and 'last Adam.' What does relationship with Him mean? In the program of God ALL are to be made alive in Christ." (End of Quote).

These two verses therefore do not teach endless punishment but do teach the following:

1. That there WILL be a resurrection of the righteous here unto ages and ages of rewards during the millennium. The unrighteous/wicked are put to death to undergo ages and ages of judgment/affliction and suffering in Hell, and then are resurrected at the end of the thousand years for the last resurrection and great white throne judgment.

2. There is no such thing as cessation of existence after death.

3. Justice/punishment/rewards will be meted out in both groups on and on for an indeterminate unknown period of time during the kingdom age which age begins with Christ's return to earth to begin His millennium reign.

4. The entire chapter Matthew 25 is plainly and irrefutably dealing with the return of Jesus in glory (vs.31) and gathering the nations together for judgment unto rewards, and judgment unto death and punishment, *just as the world is about to enter the kingdom age for 1000 years.*

5. It therefore is easy to understand how the underlying Greek word "Aionios" is used in this type verse to convey "ages and ages" rather than "eternal/endless," since it refers to the kingdom age. The fact that all men will exist and live endlessly, is a fact taken for granted by our Lord throughout all the scripture. Otherwise Isaiah (45:22-25) could not have said, "….and **ALL** of the seed of Israel shall be saved." Remember, man is/was created in the image of God, God cannot ever cease to be, neither can man!

The Watchtower heresy of annihilation further exposed and put to rest by the Words of Jehovah! (Some falsely teach that the wicked will suffer ages and ages of punishment, and then be annihilated. Such would make no sense for God to waste his resources in "punishing" or "teaching the wicked a lesson," a lesson that they would naturally experience in Hell fire, only to then turn around and cause them to "cease to exist.")

6. Then lastly we mentioned Mark 10:30. "But he shall receive an hundred fold now in this time, houses and brethren and sisters, and mothers, and children, and lands with persecutions and in the world to come eternal life." Here again if the word 'eternal' were supposed to be 'endless' referring to the security of our present salvation then the 'eternal' here would not be referenced as to be coming or beginning in the future or '…in the world (aion/age) to come.

'As in John 3:16 we have 'continuous' (aionios) life, which refers to quality of life and not 'quantity' since all people were created to live endlessly for eternity. John 3:16 as well simply is saying that those who receive Jesus now, will not cease having continuous life in Christ, and so will not 'perish' and be lost in Hell, which is a terrible quality of life.

Is it any wonder that such misunderstanding concerning a word in the English translation of the Greek can cause certain heresies to arise? No doubt the Watchtower doctrine of "eternal annihilation" was spawned by the "eternal equals endless/never ending" erroneous translation! The very idea that "eternal/everlasting" as is used in the English Bible supposedly means "endless duration" creates the illusion that God indeed does torment sinners in Hell and the Lake of Fire endlessly. Eternal infinite punishment for finite sins committed by finite mankind? The Word of God certainly does not reveal that type of God. That distorted view of the Lord makes God to be unjust/uncompassionate and even unloving towards mankind, many of whom die in their sins never having heard the name Jesus.

The Watchtower no doubt seeing that mistranslation quickly and naturally embrace the annihilation doctrine, while overlooking the truth of eventual universal salvation for all. Along with that they as well do not see the value of God severely punishing man for aionios and aionios or ages and ages in that place called Hell (making Hell to be only to be a symbolic not literal place).

It must be remembered that "Sheol/Hades" is (in this dispensation after the resurrection of Jesus) strictly speaking the world of departed **unredeemed** spirits. Indications are that Hell/Sheol has places of terrible fire, suffering and isolation for the wicked, but it is also the abode of those of much lesser sin, deserving little if any pain and suffering. "Wondering stars *(souls)* to whom is reserved the blackness of darkness forever." Jude 13. (This also explains where some will be cast into outer darkness where there will be pain and gnashing of teeth. Matt. 25:30). Clearly not all of this spirit world is of equal value in pain and suffering, but it is a place of "learning by experience" and then these souls will culminate their stay at the 2nd resurrection, where the final duration of suffering will be set at the White Throne Judgment (according to their works).

Chapter Four | Translation Correction of Matthew 25:46

Dr. Richard D. Dehaan in his booklet "The Eternal Fire," makes an amazing admission. He says clearly and plainly (and correctly) that "…tous aionia ton aionon…" contains the words from the Greek which means "age or ages," i.e. which of course is "Aion/Aionios." Revelation 14:11 states clearly in the K.J.V, "And the smoke of their torment ascendeth up forever and ever, and they have no rest day nor night, who worship the beast and his image, and whosoever receiveth the mark of his name." Matthew 25:46 states that, "And these shall go away into everlasting punishment, but the righteous into life eternal."

He then strays from the truth by saying that due to the *use* of the word "Aionios" it must be translated as "Eternal." He claims further (in error) that the life of the righteous in Matthew 25:46 is said to be "Aionios" which must mean "Eternal" in the English, and that being the case the same must be for the unrighteous, i.e. "Aionios" meaning eternal in regards to the length of their punishment. Following are irrefutable points to further clear up this problem and mis-translation.

1. The Greek word "Aionios" (ages) is *not* the same Greek word "Aidios," (eternal [endless] or everduring forward or backward, see Strong). Just as in English, two separate words describing something entirely different one from the other, are not the same and should not be considered the same, and *must not* be translated into the English as the same!! "Automobile" is not the same as "Bicycle" and "Bird" is not the same as "Snake." Both an auto and bicycle are similar in use, but vastly different in abilities, not the same and not interchangeable. True they both are vehicles of travel, but one is vastly limited in travel, speed and duration.

   Speaking of going on a trip, either could be used without mentioning which one (I could say 'I traveled to see my mother'), but when traveling speeds and distance (say I used a vehicle to go 70 m.p.h. for four hours) then for clarity, which vehicle would need to be named. To use a pre-fabricated doctrine, as endless punishment to "interpret" a Greek word into the English is to clearly change the meaning of the Words of God. The scripture in the original inspired tongue did *not* say "Aidios" punishment! Jesus said "Aionios" punishment. Punishment for ages and ages! Can that not settle the issue?

2. Rev.14:11 and Matthew 25:46 clearly have to do with "time" and not eternity. Vs. 11 clearly states, "...and they have no rest ***day nor night***..." Day and night are obviously related to the movement of the heavenly bodies, sun, moon, and stars. Time is not eternity, eternity has no time value.

The point at which these scriptures are fulfilled is at the return of Christ as the thousand year millennial reign of our Savior is about to begin. I.E. ages and ages to continue on for a thousand years, **TIME** measured by the sun moon and stars for this period. When someone says, "Why I haven't seen you for ages," they are not giving an exact period of time, but rather an indeterminate/unknown length of time. The same with the scriptures.

3. What these verses say are very plain, that the righteous are going into reward for ages and ages into the millennium, and the wicked are going into punishment for ages and ages into the millennium. The question of course is asked, "Do we not have eternal life as Christians which means we will dwell with Christ forever or endlessly enjoying permanent salvation?" To which we answer, "Of course we do, but we must not change the Words of God to mean something it does not mean.

Some may well say that in these verses the Saints are going into endless/eternal life so what difference does it make. To this we answer as follows: To say the Greek teaches that quality (endless life) here, rather than (quantity) ages and ages of entering happiness and rewards in the millennium, would force the Greek to say what it ***does not say*** about the unrighteous, (i.e. that they supposedly are going to be punished endlessly) is totally false! The word of God must speak for itself!

4. Another very interesting note is that in these verses (according to the K.J.V.) the righteous are said to be "***going into*** life eternal." "*Go-*

ing into life eternal" clearly cannot be since that translation would teach the saints do not *have* eternal life until this judgment, and then receive their salvation as they *enter* the millennial age. No, we "HAVE" eternal (Aionios) life now. Jn. 5:24. Thus these verses must be translated as "Ages and Ages" as the Greek demands, or the saints "Going into *ages and ages* of life."

Dare we tamper with word meanings, if when we do so we change a doctrine of the Word of God, or falsify the true character and intentions of Almighty God? While we know that God is represented as a "consuming fire" should we not understand that He is a compassionate God as well?

Actually, God as a "consuming fire" (Heb. 12:29) defines the fact that in judgment the fire consumes that which is dross, yea wood, hay, or stubble and all that is evil and bad, leaving the gold and silver to ever more glorify Jesus Christ.   Should we overlook the fact the scriptures teach that "... His mercy endureth forever..." Sin must be punished, legally, judicially, and through chastening.

No doubt the fires of Hell are akin to the refiner's fire, which if negated would bring failure in the plan of God to *teach* mankind the reality of His hatred and aversion of sin in man. Hell then becomes that refiner's fire, to punish man in direct proportion to his sins. Does not the Scripture teach that man will be judged "... according to his works, and whosoever was not found written in the book of life was cast into the Lake of Fire..." Rev. 20.

Dehaan in his booklet further claims as follows: "In Matt.25: 46.... If the life is endless, then the punishment must also be endless." To which we answer "That is correct, *unless* the underlying Greek supports the word 'age' by using the Greek equivalent 'aion!' which it emphatically does. This cannot be refuted.

Dehaan furthers his argument using the verse saying that Hell is a place where the fire is never quenched, and the worm dieth not. To this we answer simply as follows: True, parts of Hell are places of continuous (aionios not aidios/endless) intense suffering in fire, and a place where the soul cannot die or cease to be, as it would if it were a physical entity and could be destroyed by fire. The simple fact is that this verse is not addressing the idea of "endless punishment" or not, but is rather addressing

   a. The fact that the fire in Hell is not a fire that can be extinguished.

   b. The fact that the souls there are not "destroyed" but live on and on.

   c. The fact that he is *not* speaking of "*duration of suffering or length of time of suffering*" in that terrible place, but *only* of "a" and "b" and *nothing else!*

Another verse which shows plainly in the English language that "Aionios" could not mean "endless or eternity without end" is John 10:28.

> "And I give unto them *eternal* life, and they shall *never perish*, neither shall any man pluck them out of my hand."

Here if "eternal (Greek-aionios)" meant "endless" then Jesus would not have qualified the word "aionios/eternal" here with the adjective "never." Plainly, "eternal" coming from the Greek "Aionios" only has the same equivalent meaning as "continuous" in the English. "Continuous" can mean two things then. It can mean on and on with indeterminate/unknown duration when not modified, or it can mean "endless/never ending when clarified" as it is here by "never ending." Had our Lord felt that "Aionios" meant "endless," no doubt he would not have added "never perish." John 3:16 follows the same reasoning in translation. "Shall not perish" clarifies the noun "Aionios" to mean "everlasting/never ending." The K.J.V. word "everlasting" "Greek- aionios" meaning "on and on with no determinate duration now becomes "endless" due to the qualifying terms "never perish."

Clearly the English word "continuous" is a very good equivalent to the Greek word "Aionios." "Continuous" can certainly mean "eternal, everlasting/temporarily continuous like "I am having a continuous bout with the flu," on and on with no definition of length of time, forever and ever," in the English just as "Aionios" can in the Greek *according to context, and how it is modified*, in both languages! (Naturally when "Aion/Aionios is used with "God" it must take on the meaning of the eternal or endlessly existing God, but when used of man and his duration of physical life or punishment it is only used in the Greek as ages and ages).

Considering all of this, it must be remembered that even if "continuous/never ending/is used, the thought still may not be literally "endless" (literally endless- never ending for eternity) after all. I could say, "Due to my accident, my back has a continuous/never ending pain, and I am forever to suffer with no relief in sight." The context therefore must be regarded. Remember, Aion is not Aidios, and Aidios is not Aion, they are two separate and distinct words, and as well the context must be used to illuminate their use.

Interesting it is that the K.J.V. many times uses the words, eternal, everlasting, and eternity when there are no underlying Greek word equivalents. The word "Aidios" in the Greek certainly *does* mean "ever enduring or literally endless forward or backward." The pagans and some groups of the Jews who lived during the time of Christ, held to the false doctrine of "endless punishment" (Greek-"Aidios or Adialeipton Timora" i.e. Endless torment).

In further examining Matt.25:31-46 it becomes evident that this judgment indeed is not referring to everlasting/endless punishment! Professor A.T. Robertson and A.B. Bruce, famous Greek scholars, both agree that "kolasis aionion" (punishment on and on) has a literal meaning of "age lasting correction." The Greek word *kolasin*, rendered punishment, should be rendered chastisement, as reformation is implied in its meaning. (Certainly not endless/eternal/everlasting punishment.) G. Campbell Morgan states very clearly...

"Let me say to Bible students that we must be very careful how we use the word "eternity." We have fallen into great error in our constant usage of that word. There is no word in the whole Book of God corresponding with our word eternal."

The simple fact is that from about 1600 A.D. on, many theologians began to teach the doctrine of "endless" punishment. How many have been raised with the K.J.V. and have had it presented it to them as a perfectly translated manuscript, perfectly representing the original Greek and Hebrew manuscripts as the infallible Word of God? The fact is there are many words "invented' in the English language that did not exist in the first century Greek/Hebrew. "Eternity, everlasting, eternal" are to be included as just stated above. Other examples are the words, automobile, computer, hard drive, airplane etc, etc.

During the period of man's probation, and the different ages which come and go God is of course looked upon as the supreme "God of the Ages" or the "Aionios/ages God, and (in 1611 English) the eternal God." Therefore in Jn.3:16 it is easy to say that those in Christ receive "everlasting life" now and as well are promised ages and ages of continuous life which begins after the resurrection, life which is uninterrupted by that enemy "death."

"Shall not perish" simply refers to the fact that man who rejects Jesus is consigned to "perish" to a place of suffering and uselessness in Hell for "aionios and aionios" or ever and ever or for "aions and aions….forever and ever, or for indeterminate ages and ages uninterrupted. Certainly not for "eternity or endlessly" in the English. (An important point to remember is that *if* the wicked are to suffer endlessly in Hell/the Lake of Fire, then why would God want to have such a horrific place where the souls of the damned are screaming and moaning in pain for endless eternity? Why not rather for Him to just as well "speak them out of existence" just as he "spoke them into existence?"

Are we to believe the unsaved are to be tormented endlessly in fire and brimstone as an eternal/everlasting memorial to their failure to be saved, or for the church/Christ to reach them? No doubt herein lies the basic reason for the Watchtower to invent the idea of "everlasting death" or that the wicked cease to exist when cast into the Lake of Fire. Hell/the Lake of Fire as an eternal endless reminder of Jesus failing to reach the majority of humanity with salvation? Certainly the scriptures do not teach such. Jesus cannot lose this battle, nor allow Satan final victory due to a vastly weakened church (yes the church does fail in all centuries to win all) in failing to win all the lost to Himself! Jesus plainly said, "And I, if I be lifted up shall draw ALL men unto myself," so how can He fail to complete what He started on the cross? The scriptures also plainly say, "…because we trust in the living God who is the Savior of all men, especially of those that believe," I Tim.4:10.

Origin of the Words Eternal, Everlasting, Forever, Eternity, In the A.V. K.J.V. 1611

Good and godly people who strictly follow the A.V. 1611, have reason to believe in endless damnation for the unsaved due to the use of the above terms. It must be understood however these terms which normally mean 'endless' in the English language *do not* have the underlying Greek of 'endless' to support such a notion. The underlying Greek for these words is "aionios" or 166 which root is shown in Strongs as #165: **aion** {ahee-ohn>}. Strong then proceeds to wrongly define the term **aion** as 'Forever, an unbroken age, perpetuity of time, eternity, the worlds, universe, period of time, age.' Furthermore 'Aion' which is the root word of 'Aionios' he says, as well can mean 'never,' and a period of time such as 'an age!' *(???! Ed)*

Strange this word can have *nine* sometimes contradictory and different meanings!? (Reader please study chapter 8 of this book to clarify the meaning of Aion/Aionios by Greek scholar J. W. Hanson). Could someone say, "I'll see you in an hour," but really mean "I'll see you in a month," or really mean to say "I'll never see you again?" Of course not. 'Aion' is a 'time word' literally meaning 'age,' just as *'Aionios' is a time word as well, and does not mean endless unless it is modified* as such by saying "We have an Aionios God or a continuous God, or a God of ages and ages." St. Jerome (Roman Catholic priest/confessor) or 'Hieronymus' which is the Greek and Latin form of the given name **Jerome** and means "sacred name" (A.D. 347-420) translated the Bible into Latin, (now a dead language) the common language of those living in North Africa at that time.

Eusebius Hieronymus or Jerome (c 342 -420) was commissioned by Pope Damasus to begin translating the New Testament from Greek into Latin. He continued the task after Damasus' death and began the translation of the Old Testament from both Greek and Hebrew, completing this by the year 404. This was the Vulgate or "common" Latin Bible of the Roman Catholic Church.

Other North Africans translated the Greek word 'aion' into the Latin, 'saeculum' (or 'world' or 'world order' the chronological order of things) and 'aeternus' (in Latin more of an era or age lasting perhaps a lifetime). Unfortunately these words became the sources for the English words 'everlasting, eternal, forever and eternity.' The simple fact is that when the Latin Vulgate was translated into English these words were often wrongly translated as 'eternal, eternity, everlasting, and forever.' Since the Church of Rome traditionally threatened wandering parishioners with endless damnation for mortal sin, or for leaving the holy mother church, the translation was well suited for universal Catholic parishioners to hold them in check.

While Eusebius improved many flaws in the Greek to Latin translations, he erred in not correcting these two words. North African translators had already misrepresented, 'saeculum' and 'aeternus' neither of which meant endless, or forever endless, eternal, or eternity! Hieronymus translated the Vulgate in 380 A.D. and while attempting to be true to the Greek text, already the doctrine of endless damnation which the Babylonians and some sects of the Jews at the time of Christ held, had begun to corrupt the Latin and Greek languages. Notice as follows from

"On Line Etymology" the point of origin in history of "eternal/everlasting/eternity in the English language.

Eternal/Everlasting/Eternity from, "On Line Etymology"
eternal

> c.1366 (in variant form *eterne*), from O.Fr. *eternal,* from L.L. *æternalis,* from L. *æternus* contraction of *æviternus* "of great age," from *ævum* "age." Eternity first attested c.1374. In the Mercian hymns, L. *æternum* is glossed by O.E. *ecnisse*

eon

> 1647, from L. *æon,* from Gk. *aion* "age, vital force, lifetime," from PIE base **aiw-* "vital force, life, long life, eternity" (cf. Skt. *ayu* "life," Avestan *ayu* "age," L. *aevum* "space of time, eternity," Goth. *aiws* "age, eternity," O.N. *ævi* "lifetime," Ger. *ewig* "everlasting," O.E. *a* "ever, always").

Naturally it follows that if the scriptures *do not* teach that the eternal/endless fate of the soul is permanently fixed at death, and as well that "punishment for the unsaved" is not endless then it stands to common sense and logic that eventual universal salvation for all must be true. The distortion of the Bible doctrine of punishment in Hell forever is very serious indeed. Is God one who consigns any and all unsaved to be tormented in the fires of Hell for eternity, and that being "never ending," while saving only a few precious souls?

Or is He a God who has decreed and designed the eventual salvation of all souls after exercising His anger and wrath upon the wicked unsaved in the fires of Hell for an unknown period? Then do not the severe punishments, yea the horrors and pain of the lower levels of Hell force shame/humiliation/disgrace upon them, ultimately bringing them to admit to their guilt, giving them every legitimate reason to embrace the free salvation they spurned/neglected or were ignorant of during this life on earth?

Certainly sin is against God and cannot be forgiven without the shed blood of Christ being applied to cleanse away sin. These questions can be easily answered providing a proper understanding of Hebrew/Greek words and of course the English as well. Whatever words are used in the original Scriptures have meanings, and to (a) add to their meanings, (b) to detract from those meanings, (c) to change those meanings, is to corrupt and change the Word of God. This certainly is what has happened in regards to the doctrine of the "eternal punishment" of the unsaved wicked by the unclear English translations!

It is this authors firm belief that any man, anywhere, of any age or century while alive on this earth, if he be presented with the proper light, truth, and understanding of God and his relationship to God, (which of course can only come from the Word of God), positively will come to Christ repent and be saved. The hearts of all men are like unto a lock, which only the correct key with the correct notches and indentations in it can open it to Christ. Once the heart of a man has that correct "key" placed in it, the door must open of its own accord and Christ will be welcomed in!

Jesus said, "And ye shall know the truth, and the truth shall set you free." Notice when the lost would be set free. "When they know the truth." Does false doctrine give the "correct key" to open the unsaved man's heart? Absolutely not. Thus it is so important to understand that God does not, nor can honor a false plan of salvation. False doctrines corrupt the gospel, Catholicism, Watchtower, Calvinism, Christian Science, Mormonism, the Church of Christ with its baptismal regeneration, and on and on all have a different plan of salvation, and thus close the door of salvation to hungry hearts.

The four basic "Gods" presented by general Christendom are as follows. First the God of the Calvinists, one who sovereignly chooses only a select few to be saved, and then consigns the rest of humanity to be tormented endlessly in the fires of Hell for eternity. Second the God of mainstream Christianity today who saves only a few who are fortunately reached by the church with the gospel and sends the rest to be tormented endlessly in Hell fire. Thirdly the God of the Bible, who designs for all men to be saved, allows for the wicked to be tormented for their sins for an unknown period of time to shame/humiliate and convince them of their wickedness and the truth God's Word. Then allows them to bend their knee and confess and embrace the Savior and thus ultimately brings all souls into His kingdom by the new birth and their final acceptance of Christ.

Then lastly, the God of liberal theology which theology paints God, as one who will save all, and take all to heaven regardless of their theological positions. Perhaps Unitarianism Universalism would be best to represent that "God." Now only one theological "God" can be correct It is important to note first that nowhere in the scripture, nowhere does the Greek support wording used as "<u>endless</u> punishment." Nowhere does it say nor does it teach in the **ORIGINAL LANGUAGES** that God punishes/torments souls in Hell or the Lake of Fire <u>endlessly</u>.

Nowhere at all. Yes the *translated* scriptures do say that they are punished "eternally, everlastingly or forever and ever," but never "endlessly" in the Greek/Hebrew. What is the difference, no doubt one is asking, between endlessly and eternally. This is the problem that must be addressed here in order to understand what kind of God rules the universe. Shortly we will give examples of usage of these terms including "infinite" as well. But first it needs to be stated as follows:

1. Due to the underlying Greek words, terms "eternal, everlasting, forever and ever, and infinity or infinite" in the K.J.V. cannot be locked into one single meaning, of *"time without end/ forever never ceasing, or on and on forever never ending."* This simply cannot be refuted.

2. These terms in fact many times do not give any indication of "duration" but rather of "unknown duration." Yes, they also may give indication of "never ending" duration if properly drawn from the Greek and modified as such.

3. These terms give "indications" of several possible "durations" which must be drawn **from the context** of the scripture (and from the Greek) in which they are used.

4. The two and only two possible "durations" which they may point to are first "on and on endlessly for all eternity future (or eternity past as well which would be the case when the word eternal/everlasting/infinite is used to define God)." Or secondly "on and on, ages and ages but unknown as to length of time involved."

Herein lies the confusion, and misunderstanding of the nature and plan of God for man. Following are several simple examples where the underlying Hebrew/Greek terms for everlasting/forever are used to denote opposites, i.e. "A limited/indeterminate (*unknown*) period of time" as opposed to "endless duration." Here after "L.I.D." is "limited/indeterminate duration," while "E.D." is "endless duration."

L.I.D. Genesis 49:26. "...unto the utmost bounds of the *everlasting* hills..."

E.D. Ps. 41:13. "...Blessed be the Lord God of Israel, from *everlasting unto everlasting*..."

L.I.D. Ex. 21:6. "...and his master shall bore his ear through with an awl, and he shall serve him *forever*..."

E.D. Jn. 3:16. "...and whosoever believeth in Him shall not perish but have *everlasting* life..."

L.I.D. Nahum 3:9. "...Ethiopia and Egypt were her strength, and it was *infinite*..."

E.D. Ps. 147:5. "...Great is our Lord, and of great power, His understanding is *infinite*..."

Readers note: Eusebius Hieronymus, called Jerome (c 342 -420) was commissioned by Pope Damasus to begin translating the New Testament from Greek into Latin. He continued the task after Damasus' death and began translation of the Old Testament from both Greek and Hebrew, completing this by the year 404.

This was the Vulgate or "common" Latin Bible of the Roman Catholic Church. The Church of Rome under Justin the emperor of the East-Roman Empire, evidently was the first to issue a council edict, (Constantinople in 553 A.D.) to dogmatize the doctrine of endless damnation to and for the Church to strictly adhere to. He wrote: The holy church of Christ teaches an endless (eternal) aionic (ateleutdtos aionios) life for the just and an endless (eternal) punishment (ateleutetos kolasis) for the wicked."

L.I.D. Hab. 3:6. "...The *everlasting* mountains were scattered..."

E.D. Hab. 1:12 "... Art thou not from *everlasting* O Lord..."

L.I.D. Lk. 16:9. "...Make to yourselves friends of the mammon of unrighteousness, that when ye fail they may receive you into *everlasting* habitations..."

E.D. Lk. 18:30. "... And in the world to come life *everlasting*..."

Certainly the above shows that the terms everlasting and eternal (etc etc,) as translated in the K.J.V. are *sometimes* used to point to eternal never ending duration, but *not always* should they mean that. That fact in itself is irrefutable, and cannot be denied. Now take usage of the same terms in the English language to show "L.I.D."

L.I.D. Someone says, "My back is *forever* hurting." Or, "Why it's been an *eternity* since I saw you last." Or, "Why are you *forever* begging me for money." Or, "I'll hate you *forever* if you betray my trust." Or, "Go ahead and commit that crime, you'll go to prison *forever*."

E.D. Then when a minister in his sermon, or someone in his witnessing to the lost, uses the word eternal or forever to describe Hell (falsely thinking that Aionios/eternal/everlasting only can mean "without end") he says to the unsaved, "If you reject Christ you will die and go to Hell forever (meaning endlessly)."

The above examples from scripture, in the usage of eternal etc, prove without a shadow of doubt, that these words in dispute emphatically do not, in themselves have only one certain definition!

While the English K.J.V. is a wonderful and blessed book of God, it is only a "vehicle" to bring us the original Words of God. Certainly it is flawed in some of its translation, as any translation is bound to be since it is translated by fallible "man" and not "God." No doubt the reason the original manuscripts do not exist today is plain and simple. Were they to exist, they would be worshipped as "Divine Relics" and the Catholic church would have them placed in a glass case for the seers to be blessed by in seeing and touching yea of only the glass case alone. This writer certainly is a somewhat "flawed" person, but as a vehicle to carry the message of salvation to the lost he can do a perfect job in that regards. Thus the same with the K.J.V.

While as a "vehicle" meaning the paper, the pages, the type translation it is, may well be flawed in some aspects it still is a perfect means to bring the gospel to a lost and dying world. No, we are not saying there are "flaws" in the Word of God, but only in the vehicle which man has designed to bring the truth by. Thus the need for going into the Greek and Hebrew to "clarify" some few difficult and hard to understand parts of the translation.

There are those, such as the sadly misled 'Ruckmanites' who claim to tamper with the A.V. 1611, is to attack the Word of God. To which we simply say that, "No, never do we attack the Word of God in a translation," but rather seek to clarify any credible translation (except for of course the Watchtower N.W.T.) using the original languages as a guiding light. To those who falsely claim that the K.J.V. is the only perfect translation of the Word of God from the Greek and Hebrew we can only say if that were the case, then for 1600 years, until King James, the world did not have the Word of God!(?) Wrong! Jesus said that "...the gates of Hell **would not** prevail against the church" simply meaning that in all times and centuries, the world has had the Inspired Word of God. Away with Ruckmanism, to the scrap heap of irrational and foolish reasoning.

The adjective "Aionios" comes from the noun "aion" and means "age-lasting." This simply cannot be denied. A common rule of any language is that an adjective can have no more force that the noun from which it is derived. Just how long is an age? That could well widely vary from months to years, to centuries. Age/Aionios simply means "an indeterminate/unknown period of time, nothing more and nothing less. Since "Aion" irrefutably means "Age" as a noun, then its adjective can mean nothing more or less than the noun it modifies. Then going one step further back, beyond Aion as to its source we find the Greek term "Aei." "Aei " means- always, ever, duration, regularly etc.

Here again, absolutely no indication of "endless." "Aionios", "Aion," "Aei," absolutely and positively do not mean "endless" or eternal in the endless sense. They simply are indicative of an "indeterminate or unknown period of time, or time with no definition of length. Is there a Greek word specifically used for "endless?" Absolutely, and it has no kindred connection with "Aionios." (Clear it is, scriptures in all languages need revising and correcting in regards to 'aionios vs aidios' etc, to prove God is not a sadist.) Plainly then, it is impossible to equate, 'aionios life' with 'eternal/endless life.'

Revelation 14:9-11 and J. Preston Eby Comments

"...and if any man worship the beast and his image and receive his mark in his forehead or in his hand, the same shall drink of the wine of the wrath of God which is poured out with mixture into the cup of his indignation, and he shall be tormented *(afflicted, punished, ed.)* with fire and brimstone in the presence of the holy angels and in the presence of the Lamb: And the smoke of their torment ascendeth up forever and ever, (which is 'continuously,' aionios ton aionios), and they have no rest <u>day nor night</u> who worship the beast, and his image, and whosoever receiveth the mark of his name." Plainly here 'continuously' is not 'endlessly.'

J. Preston Eby (P. O. Box 371240 - El Paso, Tx 79937-1240) has an interesting take on these verses as follows:

Tormented in the Presence of the Lamb

The words torment, tormented, tormentors, and torments occur twenty-one times in the King James version, and all in the New Testament. Three of these are in connection with the lake of fire. Let me give you the quotations. "The same shall drink of the wine of the wrath of God, which is poured out without mixture into the cup of His indignation; and he shall be <u>TORMENTED</u> WITH FIRE AND BRIMSTONE IN THE PRESENCE OF THE HOLY ANGELS (MESSENGERS) AND IN THE PRESENCE OF THE LAMB: and the smoke of their <u>torment</u> ascends up forever and ever (Greek: unto the ages of the ages): and they have no rest day nor night..." (Rev. 14:10-11).

"And the devil that deceived them was cast into the lake of fire and brimstone, where the beast and the false prophet are, and shall be <u>tormented</u> day and night forever and ever (Greek: unto the ages of the ages - see Part One of this series -'Just What Do You Mean ... ETERNITY!')" (Rev. 20:10).

Notice please, in both instances, the subjects are tormented with fire and brimstone, and we have previously established what the fire and brimstone are. But Rev. 14:10 sheds further light, those are also tormented by and through another agency, which in reality sums up and constitutes the fire and brimstone, and that agency is THE PRESENCE OF THE LAMB and the holy angels, or messengers. What an amazing divine paradox! The Lamb - precious embodiment of the very character of innocence, patience, meekness, gentleness, holiness, sacrifice, and redemption - being made TORMENT to men for whom He died! The very thought seems incongruous. You see, dear ones, IT IS NOT THE NATURE of a lamb to torture anyone. It is simply not in the nature of the lamb to want to hurt in any way. Really! What could a lamb do to torture anyone? It has no capability for such a thing. And so it is with the LAMB OF GOD! The Lamb of God has no desire, no ability to inflict torture in any way - His desire is entirely redemptive - that men might have life and have it more abundantly! I cannot imagine One with the nature of a lamb packing poor lost souls like brick into a kiln, standing there blowing the fires of Hell through them forever. Such a grotesque representation charges the blessed Redeemer with crimes more heartless than those of Adoph Eichmann. Ah, the torment comes not from the Lamb. The torment lies within the bosoms of the tormented. The Scripture does not say that the Lamb torments them! If you think it does, you are mistaken. It states that

Chapter Four | Translation Correction of Matthew 25:46

THEY ARE TORMENTED IN THE PRESENCE of the Lamb. What a thought! TORMENTED IN THE PRESENCE. The Lamb is merely present. He does not torment. The condition is within themselves. Because they are wrong and sinful in nature, wicked in their hearts, selfish in their minds, and impure in their desires, they are CONDEMNED IN THEIR CONSCIENCES by the very PRESENCE of the pure, holy, sinless, selfless, sacrificing Lamb of God. Hell is at its fiercest when it sees heaven, and not till then. When these realize the presence, or the character of the Lamb, they are tortured in their consciences, for in the Light of the Lamb they see themselves for the wretched little devils they are. The very PRESENCE of TRUTH torments the deceitful and the liar. The very PRESENCE of HOLINESS torments the immoral and corrupt. The very PRESENCE of LOVE is torment to the mean and hateful. The PRESENCE of Him who is the PRINCE OF PEACE is torture to those who live by violence and the sword. The very PRESENCE of the LIFE OF THE LAMB is the most awful torment and torture to all the opposing forces, both deceiver and deceived, until all the deceit and hostility has been taken out of them, and they come to KNOW THE LORD. When these have been exposed for a sufficient time to the PRESENCE of the Lamb, the Lamb will overcome them; His love and power will conquer their hearts; the rebellion and waywardness will be taken from them and they will at last ENJOY the Presence of the Lamb!

Suppose a few filthy, vile men and a few immoral women from some house of prostitution were *forced to sit* in the midst of a large congregation of singing, shouting, worshipping saints. *This certainly would he torment to most of them.* They would be tortured in the flames of the blazing glory of God in that place! If they were not held in their seats *by force*, most of them would rush out of there. I have been in meetings where I witnessed three responses to the glorious manifestation of the Lord's presence. First, the saints who loved the Lord rejoiced and adoringly worshipped. Some who were not Christians, but whose hearts were tender toward the Lord, came under deep conviction and, weeping and broken, gave themselves into the loving hands of Jesus. But others, filled with self, haters of righteousness, I have seen jump up and literally *run* out of a meeting - TORMENTED IN THE PRESENCE OF THE LAMB! Sure, they would rush, even run to get away from the convicting power of the Holy Ghost! I have seen it, and so have you. To the unsaved, HIS GLORY is a LAKE OF FIRE AND BRIMSTONE - divine, cleansing, purging, purifying, consuming fire! In ages yet unborn God shall expose ALL MEN to the sweet abiding presence of the Lamb. They will come under such severe processings, under such profound conviction that they will be tormented and have no rest day or night until they finally yield. And when they do, many fountains of tears will flow with weeping, praying, and calling upon the Lord. I believe it! God hasten it! (End of quote).

So there you have it. Two distinct views on torment concerning the Lake of Fire. One where the presence of Christ torments the wicked while they reside there, and the other where there is actual torment resulting from the Lake of Fire itself. The difference is probably irrelevant. The thing to remember is this. There will be an actual Lake of Fire, and those placed there will be tormented/afflicted during that time, and that punishment certainly will not be vindictive/sadistic, but rather remedial, restorative and purifying. (No not salvation, but definitely bringing the lost to repentance and eventually to the bended knee and new birth into the family of God.) Punishment according to works, not eternal/endless torture. Moving on to Revelation 20.

Revelation 20 and Endless Punishment?

There is not one verse in Chapter 20, which says that, the souls who stand the White Throne Judgment are to be tormented endlessly eternally. No not one. First though, true it is, that those under the reign of antichrist, who worship the Beast and his image and as well receive his mark in their forehead, will be tormented/afflicted/punished, but notice now the 'time element' of day and night, forever and forever (aionios and aionios or 'indefinite not known period of time,' not aidios and aidios/on and on 'endlessly').

Revelation 20:13-14
"And the sea gave up the dead who were in it and death and Hell delivered up the dead which were in them and they were judged every man according to their works. And death and Hell were cast into the Lake of Fire this is the second death and whosoever was not found written in the book of life was cast into the Lake of Fire."

Paraphrasing this Verse as Follows

"And the sea gave up the dead bodies which had perished there; death or the grave gave up the dead bodies which were there. These bodies, which are resurrected, are bodies, which will live without decay for eternity. Hell/Sheol the spirit world, the world of the departed spirits gave up the spirits or souls of those who were imprisoned there so body soul and spirit could be re-united and then stood to be judged according to their works. After judgment the bodies and souls of the deceased who were resurrected, were cast into the Lake of Fire, and as well so were those not found written in the book of life to be punished (tormented or afflicted) for an indeterminate period of time."

Eby Has a Very Telling Picture of These Verses as Follows:

What is the second death? It is the first death and Hell cast into the lake of fire! This fact is very IMPORTANT. The second death is not merely the lake of fire. The second death is not men being tortured forever in the lake of fire. The Holy Spirit has made it very simple and plain. The second death is the first death and Hell CAST INTO THE LAKE OF FIRE. That is the Holy Spirit's definition, not mine. Can we now open the eyes of our understanding to see that everything cast into the lake of fire pertains to DEATH? Death itself is cast into the lake of fire. Hell, the realm of the dead, is cast into the lake of fire. And those whose names are not written in the *Book of Life*, those who are *dead*, in trespasses and in sins, who inhabit Hell, are cast into the lake of fire. That is the end of death and Hell and sin, for God shall destroy death in the lake of fire, He shall burn up Hell in the lake of fire, and He shall consume sin and rebellion in the lake of fire. How I long to see the end of sin and death and Hell! The time is coming, praise His name! when God's Kingdom shall be All in All, and there shall be neither sin, nor sinners, nor death, nor Hell. It is clear that God does not destroy *men* in the lake of fire, nowhere does it say that, for that would be a contradiction of terms. How can you destroy death by creating death? How can you abolish death by bringing men under the power of eternal death from which there is no escape? Oh, no, it is not men who are destroyed in the lake of fire - it is SIN and DEATH and HELL that are destroyed. "And the last enemy that shall be destroyed is *death*" (I Cor. 15:26). Thus, the lake of fire is nothing more nor less than THE DEATH OF DEATH! (End of quote).

Death meaning the physical body, and Hell meaning the spirit of departed man, so the physical body from the grave is rejoined with the departed spirit of from Hell, is judged and then he/she is cast into the Lake of Fire. Remember this 'second death' judgment takes place at the end of the 1000 year reign of Christ after the nations were gathered together under the deception of Satan to compass the holy city of the saints the number of whom were as the sand of the sea, millions maybe billions, who knows? Scripture says they compassed the holy city and fire from God comes down and devours them, i.e. they are incinerated, totally so.

Who are these millions/billions of people again? They are of the stock/ or descendants of those 144,000 Messianic Jews who accepted Jesus as their Messiah and then repopulated the earth after the rapture and His second coming. They are lineage from the stock of the restored 12 tribes of Israel, or the 144,000 who escaped the terrors of the wrath of God (in the last half of Daniel's 70th week) by being 'sealed' (the 144,000 Jews of Revelation). Now this 'Lake of Fire' has already received the beast and false prophet who are being tormented/afflicted/punished, who were cast there earlier in Revelation.

Now however, these millions/billions that have repopulated the earth during the millennium and have never had the influences or temptations of Satanic evil are suddenly brought under such temptations by the release of Satan from the bottomless pit. Remember, these souls have been living a thousand years under the righteous blessed iron rule of Jesus from His throne here on earth. A rule against all evil and injustice, as we His saints rule with Him. They have never been subjected to the influences of Satan but suddenly are and are deceived, just as our first parents in Eden were. Again, Satan deceives them, they foolishly compass the Holy City of the saints, the place where Jesus rules from, and they are incinerated.

These are also ones who experience the second death along with all unsaved who died from Adam on. They die the first time as they surround the holy city, and then the second time immediately after they are cast into the Lake of Fire, where the beast and false prophet are. This is why the second death has no power over us as Christians who live on this side of the millennium, we will be raptured, and if deceased when He comes will be resurrected to meet Him in the air, forever to be with Him.

It must be remembered that the law of *physical death* was suspended in those days and for the beast and false prophet as well. Rev. 9:6 tells us, "And in those days men shall seek death and shall not find it, and shall desire to die and death shall flee from them," so that when they were cast into the lake of fire (Rev. 19:20), they continued to 'live physically' but in a state of suffering and pain. Such will be the fate of those who are cast into the same lake of fire *after* they are physically resurrected and judged according to their works. Does the scripture say they will be judged or damned eternally? No! What does it say??? Do not add to scripture, it plainly says they will be judged ACCORDING TO THEIR WORKS.

All are judged according to their works and all are rewarded according to the same, the Christian at the Bema Seat of Christ, the unsaved at the Great White Throne Judgment. Christians will receive different degrees of reward in Heaven, while the unsaved will receive different degrees of punishment in Hell and the Lake of Fire. The same with those who stand the last Great White Throne Judgment. Once their judgment is past or completed, they will happily bow their knee, and make confession unto salvation and the new birth.

Then it truly can be stated that the last enemy is truly defeated… "Death is swallowed up in Victory" I Cor. 15:54, and the "Last enemy to be destroyed is death" I Cor. 15:26. If endless damnation were true, then "death" would reign victorious and never be destroyed. To destroy death, is to totally defeat it and put it away endlessly/forever.

Revelation 21:4
> And God shall wipe away all tears from their eyes, and ***there shall be no more death,*** neither sorrow, nor crying, neither shall there be any more pain for the former things are passed away.

Now it becomes apparent that should the doctrine of "endless suffering" in the Lake of Fire for eternity be true, then it could not be said that Jesus one day is going to abolish death as the "final enemy." Souls "dead in trespasses and sins" and writhing in pain and anguish endlessly certainly must be said to be separated from Almighty God! No! Those souls partaking of the judgment of God in pain and anguish for their sins, will find the fires of the Lake of Fire to be as stated so well by Eby as follows: "The Hell of tradition is hopeless and eternal, while the Hell of the Scripture like every judgment of God is corrective, remedial, and restorative."

Then one day, known only to God, will those souls be loosed from their bonds in the Lake of Fire after experiencing their portion of suffering for being "judged each according to his works." Differing lengths and degrees of suffering for all who are so unfortunate to neglect salvation unto their damnation/judgment! Thank the Lord though, "<u>Every knee</u> shall bow and <u>every tongue</u> shall confess that Jesus Christ is Lord to the glory of the Father." All will embrace the risen Savior, and all will become born again, blood washed saints. Did the suffering/pain and anguish of torments in the Lake of Fire cleanse away their sins? Absolutely not, it rather prepared their hearts to bend the knees to the Savior!

No More Death for Endless Eternity!

"And I heard a great voice out of heaven saying, Behold, the tabernacle of God is with men, and He will dwell with them, and they shall be His people, and God Himself shall be with them, and be their God. And God shall wipe away all tears from their eyes; and there shall be NO MORE DEATH, neither sorrow, nor crying, neither shall there be any more pain: for the former things are passed away. And HE that sat upon the throne said, Behold, I make ALL THINGS new. And He said unto me, Write: for these words are *true and faithful*" (Rev. 21:3-5).

These verses plainly and totally refute the fundamentalist damnationists false doctrine of endless pain and suffering in Hell/Lake of Fire after the White Throne Judgment! In the new heaven and new earth there will be no more, DEATH/SEPARATION FROM GOD, no more, SORROW OR CRYING, no more, PAIN!! Why? No more Lake of Fire/Hell, no more suffering therein, because these were FORMER THINGS WHICH PASSED AWAY! No more separation from God in torments since all knees were bent and every tongue confessed (*people in resurrected bodies*) unto salvation, redemption and the new birth in Christ Jesus. God said it, I believe it, and that settles it.

If the Greek word 'aionios' means endless without needing to be modified to indicate such, then 'endless/everlasting eternal death' must mean the same as 'annihilation.' i.e. Eternal endless death would be a state of total and complete separation from God, from all that God is to a person, and as well total separation from all that a person receives from Him. Therefore that lost soul could not continue to even 'exist' since their very existence is directly linked to and dependent upon God. Thus if 'aionios' means endless then eternal death would have to be total annihilation and the Watchtower would be exonerated in believing as they do that the wicked will cease to exist in the Lake of Fire.

John 3:16 Clarified

Strong and others give definitions to Greek words that the translators translated them as in the A.V. etc. So sometimes these definitions need clarification, sometimes they do not. Further in Jn. 3:16 the words 'everlasting life' do not point to "quantity of life" or such as in the endlessness of life, (yes everyone lives endlessly) but rather to the 'quality' of life, that being either to "perish" and be lost and suffering in Hell a terrible quality of life, or to be saved and enjoy a wonderful quality of life in Heaven and later ruling on earth with Christ for a thousand years.

Clearly then, aionios or ages and ages/continuous with no known duration does not mean endless. John 3:16 in the Greek paraphrased easily says "...whosoever believes and accepts Jesus as Lord/God shall not perish (die and go to Hell which is a terrible **quality** of life/existence) but will have continuous blessed life with Christ (quality again) without the fear of being lost." No need for the Greek to say aidios (endless) here since only **quality** of existence of life is being referred to here, and as well neither Jesus nor His disciples ever taught "endless punishment." Again, everyone saved or lost lives endlessly/everlastingly, the scripture clearly indicates we were created in the image of God who lives endlessly, so Jn. 3:16 is not dealing with "duration" but of "quality." Also, if everlasting in this verse must mean 'endless' then the Watchtower could have a valid point to believe that to 'perish' here would mean to 'permanently cease to be or to perish endlessly by annihilation.

The sad fact is that the majority of damnationist Christians have been so totally brainwashed with the idea that 'everlasting' (aionios) means endless, that any time the scriptures use the term 'everlasting life' or 'everlasting punishment' then automatically they can only think of 'endless life' or 'endless punishment.' As it is clearly stated above, all of humanity lives endlessly, without exception, saved or lost! Here again, the inescapable conclusion is that 'everlasting'/'aionios' here does not mean, nor can mean 'endless,' unless it is modified to mean such. See pages 107-109.

Furthermore, for those adamant that 'everlasting like in Jn. 3:16 etc. must mean endless in and by itself, one needs only to notice Luke 16:9. "…when they fail they may receive you into *everlasting* habitations." In the first, (Jn. 3:16) no doubt 'aionios' does indicate endless since being 'in Christ' is an endless relationship, but in the second the 'habitations' are only temporal dwellings showing aionios there means 'continuous' with no indefinite duration but not endless.

In summation, it is very common for we who are soul winners, to ask the unsaved if they want to be saved from their sins and have eternal life, or be lost and go to Hell forever. Strictly speaking this question is unscriptural as denoted above.

The term 'eternal (endless) life cannot be wrought solely from the underlying Greek term "aionios" in no way! 'Eternal/endless should never represent 'aionios' in translation unless it is modified to mean such. Yea rather 'continuous' to counter the idea of 'perishing' without Christ, so that not 'perishing' or dying without Christ means 'continued' life with the Lord Jesus Christ by believing in, and accepting Him as personal Lord and Savior. That is what John 3:16 is saying, and of course we who believe the Word of God believe in the security of the believer which of course is truly endless in Christ Jesus.

While we do have 'endless/permanent security in salvation through Christ, in no way should those terms be substituted for 'aionios.' Remember again, strictly and theologically speaking, everyone, saved or lost, has endless/eternal life and can never perish or cease to exist. The Greek reigns supreme in revealing the truth. To be theologically correct then, it is best simply ask the unsaved if they are willing to accept Jesus to have their sins forgiven, or pay for such themselves in the Lake of Fire in terrible punishment and isolation after death, i.e. something to that extent.

English Equivalents to 'Aionios' in the Greek
There are quite a number of ways in which we who speak English, express the idea of 'limited duration' or indefinite duration of time, using

words which many people usually take to mean 'endless.' Notice the following sentences.

1. It has been *forever* since I last saw you.

2. It has been an *eternity* since I last saw you in high school.

3. I have this headache, which the doctor said I would have *eternally* if I did not stop drinking.

4. It has been *ages* since I last saw your son.

5. Why do you *continuously* refuse to go to work?

6. Why do we have this *never ending* strife go on and on *forever*?

7. I guess you will *never* stop aggravating me with your foolishness.

8. That child goes *nonstop* around the clock with his crying and fussing.

These words can only be used to mean 'endless' or 'never ending' *if* the context demands such, or if they are modified by a subject to indicate such, example being, "The God who exists forever in eternity and who is the eternal God of the ages." Again it must be remembered that nowhere did our Lord or His disciples ever teach 'aidios'/'endless punishment, yea rather 'aionios' or continuous without indication of duration punishment!

The Word of God Mishandled

Do you allow the Word of God to speak to you, or do you interpret it by the theological system into which you have been groomed? In the October 16, 2012 Daily Bread published by R.B.C. Ministries, a powerful message was given against doing the latter. Quoting, "We may try to make it *(the Bible)* support what we already believe is true instead of allowing it to speak to us with God's intended message. Some people use the Bible to defend one side of an issue while others use the Bible to attack that same issue. Both quote Scriptures to support their views, but both can't be right." (End of quote). The article continues to correctly note that in mishandling the Bible in such fashion misrepresents God's character.

Certainly this is so true of the use of the English words, <u>eternal, everlasting, forever</u> and <u>eternity</u> which have absolutely no support in the underlying Greek Biblical text (regarding duration of punishment for the unsaved) since these words (a) generally denote endless in the English, (b) they were introduced into the English language *(discussed more fully in chapter 4)* in the 1300's, (c) the underlying Greek for these words is really 'Aionios' which irrefutably means 'continuous' a measurable time word, with no indication of duration, for ages and ages etc, but certainly not 'endless or endlessly.' The simple fact is, neither our Lord nor His disciples ever used the Greek terms which absolutely do mean 'endless' in reference to punishment in Hell/Lake of Fire.

Here we find the two extremely conflicting views of the character of God. The endless damnationist view being freshly and erroneously manufactured actually represents our Lord and Savior Jesus Christ as a sadist, one who ultimately comes to the end of His resources in His attempts to win all of men to Himself and thus consigns them to be tormented in fire and brimstone for eternity. On the other hand, we have the truly Biblical view of God (who certainly does give humiliating long term *[but not endless]* and severe punishment to the unsaved wicked) in true everlasting love and compassion, reaching out, wooing and winning every lost soul to Himself, to the exception of none.

Readers note: No man can make an objective proper decision concerning anything unless that decision is based on what he knows, and has experienced as truth. Unfortunately, no one can know what 'truth' is unless they have experienced 'truth' and conversely fully understands the implications and penalties of 'error.' As a small child grows from innocence into being responsible or chargeable for his actions, he does so naturally by trial and error. Paul noted this in Romans, "I was alive without the law once but when the commandment came sin revived and I died, and the law which was ordained to life I found to be unto death." The point here is simply that there can be no possibility of salvation for anyone without the conviction of the Spirit of God in direct relation to the one and only true gospel of Christ. Countless souls perish daily, having never heard the true gospel so this

Biblical fact of accountability plainly negates the possibility of anyone going into endless damnation beyond their justified temporary sentence in the Lake of Fire. Being created in the image of God, every human will live endless eternally as there can be no possibility of annihilation.

This punishment in Sheol/Lake of Fire is not done sadistically, but for correction and justice, and is reformative unto eventual repentance and conversion. The mishandling of these words has been such a grave injustice to understanding just what kind of God we really serve!

The Daily Bread article continues, "This is why Paul challenged Timothy 'Be diligent to present yourself approved to God, a worker who does not need to be ashamed rightly dividing the Word of truth.' 2 Tim. 2:15. A key priority for unashamed approved workers for Christ is to accurately interpret or rightly divide God's Word. As we study we can depend on the Spirit who inspired it, to give us understanding and wisdom.

Through our words and actions we have opportunity to give us understanding and wisdom." The 'endless damnationist' doctrine thus fully and unfortunately entered the English language in the 1300's! It ought to be very clear now, that John 3:16 which proclaims 'everlasting life' to those who believe on Jesus is a faulty translation with the use of the word 'everlasting.' Why so one may say? Simple. The fact is that every human being saved or lost, has 'endless/everlasting life,' being created in the image of God. Annihilation simply is not taught in the Word of God. The word 'everlasting' is thus shown to be an erroneous translation of the underlying Greek word, since we all know that everyone lives forever endlessly with no exceptions.

This underlying Greek word again is 'Aionios' which means 'continuous' and therefore must indicate 'quality of life' one has *in Christ* (whosoever believeth in Him or is in Him which is the subject here) rather than 'duration' of life especially since the verse is contrasting 'Aionios' with the idea of 'perishing' (i.e. not being in Christ at death). Simple it is therefore that if Aionios means 'endless' and should have been translated eternal/everlasting then the underlying inference for 'perish' (after dying and not believing in Christ) must mean endless 'annihilation.'

Baptizo-Aionios Unclear Translation by the K.J.V. Translators

It is well known, that the Greek word 'baptizo' or 607 in Strong's, clearly means to immerse, plunge, bury, or cover up. For whatever reason, the translators did not translate this word with an English equivalent, but rather Anglicized the word to say 'baptize or baptism.' Certainly it cannot mean 'sprinkle' to be true to the original language. We do not 'sprinkle' dirt upon one whom is being buried, but rather completely cover the body; such is baptism, a picture of being buried with Christ, and then being raised to walk in newness of life. Naturally when one unfamiliar with the original languages reads the word baptize he of course interprets it according to the teaching of the church in which he worships. Most Baptist type scholars or those who hold that baptism means immersion have traditionally been comfortable ignoring this unclear translation or Anglicizing of a truly Greek term. This is the same most Christians do with the words, everlasting, eternal, forever etc. This illuminates the fact they completely misunderstand the true meaning of God's Word. While these words certainly do have place in the English language, they have been misapplied many places in the K.J.V. A true mishandling of the Word of God.

Readers note: No man can make an objective proper decision concerning anything unless that decision is based on what he knows, and has experienced as truth. Unfortunately, no one can know what 'truth' is unless they have experienced 'truth' and conversely fully understands the implications and penalties of 'error.' As a small child grows from innocence into being responsible or chargeable for his actions, he does so naturally by trial and error. Paul noted this in Romans, "I was alive without the law once but when the commandment came sin revived and I died, and the law which was ordained to life I found to be unto death." The point here is simply that there can be no possibility of salvation for anyone without the conviction of the Spirit of God in direct relation to the one and only true gospel of Christ. Countless souls perish daily, having never heard the true gospel so this

Biblical fact of accountability plainly negates the possibility of anyone going into endless damnation beyond their justified temporary sentence in the Lake of Fire. Being created in the image of God, every human will live endless eternally as there can be no possibility of annihilation.

Mark 9:43-48 Absolutely Prooves Jesus Taught Endless/Eternal Torment in Hell/Lake of Fire??

And if thy hand offend thee, cut it off: it is better for thee to enter into life maimed, than having two hands to go into Hell, into the fire that never shall be quenched: where their worm dieth not, and the fire is not quenched: Where their worm dieth not, and the fire is not quenched. and if thy foot offend thee, cut it off: it is better for thee to enter halt into life, than having two feet to be cast into Hell into the fire that never shall be quenched: where their worm dieth not, and the fire is not quenched. and if thine eye offend thee, pluck it out: for it is better for thee to enter into the kingdom of God with one eye, than having two eyes to be cast into Hell fire: where their worm dieth not and the fire is not quenched.

Following is Proof to the Contrary and Clear to Honest Students of the Word of God

1. All damnationists know and believe that Hell, which is what our Savior referred to in these verses, *will one day come to an end and be no longer. Revelation 20 plainly tells us that Hell will be emptied and the souls therein will be cast into the Lake of Fire.* Damnationists are thus dishonest when they say that someone who is not saved will 'go to Hell for eternity.' Conclusion therefore is that our Savior does indeed limit the duration of Hell. He said "...where the worm dieth not and the fire is not quenched." The fire will be quenched when its usefulness is fulfilled and the final Lake of Fire receives the lost for their final punishment according to their works!

2. This author will readily agree that a casual reading of these verses in the 1611 K.J.V. seem to teach that the lost will spend eternity in Hell. True it is if these verses were the only ones in the Word of God explaining Hell and punishment therein, then yes possibly the lost would be there eternally. However, Revelation 20 proves these verses are improperly interpreted by damnationists. Hell will have a permanent conclusion when its designed purpose is fulfilled.

3. The only things these verses teach are, a. Hell is a terrible place of punishment so avoid it at all costs, and this is also a great motivation for the church to evangelize. b. There will be terrible conscious suffering there for the wicked in the lower parts of Hell. c. The fire there is of a type that no man can quench it or put it out. Our Savior designed and ignited its flames and He will be the one to extinguish them when their use is fulfilled.

These verses can therefore easily be paraphrased according to correct Biblical exegesis as follows:

> If any part of your body is uncontrollable, and since it could bring you to being lost outside of Christ, take heed and remove that member since to be lost would mean you would be consigned to Hell and terrible suffering therein. Remember to lose that member and thereby be able to enter into life in the kingdom of God is better than keeping that member or members and as a result be lost and cast into Hell where your soul lives on and on, that place where no one dies, and that tormenting fire is unquenchable.

To say these verses teach 'endless' damnation, is to therefore add to the Word of God. A following word of rebuke to our damnationist friends needs to be spoken:

"As damnationists you all need to realize that the only possible reason for God to inflict endless pain and suffering in Hell fire and brimstone on anyone, would be that He as a god of sadism, totally gives up in frustration and

defeat against the powers of Satan in attempting to win those lost souls to Christ, i.e. a dysfunctional God!.

To inflict such horrific pain and suffering on lost souls for eternity not to **teach any lessons** *to them, can only be due to God supposedly being a sadistic God who delights in inflicting pain and suffering for no reason. Evidently your god is that type god, mine certainly is not." God is not willing that any should perish but that all should come to a knowledge of the truth! II Peter3:9, "The Lord is not slack concerning his promise as some men count slackness but is long suffering toward us, not willing that any should perish, but that all should come to repentance." I Timothy 2:3-4, "For this is good and acceptable in the sight of God our Savior, who will have all men to be saved and to come to the knowledge of the truth."God said it, I believe it, and that settles it!*

Is It Wrong to Ask the Unsaved "Do You Have Eternal Life?"

A very common question soul winning Christians ask non-Christians is, "Do you have eternal life?" On the surface this seems to be a very fair question, and it is good to be pointed in personal evangelism. Everyone basically understands *what is really being asked* is, "Are you a born again Christian" or "Are you saved" or "Are you going to heaven when you die?" However the fact is that he who asks the question really reveals the following:

1. He is not asking the person if he is simply going to 'live forever.' Everyone knows (of course not including those who hold to annihilation after death) that all people without exception live forever/endlessly/eternally being fashioned in the image of an eternal/endless God. Asking whether one has 'eternal life' or not in the context of being 'in Christ' is fine, but that does not make 'aionios' automatically always mean endless!

2. That the blessedness and happiness of being saved is a present reality, so the real question being asked is "Are you a born again child of God with the Spirit of God living in you, which will ultimately take you to heaven?"

3. The above two points prove that people asking the first question are unwitting admitting that the K.J.V. etc., with the use of 'eternal life' really means 'continuous glorious quality of life with Christ in this life and the next' as opposed to misery and suffering in this life and a place in Hell in the next, all a poor quality of life.

Therefore it should be easy to understand why 'aionios' which is the underlying Greek term wrongly translated for 'eternal etc.' should *not* always have been translated as 'eternal/endless, forever/without end or permanent.' Going again back to John 3:16 any unbiased honest Bible student should therefore admit that 'everlasting' in this verse cannot possibly be truly representative of the underlying Greek. Someone asks, "But are we not endlessly secure in Christ when we have salvation." To which we answer "Of course we are" but our security in Christ does not prove endless punishment for the unsaved. It simply is not taught in the scriptures. Interesting it is therefore that one can scripturally say that 'In Christ we have aionios permanent/endless life in and with Him, but the unsaved have aionios/continuous but not permanent suffering in the Lake of Fire.

Following is a hypothetical conversation between a damnationist and one who follows universal Christian redemption discussing 'eternal' in the K.J.V. 1611.

Damnationist. Jesus in many scriptures said that the salvation He offered was 'eternal life.'

The following scriptures prove it. Matthew 19:16 Mark 10:17 Mark 10:30 Luke 10:25 John 3:15

And so on in the scriptures of the KJV. To have eternal life is just simply knowing the Father through Jesus. John 17:3 says: "And this is life eternal, that they might know thee the only true God and Jesus Christ whom thou hast sent."

Christian Universalist. The English translations here are credible and correct, but that certainly does not establish the correct meaning of the underlying Greek word 'aionios.' The fact is that the word 'eternal' (also eternity) in the English language means endless/permanent/forever without end. The 'The Free Dictionary' gives the following definition as following; Being without beginning or end; existing outside of time. See Synonyms at infinite. 2. Continuing without interruption; perpetual. 3. Forever true or changeless.

Of course this word can be used as a hyperbole which under definition from Wikepedia is as follows: "Hyperbole is the use of **exaggeration** as a **rhetorical device** or **figure of speech**. It may be used to evoke strong feelings or to create a strong impression, but is not meant to be taken literally." You and I both know that in the verses you quoted that Jesus was not using 'eternal' as a hyperbole.

Damnationist. Yes, I know, so that should prove that in Christ we have eternal/endless life!

Christian Universalist. Of course we have eternal/endless life in Christ. However just saying someone has 'endless/eternal life' in itself is really saying nothing since we all know (of course except the annihilationist) that we already all, *saved and lost* have eternal/endless life being made in the image of God, and nothing more. You damnationists certainly believe such since you teach everyone will live forever/endlessly, either in Heaven or in the Lake of Fire! Since such is the case this proves that 'eternal/underlying aionios' in these verses must be modified to mean such by the context.

The context of these verses plainly is that of being one with Christ in salvation, so therefore aionios translated eternal indicates endless and without end! When the rich young ruler came to Jesus and asked Him what he must do to inherit, not 'eternal ('aidios') life in the Greek but inherit 'aionios/continuous' life, he simply wanted to continue living on and on in his wealth and prosperity. He was fully aware that one day his life would be interrupted by death and the grave. Jesus was aware that the stumbling block to the man's coming to repentance of sin and conversion, (and thus to salvation) was his wealth, which the man had made his idol or god. He of course went sadly away.

Also, notice the English definition for 'eternal' was given as 'Continuing without interruption; perpetual.' We as Christians have 'aionios' physical life or life which indeed goes on and on, but is in fact interrupted briefly by the death of the body. Our spiritual oneness with Christ on the other hand is ('aidios') endless, perpetual and uninterruptable. If you say since 'aionios' was used in the afore mentioned verses in the Greek so then it must mean 'eternal/endless simply is false. The simple fact is 'aionios' certainly can mean 'endless' provided it is modified to mean such as saying "We have an 'aionios' God," but can easily mean 'continuous but not endless' such as saying "The 'aionios' (everlasting/eternal) mountains shall endure forever and ever." We all know that one day there will be no more mountains or hills in the new heaven and earth.

Damnationist. Well, I hold to the K.J.V. 1611 version, and what Jesus said is what I stand for.

Christian Universalist. I say for you to hold the English translation (which is accurate in these verses), higher and more accurate than the original Greek (and verbally inspired of God manuscripts) is to add to the Word of God. That is something no Christian should be guilty of! I may well add that for you to attempt to make some scriptures which indeed do teach the doctrine of endless security in Christ to give 'aionios' the absolute meaning of endless *wherever* it is used is to add to the Word of God! Again remember this, 'aionios' can mean either 'continuous' or 'endless' depending on how it is modified.

Readers note: A Steve Jones, http://www.auburn.edy/-allenkc/univart.html gives some interesting answers to a damnationist concerning universal Christian redemption, as follows:

Objection: What if you're wrong about this? What if universalism isn't true?

Answer: Well, then I'm wrong. Any person with an ounce of humility will consider this a real possibility about a given belief. No one is infallible. But if I am wrong, I would rather err on the side of mercy than wrath. I would rather be guilty of making God too loving than too condemning.

Objection: True. But for the wicked, that confession will not come from the heart — only from the almighty, subjugating power of Christ. (Ed. i.e. the final bending the knee for the wicked and confessing that Jesus is Lord.)

Answer: A coerced confession would not be "to the glory of God the Father."

Objection: If the authors of Scripture were universalists, why didn't they just say it plainly? Why do they write things so apt to be misunderstood?

Answer: The Psalmist wrote, "All flesh will bless his holy name forever and ever." (Psalm 145:21) How much plainer can you get than that? The same kind of language occurs in the New Testament. It is true, however, that the Bible is not a universalist catechism or primer. The latter Scriptures give us a glimpse into the faith of the early church, but not a full explanation of everything Christians believed from the ground up. The New Testament is concerned mainly with (1) the proclamation of Jesus as Messiah, (2) the proclamation of the long-awaited kingdom of God, (3) the healing of problems in the early churches. It does not answer all our eschatological queries with unmistakable plainness. Besides that, Paul tends to be difficult to understand — even another biblical author thought so. (2 Pet. 3:15-16)

Objection: If universalism is true, that means Hitler will enjoy the same eternity as the most pious saint.

Answer: Where sin abounded, grace abounded much more. That was the belief of Paul.

Objection: Jesus said that "God is able to destroy both body and soul in Hell." (Matt. 10:28) Doesn't that pretty much refute universalism.

Answer: To say that God has the power to do something is not the same thing as saying that He WILL do it. For example, John the Baptist declared that "God is able of these stones to raise up children unto Abraham." (Matt. 3:10) No one expected that to happen, of course. Jesus' utterance is part of a send-off to his missionaries who were ready to preach the kingdom of God and face severe opposition. The point was this: Do not be consumed by the fear of men, but instead fear the one who truly holds the power of life and death. It need not be viewed as a definitive statement of "what happens when non-Christians die.

Objection: Won't people live carelessly if you teach such a thing?

Answer: I can't help that. People live carelessly under the threat of endless torments, too.

Objection: Most Christians throughout the course of church history — and even today — would strongly disagree with you on universalism.

Answer: Majority vote does not determine truth. More often, it's the other way around.

CHAPTER FIVE

THE CHRISTIAN, THE JEW, AND ETERNAL DAMNATION

Jesus and Hitler Endorsed the 7 Death Camps of WWII?? Then Jesus Inflicts His Own Holocaust of Endless Pain and Suffering? Would Not This Make Jesus a Greater Sadist Than Hitler?

WWII saw the creation of seven death camps, Auschwitz, Treblinka, Birkenau, Chelmno, Belzec, Majdanek, and Sobibor in Nazi Germany. It is estimated that approximately eleven million people suffered and died in these camps from gassing, starvation, overwork, shootings, disease, horrific medical experiments, etc. The Nazi "Final Solution" was the extermination of all Jews, and of course those unlucky enough to be thrown in with them. It is only fair to estimate that probably only a small minority of those poor souls were evangelical Bible believing, born again Christians.

Knowing that most, or a large majority were Jewish, it would be evident that they certainly did *not* recognize Jesus as their promised King and Redeemer. Where is all of this leading in regards to the doctrine of "endless punishment?" Simple. The true "endless punishment fundamentalists" teach that all of these unbelieving souls, instantly, (upon their demise in the camps), were sent by Jesus to be tormented in burning Hell, and then later the Lake of Fire for all of endless eternity. No hope, signed sealed, and forever damned eternally.

If you the reader are a believer in endless damnation for the unsaved, then just go to the surviving loved ones of those gassed in Nazi death camps, and tell them that Jesus took their loved ones after death and sent them to burn in Hell's fires and the Lake of Fire for eternity after they were so viciously tortured and put to death by Hitler's depraved guards! Augustinian theology's monstrous accusation against Jesus our compassionate Savior! Yes, someone says, Jesus said He was/is the only way of salvation, and one cannot go to Heaven unless he comes by the way of the cross. To which we heartily agree, the Bible is plain on that point. Enlarging on where this is leading, does not the Lord Jesus know the end from the beginning? Is He not the creator of all things, the creator of Heaven and Hell as well?

Now since Jesus knew the eleven million souls were going to be exterminated before it happened, then when it did happen those eleven million souls were exterminated under the watchful eye of Jesus. Upon arriving in these death camps, women with children, children, elderly and unable to work, were immediately sent to the gas chambers, while able-bodied men and women were sent to work at slave labor. Just think of the thousands and hundreds of thousands children of all ages tortured and put to death, precious children for whom Jesus died, and of whom He said "Suffer the little children to come unto me for of such is the kingdom of heaven." These children raised by Hebrew Jews who rejected Jesus as their Messiah being sent to eternal/endless damnation for not believing in Jesus!?

Children 4-10-12-16 years of age fully aware of what sin is and following the religious customs of their Jewish parents suddenly having their precious lives wickedly snuffed out in the gas chambers, we are to believe Jesus therefore ordered their eternal/endless torment in fiery halls of Hell and later the Lake of Fire upon their demise? Would not such an act by Jesus be an additional "holocaust" upon those souls, and millions of times worse than what the Nazis did to them? The teaching of eternal/endless damnation certainly gives rise to a 'Jesus inflicted holocaust' upon those poor souls! I am sure our Savior is deeply grieved and offended by such theological nonsense especially when He died on the cross that all could be saved.

Scripture says Jesus is the "Savior of all men, especially of them that believe (I Tim. 4:10), and also that Jesus/God the one who is not "willing that any should perish but that ALL should come to repentance." (II Pet. 3:9). Is He not the one who is the "light that lighteth every man that cometh into the world?" (Jn. 1:9). If all does not mean 'all' then what does it mean pray tell? Is not Jesus the Savior who would "... have all men to be saved and come to the knowledge of the truth?" Did not the scriptures prophecy in the O.T. that "... and ALL Israel shall be saved?" Isaiah 45:22-25.

Now according to the doctrine of endless damnation, Jesus must have not only been in sympathy with their execution but fully endorsed it since they were dying without salvation anyway. The purveyors of the doctrine of endless damnation certainly teach that post mortem salvation cannot possibly be. The scripture is plain that He even notes when the sparrow falls! According to the doctrine of endless damnation they could not have had any possibility of salvation anyway, not believing in Jesus, so our Lord knowing they were heading for the gas chambers and execution, (and of course supposedly to the fires of Hell (and the LOF) endlessly forever) therefore had to turn a blind eye to their plight and willingly endorsed their gassing and subsequent eternal/endless damnation.

Are we to believe that Jesus upon seeing the coming execution of eleven million souls did not have the resources, the power, or the ability to stop this that they could possibly have more time to come to salvation especially the children? Are we to believe that Jesus, who is the all powerful God, could have stopped this atrocity, but chose rather to endorse the gassing of these Jews, full well knowing that they would enter the endless damned state? The doctrine of "endless damnation" therefore unwittingly teaches Jesus was the consenting (?) power behind the Holocaust and of the subsequent entrance of millions of Jews into Hell fire for endless eternity! No! Jesus was not involved in any way with the crimes of the Nazis, and to say that the doctrine of "endless punishment" (at the hands of Jesus since He created Hell) is true is to teach Jesus endorsed the Nazi war crimes.

If endless damnation were true, then Jesus brought the worst horrors imaginable upon those poor souls, much worse than the gassing they experienced by sending them supposedly into endless suffering and damnation at death. So in that case Jesus supposedly brought a much worse holocaust upon the Jews after death! Were we not shocked during WWII at the terrible conditions in these death camps? Were we not shocked at the screams and crying heard in the death ovens as women and children were viciously gassed, screams which guards tried to mask by releasing flocks of geese at the same time?

Now pray tell who was the most vicious tormentor(s) of these poor souls, (A). the Nazi death camp guards as they told these millions they were going in for showers and then turned on the gas, or (B). the "Jesus" who supposedly designed the endless furnace of Hell fire to torture these lost souls for endless eternity? Being gassed only lasted for approximately 30 minutes until all were dead and out of that miserable state forever, but then the eternal/endless damnation "Jesus" supposedly takes over and consigns these same souls to a fiery furnace of unimaginable pain and suffering for endless eternity, a furnace called Hell which He designed for the damned.

This "Jesus" is the "Jesus" of the Bible? NOT HARDLY. The Jesus of the Bible wept over wicked unbelieving Jerusalem, so it is no doubt He also wept over those entering the ovens in the death camps! All fundamentalists (who believe in eternal/endless damnation) hesitate to tell orthodox Jews their dirty little secret that they believe those Jews, men women and children, gassed in WWII certainly went on to burn in Hell fire for endless eternity since they could not have been born again. Why not? Simply, they refused to embrace Biblical Christianity and Jesus as Messiah!

So it is no wonder that the Jews, the true Orthodox Jews, find "fundamentalist Christianity which teaches the Augustinian doctrine of endless punishment to be so obnoxious and offensive. The idea that Hell/the Lake of Fire is endless for those suffering there can breed no other implication than the suffering there is not for correction, remedy, and purification but rather for endless retribution, torture pain and suffering, nothing else!

This author needs to remind the reader that certainly there is terrible suffering in *parts* of Sheol/Hades, but that it is controlled, corrective, remedial and for purification, or a burning away of the dross by 'attitude adjustment' but not salvation, though those going there will certainly eventually be saved or born again. (Only the blood of Jesus Christ can truly cleanse away sin) The Lake of Fire is not 'aidios' (endless) but rather 'aionios' or of indefinite duration. Certainly the length of time one lost soul must spend there would vary from person to person, according to their works or wickedness. As well we know that innocent deceased children go immediately to heaven. The 'Jesus' of the Bible was not the 'god' of the death camps, Satan was, plainly so!

Similarities Between the Jesus of Damationism and Hitler

If our Savior the Lord Jesus Christ is indeed the same Jesus who supposedly orchestrated/allowed or even caused ('caused' as no doubt the Calvinists would arrogantly claim, since they claim that 'God intended for man to sin' see Calvin's Institutes Chapter 23, 3:7&8. Calvin's Institutes) the holocaust, then the two (Hitler and Jesus) would be twins in possibly the most terrible savagery ever to be committed against mankind. In such a case Jesus and Hitler would not only be equals, but Jesus would be infinitely worse as a sadist, yea even the worse sadist possibly since He would be burning and tormenting souls for endless eternity in liquid fire and brimstone.

Here it must be reemphasized that Hell/Sheol is the underworld place of those departed spirits who while not yet partakers of Christ's righteousness in the new birth unto salvation, are there in 'holding' until such time as they stand the Great White Throne Judgment to be judged and punished '...according to their works.' (Damnationists, of course in ignorance, corrupt the scriptures and change this to mean 'Judgment and punishment in fire and brimstone endlessly for eternity.') As well it must be remembered that Hell/Sheol is composed of a number of sections/levels with various conditions therein as discussed elsewhere in this book. No doubt the lowest Hell, is a place of fire and severe punishment therein as shown in Luke 16, while the other levels are lesser in degree, until probably the upper level(s) have little if any suffering, but yea rather isolation etc.

In some of these areas there will be outer darkness as the scripture says with weeping wailing and gnashing of teeth. Here again, as stated elsewhere, this place will be to whatever degree needed, remedial, corrective, and purification of attitude. It can be nothing less since whatever God does, He does for good and righteous reasoning, but never sadistically. Again, some foolishly say, "Oh, then this is really the Catholic purgatory where sins are burnt away as dross," to which the answer is, "Absolutely not, Hell/Sheol is a place of attitude adjustment and as well only the blood of Jesus Christ can cleanse away sin." Sadly Rome has made vast fortunes in bleeding its followers of money to supposedly free their loved ones from the fires of an imaginary purgatory. So just what similarities are there between Jesus and Hitler if indeed Jesus does torment souls in fire and brimstone sadistically endlessly for eternity? Note as follows:

1. Hitler was a powerful influential leader of his day. So was Jesus.

2. Hitler had a 'plan' which he considered to be the 'only way' or the 'final solution.' So did Jesus. They both said 'I am the way/I have the only way.'

3. Hitler's government would tolerate no variation of his doctrines. Jesus said His coming government was absolute and without error, ruling with a rod of righteousness.

4. Hitler's ultimate punishment for refusing to obey him was slavery, pain, anguish, horrible suffering, torture, separation from family and then a horrible death. No mercy with Hitler. Jesus' (the damnationist Jesus) ultimate punishment for refusing to be 'one of his true followers' is the same as Hitler's except one step further. Hitler's ultimate punishment to his enemies permanently ended their pain and suffering by and at physical death. On the other hand, the ultimate punishment the damnationist Jesus gives 'begins' at death and extends for endless eternity, time without end, in liquid fire and brimstone upon the souls of His enemies! The damnationist Jesus and Hitler the same, no possible mercy!!

Cannot one see that if such is true about Jesus then He and Hitler would be equals in wickedness and depravity?! You the reader should be aghast that this false doctrine of endless damnation torment in fire and brimstone has so slandered our blessed merciful and compassionate Savior the Lord Jesus Christ and made Him a depraved sadist, equal to and infinitely worse than Hitler!! God save us from Romish Augustinianism. Just what kind of love is it, for Jesus to tell the unsaved that He indeed loves them and died for them, ut if they don't receive Him then He'll burn them in fire and brimstone for eternity?? That is love?? "That is like a man telling his sweetheart, "Marry me or I'll kill you." No! Rather such nonsense breeds atheism and rejection of the Bible, and voids reciprocal love from man to God!'

Evangelizing the Jews

Evangelizing USING the FALSE CLAIM "your orthodox Jewish ancestors are all no doubt burning in Hell endlessly/forever" will bring the Jewish communities to Christ???

How many lost souls no doubt, who have been raised in say perhaps very strong orthodox Jewish homes, are deeply offended and driven away from the claims of Christ when the false idea of eternal/endless damnation is applied to their deceased ancestors. These persons, having come from many, many generations of devout Jewish ancestors, when suddenly confronted with the claims of such false Christian doctrine as stated above, naturally are repulsed and are thereby driven *away from* Biblical salvation. We have seen plainly in the Word of God that "All Israel shall be saved," At the name of Jesus every knee shall bow, of things in heaven and things in earth, and things (those in Sheol/Hades) under the earth; And that every tongue should confess that Jesus Christ is Lord, to the glory of God the Father.

Not One of the Seed of Israel Shall Be Lost!

Isaiah 45:22-25

Look unto me, and be ye *saved all the ends of the earth*: for I am God, and there is none else. I have sworn by myself, the word is gone out of my mouth in righteousness and shall not return, That unto me *every knee shall bow, and every tongue shall swear.* Surely, shall one say, in the Lord have I righteousness and strength: even to Him shall men come and *all that are incensed against him shall be ashamed. In the Lord shall all the seed of Israel be justified*, and shall glory. ALSO NOTICE…

Ro 11:26 And so *all Israel shall be saved*: as it is written, There shall come out of Sion the Deliverer, and shall turn away ungodliness from Jacob:

Now in the face of such incontrovertible evidence, who should dare make such a false statement as the heading in this section that "…Jewish ancestors are not doubt burning…"? Preaching/teaching that "all" souls, including those who have died rejecting the Jewish Messiah will ultimately be saved whether in this world or the world to come certainly will increase the possibility of winning our Jewish friends. Yes, all will eventually embrace the Savior in repentance and experience the new birth either in this life or the one to come!

Now who, under heaven, could possibly say that these scriptures will not be fulfilled? Can the Lord Almighty send forth His sworn Word, sworn in His righteousness, to save "ALL" of Israel's seed, and not see it come to pass? What force possible could there be to thwart the will of God Almighty? If there are going to be countless Jews/Israelites to be tormented in the fires of Hell for eternity/infinity, while only a small minority are to be saved and accept Jesus as Messiah then these verses are a plain lie. Who can possibly deny it! For those who claim that the Israelites are included in the N.T. church and vice versa, then it should be very plain that eventually "all will come to repentance." Certainly if God has sworn that all Israel will be saved, then no doubt all gentiles will eventually be saved as well! No need of anyone to go for infinity/eternity to Hell/the Lake of Fire. Pain bringing sorrow, humility repentance & salvation a blessing indeed.

Luke 12:47-48 Teaches Endless Punishment?

"And that servant, which knew his lord's will, and prepared not himself, neither did according to his will, shall be beaten with many stripes. But he that knew not, and did commit things worthy of stripes shall be beaten with few stripes. For unto whomsoever much is given, of him shall be much required; and to whom men have committed much, of him they will ask the more." Luke. 12:47-48.

John R. Rice, wonderful soul winning evangelist certainly thought so. In his booklet (which clearly teaches endless/eternal damnation for the lost) "Hell What The Bible Says About It," says these verses "…clearly teach that the greater the enlightenment and opportunity which a sinner has the greater punishment will be if he rejects it." He earlier states that "…Judgment will be on the basis of what men deserve. People go to Hell because they deserve to go; some have a worse Hell because they deserve a worse Hell. They will be judged accurately according to God's records of their works and punished in Hell accordingly." (End of quote.)

Naturally the question begs to be answered, where in these verses does it say that the unprofitable servant will be beaten endlessly for eternity? Of course it states that they certainly will be punished, but not endlessly so, and further they are to be punished differently according to light etc. Since the idea here is "length of punishment differs" it stands to reason that they will not be beaten forever/endlessly! Not only that but this scripture does not indicate anything such as endless punishment (damnation) in these verses.

If anything, these verses definitely teach first, that sin will be punished, secondly that the sin will be punished according to its degree, thirdly that the punishment will not be endless ("many" stripes are not "endless" stripes.) No doubt this is a parable, but a parable in itself still is a realistic true story drawn from real life, and no one believes that a dishonorable servant should be beaten continuously for eternity.

These verses plainly and irrefutably teach temporary severe punishment according to their sins. Another point, is Rice claims that "Hell" is the place where man is punished according to his sin/wickedness, and while it is true that there are various levels of Hell in the underworld, Ps. 86:13, (no doubt each level with much, some, little, or little if any suffering) the only place man truly is judged and punished according to his personal sins is in the Lake of Fire Rev. 20, and that punishment is clearly stated to be according to their "works" and not punishment "endlessly and for eternity."

Rice further (in error) states "…how freely men will be permitted to indulge their sinful appetites…" *(In Hell. ed)*. Sorry, no truth here. The wicked will have no means of exercising their sins, but will be thoroughly humbled with excruciating pain and suffering. It is plain even in this life, that when any person is enduring severe pain and suffering he/she will have no interest in committing sin. People in Hell will have no interest in sinning, but rather will anticipate the eventual coming end of their justified suffering, when every knee shall bow and every tongue shall gladly confess before the Savior.

Lastly he states, "We may be sure that most of the people in Hell did not expect to go there..." While no doubt this is true, we can be sure that as Revelation 20 plainly states, "...and the Devil that deceived them was cast into the Lake of Fire." To believe that God would allow man to be deceived by Satan and then burn/torture/punish him in endless fire and brimstone for eternity is too much to believe. The Bible simply does not state such. At the Great White Throne, all souls standing this Judgment will be "...judged according to their works," (not endlessly/eternally judged) which clearly indicates varying lengths of time for punishment, certainly not endless eternity!

To use the old argument that 'God doesn't send anyone to Hell, they send themselves there,' sounds good, but the reality is that first, God/Christ did indeed create/invent Hell and all the punishment therein, and secondly the Lord does indeed send souls there for their rejection of salvation, and thirdly there is no justice in giving infinite punishment for finite sins, and especially so for those who were deceived ('tricked' a good word) by Satan.

For Rice who believes in endless/eternal damnation in Hell fire, to say these verses refer to lost souls in Hell simply does not wash. In noticing the preceding context it is easy to see that there is a 'servant/lord' works relationship being examined, and we know that 'works' does not bring salvation from damnation, since we are saved by grace through faith. Eph. 2:8-9. In all probability these verses are referring to the Christian's judgment at the Bema Seat of Christ, where our works are placed before us for reward or rebuke. See II Cor. 5:10 & I Cor.3:11-15.

Rice states Chapter 5, "Keeping People out of Hell: The Soul-Winning Motive" is the reason we should win souls to Christ.

While this is absolutely true, some will ask if Hell/Lake of Fire is not endless then no need to have such concern. To which we answer that even in this life, we as compassionate human beings seek to alleviate pain and suffering whenever and wherever we are able, 'loving our neighbor' as ourselves. For us to help the wicked unsaved find salvation and redemption in Christ, freedom from the enslavement of sin, and all the happiness and joy the Christian life brings with it upon conversion and salvation, must be paramount to allowing the lost go on in their sin, misery and shame with only tremendous suffering after death to come. Any Christian who is unconcerned about the unsaved and the horrors they face in Sheol/Hades in the next life, cannot be right with the Lord.

The False Guilt Trip of the Damnationists

A very strong doctrine of the Damnationists to encourage fervent soul winning is to teach and preach that we as Christians could well be the reason someone will spend endless eternity in Hell-fire if we don't attempt to win them to a saving knowledge of Christ. The point is often made from such churches that many many souls have died and gone to a Christless grave and on to endless damnation due to our failure to reach them in soul winning with the gospel. Nothing could be further from the truth. While yes it is true, that if we fail to win a person to Christ, they will undoubtedly be sent to Hell/Sheol/Hades to await their sentencing at the White Throne Judgment.

As well they will miss the rapture/translation of the church, and in being here to rule and reign with Jesus for a thousand years in the Millennial age. Such false theology as above in *our* sending anyone to endless Hell fire/damnation certainly does load followers of such doctrine with extreme guilt ridden motivation and fear for the lost, but it is still a lie!

1. No lost person will be able to say "So and so didn't witness to me so I was lost." Yea rather the Word of God is quick to set the record straight by saying, "He that believeth not shall be damned," and thus putting the final blame not on us, but on the lost sinner. If a lost man could use the afore mentioned as an excuse, then no doubt God on judgment day would not be justified in sending him to Hell fire. In fact if death is the final determining point of salvation or damnation, then many untold millions and millions would be justified to give Jesus the simple excuse, "I never had a chance to be saved due to the

failure of your Church but would been saved had they witnessed to me, I was totally ignorant of the true plan of salvation."

2. Dr. John R. Rice, great soul winning evangelist of the last century related a story in one of his booklets concerning his failure to win a man to Christ, a man he felt led to witness to but did not, and soon thereafter the man died, to all appearances unsaved. He related that he felt that due to his failure to win the man, he would be guilty of the man's eternal never ending damnation according to Ezekiel and the 'bloody hand warning.'

Ez. 33:7-9
"...I have made you a watchman for the house of Israel, therefore you shall hear a word from my mouth and warn them for me. When I say to the wicked, "O wicked man you shall surely die," and you do not speak to warn the wicked from his way, that wicked man shall die in his iniquity, but his blood I will require at your hand. Nevertheless, if you warn the wicked to turn from his way, and he does not turn from his way, he shall die in his iniquity but you have delivered your soul.

Now the only thing that this scripture clearly teaches, is that if we as Christians do indeed fail to win the lost to Christ when we have the opportunity, and refuse to do so, then we become guilty in 'aiding and abetting' their rejection of Christ, which for a Christian is a sin and an extremely serious matter. And yes we certainly will have guilt having their 'blood' on our hands, but won't be sending them to an endless eternal suffering in Hell-fire.

3. Now if the damnationists doctrine of endless damnation in Hell fire be true then for a Christian to stumble, or cause an ignorant man to go to Hell by not witnessing to him would cause a huge problem. The problem would be a question which must be answered. The question simply is this. What pray tell, should be the Christian's punishment for sending that poor soul to endless damnation,

if endless damnation be true? What sin could a Christian commit which would rise to the level of sending a poor ignorant soul to a burning Hell for eternity? Murder? Adultery? Pedophilia? Apostasy? The answer to that is NONE. Absolutely NONE!! Should not the punishment fit the crime?

Does not the Word of God teach capital punishment for serious sins? IF, and we say IF a Christian could possibly send another man to Hell for eternity by not witnessing to him, or failing to do so, then there could be no greater sin he could commit than that! So what should be *his* punishment? To be consistent it should be capital punishment!? Here you would have a poor ignorant soul for whom Christ died, dying and supposedly being sentenced to burn in Hell fire for eternity because some Christian did not witness to him, but the Christian who failed to witness goes on to spend eternity in Heaven, but only losing some 'rewards' at the Bema Seat of Christ!? Does that at all make any sense?

Then the big question looms, "Which person has sinned greater, the poor lost soul who died in ignorance, or the Christian who failed/refused to witness to him, supposedly causing him to go to endless damnation?" The answer to that is the <u>Christian</u> would be guilty of not only a sin which completely overshadows that sin of the lost soul, but of an infinite sin since it caused an infinite amount of pain and suffering to that lost soul! So put the Christian to death?

4. Then again, another very serious question on the heels of the previous "3" question of justified punishment due to the Christian who refuses to go soul winning and engage the lost in personal witnessing. What should the church do regarding punishment for such Christians which fail to evangelize and win souls if endless damnation is true and the lost are stumbled into endless torments by them? Certainly if E.D. is true then the church must enforce the greatest punishment possible upon the guilty church members who fail to evangelize and win souls. Such sin would again be greater

than fornication/adultery murder etc. and as such would demand to be severely punished to the highest degree!

If such sin should not be punished, then the lesser sins mentioned must not be punished and who would believe that?! Most evangelical churches today are nearly destitute of members who are strong personal soul winners! The same with pastors, teachers, and evangelists. These churches that hold persons who have been through a divorce and have remarried in the shadow of adultery, refusing them to hold leadership positions in the church, yet are themselves often very weak in personal soul winning and evangelism. So if E.D. is true, and poor ignorant souls can be stumbled into Hell-fire by those who do not win souls (or try to), then the greatest punishment possible should be levied against all in the church who fail to win souls.

That would be most of the congregation no doubt, and soon after such punishment these churches would have empty pews. What hypocrisy! No! The false idea that we can "stumble" someone into endless Hell-fire is totally false. What is true though is that we *can* possibly stumble the lost into Hell by refusing to witness to them, but that Hell is not going to be endless! Now this last point is absolutely intolerable for a Christian/parishioner to sin in regards to.

Our motivation for winning the lost is that we are commanded to do so. Salvation will bring them to a blessed life in Christ Jesus freeing them from sin and sinful habits, bringing glory to God, and keeping them from the pain and suffering of Hell for their sins. These are the main reasons for soul winning. No Christian is right with the Lord who refuses to share the good news of the Gospel. Think about the Day of Judgment, when that lost soul stands before God, (and supposing endless damnation is true) he hears his sentence for eternity in the Lake of Fire. His answer to God? "Lord, you must have mercy on me since I died in ignorance and unbelief because this Christian did not witness to me.

Also as well, since he failed to warn me, now HIS failure to do so is about to cause me endless suffering in Hell fire, while HIS 'reward' is to spend eternity in Heaven and mine in the Lake of Fire. Am I about to get infinite punishment for HIS infinite sin against me while he goes to Heaven forever and me to Hell fire endlessly forever? Is that just and fair?" Any Christian who thinks that would be fair and just for such to be has a perverted sense of justice!

No! The damnationist's doctrine of endless damnation here as always, fails the scriptural test of reason, the Bible and sanity. This doctrine of E.D. breeds the worst feelings towards those who the damnationists hold as being without hope, and incorrigible. Rather than pray and continually work for their salvation, they give up the struggle to win them to Christ, and often rejoice when that soul dies and goes to Hell. Yea rather they should never give up on praying and working for the salvation of any lost soul!

Lastly, we in no way wish to lessen the concern Christians should have for the lost and winning them to Jesus. The lost will go to suffer in Hell fire for their sins, and as well the Lake of Fire but thankfully the Word of God states the universal salvation of all men regardless, and that of course after severe punishment, humbling, and a bowing of the knees before Jesus and receiving forgiveness and the new birth into the family of God.

Lastly, is it any wonder many people are naturally offended when we as soul winners ask them, "Are you saved?" Why so? Simple. For hundreds and hundreds of years, fundamentalists have ignorantly held to the false doctrine of endless damnation based on the corruption Augustine introduced into the early Christian church, which corruption has continued even down to this day. Who among the unsaved, non churched are *not* aware that modern fundamentalist type Christians generally hold to the Augustinian perversion of God's punishment for the wicked/

unsaved, namely that God supposedly inflicts *infinite* endless pain and suffering in Hell-fire for *finite* sins for eternity?

When any unsaved/liberal rational thinking person logically weighs out such an injustice, naturally he or she can easily dismiss such a god, and the question asked. Naturally they easily scoff at the question asked them, "Are you saved?" since the fundamentalist is not asking if they are saved from God's punishment for their sins, but in reality are asking "Are you saved from God's endless/eternal punishment?" Little wonder that in that sense they feel right in answering that they reject such a question asked of them since it denotes the unjust/false doctrine of endless punishment. Sadly, no doubt their conscience congratulates them for rejecting such a god, (which it should).

In reality they should be concerned that indeed severe, yea maybe even horrible punishment is awaiting them after death at the hands of a truly just God. Someone needs to explain just why the damnationist believes anything **less** than endless torment in Hell-fire and brimstone would not be, or is not sufficient punishment for the unsaved dead!

Is it any wonder that so many lost souls readily scoff at the 'Are you saved' question considering that such question is most always readily connected to the damnationists false concept of God and endless damnationism. As well, no wonder so many of these die lost, perceiving that this God is not worthy of bowing before due to His supposed injustice of infinite punishment for finite sins. A shocking question then arises which is, 'Are the damnationists bowing before a false god, and if not then just what god do they really worship since the god of endless damnation is a false god, and simply does not exist except in doctrinal fantasy!?'

CHAPTER SIX

THANK GOD FOR HELL? YES!

Death's Improvement of the Wicked

The wicked in this life, atheists, agnostics, reprobates etc, sometimes do from the result of God severely dealing with them, come to Christ and are gloriously saved. On the other hand, sometimes they are so hardened in sin and unbelief that nothing outside of a divine revelation can force them to see and give ascent to the truth.

I may have a wild untamable lion, which I house in my garage etc, and my neighbor could adamantly be in unbelief of the same, but if I am to cast him into the room he forever becomes a believer if he can get out alive. The same with the wicked in this life. They may well be in adamant disbelief of God, they may be tyrants, despots, dictators, incorrigible drug dealers, thieves, murderers, adulterers etc, but upon death, and entering that terrible place of torment/affliction in Hell-fire, they suddenly and instantly begin to improve. How so?

1. They are instantly and eternally transformed into believing in the existence of God, they no doubt meet Him face to face in judgment. Improvement 1.

2. They as well know then (and are forced to admit) without doubt that Jesus Christ is God, and God the Son. He who sits at the Fathers right hand. Improvement 2.

3. At death they instantly recognize, and are forced to admit that they were wrong in being what they were and in doing what they did as they stand before the Righteous Judge of the Universe, and who, who can argue against Jehovah, the all knowing God? Improvement 3.

4. At death, the wicked will no doubt, (unhappily of course) come to be in total agreement with their damnation or judgment, and the righteousness of God's judgment. His wisdom and judgments are unquestionable, cannot be argued against, and the wicked will be forced to accept them. They will be forced to acknowledge the error of their ways and the justice of their coming damnation in Hell. The simple fact is that it is either 'God's way or no way' as there is no other way! They cannot disagree in that day. God will not allow anyone to go to Hell in ignorance. Improvement 4.

5. The wicked will be fully aware that their damnation or judgment is "aionios" or "on and on" with indefinite duration (or length of punishment) known only to God. They will understand the necessity for retribution or punishment meet for their sins being outside of Christ. The Lord will see to that. Improvement 5.

6. Improvement Improvement Improvement, but of course no salvation... yet...!

Praise and Thank God for the Pain and Suffering Sinners Receive when Going to Hell!

A shocking sadistic statement to make? Well *yes*, if sinners are to be tormented for an endless eternity to give them retribution for their sins, (we ask here, is it really just to give *infinite* punishment for *finite* sins, sins committed in a short space of say 10-70+ years?) But *no*, not sadistic if sinners are there to suffer the punishment due them for their sins, and through this terrible trial and affliction they are fully brought to a place of total submission, humility and as well are brought into full agreement with God concerning the seriousness and wickedness of their sins.

And then again *no,* if they as a result of dying and going to Hell, are finally brought with a willing broken and contrite heart to turn to Jesus Christ for the salvation they spurned while alive on earth. I can hear some complain that those lost had a complete life of maybe threescore and ten to find the Lord. To that I ask, "What about those who lived in the antediluvian age who had 2-3-4-5-6 hundred years to learn the truth of Jehovah?" Why should they, (if endless torment in Hell/Lake of Fire is true), have had that much time to learn the truth of the Lord and be saved, but yet were still damned by the flood?

Tell me fellow Christian, just who is a better Christian? One who delights to know or believe that God consigns souls to eternal endless torment as a "payback" for their wickedness? (What else could it be?). Or one who delights to know that the pain and suffering in Hell and the Lake of Fire is a carefully measured invaluable tool, designed by God Almighty Himself to punish and irrefutably forever prove to that sinful soul (1) the seriousness of its depraved inclinations toward sin and wickedness, (2) the truth of God's Word, and then (3) later that pain and suffering proved to be the turning point in that sinners receiving of Jesus Christ and free salvation?

Now herein lays the real problem. Augustinian theology with its "eternal/endless damnation paints a picture of a God who one day finally has every lost damned soul in the universe on bended knee, willingly so, and they in full knowledge giving total ascent to all the truth of God, His scheme of redemption, and at His full disposal and total submission. On their knees (as the scripture plainly states Phil. 2:10, "…every knee shall bow, and every tongue shall confess that Jesus Christ is Lord to the glory of God the Father…") they make a true fully believing confession that Jesus Christ is Lord (and God), and of course it follows they as well have come to believe that He was raised from the dead. Then this aberrant theology teaches that God sends them screaming into the burning halls of the damned in Hell's fires for endless eternity after their total submission and confession of Christ!

Now does not the scripture plainly teach "That if thou shalt confess with thy mouth the Lord Jesus, and believe in thine heart that God hath raised Him from the dead, thou shalt be saved?" Rom. 10:13. Is not Jesus Christ 'the same yesterday, today, and forever? Heb. 13:8. Would He not willingly save that humbled, repentant spirit in the next life when called upon in truth and submission?

Would not their supposed damnation then (in the next life), be the same as if a wicked reprobated sinner in this life were to be totally humbled and subdued by say a very painful God sent experience, then on bended knee confess his sins and confess to Christ that He is indeed God the Son, only to find himself to being slain and cast into Hell-fire for endless eternity? Is that the kind of God who rules the universe, one who totally defeats the enemy, brings him to total submission and ascent of the truth, after hearing a willing confession of Christ and then He sends him to burn in torment in Hell-fire for eternity?

Augustinian theology certainly thinks so. The Christian church today is steeped with such a false theology.To quote the scripture (Heb. 9:27) "…as it is appointed for all men to die, and after this the judgment…" to show that there is no 'post mortem' possibility of salvation does not fit. The 'judgment' here of course is 'Hell' for the unsaved, and 'Heaven' for the saved. Nothing more, nothing less. The judgment for the unsaved is certainly a judgment unto eventual submission, and confession of Christ, after enduring retribution/punishment for their sins. "Every knee shall bow…Every tongue shall confess…" Ph. 2:10. The 'judgment' for the true believer after death is Heaven, and the 'judgment' for the unsaved soul after death is affliction in Hell. Someone asks, "Well does not the scripture say that if one is not born again in this life he cannot see the kingdom of God?"

Chapter Six | Thank God for Hell? Yes!

To which we answer of course it does! The Kingdom of God however, is not set up on this earth until the 1000 year millennial reign of Christ. That is a 'time period' and not of an endless eternal duration. Those not born again in this life, will miss that millennial reign of Christ, and not be raised from the dead until the second resurrection, at the Great White Throne.

The bottom line in the salvation or damnation of man is, if "aionios timoria" or "punishment/torment of indefinite duration" is indeed what the Greek says, then it naturally follows that repentance beyond the grave, or perpetual probation is indeed a fact, and that fact precludes the modern error that the soul's destiny is endlessly/eternally decided at death. On the other hand, if "aidios timoria" is what the Greek says, then there is no post mortem salvation possible. This author holds to the belief that Augustinian theology of endless damnation was favored over "aionios timoria" due to the mistaken idea that the people would be better held in check by endless damnation type theology (the Roman Catholic Church has certainly always thought so).

It has already been pointed out that Jesus and His disciples never used the term "aidios" in relation to punishment after death. It also has been pointed out that while the Bible being translated into English, does indeed seem to teach 'endless' damnation, the Greek does not. Which is to rule our thinking, the modern day English and newly created words from the 1300's such as 'eternal/everlasting, or the original Greek words? It has been clearly pointed out that in the early centuries of the church; "Eventual Universal Salvation" was the norm of theological belief that is when and where Greek was the language of Christendom.

On the other hand all countries of the world during early centuries of the church in which Latin was the predominant language, were steeped in ignorance and darkness, and were of the most corrupt and ignorant ages of the church! For the first three hundred years of the church, the doctrine of "universal restoration and salvation" was clearly believed and taught. The greatest of the church fathers in the first three hundred years of the church all believed in universal salvation/restoration. As well absolutely no creed of the first five hundred years of the church expresses any idea contrary to universal salvation and in favor of eternal/endless damnation.

It is interesting to note that the first advocates of eternal damnation, Minucius, Felix, Tertullian, and of course Augustine were Latins who were all ignorant of the Greek and much less competent to interpret the meaning of Greek Scriptures than were the Greek scholars. The first advocates of universal salvation after the apostles were the Greeks, in whose mother tongue the scriptures were written. They found their universal salvation in the Greek Bible so who should be correct, the Greeks or the Latins?

J.W. Hanson tells us "…all ecclesiastical historians and the best Biblical critics and scholars agree to the prevalence of Universalism in the earlier centuries." From Hanson's 1899 book on "Universalism the Prevailing Doctrine of the First 500 Years of Christianity." The darkest periods of church history overwhelmingly held the doctrine of endless damnation, while the most enlightened held to universal restoration.

J.W. Hanson gives an interesting view of the "fire of God" in regards to its application to the wicked, quoted as follows:

He is a "Refiner's Fire"

"He burns to purify."He shall sit as a refiner and purifier of silver." Could the melting metal feel, how might it misunderstand the process through which it is passing. The unrelenting fire burns beneath the crucible, and the dirty, unsightly ore becomes like liquid light, and circulates as useful coin, and sparkles on the fingers of happy brides, and shines on the scepters of kings, and in the coronets of queens. And all because the severe and purifying fire of the refiner has tried it. Inasmuch as the consuming fire of God is refining, we learn that it only destroys the dross of sin, and leaves the spiritual gold, the immortal soul, unscathed and pure when its blessed work is finished.

One infidel (Celesus) in a debate with an early church father charged that the Christian God was cruel since He punished with fire. To which came the answer, "...God's fire is curative that He is a consuming fire because He consumes sin and not the sinner." End of Hanson quote. *(Ed. No, only the blood of Christ can "consume" sin, though the fires of Hell certainly can be curative of disbelief and rebellion etc.)*

The Doctrine of Endless Damnation Discourages the Death Penalty

Our country being founded on Judeo/Christian principles naturally reflects the Word of God underlying our most basic laws. Society today, no matter what Christian denomination saving a few, such as the Watchtower etc., holds to the Augustinian doctrine of endless damnation. Naturally judges and juries could be hesitant in applying the death penalty to those convicted of crimes worthy of death since in their view (if they hold to the doctrine of endless damnation) that convicted criminal once put to death would be ushered into a state of fire and brimstone endlessly for eternity.

As stated earlier, traditional/Augustinianism teaches death is final in bringing the lost soul into endless ruin and suffering, while the Word of God teaches that Hell/Lake of Fire in the Word of God purifies, is restorative in nature bringing limited and controlled suffering and pain to the wicked and as well easily brings him to true sorrow and repentance. Now how many judges and juries, are naturally swayed away from sentencing someone to such a horrible fate as physical death/endless damnation, hoping that one day (if they let them live) that lost soul will find repentance and faith in Christ? Were they to understand the *value* of the unsaved going to Hell, no doubt the death penalty would be more readily applied, and many would hesitate committing crimes for fear of being sentenced to death!

Hell/Lake of Fire the Place of Purification Unto Sorrow-Repentance-Salvation-Restoration

A Tale of Three Kingdoms

Once upon a time, there were three magical dream land kingdoms divided evenly between three very righteous Kings who were also brothers. These kings were the epitome of righteousness and goodness, and zealously ruled their kingdoms with truth and righteousness. All was well in the three kingdoms until one day there were found the seeds of wickedness and rebellion being sown by an enemy. Little by little, sin began to filter in and through these previously innocent kingdoms. Many of those who were once faithful and loyal to their Kings were now rebellious and constantly involved in crime and corruption, and as well sought to seduce others to their pernicious ways, murder and immorality began to run rampant. Fortunately there were those few, very few who remained loyal and obedient to their Kings in each of the three kingdoms.

The three Kings, seeing their subjects heading toward a total civilization collapse, decided to hold an urgent meeting, to determine what would be the best course of action to take in resolving these problems. The first King's decision was that of painful fiery annihilation for the wicked. The second King decided to inflict horrible endless suffering forever and forever on the wicked in a huge canyon of liquid fire and brimstone at the most further corner of his kingdom.

The third King decided (due to his love and concern for all of his subjects) to: First, severely and painfully punish the wicked exactly in proportion to their wickedness, and that being no longer than needed to perfectly convince them of the error of their way, and the justice of their punishment. He as well reasoned that their punishment was to be so severe that it must be permanently etched in their memory, so they would never again want to stray. Secondly to give them perfect understanding of his will in doing such, and of his love for them and his desire for their redemption/restoration. Thirdly, once they fully learned their lesson and were brought to bended knee in total sorrow and repentance, to restore them to eternal happiness and joy in his kingdom once their sentence and redemption was completely carried out.

The First King
The King of Annihilation

The first King meeting and discussing with his brothers, told them as follows. Yes, I cannot tolerate the sin and rebellion of the wicked in my kingdom. I shall take all of those who are guilty of sin and crime, and who do not repent, to the huge canyon which lies just outside my kingdom. I have established a deadline (unknown to my subjects) and if they pass that deadline without totally repenting, then and there I shall force them into the canyon, fill it with those unrepentant wicked sinners.

Then I shall fill the canyon with the most flammable liquid I can find, ignite it and while hearing their cries screams and pleas for mercy, happily destroy every one of them for eternity, never to be heard of again. I know who the enemies are, and they will have the same fate. My patience has come to an end with the ungodly, and I am totally forever giving up on them. This will be a wonderful lesson for those few who have remained loyal and faithful to me. They will love me forever and never cause my kingdom any trouble.

The Second King
The King of Endless Punishment

After listening intently, the second King said, "Well, I have one better than that! Yes, while I am giving up on the ungodly forever as well after a secret deadline, what I am going to do will top that." I am going to do exactly the same thing as you but with one major difference. I am not going to allow them to die and cease to exist, but rather am going to magically cause them never to perish but to be consciously tormented in the same fires, continually for all eternity. They will never die, never have food, water or comfort, will be swimming in that liquid fire and brimstone never ceasing, screaming, cursing and begging for mercy for all eternity, but I will not respond with any type of favor towards any of them. I will forever/eternally seal such as their fate.

The Third King
The King of Universal Redemption

The third King, upon listening to his brothers, and upon deep reflective thinking said the following. I, my brothers, am going to take a totally different course of action with my subjects. I must say that I have deep concern and a true love for all of my subjects, even the ungodly ones and I will not 'give up' on even the worst of them. If a man has learned to do wrong, and wickedness, and has experienced severe punishment in the same proportion to his sin, then he as well can learn to do that which is right. I shall therefore measure out his punishment, which of course will have to come in painful suffering since he lived in pleasurable sin, and make him suffer until I am fully persuaded that he will never want to offend and live in sin again.

So, I will design a place of suffering as well, but it will be a place of measured suffering for all who enter therein, measured according to their wickedness and sin. In that place I will withhold all of the comforts of life. There will be no rest day or night, no food no water, there will be extreme heat and as well the wicked will fully understand the justice of their being in that terrible place.

No I will not punish them endlessly/forever. I will not punish them beyond what they deserve, and after their deserved measured suffering will release them to stand before my judgment seat, and I am quite certain that they will bend their knee in gratitude and thanksgiving yielding to my absolute rule and authority. Thus they will all without exception, gladly and happily embrace my power authority and rule. My love will conquer their rebellion and wickedness, though they will go through great suffering and trial in yielding to my righteous rule.

Chapter Six | Thank God for Hell? Yes!

The Plans Executed and the Aftermath

The first King proceeded to execute his plan. He had one million subjects and about eighty percent had become profligate and wicked. Using his powers he swept away the eighty percent to that terrible canyon of fire and brimstone. Instantly the wicked were gathered together by his soldiers and thrown screaming and fighting into those terrible fires of brimstone and fire totally consumed and never to be heard from again. True it was there was no more sin and wickedness in his kingdom, but the fact he had forever lost 800,000 souls forever deeply saddened him and those related to those destroyed. Fathers and mothers forever lost children, husbands forever lost wives and vice versa. Not a single family of his kingdom was untouched with sorrow and sadness from the loss. Tears and sorrow continued to abound day after day in his kingdom. I wonder" said he, "perhaps there would have been a better way… maybe so, maybe so."

The second king proceeded to execute his plan. Once his secret deadline was crossed, he as well gathered together all of the unrepentant/ungodly and placed an endless curse of never ending conscious physical existence upon them, forever to be tormented in that same fiery canyon. One difference was however, he did judge them according to their works and leveled the degree of pain they should endure accordingly for all eternity.

All who were ungodly, the heathen who died somehow having never been aware of his commands and edicts, men women and children of all ages from the age of reason up, those who were secretly deceived by Satan through false religion, and those wicked who were hopelessly enslaved to their sins and vices, after this terrible judgment, were gathered together by his soldiers, and cast alive screaming into the canyon of liquid fire and brimstone to be tormented endlessly forever. "Now," said he, "These wicked shall forever endlessly know and realize that they should not have been wicked and ungodly, and should have submitted to my righteous rule." Again, after executing his plan, the same realization crept in to the King's heart.

Nearly eighty percent of his kingdom lost forever. Mothers loosing children, children loosing parents, brothers and sisters forever endlessly separated, and thus no one remaining in his kingdom was untouched with unfathomable sorrow for the loss of loved ones. Not only that, but now, for eternity he would have to hear the screams, moaning and shrieks of those in the infernal canyon. It would thereby be an eternal/endless monument of failure to his rule of righteousness over all his subjects and the failure of the majority to submit to his perfect rule. Here again, tears of sorrow, sadness and pain continued to abound from those subjects remaining behind, sorrow and pain which would not seem to go away. I wonder" said he, "perhaps there would have been a better way... maybe so, maybe so."

The third King proceeded to execute his plan. This King loved all of his subjects without exception and had no desire to lose even one. Though these wicked servants deserved punishment he still loved them all, in spite their sins, but certainly not because of them. This King believed that full reconciliation, restoration and forgiveness was more to be desired than to torment these souls for all eternity. Therefore all of the wicked/ungodly without exception were swept away by his soldiers to his judgment halls.

This King created a prison setting which was one of confinement, fair and just pain and suffering for differing degrees of sin and wickedness. One by one they were judged, and sentenced accordingly, all to long terms of confinement in differing degrees of pain and suffering, but all judged accordingly, and according to their sins and wickedness without exception. None of these had any sense of time during their confinement so each had no idea of how long they would have to suffer. Each knew however, that his/her confinement suffering and pain was just fair and righteous. Year after year, those who were wicked and ungodly were punished, until one day they were released to once again stand his judgment.

This time however, all who had previously rebelled and lived in wickedness under his rule, gladly bent their knee in total submission and gladness to be reconciled not only to their King and kingdom, but to their families as well. Joy was everywhere, the kingdom erupted with gloriously jubilee, families reunited, and thanksgiving for the sinners come home, soundly converted to righteousness and not one lost. The other two Kings, seeing all of this, said between themselves, "Certainly this was a better way; we have lost the majority of our kingdom subjects to fire for eternity, while our brother has used his fire for purification unto repentance and restoration to his kingdom."

Of course the above "Tale of Three Kingdoms" is limited in its scope and in parallels, but it does clearly show the rationale in the wisdom of God for not only sending Jesus to die for the sins of all people, but providing the means for all to come to Jesus whether in this life or the next. Who could possibly fault God with bringing all men to; Pain, suffering, remorse, sorrow, repentance, salvation, and finally permanent restoration to eternal happiness and life in the Kingdom of God?

Post Mortem Salvation?

Christendom is saturated with the idea that there is absolutely no post mortem salvation possible. Millions die, and have died over thousands and thousands of years, having never heard the name of Jesus, or the story of the wonderful plan of salvation. The Word of God is very plain that there is absolutely no salvation possible outside of saving faith in the Lord Jesus Christ. No doubt the reason so many Christians have reached such conclusion is that death ends all of earthly contact with the deceased, and the church has vociferously held that "It is appointed unto man once to die, and after that the judgment" to mean that once a man dies, the only thing left is for him to go to judgment, to Heaven or to Hell with no further possibility of redemption.

Now a casual reading of this verse, may indeed lead one to believe such, but certainly there is a deeper meaning here. We heartily agree with this verse, that man is destined to die once, and then he is brought to judgment. It must be remembered however that nowhere in the Word of

God does it say that after this judgment, man is consigned eternally/endlessly to Hell if he is not saved. Quite the contrary, the Word plainly teaches, that in the end, "Every knee shall bow, and every tongue shall confess that Jesus Christ is Lord *(God)* to the glory of God the Father."

The 'damnationists' (those believing in endless/eternal damnation) claim that the White Throne Judgment in Revelation 20 is the final/endless state of the unsaved wicked. However they need to read the next chapter. Revelation chapter 21 plainly shows God has created a new heaven and earth. The former creation (with the temporal Lake of Fire and its pain and suffering) shall pass away, or be ended/dissolved by fire. The plain inference here is that once those souls who were cast into the Lake of Fire were sufficiently punished, duration according to their works, they are delivered on bended knee in repentance, remorse, the new birth, and restoration to the Kingdom of God.

II Peter 3:9-13

> The Lord is not slack concerning His promise as some men count slackness but is longsuffering to us-ward, not willing that any should perish, but that all should come to repentance. But the day of the Lord will come as a thief in the night, in the which the heavens shall pass away with a great noise and the elements shall melt with fervent heat, the earth also and the works that are therein shall be burned up. Seeing then that all these things be dissolved, what manner of persons ought ye to be in all holy conservation and godliness, looking for and hastening unto the coming of the day of God wherein the heavens being on fire shall be dissolved and the elements shall melt with fervent heat. Nevertheless we according to His promise, look for new heavens and a new earth, wherein dwelleth righteousness.

Revelation 21:4

> And God shall wipe away all tears from their eyes there shall be no more death, neither sorrow, nor crying, neither shall there be any more pain for the former things are passed away.

Interestingly, here the annihilationist could falsely claim using II Peter 3:10-12 that the wicked are burned out of existence. As well in this chapter pain, suffering, death and separation from God will be no more. This clearly pictures that God has then had ultimate victory over sin, Hell and the grave, with every knee bowing in reverence and acceptance of His Son, the Lord Jesus Christ. Once an unsaved man dies, he without any doubt faces God in judgment for his sins, and whom do you suppose that he will stand before to receive his sentence? Who shall judge the quick (living) and the dead?

When he faces Jesus seated at the right hand of God, how can he not perfectly understand the gospel that Jesus died for his sins, was buried, and was raised from the dead three days later, ascending back to Heaven? Such a personal revelation at that time will be irrefutable to his sinful soul, but it will be to late not to be sent to Hell/Sheol and later the Lake of Fire for punishment for his sins. This terrible consequence of dying unsaved should surely motivate us to win the lost at any cost! Post mortem salvation? Absolutely, eventually but not immediately. Thank God for His victory and the restoration of all things.

Isn't it strange that the damnationists insist that pain, suffering and death in that terrible Lake of Fire will continue past Revelation 20 for all eternity, when this verse 4 plainly contradicts such a notion? That being the case, and then they claim to vociferously believe 'every jot and title' of God's Word! To use the argument that verse 8 is included in chapter 21 after the creation of the new heaven and earth which merely *restates* the coming penalty of the Lake of Fire to the wicked, is however just that and nothing more. For whatever reason, John under inspiration while giving facts concerning the new heaven and earth issued the verse 8 warning (again), as it was given in chapter 20. This verse no doubt was not meant to be chronologically exact in the chapters. To further quell the notion that the Lake of Fire is to endlessly punish the wicked we turn to Jude to find out the true reason for this last judgment.

Jude 14-15

> And Enoch also the seventh from Adam, prophesied of these saying, Behold the Lord cometh with ten thousands of His saints to execute judgment upon all, and ***to convince** all that are ungodly among them of all their ungodly deeds which they have ungodly committed and of all their hard speeches which ungodly sinners have spoken against Him.*

How much plainer could it be? Jesus is coming again to cast the wicked into Hell fire the Lake of Fire to torment them endlessly forever eternally? No! He is coming (which coming begins at the opening of the sixth seal, the period called 'The Day of the Lord') to severely punish them with the trumpet and vial judgments culminating in their final judgment according to their works in the Lake of Fire to what?? To:

> **Convince all that are ungodly among them of all their ungodly deeds which they have ungodly committed and of all their hard speeches which ungodly sinners have spoken against Him.**

Yes, a merciful God indeed! A God of true love and compassion, a God who does not design the endless eternal damnation in unimagined pain and suffering for the wicked, but a loving and compassionate God who must pour out his anger and wrath upon the ungodly in pain and suffering designed by Him to convince/convict the wicked that they were wrong in first their ungodly deeds, and secondly their ungodly speeches against Him. If God has designed these horrific punishments to accomplish such an 'adjustment of attitudes' you can rest be assured it will do just that, and nothing less. It will certainly therefore end in their sorrow, remorse, repentance, conversion and restoration.

It can do nothing less. "Every knee shall bow and every tongue shall confess…" The damnationists teach that the mercy of God ends for the wicked at their death if they do not receive Christ in the new birth experience. That is false. The mercy of God is infinite since it issues from the attribute of God which is just that...He is a merciful God and His mercy endures forever and that does not mean just this side of the grave. The last point here is since being merciful is an attribute of God, and an unchangeable one at that, if the lost were to be tormented endlessly/eternally then from the White Throne Judgment onward forever it could not be said God was a merciful God.

To punish someone endlessly beyond what it takes to 'convince/convict of the truth' would certainly make God, a God of injustice. As well it would dishonor God's ability to bring souls to truth and repentance. Post mortem salvation therefore is a truth from the Word of God. One simple fact the damnationist overlooks is that any human being who has ever lived or ever will live, can be subjected to an experience which will permanently and forever alter his/her behavior, and which can set his endless destiny in the right direction.

That experience may well need to be to spend time in that place of isolation and suffering, that place called Hell/the Lake of Fire. Yes, the anger and wrath of God is exercised in consigning wicked unsaved souls to suffering there, no doubt about that! But on the other hand that place still becomes a place of *mercy* where our Savior inflicts remedial punishment upon them for an indefinite period of time to permanently turn their attitude from sin, and redirect their endless destiny to repentance the new birth and salvation. Our God is a merciful God, and His mercy endures forever.

Damnationists Brainwashed with False Concepts of Hell and the Lake of Fire

1. That the Lake of Fire is to exist for eternity.

2. That Hell/Lake of Fire is the place God sends those whom He has in frustration and defeat given up on.

3. That Hell/Lake of Fire is the place where those whom have defeated God's desire for their salvation will be for eternity, a place where

God puts those whom He has failed to reach through the church, evangelism, or any other means..

4. That Hell/Lake of Fire is the place where those deceived lost souls who were misled by Satan will spend eternity, *not* being punished with a view of correction/improvement unto later salvation, but a place where God torments/afflicts and applies excruciating pain solely for the purpose of showing the wicked lost His true hatred of them for rejecting Jesus, and thus vindication in placing them there and tormenting them for endless eternity. (This concept further breeds a vicious attitude of the damnationist towards those who seemingly are unreachable/unteachable for Christ. Thus rather than be sorrowful prayerful and compassionate toward these incorrigibles they become happy they will 'burn in Hell-fire for eternity.' ed.)

5. That if there were to be eventual post mortem salvation, then Hell/Lake of Fire would be nothing more than a type of purgatory.

6. That if there was a 'second chance' after death, then many many people would be more willing to live in sin and depravity in this life, to enjoy the pleasures of sin for a season knowing that one day they would be brought to a saving knowledge of Christ.

7. That the horrors of Hell fire and brimstone for eternity are extremely useful in frightening people into accepting Jesus as their personal Savior. (*Thus instilling 'fear' in the unsaved of burning in Hell-fire for eternity becomes a main motivating factor to move souls to repentance, rather than '…Godly sorrow which works repentance unto salvation, not to be repented of but the sorrow of the world worketh death." See II Cor. 7:10. ed.*)

8. That the heathen in foreign lands, who have died without Christ and having never heard the gospel, will be judged and damned endlessly eternally solely on the basis of the violation of their conscience. (*They erroneously base this on Romans chapter one. ed.*)

9. That Hell/Lake of Fire is God's torture chamber, which was created by our loving caring Savior Jesus Christ, to burn the unsaved endlessly eternally in liquid fire and brimstone for not understanding/believing or accepting God's simple plan of salvation.

10. That whatever God does he does it forever and nothing can be added to, nor taken away from it. *(This they falsely apply to souls in Hell fire and brimstone. ed.)*

CHAPTER SEVEN

LIMITED…THE GOD OF THE DAMNATIONISTS THE GOD OF ETERNAL ENDLESS DAMNATION!

God's Desire Is Not for Only a Small Part of Humanity to Be Saved, but That All Consider: There Can Be Absolutely No Limitations on God and His Dealings with Man

1. God/Christ/the Holy Spirit being omnipotent/omniscient/omnipresent have all the resources they need to win any man woman boy or girl to Christ, at any point in human history.

2. Jesus indeed died that all could have opportunity to come to Christ and be saved.

3. His substitutionary death on the cross has a scope, which indeed also can easily include all of humanity ever to have lived or ever will live.

4. All men regardless of who when and where, can be saved and come to a knowledge of the truth.

5. All four above irrefutable facts drawn from Holy Scripture clearly indicate that all and literally all persons young and old of all ages

therefore must be included in the desire of God for salvation, and if in the desire of God, then certainly they must somehow have the opportunity to be saved some time and somewhere.

6. It is an irrefutable fact that millions die every year, and have for every century, without having ever known of the true plan of salvation. On these six irrefutable facts comes the conclusion that for God to treat all men equally, and give all a chance to be saved, especially when such provision has been made available, then these mentioned in this point "6" must have an opportunity to come to the knowledge of the truth in Christ Jesus and be saved at some point during this life or yes, after death. "Natural Revelation" is not enough to bring them to Christ "after death."

7. It is simple to understand that God cannot ever be defeated, suffer defeat, or expect defeat due to the fact that "all truth" concerning everything concerning the eternal destiny of man will ultimately reign supreme over any and all objections of sinful man to yield to Almighty God. That thought in itself is enough to prove that in the "end" all men will be convinced humbled and subdued, and that being in accordance with their consent, that they must be saved and submit to God's plan of salvation. Therefore ultimately all will be saved…eventual universal salvation!! Were God to "lose" in winning one precious soul to Himself, then Satan would be the ultimate victor over sin Hell and the grave. To lose is to lose, and for that fact alone, God cannot lose to Satan, never nor for any reason.

Following are some thoughts presented by an unknown writer concerning Clark Harold Pinnocks views on eventual salvation for all men. (Pinnock, also an annihilationist now deceased, was a theological professor, and writer who held to "open theism." A doctrine that has problematic conclusions, but cannot be discussed in this brief discourse.) The writer states as follows: "…Secondly, I agree with Pinnock, that we have to think about those who have never heard the Gospel or the name of Jesus, even once, in their whole lives. It is naïve for me to answer this question by rushing to say that they surely will be cast into Hell. Logically, our theology is completely unfair. Why will so many people be punished for something they have never known or realized? It is not fair. Pinnock's suggestion helps me to understand this problem. He said, "God will not abandon in Hell those who have not known and therefore have not declined His offer of grace." I think that it is also biblically true that Scripture gives many plain statements that God wants all people to come to Him. He maintains that God is the One who has a wideness of mercy, therefore, He will make the redemptive work of Jesus Christ available to all humans. God gives his general revelation and also an opportunity to believe after they die (postmortem opportunity). God does this because he loves the world and wants no one to perish.

My suspicion is that we have narrowed the motivation for missions down to this one thing: **deliverance from wrath**. We have made it the major reason for missions when it is not. I object to the notion that missions is individually oriented, Hell-fire insurance. Sinners are not in the hands of an angry God. Our mission is not to urge them to turn to Jesus because God hates them and delights in sending them to Hell. Jesus did not come to condemn but to save the world (John 3:17). No, our mission is to announce the wonderful news of the kingdom of God (Mk 1:14-15). It is not based on the assumption that now there is grace where was not grace before. Rather, it is news of an event that had not happened before, the news of God reconciling the world to himself in Jesus Christ and the beginning of the age of salvation. Basically Pinnock answers that there must be an opportunity for those who have never heard the Gospel to be saved. "If Christ died for all, while yet sinners, the opportunity must be given for all to register a decision about what was done for them (Rom. 5:8). What is the fate of the unevangelized or those who have never heard about the redemptive work of Jesus Christ? We can say that obviously this is a question about the eternal destiny of a very large number of people throughout history. He said that this Augustinian thought has been pessimistic concerning admitting God's grace outside the church. According to Pinnock, this understanding implies that God reveals himself to all people, not to help them, but to make their condemnation or punishment more ruthless. He states, **"What kind of God is it who would reveal himself in order to worsen the condition of sinners and make their plight more hopeless?"**

The adequacy of general revelation makes possible the existence of holy pagans. They are people who seek God enthusiastically through their general understanding. God, however, will save them based on the work of Jesus Christ. Pinnock's key assumption here is that **"If God really loves the whole world and desires everyone to be saved, it follows logically that everyone must have access to salvation."**

The universal axiom is based on biblical texts that speak strongly about God's desire to save everyone. Pinnock calls this axiom "the global reach of God's salvation." This is the foundation of his theology of religions. Basically we can say that the first axiom is about lifting up the universal salvific will of God. This is pointing to God's stated (and therefore serious) desire to save the entire race that is lost in sin. The purpose of this axiom, for him, is to determine whether an optimism or a pessimism of salvation conditions our thinking and whether we are full of hope or are hopeless in respect to the multitudes of non-Christian people. Pinnock sees himself as a theologian who is conditioned by an optimism of salvation and full of hope.

Furthermore, Pinnock sees that the Bible clearly articulates this axiom to a knowledge of the truth." He quotes some simple statements in the Bible that cannot be denied by any theologian. The apostle Peter says, "He is patient with you, not wanting anyone to perish, but everyone to come to repentance" (2 Peter 3:9). In 1 Timothy 2:4, Paul states plainly, "God wants all men to be saved and to come…" Another passage that Pinnock assumes as speaking plainly is Romans 11:32. It reads: "For God has bound all men over to disobedience so that he may have mercy on them all."

Pinnock is also struggling with the question about who God really is. Is he a God who would be capable of sitting by while large numbers perish, or is he a God who seeks them out patiently and tirelessly? ***Does***

God take pleasure and actually get glory from the damnation of sinners or is God appalled and saddened by this prospect? But Pinnock answers, "My reading of the Gospel of Jesus Christ and my control belief causes me to celebrate a wideness in God's mercy and a boundlessness in his generosity towards humanity as a whole." This boundless mercy of God makes optimism of salvation possible. Besides that, in the universal axiom, God also will make the salvation available to everyone.

To say that death absolutely ends God's dealings with man in a positive way is but to forget the original design under which man was created. Was not man created (yes made) in the image of Almighty God, and that he was to live in complete harmony with Him for all of eternity? The reason for the "death" of his body was of course due to sin. God could have simply decided to cause man to continue to live in a sinful body, for eternity/infinity, but that course was not taken for whatever reasons known to God.

The simple fact is that man indeed does continue to "learn" after death as was previously shown by the account of Lazarus and the rich man in Luke 16. In learning it is easy to note that the Lord does see to it, especially by the fires in Hell, that unsaved/unregenerate man "learns a very hard lesson" indeed! Take for instance the eternal everlasting, yea infinite *effects* the torment of Hell has on the soul of the damned.

1. First that soul looses all of the things in life that it relished as "good, lovely, enjoyable and desirable," and finds itself in a place of unutterable horror. Now that soul can "experience" just how serious that a sinful unregenerate/unrepentant life is against God and how much God hates it and the just punishment it deserves. Thus the punishment and pain sin deserves in the soul of the lost is meted out each according to his wickedness/sinfulness or depravity, as well as its length and duration.

2. Second. That soul now in torment/affliction learns that without God there can be no true happiness, contentment or peace. Now he

experiences wretched painful existence in Hell without the blessings of God that he experienced in his previous life.

3. Third. That soul "experiences" the wrath of Almighty God for his sins, and finds out just how much God really hates sin and rebellion. Now the "wrath" or anger of God is truly felt. Now feeling for Aionios/forever or on and on the wrath of Almighty God.

4. That wrath is felt in such an excruciatingly painful way that the sinner will "forever and forever" for all of eternity/infinity never forget it. Thus the pain of Hell becomes everlasting/eternal/infinite in its lesson to him of God's hatred for sin, and the need for him to avoid it at all costs. Hell's fires thus have an eternal/infinite purpose, and that purpose is carried out on the lost damned (judged) soul.

5. That experience in the fires of Hell becomes a permanent "imprint" upon the soul of the damned, yea an eternal imprint which will mean that sinner has had the vengeance of eternal/aionios Hell, i.e. on and on suffering, with no definition of length, (since all must be judged according to their works, and sentenced differently). That sinner will truly be given an eternal/infinite lesson, one that will never be forgotten, for all of eternity! Do we as Christians not have devastating circumstances come upon us in this life? Horrific terrible things, which leave a permanent mark on us, lessons that we will never forget? Absolutely yes. Thus the same with the unrepentant sinner, when he finds himself in Hell at the end of a godless life, he finds suddenly that everything the Bible taught was indeed a fact. He suddenly becomes a believer in the Word of God, but now must suffer the pangs of the damned.

Of course there are those who claim that Hell is a type of purgatory, where sins are "purged" away. No, no such thing. Only the precious blood of Jesus Christ can cleanse away sin. The simple fact of Hell is that it does have purpose in the afterlife of the unregenerate. First it is a temporary "holding cell" for the lost until the time of judgment. Second it serves as a place of "punishment pain and anguish" for the rebellious lost soul. Third it serves as a place of "learning" showing the unsaved the hatred of God for his sins. Hell does have its end, "... and death and Hell were cast into the Lake of Fire, this is the second death and whosoever was not found written in the book of life, was cast into the Lake of Fire." Jesus said that Hell was a place where the "worm dieth not and the fire is not quenched." Theologian J. Preston Eby wrote the following concerning the "unquenchable fires" in the Word of God;

More than 2500 years ago the Holy Spirit warned the wicked inhabitants of Jerusalem that God would kindle a fire at Jerusalem's gates which would devour her palaces. "But if you will not hearken unto Me ... then will I kindle a fire in the gates thereof, and it shall devour the palaces of Jerusalem, and it shall not he quenched" (Jer. 17:27). Did not God say this fire "shall NOT BE QUENCHED?" This prophecy was fulfilled and the fire did occur a few years later and it did destroy all the houses of Jerusalem (Jer. 52:13). Since God said no person or thing would "quench" this fire, did that mean that it would burn forever? Since it accomplished the work it was sent to do, and since it is NOT BURNING TODAY, it obviously went out by itself after accomplishing its purpose!

Unquenchable fire is not eternal fire - it is simply fire that cannot be put out until it has consumed or changed everything it is possible for it to change! It then simply goes out, for there is nothing more to burn. Yet I hear the preachers ranting and raving about poor souls being cast into bell fire where "their worm dies not, and the fire is not quenched" and this, we are told, means eternal, unending torment. How foolish, illogical, and deceptive! Such a view contradicts the plain meaning of the term "unquenchable" and its use in the Word of God. End of Eby quote.

Jesus plainly taught that Hell should be avoided at all costs, yea, "... if thy hand offend thee cut it off, for it is better to enter life maimed than to have the whole body cast into Hell ..." Mk. 9:48. What may take an unconverted wicked sinner all his life to learn, that he does need to be saved, and that the Bible is indeed the Word of God, (if he fails to learn it now in this life), he certainly does instantly and in a few seconds, learn it by the blazing revelation of finding himself in Hell, being tormented/afflicted in punishment for his sins! God did not create Hell to torment/afflict man for eternity.

It must be understood that "torment" as used in the Greek is not an evil word in regards to its application of the pain in Hell to the souls of the damned (yes righteously "judged" souls). Strongs 928-929 gives the words, "Basanizo and Basanimos" which mean vex, afflict, torment, torture. "Torment" simply means "extremely painful affliction" which of course could mean in mental or physical sense or both. God cannot be unrighteous in His judgments on the unsaved when they perish. This author's grandmother would often reply to my grandfather's sometimes aggravating jesting as his being "tormenting" etc.

The words "torment or torture" as commonly used in the English language today are mostly applied to "unjust suffering" such as some boys "cruelly mistreating or tormenting a cat." God does not "cruelly mistreat anyone for any reason ever. His absolute holiness and justice prevents that! Now who would not say that wicked men do not need to be severely punished after death, and as well in this life? Are not Christians "punished" severely sometimes for their waywardness and sins yea even to the point of physical death? (... "if any man defile the temple of God him shall God destroy," 1Cor. 3:17, and ... "there is a sin unto death..." 1 Jn. 5:18) Of course they are, it is called "chastisement."

Is not the blood of Jesus cleansing them from their sins as 1 John Chapter 1 tells daily? Of course it is. Can it be said that chastisement in the case of the Christian, or Hell in the case of the sinner is a purgation or the cleansing of sin? Of course not, only the precious blood of Jesus can achieve that! So it is plain that the lost souls in Hell are there "not having their sins purged away" but are rather being "punished" or receiving retribution or vengeance for them. Only the blood of Christ can cleanse sin away, and if it were not for that no doubt the sinner would have to stay in Hell endlessly! We have already shown that in the afterlife in Hell, as in Lk.16, that there is "learning" taking place after death.

Anything a person learns in life, certainly can and will benefit him in some way. Learning to walk, learning that the law of gravity must be obeyed, learning that undeserved pain and suffering will come if not careful etc, etc. How much did the rich man learn immediately after death? Read the afore mentioned points on Lk.16. Some probably will say, "No, man cannot pay for his sin, only Christ can do that on the cross of Calvary." To which we heartily say "AMEN." BUT... Hell is not a place to settle a legal sin debt against Almighty God, but rather a place to "experience" and understand the wickedness and seriousness of sin by pain and suffering.

(One writer aptly put it in proper perspective by saying, "If I inflict severe pain on someone simply to satisfy my anger against them without wanting to teach them a lesson, and with absolutely no intent on making them want to correct their behavior, what kind of person would I be? And what kind of God would the Lord be if He acted in this same manner?") Lower Hell is such a terrible place, that 5 minutes there will no doubt convince the most hardened/atheist that God was just in putting him there.

The atheist wants an existence without God, so therefore an existence without God and His bountiful provisions, (and as well as a place opposite the comforts of life on earth) will be given to him. (Horrible suffering in the lower parts of Hell).

As a former believer in endless Hell, the following thought (at that time) would continue to occur to me. If say a Christian mother or father etc lost a son or daughter to an early death, and that loved one was not saved, then when in Heaven, how could that Christian parent not grieve eternally/endlessly for that precious soul in Hell? How could they *not* be devastated endlessly for eternity over the screams, shrieks, and groans of their precious loved one suffering in the tormenting fires of Hell?

(How sick it is that the Calvinists have "God" deciding for people who will burn in Hell fire and who will not for endless eternity, and therefore forcing people to be saved or lost.) Then on the other hand, that precious Christian mom, who lost her wayward son or wicked husband to Hell can truly rejoice in the pain and suffering their lost loved one is experiencing in Hell, since it will certainly be the tool to fully persuade and convince him to turn to Christ. Call it forced salvation if you will, but it is certainly "forced reality." How wonderful it is that the Lord has planned to bring all lost souls to Himself for salvation! Let me ask you.

After death do souls lose their ability to think, reason, rationalize, regret, etc? Certainly not. Again consider the rich man in Hell, and the points enumerated above. It must be remembered that man was created in the image of God, and that he was created to live endlessly with God in a body of flesh and bone. Temporarily losing his body to death certainly does not cause his mental/spiritual faculties to cease, no they will go on for eternity, and he will continue to learn for endless eternity. Romans plainly tells us concerning the salvation of ALL. Notice as follows. Ro 11:26 "And so **ALL Israel shall be saved**: as it is written, There shall come out of Zion the Deliverer, and shall turn away ungodliness from Jacob."

Consider Satan in Revelation 20. "…and the devil that *deceived* them was cast into the Lake of Fire and brimstone, where the beast and the false prophet are, and shall be tormented day and night forever and forever." Now *when* were these poor souls deceived who so foolishly followed Satan, the beast and false prophet? They were deceived while alive on planet earth. Now if a person is deceived does that not mean that he is convinced that a lie is in reality the truth? Absolutely so. Now how many people who have ever lived, have been deceived by Satan and false systems of worship? They have lived their lives out in that deception, raised their children in that deception, and then finally at the end of life died in that deception, fully believing that what they believed was the truth!?

Are we to believe that all of these poor deceived souls were to be infinitely punished in Hell fire and brimstone, and totally abandoned by Jesus for eternity because the Devil deceived them? Absolutely not. What is going to be going on in the lives of all who live say 16,000 years after the final chapter in Revelation? Does the Word of God say? Of course all will be gloriously happy, no doubt, but Revelation does not tell us much if anything about that. To say that poor lost souls deceived by

Satan do wake up in burning Hell to be tormented/afflicted forever and forever, for ages and ages upon ages, or for Aionios and Aionios, is in accord with Scriptures and indeed is a fact.

To say that the poor souls who were deceived by Satan, and suddenly wake up in a burning Hell are totally abandoned and rejected by God for eternity/infinity, is simply not in accord with Holy Scripture. Have they not at that point been forced to admit the seriousness of their deception and error, and as well now have come to realize the truth and truths which have saved millions and millions of others? Does not Jude plainly say that the reason for the coming of Christ in judgment is to "Convince" the wicked of their error?

Jude vs.14-15. "And Enoch also the seventh from Adam prophesied of these saying, Behold the Lord cometh with ten thousands of His saints. To execute judgment upon all, and to **convince all** them that are ungodly among them of all their ungodly deeds which they have ungodly committed, and of all their hard speeches which ungodly sinners have spoken against Him." Does not "convince all" mean "all" without exception? If "all" become "convinced of the error of their ways and doctrines, then they naturally become candidates for mercy and pardon after their punishment and upon their confession on bended knee!

Next notice 1 Cor. 15-22. "For as in Adam all die, even so in Christ shall all be made alive." Now how many "die" in Adam? 'ALL!' So then the opposite in Christ for ALL... ALL shall be made alive! If words mean anything, then eventual universal salvation must be fact. Are we to believe here that God/Christ is going to come in judgment, to convict/convince the ungodly/unsaved that indeed they were speaking and teaching lies about the Almighty, and to force them to admit that they were indeed worthy of damnation in order to righteously consign them to the Lake of Fire for a never ending eternity?

Was not the Apostle Paul given irrefutable revelation on the road to Damascus, such revelation which caused him to be instantly converted to Christ. That God did in fact move in such a way towards Saul of Tarsus, indicates that the Lord will in His time move in such a way toward ALL men everywhere to gain their salvation, and to turn their eyes upon Jesus! It is a fact that at some point, whether in this life or the next, all will be will be shown that truth in such an irrefutable light that they will instantly and willingly be converted to Christ.

Are these poor souls not to be punished, tormented, afflicted with pain forever and forever? Of course they are. For "Aionios and Aionios" for ages and ages or on and on with no known length or duration of pain and suffering since only God knows what that length of suffering will be, but certainly not for a non ending eternity/infinity.

The Cup of Wrath Will Be Full

Ps. 75:8
> For in the hand of the Lord there is a cup, and the wine is red, it is full of mixture and he poureth out the same: but the dregs thereof all of the earth shall wring them out, and drink them.

How full can a cup be filled? Can a cup be only partially filled and yet be called "full?" Of course not! Can a cup be filled to the rim and be overflowing? If a critically ill person needs a full cup of medicine crucial for his healing then what use is it for the cup to only be half full? That would only cause a lack of complete healing to the one drinking, and as well could cause serious consequences if he is denied the balance. On the other hand if the cup is continually and eternally overflowing and he is forced to forever/endlessly drink on and on, then the effects could just as well be as disastrous.

Now the point is simple. God will not be satisfied unless His full measure of justice and wrath is administered to the unrepentant/wicked. That He will force the wicked, those who die without Christ, to drink the full cup of His indignation must go without debate. Rest be assured, when the wicked are in Hell/the Lake of Fire, they will certainly be forced to drink the full cup of the fury and wrath of Almighty God, in torment, and they will drink every terrible drop until that cup is empty. To say that for the unsaved to drink that cup will be a horrible experience goes without saying, but it must be remembered that the healing medicine administered to the sick, whether by radium for cancer, or under the surgeon's knife or other, no matter how unpleasant, paves the way to healing and recovery.

Certainly that lost soul in Hell, once he drinks the full cup of God's anger and wrath, (and that being no greater measure than God determines for each lost soul is needed), will be forced to willingly, humbly and gladly give ascent to all of the truths of the precious Word of God.

What kind of healing can be expected in drinking fully from the cup of God's wrath? Simple.

1. The complete, final, and permanent renovation of the wicked mind to fully accept guilt for his sins and due punishment for them.

2. To experience the displeasure and wrath of God in pain and anguish thereby leaving an eternal/everlasting/endless remembrance that God will have full satisfaction seeing them embrace Calvary and Calvary alone for their salvation.

3. That sin must be forever abandoned, and that Jesus Christ is the only way of salvation.

Once that lost sinner is emptied of himself, his ego, his rebellion, pride, foolishness, yea, yes even his false doctrines, his mind then necessarily as an empty purified vessel can truly embrace and be filled with the truth of God's word and only plan of salvation. When that punishment is completed, then the only result can be instant repentance and acceptance of Jesus in the new birth experience.

Certainly in this life over the ages, millions have not found the truth concerning salvation, and those millions have died and continue to die every day to face God in eternity. Naturally they must be denied entrance to the portals of Heaven. They have died embracing all forms of false religions, Watchtower, Mormonism, Buddhists, Hindus, on and on, and as well wicked unrepentant sinners enslaved by all forms of vice and depravity, and as well those who knew the truth of salvation by the new birth and faith in Christ but procrastinated in making that decision. Yes they are lost, but......in the next life, drinking fully of the cup of God's wrath, and being emptied of themselves and their wickedness, then and only then can they as a fully empty vessel instantly become candidates for being filled with the truth of God's simple plan of salvation. There can be no doubt that upon death, all must stand before the courts of Heaven, and the judgment bar of Almighty God.

The sentence must be passed, "Lost and consigned to punishment in the fires of Hell." At the judgment bar of God, who will be there? The Lord Jesus Christ who will be arrayed in all of His glorious majesty, clearly showing His deity, His resurrection to the right hand of God, and that and that alone will sweep away all false notions or doctrines from the doorsteps of those lost sinners. At that time it will be crystal clear to those lost souls that salvation by faith and faith alone in Jesus Christ was the only true way of salvation, but it will be too late to escape punishment and retribution.

Unfortunately for them, the scripture plainly teaches, "Except a man be born again, he cannot see the kingdom of God," so they cannot enter heaven at death but will experience some degree of that terrible place called Hell. That there are degrees and levels of Hell has been established by the Word of God. While they may not experience the same level of pain and suffering as a very wicked person, they will still experience suffering, separation from God and life's blessings and as well will drink that same cup God deems necessary (to whatever degree), in punishment for their sins. In this life, do not many sinners experience horrible and tragic calamities, which do have a positive effect on their becoming a child of God?

Do not many of these same people finally, before death, learn the doctrines of salvation and with the trials they went through finally with broken and repentant spirits embrace the Savior and become born again? Of course! We all know cases of such. Once they became fully convinced of the truth, and were sufficiently humbled they gladly gave their hearts to Jesus. Now how could God treat those in the next life with distain, those who have fully drunk of the cup of His wrath in Hell, and have finally yielded to the truths of God's word in humility and shame?

Does the truth of God's spoken word end at the grave? Does not the scripture plainly teach "Whosoever shall call on the name of the Lord shall be saved?" Does not the scripture plainly teach that:

Philippians 2:10-11
At the name of Jesus every knee should bow, of things in heaven and things in earth, and things *(those in sheol/hades)* under the earth; And that every tongue should confess that Jesus Christ is Lord, to the glory of God the Father.

Are we to believe that those in Hell will be making a false/cynical confession of faith of who Jesus is especially when they have been fully punished/humbled and forced to see what the truth really is? Are we to as well believe that God honors and saves one in this life when they call upon Jesus out of a humble, contrite and fully convinced heart of the truths of God's Word, but in the next life when a person reaches that same point He turns His back on them and allows them to burn in torments endlessly for eternity? When the lost are taken from Hell at the end of their punishment are we to believe that they will be dishonest in their confession while on bended knee before Jesus Christ as He sits in all of His glory and majesty before the entire universe? Of course not! There will be no hiding place, no place of refuge for that lost soul except for him to embrace the healing salvation of the Savior.

One of the arguments the Watchtower, (as well as the skeptics) has against Hell and the Lake of Fire, is the issue of the conscious aionios/eternal, everlasting (supposed/never ending) punishment of the damned/judged. The Watchtower, rightly claim, that the Lake of Fire *(yes is a totally different place from Sheol/Hades- the spirit world of the departed spirits. Remember that "death- the body risen from the grave, and Hell-the spirit from the spirit world being reunited occurs, Rev.20:13 "... and death and Hell delivered up the dead which were in them, and they were judged..."*) is a literal/physical lake of fire and brimstone, but then err in believing that when the wicked are cast there they are instantly "disintegrated" or "burned up" i.e. annihilated or cease to exist.

They have overlooked a very simple Biblical fact, that is, in Rev. 9:6 under the sounding of the fifth trumpet by the angel, the powers of death and dying are miraculously suspended. The fundamentalists who believe in eternal never-ending punishment of course see the lake as a spiritual entity/reality where the wicked are consciously tormented forever and ever endlessly. Interesting it is that both camps are partially right.

The Watchtower in that it is a "physical lake," and the fundamentalists that those lost souls are consciously tormented on and on, for Aionios and Aionios or forever and ever (*but not endlessly ed.*) with no prospect of "annihilation". The scriptures are plain that the wicked are "raised from the dead," i.e. that their souls and spirits are reunited with their resurrected bodies and then are judged "according to their works."

Immediately then thereafter, they are accordingly cast into the Lake of Fire, to undergo the same fate as the beast and false prophet earlier in Revelation, where they were to be tormented (note again not annihilated) with fire and brimstone in the presence of the throne of God. See Rev. 14:11, 19:20, and 20:10. Having said all this, just what is the problem the Watchtower has with this doctrine of "conscious" Aionios everlasting/eternal punishment? It is the torment/affliction pain part.

It is important to consider one aspect of Hell or the Lake of Fire, and that is "pain." Pain is something that no one desires or wants in this life or the next. The Watchtower sees the fundamentalist doctrine of suffering and pain in Hell or the Lake of Fire, as a proof at least to them, that God could not possibly allow such to happen since that would make Him sadistic and cruel, akin to a man putting red hot coals in the eyes of a dog. That analogy of course is indeed flawed to begin with.

First the dog is an innocent creature, with not enough intelligence to understand right from wrong in a moral sense, nor to do anything except by pure instinct alone. There could be no sane reason for anyone to torment a dog in such a matter ever! But the matter of pain? One needs only to understand that pain is a necessary evil in this world, and in the underworld, that place called Hell. Pain indeed, no matter how much people do not want to experience it, is and can be a blessed experience when administered by the gracious hand of God! Consider the following:

1. God Almighty Himself created the conditions which cause pain. God does nothing without a purpose, and yea that purpose must be in some way whatever, to bring about good, or better conditions for His creatures/creation. Pain a blessing indeed.

2. Pain comes to the human body when it is abused and misused. Thus a safeguard and a warning to stop that which is causing the pain. What damage could be done to a child who could lay his small hand on a red hot stove if he had no feeling of pain. Pain a blessing indeed.

3. Pain when administered to disobedient children, as the scriptures teach concerning corporal punishment, can turn a child from waywardness and disobedience to being a proper and well mannered child. Pain a blessing indeed.

4. The painful chastisement of God upon a disobedient Christian brings about repentance and obedience, and a desire to glorify and obey God. Pain a blessing indeed.

5. The pain of a surgery to remove a cancer, or do a heart bypass or any other operation brings about relief and healing. No pain, no surgery. Pain a blessing indeed.

6. The insufferable pain of that lost soul in the fiery halls of the damned. Forever leaving upon it a permanent/imprint and reminder of the price and punishment for sin. Pain far greater than the pleasures of

sins which sent that soul to the fiery place of suffering. That suffering soul feeling the wrath of the Almighty bearing down upon it in anger and retribution for the terrible sins it committed.

When that soul finally finds deliverance from that terrible state, sin will no longer hold any temptation to rest secretly in its bosom or to resist the laws of the Almighty (and His plan for the salvation of all). Then, upon deliverance from that fiery inferno, will all lost souls finally be able to bend their knee, and … "…Every knee shall bow, and every tongue shall confess that Jesus Christ is Lord (God) to the glory of God the Father." Does not Paul here in Phil. 2:10-11 endorse universal submission and acceptance of Jesus Christ as Lord/God?

Absolutely yes. Just how long, how many ages and ages must pass while those souls are suffering for their sins before they are brought to complete submission is unknown to us, yea only known to God. Isaiah 43:22-25 is still true, and proudly proclaims that **not** just a small portion of Israel would be saved, while the rest/majority are tormented in Hell for eternity, but that "ALL" of the seed of Israel shall be saved! (Naturally the same applies to the Gentiles). Pain a blessing indeed.

7. The pain of a burning conscience upon one doing wickedness, thereby verifying the Law of God written upon the table of the heart of man and forcing him to admit his guilt and possibly leading him to repentance and salvation in this life keeping him out of Hell. Pain a blessing indeed.

8. The painful conviction of the Spirit of God upon the sinful unregenerate soul of a lost person, convincing them of the need of repentance of sin and salvation. Pain a blessing indeed.

Pain, in the hand of an all wise, omnipotent, compassionate God, (when it is meted out carefully under the Divine judicial act of exercising His wrath on sinful/unrepentant man) is certainly and justly measured upon the soul of the damned and fairly executed! We as Christians should rejoice in the excruciating suffering souls experience in the fires of Hell! I can hear some readers (if not all) of this booklet saying "What a horrible thing to say!"

To which I answer, "Thank God for the pain and suffering lost souls experience in Hell fire since it is that pain and suffering which convinces that wicked lost soul, that God hates sin, will not tolerate sin and unrepentance, and that Jehovah will be the ultimate victor over all of mankinds sin and rebellion which will ultimately bring those lost souls to Jesus Christ in full pardon and forgiveness of sin!" Is not that everlasting/Aionios sentence of those damned/judged *fair*, when it "convicts and convinces" them of their wickedness, and allows them in the next life to experience pain according to the wickedness of their sins (and especially so when it leads them to embrace the gift of God's salvation)?

There can be no positive without a negative, no height without depth, no white without black. On the same token there can be no happiness without the possibility of unhappiness, there can be no Heaven without a Hell. Pain indeed, that purifying pain. Purifying a man from his profligacy? Absolutely yes. "Cleansing away his sins?" Absolutely not, only the blood of Jesus Christ can do that and that only with the new birth. Away with those pacifists who shun or degrade that blessed Divine doctrine of suffering forever and ever, for Aionios and Aionios, or for ages and ages in that terrible place called Hell, where **their worm dieth not and the fire is not quenched!**

The simple fact is that pain may well cause the feeling of torture, but that torture may well be in line with the condition causing it, a condition which in itself is justified in causing that pain/torture. Therefore it must be asked, just what is the source of the pain. If say a tooth is abscessed and causing great suffering, such may well be a feeling of being tortured, as would be any other similar situation.

Now to blame God, and say He is unjust for allowing/causing such suffering/torture in Hell is to forget the real reason a person is there in such a terrible place. A fair way to describe Hell and the suffering therein is simply that it is a remedy for justly punishing a person for their sins. The condition for causing the suffering/torment in Hell, as was the abscessed tooth example, is simply unforgiven sins against Almighty God by an unregenerate lost damned soul. The unsaved, lost sinner, upon his decent into Hell, suddenly experiences in reality, the anger, displeasure, and wrath of God upon himself, for his sins by the suffering and torture in Hell. God's fault he is there? Absolutely not!

Can the fires of Hell purge away his sins? Absolutely not. Only the blood of Jesus Christ can cleanse away sins. How long will the sinner suffer for his sins? For as long as it takes to "completely convict/convince him" of his error and profligacy, and allow him to suffer sufficiently for his wickedness. Forever and forever, Aionios and Aionios, ages and ages will he suffer until such a time as God sees, and only God can see when, that soul will willingly, humbly, and honestly proclaim on bended knee, that indeed "Jesus Christ is Lord to the glory of God the Father." Forced salvation and forced damnation? Not hardly.

The laws of nature, of gravity, of inertia, of hot and cold etc. etc., are laws while any person could well be ignorant of in their childhood, are laws that such children must learn, and have to learn to live safely in the physical world. A child certainly is glad to learn them is he not even though he suffers in learning them? Thus the same with eternal (aionios) Hell and the suffering and torment therein. Hell, a place of learning, a place of experiencing the wrath of God first hand, a place that forever and permanently imprints upon the tables of that sinner's heart the invaluable lesson that sin simply is not worth being on the other side of God for. Almighty God knows just exactly, in what precise measure to allow man to be tormented/afflicted/punished in Hell and for exactly for how long.

Infinite, never ending, torment in Hell/Lake of Fire being executed upon the souls of the lost? If so then we should say that God must delight in infinite torment as punishment for finite sins? Certainly not. God cannot be unjust to anyone, even to the lost! If God did not allow the wicked lost to be "punished" for their sins, yea to "experience the wrath of the Almighty and His extreme displeasure for their sins, then the command to obey God and His commands would mean nothing at all. Certainly for the righteous to be aware of such punishment/pain and suffering for the wicked is a very valuable lesson to them as well.

It is well to look at the definition of infinity, everlasting, eternity, and eternal more closely.

Notice also…
>Phil. 2:9-11. "Wherefore God hath also highly exalted Him, and given Him a name which is above every name: that at the name of Jesus *every knee should bow* of things in heaven, and things in earth, and things under the earth; and that *every tongue* should confess that Jesus Christ is Lord to the glory of God the Father."

Now to say that these people are bowing the knee, and confessing that Jesus is indeed God simply to give "lip service" to God is totally without scriptural merit. The only confession these people could possibly make would be an honest confession in the face of irrefutable revelation. The above scripture from Jude plainly says that the Lord "convinces *all*" the ungodly of their error. Now whatever God does, He does it thoroughly, and nothing can be added to it nor can anything be taken from it!

They will be totally brought around to fully understanding and appreciating the truth which they at first rejected from the teaching and preaching of the Scriptures. In further considering the fact that sinners will need to be "convinced" of their ungodly deeds it naturally follows "of their false doctrines" as well. It is well to remember that there would not need to be a "convincing" if God were giving up on them to allow them to burn in the Lake of Fire for infinity/eternity. Why would the Lord see the need to "convince" them (or "convict" them as some translators put it) of the error of their way if such were the case?

Were or had not they been deceived by false teachers, or perhaps raised in a culture of heresy which forbid the teaching and preaching of the gospel, as such is the case in many Muslim nations today? Were they not perhaps as children raised loving and trusting that their parents were teaching them "time honored family traditions and religious beliefs" and thus were deceived and bound to error by family heresies? The simple irrefutable fact is that millions in such sad state have perished in war, natural disasters and other catastrophic circumstances having never even had the opportunity of anyone attempting to "convince" them of the truth of the glorious gospel of Jesus Christ.

The very idea that God is unable to convince anyone of the truth having been reared in such circumstances, or does not have the resources to do such is to deny the omnipotence and omniscience of Almighty God. How limited are the resources of the church in reaching the heathen with the gospel is clearly shown by the fact that century after century heathen nations continue to thrive and exist and yea perish in their false doctrines while the church does indeed honorably do all in its power to evangelize them as much as is possible, but sadly still fails to reach all.

How many false denominations/cults exist in the U.S. alone and continue to thrive and grow. Consider the Mormons, who deny the deity of Jesus Christ, as well as the Watchtower founded by Charles Taze Russell commonly and erroneously called the Jehovah Witnesses. For the past plus hundred years or more they have continued to thrive, grow, and spread their false teachings! Generation after generation continues to perish enslaved in those false doctrines. Now I ask you. How long is a devout Mormon/Watchtower deceased, before he is "convinced" of the error of his denomination/church. That answer is simple.

No longer than it took for the rich man to wake up in Hell, and evaluate his condition, and that of Lazarus in Abraham's bosom. Immediately after death! Will they in such circumstances be tormented/afflicted forever and ever and ever, for Aionios and Aionios, or for ages and ages? Absolutely yes, but for infinity and infinity? Absolutely not. At the end of someone being finally "convinced" of the error of his way, lays certain eventual reconciliation to the Almighty. Are we to believe that these souls are "convinced" and finally saved without the new birth or the shed blood of Jesus being applied to their sins, or without being born again? Absolutely not!

Jesus said plainly, "Except a man be born again he cannot see the kingdom of God." Are we going to touch on the possibility of salvation after death for the wicked/apostate that die in their sins? We already are, and that is self-evident. Is the torment/affliction, which is experienced in Hell able to "purge" away sins? Absolutely not. Does not that affliction "punish" that poor soul and convince it as well that it died in a state of apostasy against God, and prove to it that Jesus was indeed God come in the flesh, and that there is no salvation outside of Him?

Absolutely so! The torments of Hell/Lake of Fire are to serve simply that. To "convince" the wicked of his sins and to bring about that change of mind by irrefutable force that indeed he must come by the way of the cross. Does not the scripture again say, that "Every knee shall bow, and every tongue shall confess that Jesus Christ is the Lord (God)." Are we to believe that God finally "convinces" and convicts all who died in a state of having been deceived of the truth of the true way of salvation, that Jesus was indeed "God come in the flesh," and then consigns them to burn in never ending Hell fire for eternity/infinity to punish them for being deceived? To say so certainly is to paint a picture of a sadistic cruel God!

This author can indeed hear the cry of some of his peers, "Well then if everybody is eventually to come to repentance, what should be the urgency to preach the gospel to the entire world?" The answer to this is simple. That as many as are humanly possible should be reached, to spare them the torments of the damned by the new birth and salvation by the blood of Jesus Christ in this life. Plain and simple, and as well bring them while alive and in this life, into a joyous victorious life in serving Jesus Christ.

This idea that God was unable to win the majority of humanity to Christ through the church, and that therefore they are consigned to burn in a never ending infinite Hell, forever reminding all of the entire universe that God failed in reaching them (and that Satan won that battle) is an impossible conclusion! God cannot fail, now or ever in anything He sets forth to do. The fact that there is a warfare going on in this world and has gone on for some 6000 years goes without argument. That Satan is contending and striving to win the souls of men to himself is unquestionable and cannot be debated. No one will deny that.

For someone to say that it is 100% man's fault that he goes to Hell is only partially true. Of course there is a real Hell with places of fiery punishment. That fact cannot be refuted except by the wresting of scriptures, and seeking to make a false story out of such as Luke 16 with the rich man and Lazarus. One needs to consider the hundreds of thousands who as young children regularly lose their lives in tornadoes, mud slides, volcanoes or other natural disasters.

These many have perhaps been raised as Buddists, Muslims, or other false religions with absolutely no exposure to the saving gospel of Jesus Christ. Are we to believe that God consigns them to burn in an infinite never ending Hell/Lake of Fire? Are we to believe that God has no compassion towards those who have never heard? Jesus wept over Jerusalem and said how He would have gathered them unto himself as a mother hen gathers her chicks to herself, but they would not, i.e. **they** were not innocent, and were without excuse! Are we to believe they were without fault and that they could obtain salvation without coming to Christ? Absolutely not! Can such people ever escape the terrible place called Hell and later the Lake of Fire, and gain entrance to Heaven without being "born again?"

Absolutely not! But to believe that these other precious souls (the above young and ignorant who perish in natural disasters etc.) for whom Christ died, though they never had a chance to hear, would be consigned to burn infinitely in a place of unutterable horror and pain is too much to charge God with, and is contrary to Scriptures and common sense.

If our Savior could have wept over a rebellious people in Jerusalem who resisted salvation, then no doubt He is/was that *much more* concerned over those who have never heard, and never had a chance to be saved! Certainly those who have never reached the age of accountability and reason such as babies and little children do indeed enter Heaven to be in the presence of God (as David said of his baby II Sam. 12:23, who died…. "He shall not come to me, but I shall go to him"), so to say those unsaved souls who are accountable but have never heard the gospel are not allowed to enter Heaven is no doubt a fact, no doubt they do go to that place for sinful/unregenerate souls, a place of darkness and separation from God called Sheol/Hades. That there are degrees of punishment is clearly taught.

In Revelation it is said that… "… And every man was judged according to his works." To further address that state in this paper is not our intention, but rather to closely examine the doctrine of torment in "never ending infinite Hell-fire." Can it be said that the will of rebellious man, was finally and eternally able to thwart the will of the Almighty? Can it really be said that the will of man was finally in the end, able to resist irrefutable truth fully and clearly revealed to the entire universe?

Take the apostle Paul, who as Saul of Tarsus was putting Christians to death for their faith. For whatever reason, God gave him a revelation so shocking and real, that it brought his instant conversion! If the Lord saw the need to do such for him, then I am sure that He in his time and providence will do the same for all men though it may well come immediately after death. Why in this life, there are many many that have not had an irrefutable revelation forced upon themselves only God knows.

However in the next life, that one second in Hell will be able to do what all of the promptings and pleadings that sinner had while alive had failed to do. That rebellious lost sinner running from God, upon the death rattle in his throat, and seconds after will suddenly find the revelation of God blazing in his face, and ultimately sealing forever his clear acceptance of the truth God was trying to show him while alive. The fires of Hell will be the "pay back" for his sinful life, and will ultimately and forever chase away his unbelief and rebellion. Will they "purge away or wash away his sins." Absolutely not. Only the blood of Jesus can do that. Then there is the fact that "Truth" cannot ultimately fail, it cannot ultimately and finally be misunderstood, nor ultimately finally and permanently rejected by any soul in the universe for eternity. Truth is Jesus, and Jesus will and must have total supremacy over all evil powers no matter whence their origin. There will never be a time in eternity future that truth will fail to reign supreme to the total exclusion of error.

It is a simple indisputable fact that if two exactly equal forces are exerted the one against the other, at the same time, there can be no gain for either side, none at all. If however, one force is greater by any degree no matter how small that degree, the weaker of the two will eventually give way and loose. The warfare that is taking place in this universe and has been taking place, and will continue to take place until God ultimately reigns absolutely over His creation, at the last put down of sin and rebellion are not two forces of equal value. Infinite punishment for finite sins? Not hardly.

God cannot be other than fair and just in the justice He meets out upon those who are His enemies. Let God be true and every man a liar. This author has finally come to the firm conclusion that the doctrine of "never ending infinite punishment" mocks the Lord God Almighty, and relegates Him and his final relationship to all of humanity to a place of utter defeat, and thus the exaltation of the powers of Satan over Jehovah's. Satan, (by the teaching of this false doctrine, in the end, and after all warfare has been fought between the forces of God and Satan, of righteousness verses unrighteousness), ultimately is seen to defeat God's divine plan of reaching all of humanity with the saving cleansing gospel of Jesus Christ. That God should loose in the end, would naturally be the goal of all satanic powers. Now it is a plain fact, that no one will deny, not one, that God is the Supreme,

Omnipotent Ruler of the universe, and that He and He alone cannot be defeated, in any form of warfare that may be devised against Him, whatever that may be, whenever or in whatever form it may come against Him and his armies! God will be the only supreme God, and the only God that will have ultimately the only absolute victory over the forces of Satan for time and eternity.

Is Hell or the Lake of Fire to contain the souls of millions upon millions of lost and damned souls for eternity/infinity and thus be an infinite never ending reminder to the Almighty, and to all of the redeemed of all ages, that sin ultimately won victory over those poor souls which God with His unlimited knowledge and resources was unable to convince of and win to the truth? Is it to be the eternal/infinite "junk yard, scrap heap of the universe" with the screams, shrieks, moans and pleas for mercy from the terror ridden racked in never ending insufferable pain, lost and damned souls?

Certainly not! Truth cannot be refuted, cannot be forever/infinitely ignored nor rejected no matter how dark the heart of wicked sinful man should be. Truth being ignored neglected, or even denied in this life may be the norm of those without the blazing light of irrefutable revelation from God, but in the next, such will not, nor can be the case.

No not for anyone. All lost souls will instantly see, and instantly understand, by waking up in the fiery halls of the damned that irrefutable revelation of God revealing their profligate wondering in the dregs of sin, shame and rebellion. Is it any wonder that the atheist/agnostic etc, would scoff at believing in the God most Christians believe in. A God who would supposedly torment/afflict innumerable lost souls of all ages in the fires of Hell or the Lake of Fire never ceasing for endless eternity.

Christians over the centuries have been unwittingly portraying their God as one who is ultimately defeated by Satan and his forces of unbelief by loosing countless precious souls for whom Christ died. No, God cannot loose, nor can He in the end loose one single soul for infinity to the fires and torments of Hell and the Lake of Fire. While those souls may well be "lost in this life" and in the next for "Aionios and Aionios or forever and forever, or for ages and ages, they will certainly be well ready (eventually) after death to fully embrace all of the revelation of Jesus Christ.

One very simple point can be made about the excruciating suffering in Hell for a lost sinner. For a sinner to experience the torments of the fires and suffering in Hell for one minute is to experience the pain of Hell-fire for eternity! Think about the following impact waking up in Hell will have on a lost soul.

1. First the shock and horror of being in such a place will totally overwhelm that spirit and consume every thought and desire of that poor lost soul.

2. Second the pain and suffering will be such as to force that soul to admit its error and neglect of the ways/salvation of the Lord, and/or that while alive on earth he was deceived and misled by false doctrines or his love for sin etc.

3. He will be forced to admit that his sentence is fair and just, and he deserved such pain and suffering. Yea for endless eternity, he will never never *forget* experiencing and learning that truth in Hell.

4. He will have no idea as to just how long he is in Hell since there will be nothing there to measure the passing of time. Thus one minute, one hour, or 10 years will not be comprehensible. One minute thus may well be an eternity, very easily.

5. As the lessons of Hell envelope him, gradually his thinking will evolve to accept his fate, that God is just, and his sentence is just, and no doubt it will be soon thereafter he will find himself out of Hell/Lake of Fire, and standing, yea bowing at the throne of Almighty God, as the scriptures plainly teach that (Ph. 2:10) "Every knee shall bow, and every tongue shall confess that "...Jesus Christ is King of Kings and Lord of Lords." Certainly this confession will not be cynical in any sense due to the overwhelming truth of this experience!

Then there is the fact that in the distant future, according to God's prophetic time clock time will cease. Endless eternity/infinity will then begin. Aionios or ages upon ages, or forever and forever will not be counted as an indefinite "period of time." An unknown time period is just that. Not known. Nor can be known. No one knows for how long a period of time someone will be sentenced to be afflicted in the underworld Hell, and later the Lake of fire. It can be easily seen in Revelation that the Lake of fire, into which the damned (judged) are cast, after being physically raised and judged, is just that, a physical lake of fire in or about this physical earth, before the new heaven and new earth.

Now yes, it is a fact that the beast and false prophet are cast there and are tormented alive on and on, Aionios and Aionios, forever and forever, for ages and ages. Those who followed him have this same fate and are tormented/afflicted as well, but notice, that they do not "cease to exist", nor are they "burned up." One has but to read earlier in Revelation where men "seek death and cannot find it." Rev. 9:6. Simply speaking the power of death over the human body is suspended earlier in Revelation, so those not written in the Book of Life are cast alive there and are tormented/afflicted along with the beast and false prophet! Who can refute that?

The Unthwartable Will of Almighty God

Are we to believe as Christians that the will of God will ultimately be defeated (or be ultimately and permanently violated) in any measure of form in even the smallest matters whatsoever? Are we to believe that when the scripture says that "God is not *willing* that any should perish, but that *all* should come to repentance," that His will should be ultimately defeated by the eternal endless damnation, or eternal endless death of the least of sinners? Absolutely not! Looking at this from another point of view, this scripture could well be stated, "God desires that none should perish, but is desirous that all souls ever created should be saved." (For God to "desire or be willing or not willing" concerning anything, certainly means He first evaluated and judged, coming to certain conclusions.)

This brings about the firm conclusion that what God desires or does not desire, must in fact be behind his will concerning whatever. I.e. first, evaluation, second, judgment, third, will in force. God's will is a definite force in whatever direction He may exercise it, and as well it has force to it, and that force yea is an endless, overpowering, yea ultimately totally victorious force, and that will backed with omnipotence eventually must and will be fulfilled. His will must then of necessity bring down the last, most rebellious sinner to glorious salvation through repentance and faith in the shed blood of Jesus Christ! Remember the "Lord's prayer, "…thy kingdom come, thy will be done in earth as it is in heaven."

Praise the Lord! He is not willing that **ANY** should perish. Are we to believe that the will of any man will ultimately rule or oversee the will of Almighty God in regards to his own eternal/endless destiny? Are we to believe that the will of any man will ultimately defeat the will of God in regards to his own salvation? Must we accept the notion that God in the end of all things is so defeated by the stubborn will of man that he must resort to endlessly tormenting man for all eternity/infinity in fire and brimstone? (I.e. Jesus saying, "You didn't accept me so I'm going to torture you in fire and brimstone endlessly for eternity!"??)

The scriptures nowhere indicates such except in the English with the mistranslation/misapplication of "Aionios" from its true meaning of "indeterminate/unknown length or continuous" to being improperly understood and used as "endless." Are we to believe that God could come to the "end of Himself" and see unsaved wicked man as so sinful and rebellious that he must give up on him for endless infinity? Does God have an "end of Himself" a point of no possibility of "going any further?" (Man surely does!) Certainly not! God's resources are unlimited and not bound by time space of even eternity. Man's will cannot go past that which is "impassable."

Are we to believe that souls in the tormenting/afflicting/punishing fires of Hell are going to have to spend endless eternity writhing in pain and anguish to "learn" that they should have accepted Jesus, turned from sin and been born again? This author certainly does not believe so, and the scriptures (except in the misapplied/mistranslated English) do not indicate such. The question must be asked here, "Cannot a person learn a permanent lesson in this life under the schoolmaster of affliction?" Of course he can!

Many many persons have had life changing experiences at one point or another, experiences which permanently altered their habits and behavior. Take a small child who is unaware of the dangers of a hot stove burner. He has been continually warned and warned repeatedly of the dangers of playing with matches or of the burners on a stove. One day out of curiosity he ignores the warnings having never been severely burnt and suddenly the truth he has ignored and not experienced becomes a reality in his life and forever changes his conduct.

Now pray tell, **_how long_** must he experience the actual pain of the fire to permanently learn a lesson he'll never forget, and as well have his conduct forever changed for the better? To say that he suffered eternal or everlasting punishment is indeed very proper. There certainly would be no need to keep his hand in "endless" pain and suffering to permanently change his dealings with matches or a stove. The same with Hell. No doubt, souls of wicked unregenerate persons must first hand "experience" the penalty of sin and separation from God in the torment/affliction of the damned in Hell fire.

How long must that soul stay there in order to learn that sin must be punished, and righteously so? Who knows? Sin can only be committed in this life, and not the next. The lost man in Hell has lost his connection to the physical world (in which we now live) wherein the option to sin lies. When in Hell, he will not be blaspheming and cursing God, no, his pain and suffering will be so intense, and his awareness will be too acute as to his deserving of being in that terrible place of punishment. No doubt when an unsaved person goes into the fires of Hell, he stays there until God reckons that he is sufficiently "educated" if that term can be used, in understanding...

1. That sin must be punished.

2. That there is no salvation outside of Jesus Christ and being born again.

3. That he will be in Hell until God sees his punishment is sufficient "payback" for his sinfulness, no doubt the more wicked, the longer and greater the pain and suffering.

4. That God's way is the only way of obedience for man to forever follow.

5. That sin can never be justified under any circumstance, by any man.

6. That sin can never be considered as a valid option in any circumstance, ever.

7. That God would much rather shower His blessings/comforts and the joys which serving Christ brings upon obedient mankind, as opposed to pouring out His wrath and indignation in fiery judgment upon the lost.

For years this author was at a loss for explanation as to the bitter attitude of some lost persons against God for "that Hell fire and brimstone" theology. My answer to them usually was that the plan of salvation was so simple as the scriptures plainly say... "...that whosoever shall call upon the name of the Lord shall be saved." Those who ridiculed the Bible on that basis this author now sees had become "infected" with the false teaching of "endless/never ending punishment," due to the misunderstood wording concerning the same in the English translation. The same with the atheist who scoffs at the idea of "endless torment in the Lake of Fire."

Certainly these groups falsely blame the Bible for this teaching. In the interest in winning these precious souls to Jesus for whom Christ died, naturally the first step is to show them the error of endless punishment, and the truth that sin must still be punished but not endlessly so. Endless punishment makes no sense whatever. Whatever God does He does for good reason, and that with a positive outcome of those plans which He executes. His plan to save all certainly is not forced salvation, but rather salvation which is eventually happily agreed upon by all souls, and thus all souls willingly coming to the Savior. Truth cannot fail.

Interesting note it is that the Watchtower Society, unscripturally known as the 'Jehovah Witnesses' who hold to endless annihilation at the Lake of Fire for all wicked, *(including Satan)* have created a huge theological speed bump for themselves there. In the second resurrection it is very clear that all wicked are raised from the dead, judged, and then are cast into the Lake of Fire *in their resurrected bodies*.

If then they are supposedly 'annihilated' or are 'totally incinerated/burnt up, then what could possibly happen to Satan who is and has always been a 'disembodied spirit?' How pray tell, can a disembodied spirit be incinerated?? Clearly, Satan is cast into the Lake of Fire with the wicked at this judgment! No, these souls, the souls of the unsaved being reunited with their bodies at this last/second resurrection will be raised in bodies that *will be* subject to pain and suffering, but **not** annihilation. These bodies will be eternal bodies which will ultimately (after suffering in the Lake of Fire according to their works rebellion and wickedness) be brought to shame, humiliation and subjection, bending their knees and confessing and embracing the Lord Jesus Christ as their Savior.

Revelations 20:10 & 14-15. "And the Devil that deceived them was cast into the Lake of Fire and brimstone where the beast and the false prophet are, and shall be tormented day and night forever and ever… And death and Hell were cast into the lake of fire, and whosoever was not found written in the book of life were cast into the lake of fire."

Damnationists Unwittingly but Willingly Violating Warnings of Adding to God's Word

Revelation 22:18-19

"For I testify to every man that heareth the words of the prophecy of this book, if any man shall add to these things God will add to him the plagues that are written in this book. And if any man shall take away from the words of the book of this prophecy, God will take away his part out of the book of life and out of the holy city and from the things which are written in this book."

How is it that the damnationists unwittingly 'add' to or 'take away' from the truth of the book of Revelation? Simple that is to answer.

1. Revelation chapter 21:1 plainly states that the first heaven and earth pass away, there is no more sea. It then enlarges on the new heavens and earth which of course include all aspects of the same by saying in verse 4, "And God will wipe away all tears from their eyes and there shall be no more death neither sorrow, nor crying, neither shall there be any more pain for the former things have passed away." Damnationists claim this verse is *only speaking to the saints while the vast majority of humanity died lost and are destined to burn in endless torment for eternity.*

2. In saying such a thing, it is plain that such a statement is an addition to the book of Revelation, since there is *no qualification in this verse limiting it only to the saints to the exclusion of everyone else* (i.e. damnationists create two eternal/endless classes of people after the white throne judgment the saved and the lost).

   This scripture (vs.4) with no qualification plainly shows universal Christian redemption/restoration! Further note that the Lake of Fire, the final judgment of pain, death and suffering upon the unsaved, has been 'done away with' since verse four above says so! "... no more death... no more pain... *for the former things (which includes the Lake of Fire, with its pain suffering and death therein, i.e. a former thing), have passed away." The Lake of Fire was a 'former thing' which passed away!*

Where is Sheol/hades today? 'Down' no doubt in the heart of the earth, (Jonah went there) and while it is a physical place, as well it's a spiritual holding cell for the lost. Luke 16 describes some conditions there. Plain it is, Sheol/Hades will be a 'former thing' which passes away, and will not be a part of the new heaven and earth. Its purpose as a temporary abode for the wicked will have fulfilled its purpose, making way for the final Lake of Fire which will as well be done away with when its purpose is fulfilled in punishing the wicked in proportion for their sins.

Damnationists contradict the Word of God and say the Lake of Fire is not done away with (has not 'passed away') but extends on future into eternity to endlessly torment lost souls isolated in spiritual/physical death pain and horrible suffering, and they thus add to the Word of God! That is not a serious thing for them to do??

3. Verse 3 plainly says, "...Behold the tabernacle of God is with *men*, and He will dwell with them, and they shall be His people and God himself will be with them and be their God." Now 'men' and 'mankind' and 'humanity' are absolutely generically indicative of 'all' to the exclusion of none!

    Plainly, 'death' and 'pain' no longer exist in this newly created universe, since the Lake of Fire and its usefulness to punishing the wicked has been fulfilled by fully punishing the lost 'according to (i.e. in proportion to) their temporal works. (Here again, no infinite punishment for finite sins) Verse 3 plainly reveals that after punishment in the Lake of Fire, 'all' have bent their knee in submission unto the new birth and salvation, "And every knee shall bow, and every tongue shall confess that Jesus Christ is Lord to the glory of God the Father."

4. Lastly, damnationists plainly contradict/add to the Word of God by saying that 'Death for the unsaved, i.e. separation from God which is spiritual death in the Lake of Fire will continue for endless eternity after the white throne judgment. This means that Jesus failed in

defeating the last enemy which I Cor. 15:25-26 says is death. Thus a plain contradiction to these verses. "For He must reign till He hath put all enemies under His feet. The last enemy that shall be destroyed is ***death***."

So here again, the paramount question must be asked and answered. Just who is contradicting the Word of God? The damnationists who say 'death' for some will last for endless eternity, or the Christian Universalists *(no not the apostate Universalist Unitarians)* who teach that Jesus will finally defeat the last enemy, the enemy called death? As well they flagrantly and proudly continue contradicting Phil. 2:10-11 and Romans 14:11. "For as it is written as I live saith the Lord, every knee shall bow to me, and every tongue shall confess to God," and "That at the name of Jesus every knee shall bow, of things in heaven and things on earth and things under the earth, and that every tongue should confess that Jesus Christ is Lord to the glory of God the Father."

CHAPTER EIGHT

J.W. HANSON

Following is the bulk of Hanson's 1875 magnificent expose of the erroneously translated/misapplied Greek Word "Aionios into the English Bible as "endless/everlasting." While Hanson was dead on target in this matter, he certainly failed to properly understand the reality of a literal burning Hell, and the deserved punishment of those entering therein in the afterlife. He wrote:

> We deny that inspiration has named Hell as a place or condition of punishment in the spirit world. It seems a philosophical conclusion, and there are Scriptures that seem to many Universalists to teach that the future life is affected to a greater or lesser extent by human conduct here" (End quote.)

We are confident him being in (heaven) the afterlife now he understands how wrong he was.

J.W. Hanson's 1875 Comments on "Aionios"

Many sensible people will, with propriety, say, "Why all this labor to establish the meaning of one word?" And the author confesses that such a labor should be unnecessary. Men ought to refuse to credit such a doctrine as that of endless punishment on higher grounds than those of verbal definitions. Reverence, not to say respect, for God, the fact that he is the Father of mankind, should cause all to reject the doctrine of endless torment, though the weight of argument were a thousand fold to one in favor of the popular definition of this word. But there are many who disregard the moral argument against the doctrine, which is unanswerable; who crush under the noblest instincts of the heart and soul, which plead, trumpet-tongued, against that horrible nightmare of doubt and unbelief; who cling to the mere letter of the word which kills, and ignore the spirit which gives life; who insist that all the voices of reason and sentiment should be disregarded because the Bible declares the doctrine of endless punishment for sinners. It is for such that these facts have been gathered, and this essay written, that no shred nor vestige even of verbal probability should exist to mislead the mind, and so seem to sanction the doctrine that defames God and distresses man; that it might be seen that the letter and the spirit of the word agree, and are in perfect accord with the dictates of reason, the instincts of the heart, and the impulses of the soul, in rejecting the worst falsehood, the foulest of all brood of error, the darkest defamation of the dear God's character that ever yet was invented, the monstrous falsehood that represents him as consigning the souls he has created to his own image to interminable torment. The word under examination is the foundation stone of that evil structure.

"Aidios" an Important Word Considered

There is but one Greek word beside *aiónios* rendered everlasting, and applied to punishment, in the New Testament, and that is the word *aidios* found in Jude 6: "And the angels which kept not their first estate, but left their own habitation, he hath reserved in *everlasting* chains under darkness unto the judgement of the great day." This word is found in but one other place in the New Testament, viz. Rom. i:20: "For the invisible things of him from the creation of the world are clearly seen, being understood by the things that are made, even his *eternal* power and Godhead."

Now it is admitted that this word among the Greeks had the sense of eternal, and should be understood as having that meaning wherever found, unless by express limitation it is shorn of its proper meaning. It is further admitted that had *aidios* occurred where *aiónios* does, there would be no escape from the conclusion that the New Testament teaches Endless Punishment. It is further admitted that the word is here used in the exact sense of *aiónios*, as is seen in the succeeding verse: "Even as Sodom and Gomorrah, and the cities about them in like manner, giving themselves over to fornication, and going after strange flesh, are set forth for an example, suffering the vengeance of *eternal* fire." That is to say, the "*aidios*" chains in verse 6 are "*even as*" durable as the *aiónion* fire" in verse 7. Which word modifies the other?

1. The construction of the language shows that the latter word limits the former. The *aidios* chains are even as the *aiónion* fire. As if one should say "I have been infinitely troubled, I have been vexed for an hour," or "He is an endless talker, he can talk five hours on a stretch." Now while "infinitely" and "endless" convey the sense of unlimited, they are both limited by what follows, as *aidios*, eternal, is limited by *aiónios*, indefinitely long. That this is the correct exegesis is evident from still another limitation of the word. "The angels — he hath reserved in everlasting chains UNTO the judgement of the great day." Had Jude said that the angels are held in *aidios* chains, and stopped there, not limiting the word, we should not dare deny that he taught their eternal imprisonment. But when he limits the duration by *aiónion* and then expressly states that it is only *unto* a certain date, we understand that the imprisonment will terminate, even though we find applied to it a word that intrinsically signifies eternal duration, and that was used by the Greeks to convey the idea of eternity, and was attached to punishment by the Greek Jews of our Savior's times, to describe endless punishment, in which they were believers.

2. But observe, while this word *aidios* was in universal use among the Greek Jews of our Savior's day, to convey the idea of eternal duration, and was used by them to teach endless punishment, he never allowed himself to use it in connection with punishment, nor did

any of his disciples but one, and he but once, and then carefully and expressly limited its meaning. Can demonstration go further than this to show that Jesus carefully avoided the phraseology by which his contemporaries described the doctrine of endless punishment? He never employed it. What ground then is there for saying that he adopted the language of his day on this subject? Their language was *aidios timoria*, endless torment. His language was *aionion kolasin*, age-lasting correction. They described unending ruin, he described it as discipline, resulting in reformation.

But observe, while this word *aidios* was in universal use among the Greek Jews of our Savior's day, to convey the idea of eternal duration, and was used **by them** to teach endless punishment, he **never** allowed himself to use it in connection with punishment, nor did any of his disciples but one, and he but once, and then carefully and expressly limited its meaning. Can demonstration go further than this to show that Jesus carefully avoided the phraseology by which his contemporaries described the doctrine of endless punishment? He never employed it. What ground then is there for saying that he adopted the language of his day on this subject? Their language was *aidios timoria*, endless torment. His language was *aionion kolasin*, age-lasting correction. They described unending ruin, he discipline, resulting in reformation.

Authorities

The oldest lexicographer, *Hesychius*, (A. D. 400-600,) defines *aión* thus: *"The life of man, the time of life."* At this early date no theologian had yet imported into the word the meaning of endless duration. It retained only the sense it had in the classics, and in the Bible.

Theodoret (A. D. 300-400) "*Aión* is not any existing thing, but an interval denoting time, sometimes infinite when spoken of God, sometimes proportioned to the duration of the creation, and sometimes to the life of man."

John of Damascus (A. D. 750,) says, "1, The life of every man is called *aión*. ... 3, The whole duration or *life of this world* is called *aión*. 4, The life after the resurrection is called 'the *aión* to come."

The definition by *Phavorinus in the sixteenth century*, is extracted literally from the "Etymologicon Magnum" of the ninth or tenth century. This gives us the usage from the fourth to the sixteenth century, and shows us that, if the word meant endless at the time of Christ, it must have changed from limited duration in the classics, to unlimited duration, and then back again, at the dates above specified!

(Interesting it is that from the sixteenth century onward, the word has been defined as used to denote all lengths of duration from brief to endless.)

Phavorinus was compelled to notice an addition, which subsequently to the time of the famous Council of 544 had been grafted on the word. He says: "*Aión*, time, also life, also habit, or way of life. *Aión is also the eternal and endless* AS IT SEEMS TO THE THEOLOGIAN." Theologians had succeeded in using the word in the sense of endless, and Phavorinus was forced to recognize their usage of it and his phraseology shows conclusively enough that he attributed to theologians the authorship of that use of the word. Alluding to this definition, Rev. Ezra S. Goodwin, one of the ripest scholars and profoundest critics, says "Here I strongly suspect is the true secret brought to light of the origin of the sense of eternity in *aión*. *The theologian first thought he perceived it,* or else he placed it there. The theologian keeps it there, now. And the theologian will probably retain it there longer than any one else. Hence it is that those lexicographers who assign eternity as one of the meanings of *aión* uniformly appeal for proofs to either theological, Hebrew, or Rabbinical Greek, or some species of Greek subsequent to the age of the Seventy, if not subsequent to the age of the Apostles, so far a I can ascertain."

From the sixteenth century onward, the word has been defined (erroneously ed.) as used to denote all lengths of duration from brief to endless. We record here such definitions as we have found.

Rost: (German definitions) " *Aión,* duration, epoch, long time, eternity, memory of man, life-time, life, age of man. *Aiónios,* continual, always enduring, long continued, eternal."

Hedericus: "An age, eternity, an age a if always being; time of man's life in the memory of men, (wicked men, New Testament,) the spinal marrow. *Aiónios,* eternal, everlasting, continual."

Dr. Taylor, who wrote the Hebrew Bible three times with his own hand, says of *Olam,* (Greek *Aión*) it signifies a duration which is concealed, as being of an unknown or great length. "It signifies eternity, *not from the proper force of the word, but when the sense of the place or the nature of the subject require it, as God and his attributes.*"

Cruden: "The words eternal, everlasting, forever, are sometimes taken for a long time, and are not always to be understood strictly, for example, 'Thou shalt be our guide from this time forth, even forever,' that is, during our whole life."

Scarlett: "That *aiónion,* does not mean endless or eternal, may appear from considering that no adjective can have a greater force than the noun from which it is derived. If *aión* means age (which none either will or can deny) then *aiónion must mean age-lasting,* or duration through the age or ages to which the thing spoken or relates."

The True Idea

Undoubtedly the definition given by Schleusner is the accurate one, 'Duration determined by the subject to which it is applied.' Thus it only expresses the idea of endlessness when connected with what is endless, as God. The word great is an illustrative word. Great applied to a tree, or mountain, or man, denotes different degrees, all finite, but when referring to God, it has the sense of infinite. Infinity does not reside in the word great but it has that meaning when applied to God. It does not impart it to God, it derives it from him. So of aiónion; applied to Jonah's residence in the fish, it means seventy hours; to the priesthood of Aaron, it signifies several centuries; to the mountains, thousands of years; to the punishments of a merciful God, as long as is necessary to vindicate his law and reform his children; to God himself, eternity. What great is to size, aiónios is to duration. Human beings live from a few hours to a century; nations from a century to thousands of years; and worlds, for aught we know, from a few to many millions of years, and God is eternal. So that when we see the word applied to a human life it denotes somewhere from a few days to a hundred years; when it is applied to a nation, it denotes anywhere from a century to ten thousand years, more or less, and when to God it means endless. In other words it practically denotes indefinite duration, as we shall see when we meet the word in sacred and secular literature.

It does not seem to have been generally considered by students of this subject *that the thought of endless duration is comparatively a modern conception.* The ancients, at a time more recent than the dates of the Old Testament, had not yet cognized the idea of endless duration, so that passages containing the word applied to God do not mean that he is of eternal duration, but the idea was of indefinite and not unlimited duration. I introduce here a passage from Professor Knapp, or Knappius, the author of the best edition of the Greek Testament known, and one in use in many colleges and ranks as a scholar of rare erudition. He observes:

"The pure idea of eternity is too abstract to have been conceived in the early ages of the world, and accordingly *is not found expressed by any word in the ancient languages.* But as cultivation advanced and this idea became more distinctly developed, it became necessary in order to express it to invent new words in a new sense, as was done with the words *eternitas, perennitas,* etc. The Hebrews were destitute of any single word to express endless duration. To express a past eternity they said before the world was; a future, when the world shall be no more. . . . *The Hebrews and other ancient people have no one word for expressing the precise idea of eternity.*"

Can anything be clearer than this, that the lexicographers and critics unite in saying that limited duration is not only allowable, but that it is the prevailing signification of the word (aionios ed.)? Do they not agree that eternal duration is not in the word, and can only be imparted to it by the subject associated with it? Thus Lexicography declares that Limited Duration is the force of the word, duration to be determined by the subjected treated, if we allow Etymology and Lexicography to declare the verdict. And yet it is possible for these to be mistaken. Incredible, but still possible, that all students and critics of the word should have mistaken its character. But there is one tribunal that cannot mislead, and that is Usage.

In tracing the usage of the word, our sources of information will be (1) The Greek Classics, (2) The Septuagint Old Testament, (3) Those Jewish Greeks nearly contemporary with Christ, (4) The New Testament, and (5) The Early Christian Church.

I. The Classics Never Use Aion to Denote Eternity
It appears that the classic Greek writers, for more than six centuries before the Septuagint was written, used the word *aión* and its adjective, but never once in the sense of endless duration.

When, therefore, the Seventy translated the Hebrew Scriptures into Greek, what meaning must they have intended to give to these words? It is not possible, it is absolutely insupposable that they used them with any other meaning than that which they had held in the antecedent Greek literature. As the Hebrew word meaning horse, was rendered by a Greek word meaning horse, as each Hebrew word was exchanged for a Greek word denoting precisely the same thing, so the terms expressive of duration in Hebrew became Greek terms expressing a similar duration. The translators consistently render *olam* by *aión*, both denoting indefinite duration.

When, therefore, the Seventy translated the Hebrew Scriptures into Greek they must have used this word with the meaning it had whenever they had found it in the Greek classics. To accuse them of using it otherwise is to charge them with an intention to mislead and deceive.

Thus it appears that when the Seventy began their work of giving the world a Greek version of the Old Testament that should convey the exact sense of the Hebrew Bible, they must have used *aión* in the sense in which it then was used. *Endless duration is not the meaning the word had in Greek literature at that time. Therefore the word cannot have that meaning in the Old Testament Greek. Nothing can be plainer than that Greek Literature at the time the Hebrew Old Testament was rendered into the Greek Septuagint did not give to Aión the meaning of endless duration. Let us then consider the Old Testament Usage.*

2. The Old Testament Usage

We have concluded, *a priori*, that the Old Testament must employ the word *Aión* in the sense of indefinite duration, because that was the uniform meaning of the word in all antecedent and contemporaneous Greek literature. Otherwise the Old Testament would mislead its readers. We now proceed to show that such is the actual usage of the word in the Old Testament.

And let us pause a moment on the brink of our investigation to speak of the utter absurdity of the idea that God has hung the great topic of the immortal welfare of millions of souls on the meaning of a single equivocal word. Had he intended to teach endless punishment by one word, that word would have been so explicit and uniform and frequent that no mortal could mistake its meaning. It would have stood unique and peculiar among words. It would no more be found conveying a limited meaning than is the sacred name of Jehovah applied to any finite being. Instead of denoting every degree of duration, as it does, it never would have meant less than eternity. The thought that God has suspended the question of man's final destiny on such a word would seem too preposterous to be entertained by any reflecting mind, did we not know that such an idea is held by Christians. Endless duration is never expressed or implied in the Old Testament by Aión or any of its derivatives, except in instances where it acquires that meaning from the subject connected with it. How is it used? Let us adduce a few illustrations:

Examples

Gen. vi:4, There were giants in the earth in those days; and also after that, when the sons of God came in unto the daughters of men, and they bare children to them, the same became mighty men which were of old, (*aiónos*), men of renown." Gen. ix:12; God's covenant with Noah was "for *perpetual* (*aiónious*) generations." Gen. ix:16; The rainbow is the token of "the everlasting (*aiónion*) covenant" between God and "all flesh that is upon the earth." Gen. xiii:15; God gave the land to Abram and his seed "forever," (*aiónos*). Dr. T. Clowes says of this passage that it signifies the duration of human life, and he adds, "Let no one be surprised that we use the word *Olam (Aión)* in this limited sense. This is one of the most usual significations of the Hebrew *Olam* and the Greek *Aión*." In Isa. lviii:12; it is rendered "*old*" and "*foundations*," (*aiónioi and aiónia*). "And they that shall be of thee shall build the old waste places; thou shalt raise up the *foundations* of many generations; and thou shalt be called, The repairer of the breach." In Jer. xviii:15, 16, ancient and perpetual, (*aiónious and aiónion*). "Because my people hath forgotten me, they have burned incense to vanity, and they have caused them to stumble in their ways from the ancient paths, to walk in paths, in a way not cast up; to make their land desolate, and a perpetual hissing; every one that passeth thereby shall be astonished, and wag his head." Such instances may be cited to an indefinite extent. Ex. xv:18, "forever and ever and further," (*ton aióna, kai ep aióna, kai eti.*) Ex. xii:17, "And ye shall observe the feast of unleavened bread; for in this selfsame day have I brought your armies out of the land of Egypt, therefore shall ye observe this day in your generations by an ordinance forever," (*aiónion*). Numb. x:8, "And the sons of Aaron the priests, shall blow with the trumpets; and they shall be to you for an ordinance *forever* (*aiónion*) THROUGHOUT YOUR GENERATIONS." "Your generations," is here idiomatically given as the precise equivalent of "forever." Canaan was given as an "everlasting (*aiónion*) possession;" (Gen. xvii:8, xlviii:4; Lev. xxiv:8,9;) the hills are everlasting (*aiónioi;*) (Hab. iii:6;) the priesthood of Aaron (Ex. xl:15; Numb. xxv:13; Lev. xvi:34;) was to exist *forever*, and continue through *everlasting* duration; Solomon's temple was to last *forever*,

(1 Chron. xvii:12;) though it was long since ceased to be; slaves were to remain in bondage *forever*, (Lev. xxv:46;) though every fiftieth year all Hebrew servants were to be set at liberty, (Lev. xxv:10;) Jonah suffered an imprisonment behind the everlasting bars of earth, (Jon. ii:6;) the smoke of Idumea was to ascend *forever*, (Isa. xxxiv:10;) though it no longer rises, to the Jews God says (Jer. xxxii:40;) "and I will bring an *everlasting* reproach upon you, and a perpetual shame, which shall not be forgotten," and yet, after the fullness of the Gentiles shall come in, Israel will be restored. Rom. xi:25-6.

Not only in all these and multitudes of other cases does the word mean limited duration, but it is also used in the plural, thus debarring it from the sense of endless, as there can be but one eternity. In Dan. xii:3; the literal reading, if we allow the word to mean eternity, is to *eternities and farther*," (*eis tous aiónas kai eti.*) Micah iv:5, "We will walk in the name of the Lord our God to eternity, and beyond," *eis ton aióna kai epekeina.*

"Ps. cxlviii:4-6, "Praise him, ye heaven of heavens, and ye waters that be above the heavens. Let them praise the name of the LORD: for he commanded and they were created. He hath also established them for *ever and ever*: he hath made a decree which shall not pass. The sun and moon, the stars of light, and even the waters above the heavens are established *forever*," *eis ton aióna tou aiónos*, and yet the firmament is one day to become as a folded garment, and the orbs of heaven are to be no more. Endless duration is out of the question in these and many similar instances.

We have found the noun *Aión* three hundred and ninety-four times in the Old Testament, and the adjective *Aiónion* one hundred and ten times, and in all but four times it is the translation of *Olam*.

The Noun

Waiving the passages where it is applied to God, and where by accommodation it may be *allowed* to imply endlessness, just as great applied to God means infinity, let us consult the general usage: Eccl. i:10, "Is there anything whereof it may be said, See, this is new! It hath been already of *old time*, which was before us." Ps. xxv:6, "Remember, O LORD, thy tender mercies and thy loving kindnesses; for they have been *ever of old*," (*aiónos*). Ps. cxix:52, "I remembered thy judgments *of old*, O LORD; and have comforted myself."

Servants were declared to be bound forever, when all servants were emancipated every fifty years. Thus in Deut. xv:16,17, we read, "And it shall be, if he say unto thee, I will not go away from thee; because he loveth thee and thine house, because he is well with thee, then thou shalt take an awl, and thrust it through his ear unto the door, and he shall be thy servant forever." And yet we are told, Lev. xlv:10,39,41, "And ye shall hallow the fiftieth year, and proclaim liberty throughout all the land unto all the inhabitants thereof: it shall be a jubilee unto you; and ye shall return every man unto his possession, and ye shall return every man unto his family.

This forever at the utmost could only be forty-nine years and three hundred and sixty-four days and some odd hours. And certainly no one will ascribe endless duration to *aión* here!

Many passages allude to the earth as enduring forever — to the grave, as man's "long home," to God's existence, as "Forever, etc." Often the language is equivalent to "to the ages," or "from age to age," and sometimes eternal duration is predicated, *never* because the word compels it, but because the theme treated requires it.

The Adjective

is applied to God, Zion, and things intrinsically endless, and thus acquires from the connected subjects a meaning not inherent in the word, as in the following passages: Gen. xxi:33; Ex. iii:15; Job xxxiii:12; Isa. xl:28, li:11, liv:8, lv:3,13, lvi:5; lx:15,19, lxi:7,8; lxiii:12; Ezek. xxxvii:26; Dan. vii:27, ix:24, xii:2; Hab. iii:6; Ps. cxii:6, cxxx:8.

No one can read the Old Testament carefully and unbiassed, and fail to see that the word has a great range of meaning, bearing some such relation to duration as the word great does to size. We say God is infinite when we call him the Great God, not because great means infinite, but because God is infinite. The *aiónion* God is of eternal duration, but the *aiónion* smoke of Idumea has expired, and the *aiónion* hills will one day crumble, and all merely aionian things will cease to be.

While it is a rule of language that adjectives qualify and describe nouns, it is no less true that nouns modify adjectives. A tall flower, a tall dog, a tall man, and a tall tree are of different degrees of length, though the different nouns are described by the same adjective. The adjective is in each instance modified by its noun, just as the aionian bars that held Jonah three days, and the aionian priesthood of Aaron already ended, and the aionian hills yet to be destroyed, and aionian punishment, always proportioned to human guilt, are of different degrees of length. The adjective is modified and its length is determined by the noun with which it is connected.

The Subject Determines the Duration Described by the Adjective.
Prof. Tayler Lewis says, ">One generation passeth away, and another generation cometh; but the earth abideth forever.> This certainly indicates, not an endless eternity in the strictest sense of the word, but only a future of unlimited length. Ex. xxxi:16; <Wherefore the children of Israel shall keep the Sabbath, to observe the Sabbath throughout their generations, for a *perpetual* covenant.' *Olam* here would seem to be taken as a hyperbolical term for indefinite or unmeasured duration." Where the context demands it, as "I live forever," spoken of God, he says it means endless duration, for "*it is the subject to which it is applied that forces to this, and* NOT *any etymological necessity in the word itself.*" He adds that *Olam* and *Aion*, in the plural, ages, and ages of ages, demonstrate that neither of the words, of itself, denotes eternity. He admits that they are used to give an idea of eternity, but that applied to God and his kingdom, the ages are finite.

The End of Aionian Things
The smoke of Idumea no longer rises; the righteous do not possess the land promised them forever; some of the hills and mountains have

fallen, and the tooth of Time will one day gnaw the last of them into dust; the fire has expired from the Jewish altar; Jonah has escaped from his imprisonment; all these and numerous other eternal, everlasting things — things that were to last forever, and to which the various aionian words are applied — have now ended, and if these hundreds of instances must denote limited duration why should the few times in which punishments are spoken of have any other meaning? Even if endless duration were the intrinsic meaning of the word, all intelligent readers of the Bible would perceive that the word must be employed to denote limited duration in the passages above cited. And surely in the very few times in which it is connected with punishment it must have a similar meaning. For who administers this punishment? Not a monster, not an infinite devil, but a God of love and mercy, and the same common sense that would forbid us to give the word the meaning of endless duration, were that its literal meaning, when we see it applied to what we know has ended, would forbid us to give it that meaning when applied to the dealings of an Infinite Father with an erring and beloved child. But when we interpret it in the light of its lexicography, and general usage out of the Old Testament, and perceive that it only has the sense of endless when the subject <u>compels it</u> [emphasized by editor], as when referring to God, we see that it is a species of blasphemy to allow that it denotes endless duration when describing God's punishments.

Applied to Punishment

A few prominent instances illustrate the usage of the word connected with punishment. Ps. ix:5, Thou *hast* destroyed the wicked." How? The explanation follows: "Thou hast *put out their name forever and ever*," (*ton aiona, kai eis ton aióna tou aionos.*) His is not endless torment, but oblivion. Solomon elsewhere observes: Prov. x:7, "The name of the wicked shall rot," while David says, Ps. cxii:6, "The righteous shall be in everlasting remembrance." Ps. lxxviii:66, "He put them (his enemies) to a perpetual reproach." Is. xxxiii:14, "Who among us shall dwell with the devouring fire? Who among us shall dwell with everlasting burnings?" The prophet is here speaking of God's temporal judgments, represented by fire. "The earth mourneth; Lebanon is ashamed; the people shall be as the burnings of lime." Who will dwell in safety amid these fiery judgments? These aionian burnings? "He that walks uprightly." Earthly judgements among which the upright are to dwell in safety are here described and not endless fire hereafter. Jer. xvii:4, "Ye have kindled a fire in mine anger which shall burn forever." Where was this to be? The preceding verse informs us. "I will cause thee to serve thine enemies in a land which thou knowest not." Jer. xxiii:40, "I will bring an everlasting reproach upon you; and a perpetual shame which shall not be forgotten." The connection fully explains this verse 39, "I will utterly forget you, and I will forsake you, and the city that I gave you and your fathers. See Jer. xx:11. Mal. i:4, "The people against whom the Lord hath indignation forever." This is an announcement of God's judgements on Edom" "They shall build but I will throw down" and they shall call them the border of wickedness, and the people against whom the Lord hath indignation forever."

Out of more than five hundred occurrences of our disputed word in the Old Testament, more than four hundred denote limited duration, so that the great preponderance of Old Testament usage fully agrees with the Greek classics. The remaining instances follow the rule given by the best lexicographers, that it only means endless when it derives its meaning or endlessness from the nature of the subject with which it is connected.

3. Jewish Greek Usage

Those Jews who were contemporary with Christ, but who wrote in Greek, will teach us how they understood the word. Of course when Jesus used it, he employed it as they understood it.

Josephus applies the word to the imprisonment to which John the tyrant was condemned by the Romans; to the reputation of Herod; to the everlasting memorial erected in re-building the temple, already destroyed, when he wrote; to the everlasting worship in the temple which, in the same sentence he says was destroyed; and he styles the time between the promulgation of the law and his writing a long *aión*. To accuse him of attaching any other meaning than that of indefinite duration to the word, is to accuse him of stultifying himself. But when he writes to describe endless duration he employs other, and less equivocal terms. Alluding to the Pharisees, he says:

"They believe that the wicked are detained in an everlasting prison [*eirgmon aidion*] subject to eternal punishment" [*aidios timoria*]; and the Essenes [another Jewish sect] "allotted to bad souls a dark, tempestuous place, full of never-ceasing punishment [*timoria adialeipton*], where they suffer a deathless punishment, [*athanaton timorian*]."

It is true he sometimes applies *aiónion* to punishment, but this is not his usual custom, and he seems to have done this as one might use the word great to denote eternal duration, that is an indefinite term to describe infinity. But *aidion* and *athanaton* are his favorite terms. These are unequivocal. Were only *aiónion* used to define the Jewish idea of the duration of future punishment, we should have no proof that it was supposed to be endless.

Thus the Jews of our Savior's time avoided using the word *aiónion* to denote endless duration, for applied all through the Bible to temporary affairs, it would not teach it. If Jesus intended to teach the doctrine held by the Jews, would he not have used the terms they used? Assuredly; but he did not. He threatened age-lasting, or long-enduring discipline to the believers in endless punishment. *Aiónion* was his word while theirs was *aidion, adialeipton,* or *athanaton,* — thus rejecting their doctrines by not only not employing their phraseology, but by using always and only those words connected with punishment, that denote limited suffering.

And, still further to show that he had no sympathy with those cruel men who procured his death, Jesus said to his disciples: "Take heed and beware of the leaven [doctrine] of the Pharisees and the Sadducees" [believers in endless misery and believers in destruction].

Had *aiónion* been the strongest word, especially had it denoted endless duration, who does not see that it would have been in general use as applied to punishment, by the Jewish Greeks of nineteen centuries ago?

We thus have an unbroken chain of Lexicography, and Classic, Old Testament, and Contemporaneous Usage, all allowing to the word the meaning we claim for it. indefinite duration is the meaning generally given from the beginning down to the New Testament.

The New Testament Usage
Aion the Same in Both Testaments

Speaking to those who understood the Old Testament, Jesus and his Apostles employed such words as are used in that book, in the same sense in which they are there used. Not to do so would be to mislead their hearers unless they explained a change of meaning. There is certainly no proof that the word changed its meaning between the Old and New Testaments, accordingly we are under obligation to give it precisely the meaning in the New it had in the Old Testament. This we have seen to be indefinite duration.

Number of Times Aion is Found and How Translated.
The different forms of the word aion that occurs in the New Testament is one hundred and ninety-nine times, if I am not mistaken, the noun one hundred and twenty-eight, and the adjective seventy-one times.

Bruder's Concordance, latest edition, gives *aión* one hundred and twenty-six times, and *aiónios* seventy-two times in the New Testament, instead of the former ninety-four, and the latter sixty-six times, as Professor Stuart, following Knapp's Greek text, declares.

In our common translation the noun is rendered seventy-two times ever, twice eternal, thirty-six times world, seven times never, three times evermore, twice worlds, twice ages, once course, once world without end, and twice it is passed over without any word affixed as a translation of it. The adjective is rendered once ever, forty-two times eternal, three times world, twenty-five times everlasting, and once former ages.

1. The Kingdom of Christ

Ten times it is applied to the Kingdom of Christ. Luke i:33, "And he shall reign over the house of Jacob forever; and of his kingdom there shall be no end." See also i:55; Heb. vi:20; vii:17,21; I Pet. iv:11; II Pet. i:11; iii:18; Rev. i:6; xi:15

2. The Jewish Age

It is applied to the Jewish age more than thirty times: 1 Cor. x:11, "Now all these things happened unto them for ensamples; and they are written for our admonition, upon whom the ends of the *world* are come." Consult also Matt. xii:32; xiii:22,39,40,49; xxiv:3; xxviii:20; Mark iv:19; Luke i:70; xvi:8; xx:34; John ix:32; etc, etc. But the Jewish age ends with the setting up of the Kingdom of Christ. Therefore the word does not denote endless duration here.

3. The Plural Form

It is used in the plural in Eph. iii:21; "the *age* of the *ages.*" *tou aionos ton aionon.* Heb. i:2; xi:3, "By whom he made the worlds." "The worlds were framed by the word of God." There can be but one eternity. To say "By whom he made the eternities" would be to talk nonsense. Endless duration is not inculcated in these texts.

4. The Sense of Finite Duration

The word clearly teaches finite duration in such passages as Rom. xvi:25; II Cor. iv:17; II Tim. i:9; Philemon 15; Titus i:2. Read Rom. xvi:25: "Since the *world* (eternity?) began." II Cor. Iv:17. " Therefore *aiónion* does not here mean eternal.

5. Equivalent to Not

The word is used as equivalent to not in Matt. xxi:19; Mark xi:14; John xiii:8; I Cor. viii:13. "Peter said unto him 'thou shalt *never* wash my feet'," is a specimen of this use of the word. It only denotes eternal by accommodation.

6. Applied to God, etc.

It is applied to God, Christ, the Gospel, the good, the Resurrection world, etc., in which the sense of endless is allowable *because* "endless/eternal is imputed to the word Aion/aionios by the subject "God." Rom. i:25; ix:5; xi:36; xvi:27; Gal. i:5; Phil. iv:20; I Tim. i:17; II Tim. iv:18 etc, etc. (*It is important to remember here that* **'all people have eternal/endless life,** *i.e. all people live endlessly forever being made in the image of God so eternal life as in John 3:16 cannot refer to* **quantity or duration of life, but rather quality of life!** *Ed.*).

7. Life Eternal

It is applied to life, "Everlasting and Eternal Life." But this phrase does not so much denote the duration, as the quality of the Blessed Life. It seems to have the sense of durable in these passages: Matt. xix:16,29, xxv:46; Mark x:17,30; Luke x:25, xvi:9, xviii:18,30; John iii:15,16,36, iv:14,36, v:24,39, etc, etc.

Passages Denoting Limited Duration

Let us state more definitely several passages in which all will agree that the word cannot have the sense of endless. Matt. xxii:22, "The care of this *world*, and the deceitfulness of riches, choke the word," the cares of that age or "time." Verses 39, 40, 49, "The harvest is the end of the *world*," i.e. age, Jewish age, the same taught in Matt. xxiv, which some who heard Jesus speak were to live to see, and did see. Luke i:33, "And he (Jesus) shall reign over the house of Jacob *forever*, and of his kingdom there shall be no end." The meaning is, he shall reign to the ages (*eis tous aionas*). That long, indefinite duration is meant here, but limited, is evident from I Cor. xv:28, "And when all things shall be subdued unto him, then shall the Son also himself be subject unto him that put all things under him, that God may be all in all." "Now to the King *eternal* (of the ages) be glory for the *ages of the ages*." What is this but an asscription of the ages to the God of the ages? Eternity can only be meant here as ages piled on ages imply long, and possibly endless duration. "All the ages are God's; him let the ages glorify," is the full import of the words. Translate the words eternity, and what nonsense. "Now to the God of the eternities (!) Be glory for the eternities of the eternities (!!) Heb.

i:8, "The *age of the age.*" Eph. ii:7, "That in the *ages* (*aións*) to come he might show the exceeding riches of his grace." Here at least two *aións, eternities* are to come. Certainly one of them must end before the other begins. Eph. iii:21, "The generations of *the age of the ages.*" IITim. iv:18, "*The age of the ages.*" The same form of expression is in Heb. xiii:21; I Pet. iv:11; Rev. i:6, iv:9, v:13, vii:12, xiv:11, xv:7, xx:10. When we read that the smoke of their torment ascends *eis aiónas aiónon,* for ages of ages, we get the idea of long, indefinite, but limited duration, for as an age is limited, any number however great, must be limited. The moment we say the smoke of their torment goes up for eternities of eternities, we transform the sacred rhetoric in jargon. There is but one eternity, therefore as we read of more than one *aión,* it follows that *aión* cannot mean eternity. Again, I Cor. x:11, "Our admonition, on whom *the* ENDS of the *aións* (ages, *ta tele ton aiónon*) have come." That is, the close of the Mosaic and the beginning of the gospel age. How absurd to "ends of the eternities!"

Here the apostle had passed more than one, and entered, consequently, upon at least a third *aión.* Heb. ix:26, "Now at an end of the *ages.*" Matt. xviii:39, 40, xxiv:4, "**The conclusion of the age.**" **Eternity has no end. And to say ends of eternities is to talk nonsense. II Tim. ii:9, "Before the world began," i.e., before the aiónion times began. There was no beginning to eternity, therefore the adjective aiónion here has no such meaning as eternal. The fact that aión is said to end and begin, is a demonstration that it does not mean eternity.**

Absurdity of Popular Views

Translate the word eternity, and how absurd the Bible phraseology becomes! It represent the Bible as saying, "To whom be the glory *during* the ETERNITIES, even TO THE ETERNITIES." Gal. i:5. "Now all these things happened unto them, for ensamples, and they are written for our admonition upon whom *the ends* OF THE ETERNITIES are come." I Cor. x:11. "That in the ETERNITIES coming he might show the exceeding riches of his grace." Eph. ii.7. "The mystery which hath been hid *from the* ETERNITIES *and from the generations.*" Col. i:26. "But now once in the end of the *eternities,* hath he appeared to put away sin by the sacrifice of himself." Heb. ix:26. "The harvest *is the end of the eternity.*" Matt. xiii:39. "So shall it be *in the end of this eternity.*" Matt. xiii:40. "Tell us when shall these things be, and what the sign of thy coming, and of the end of the eternity." Matt. xxiv:4. But substitute "age" or "ages," and the sense of the Record is preserved. The words literally mean that age or epoch, but in this instance the immortal world is the subject that defines the word and gives it a unique meaning. So when the word refers to God, it denotes a different duration than when it applies to the Jewish dispensation. That in some of the places referred to the mooted word has the sense of endless, we do not question, but in all such cases it derives that meaning from the subject connected with it.

When the word "Aionios" refers to God, it denotes a different duration than when it applies to the Jewish dispensation. That in some of the places referred to the mooted word has the sense of endless, we do not question, but in all such cases it derives that meaning from the subject connected with it. Let us indicate its varied use. Matt. vi:13:2"Thine is the glory *forever,*" that is through the ages. Here eternity may be implied, but the phrase "forever" literally means "for the ages." Mark iv:19, same as Matt. i:22. Mark x:30. "But he shall receive a hundred fold now in this time, houses, and brethren, and sisters, and mothers, and children, and lands, with persecutions; and in the *world* to come *eternal* life." Literally, in the age to come the life of that age," *i.e.,* gospel, spiritual, Christian life. We have shown that the world to come denotes the Christian dispensation.-Mark xi:;14. "No man eat fruit of thee hereafter *for ever,*" that is "in the age," meaning the period of the tree's existence.-John xii:34. "The people answered him, We have heard out of the law that Christ abideth *for ever;*" (to the age). The Jews believed that their dispensation was to continue, and Messiah would remain as long as it would last.

"And I will pray the Father and he shall give you another Comforter, that he may abide with you *for ever,*" eis ton aióna, "unto the age," that is, accompany them into the coming or Christian era.-John vi:51. 58, "If any man eat of this bread he shall live *for ever;*" eis ton aióna, into the age, that is, enjoy the life of the world that is to come, the Christian life. Its duration is not described here at all.-John viii:35. "And the servant abideth not in the house *for ever*; (to the age,) *but* the Son abideth ever." The Jews are here told that their religion is to be superseded by the Christ only. They are to leave the house because slaves to sin, while the Son will remain to the age-permanently.-John viii:51, 52. "Verily, verily, I say unto you, If a man keep my saying he shall *never* see death. Then said the Jews unto him, Now we know that thou hast a devil. Abraham is dead, and the prophets; and thou sayest, If a man keep my saying he shall *never* taste of death." Moral, spiritual death is impossible to a man as long as he keeps the saying of Christ, is the full meaning of the words.

Occurrence of the Adjective Aionios

The adjective *aiónios* occurs sixty-six times in the New Testament, be we make it seventy-two times. Of these fifty-seven are used in relation to the happiness of the righteous; three in relation to God or his glory; four are of a miscellaneous nature; and seven relate to the subject of punishment. Now these fifty-seven denote indefinite duration, "everlasting life" being a life that may or may not — certainly does not always — endure forever.

Thus the great preponderance of usage in the New Testament is **indefinite duration**. But if the preponderance were against this usage, we ought, in order to vindicate God's character, to understand it in the sense of limited when describing a Father's punishment of his children.

Aion/Aionios Applied to Punishment

How many times does the word in all its forms describe punishment? Only fourteen times in thirteen passages in the entire New Testament, and these were uttered on ten occasions only. *The Noun*, Matt. xii:32, Mark iii:29, 2 Pet. ii:17, Jude 13, Rev. xiv:11, xix:3, xx:10. *The Adjective*, Matt. xviii:8, xxv:41, 46, Mark iii:29, 2 Thess. i:9, Jude 7, Heb. vi:2.

Now if God's punishments are limited, we can understand how this word should be used only fourteen times to define them. But if they are endless how can we explain the employment of this equivocal word only fourteen times in the entire New Testament? A doctrine that, if true, ought to crowd every sentence, frown in every line, only stated fourteen times, and that, too, by a word whose uniform meaning everywhere else is limited duration! The idea is preposterous. Such reticence is incredible. If the word denotes limited duration, the punishments threatened in the New Testament are like those that experience teaches follow transgression. But if it means endless, how can we account for the fact that neither Luke nor John records one instance of its use by the Savior, and Matthew but four, and Mark but two, and Paul employs it but twice in his ministry, while John and James in their epistles never allude to it? Such silence is an unanswerable refutation of all attempts to foist the meaning of endless into the word. "Everlasting fire" occurs only three times, "everlasting punishment" only once, and "eternal damnation" once only. Shall any one dare suppose that the New Testament reveals endless torment, and that out of one hundred and ninety-nine occurrences of the word *aion* it is applied to punishment so seldom, and that so many of those who wrote the New Testament never use the word at all? No. The New Testament usage agrees with the meaning in the Greek classics, and in the Old Testament. Does it not strike the candid mind as impossible that God should have concealed this doctrine for thousands of years, and that for forty centuries of revelation he continually employed to teach limited duration the identical word that he at length stretched into the signification of endless duration? The word means limited duration all through the Old Testament; it never had the meaning of endless duration among those who spoke the language, (as we have demonstrated,) but Jesus announced the doctrine of endless punishment, and selected as the Greek word to convey his meaning the very word that in the Classics and the Septuagint never contained any such thought, when there were several words in the copious Greek tongue that unequivocally conveyed the idea of interminable duration! Even if Matthew wrote in Hebrew or in Syro-Chaldaic, he gave a Greek version of his gospel, and in that rejected every word that carries the meaning of endlessness, and appropriated the one which taught nothing of the kind. **If this were the blunder of an incompetent translator,** or the imperfect record of a reckless scribe, we could understand it, but to say that the inspired pen of the evangelist has deliberately or carelessly jeopardized the immortal welfare of countless millions by employing a word to teach the doctrine of ceaseless woe that up to that very hour taught only limited duration, is to make a declaration that carries its own refutation.

Matthew 25:46 the great proof text of eternal punishment

These shall go away into everlasting punishment, and the righteous into life eternal." We shall endeavor to establish the following points against the erroneous view of this Scripture. 1. The punishment is not for unbelief, but for not benefitting the needy. 2. The general antecedent usage of the word denoting duration here, in the Classics and in the Old Testament, proves that the duration is limited. 3. One object of punishment being to improve the punished, the punishment here *must* be limited; 4. The events here described took place in this world, and must therefore be of limited duration. 5. **The Greek word kolasin, rendered punishment, should be rendered chastisement, as reformation is implied in its meaning.**

Practical benevolence is the virtue whose reward is here announced, and unkindness is the vice whose punishment is here threatened, and not faith and unbelief, on which heaven and Hell are popularly predicated. Matt. xxv:34-45. "Then shall the King say unto them on his right hand, Come, ye blessed of my Father, inherit the kingdom prepared for you from the foundation of the world: For I was a hungered, and ye game me meat: I was thirsty, and ye gave me drink: I was a stranger and ye took me in: Naked, and ye clothed me; I was sick, and ye visited me: I was in prison, and ye came unto me. Then shall the righteous answer him, saying, Lord, when saw we thee a hungered, and fed thee? or thirsty, and gave thee drink? When saw we thee a stranger and took thee in? or naked, and clothed thee? Or when saw we thee sick, or in prison, and came unto thee? And the King shall answer and say unto them, Verily I say unto you, *Inasmuch as ye have done it unto one of the least of these my brethren, ye have done it unto me.* Then shall he say unto them on the left hand, Depart from me, ye cursed, into everlasting fire, prepared for the devil and his angels: For I was a hungered, and ye gave me no meat: I was thirsty, and ye gave me no drink: I was a stranger, and ye took me not in: naked and ye clothed me not: sick, and in prison, and ye visited me not. Then shall they also answer him, saying, Lord, when saw we thee a hungered, or athirst, or a stranger, or naked, or sick, or in prison, and did not minister unto thee? Then shall he answer them, saying, Verily I say unto you, *Inasmuch as ye did it not to one of the least of these, ye did it not to me.*"

If cruelty to the poor —neglect of them even,—constitutes rejection of Christ —as is plainly taught here —and all who are guilty are to suffer endless torment "who then can be saved?" the single consideration that works, and not faith are here made the test of discipleship, cuts away the foundation of the popular view of this text.

The Word Aionion Denotes Limited Duration

This appears in Classic and Old Testament usage. It is impossible that Jesus should have used the word rendered everlasting in a different sense than we have shown to have been its meaning in antecedent literature.

The Word Translated Punishment Means Improvement

The word is *Kolasin*. It is thus authoritatively defined: *Greenfield*, "Chastisement, punishment." *Hedericus*, "The trimming of the luzuriant branches of a tree or vine to improve it and make it fruitful." *Donnegan*, "The act of clipping or pruning —restriction, restraint, reproof, check, chastisement." *Grotius*, "The kind of punishment which tends to the improvement of the criminal, is what the Greek philosophers called *kolasis* or chastisement." *Liddell*, "Pruning, checking, punishment, chastisement, correction." *Max Muller*, "Do we want to know what was uppermost in the minds of those who formed the word for punishment, the Latin *pæna* or *punio*, to punish, the root *pu* in Sanscrit, which means to *cleanse*, to purify, tells us that the Latin derivation was originally formed, not to express mere striking or torture, but cleansing, correcting, delivering from the stain of sin." That it had this meaning in Greek

The Death of Endless Damnation

usage we cite Plato: "For the natural or accidental evils of others, no one gets angry, or admonishes, or teaches or punishes (kolazei) them, but we pity those afflicted with such misfortunes. ** For if, O Socrates, you will consider what is the design of punishing (kolazein) the wicked, this of itself will show you that men think virtue something that may be acquired; for no one punishes (*kolazei*) the wicked, looking to the past only, simply for the wrong he has done,—that is, *no one does this thing who does not act* LIKE A WILD BEAST, *desiring only revenge, without thought* —hence he who seeks to punish (*kolazein*) *with reason*, does not punish for the sake of the past wrong deed, ** but for the sake of the future, that neither the man himself who is punished, may do wrong again, nor any other who has seen him chastised. And he who entertains this thought, must believe that virtue may be taught, and *he punishes* (*kolazei*) *for the purpose of deterring from wickedness.*" Like many other words this is not always used in its exact and full sense. The apocrypha employs it as the synonym of suffering, regardless of reformation. See Wis. iii:11, xvi:1; I Mac. vii:7. See also Josephus. It is found but four times in the New Testament. Acts iv:21, the Jews let John and Peter go, "finding nothing further how they might punish them" (*kolazo*). Did they not aim to reform them? Was not their punishment to cause them to return to the Jewish fold? From their standpoint the word was certainly used to convey the idea of reformation. 1 John iv:18. "Fear hath *torment.*" Here the word "torment" should be *restraint*. It is thus translated in the Emphatic Diaglot. The idea is, if we have perfect love we do not fear God, but if we fear we are restrained from loving him. "Fear hath restraint." The word is used here with but one of its meanings. In 2 Peter ii:9, the apostle uses the word as our Lord did: the unjust are reserved unto the day of judgement to be punished (*kolazomenous*). This accords exactly with the lexicography of the word, and the general usage in the Bible and in Greek literature agrees with the meaning given by the lexicographers. Now, though the word rendered punishment is sometimes used to signify suffering alone, by Josephus and others, surely Divine inspiration will use it in its exact sense. We must therefore be certain that in the New Testament, when used by Jesus to designate divine punishment, it is generally used with its full meaning. The lexicographers and Plato, above, show us what that is, suffering, restraint, followed by correction, improvement.

From this meaning of the word, torment is by no means excluded. God does indeed torment his children when they go astray. He is a «consuming fire,» and burns with terrible severity towards us when we sin, but it is not because he hates but because he loves us. He is a refiner›s fire tormenting the immortal gold of humanity in the crucible of punishment, until the dross of sin is purged away. Mal. ii:2,3, «But who may abide the day of his coming? and who shall stand when he appeareth? for he is like a *refiner's fire* and like fuller's soap. And he shall sit as a refiner and purifier of silver: and he shall *purify* the sons of Levi, and purge them as gold or silver, that t*hey may offer unto the Lord an offering in righteousness.*" Therefore *kolasis* is just the word to describe his punishments. They do for the soul what pruning does for the tree, what the crucible of the refiner does for the silver ore.

Even if *aiónion* and *kolasis* were both of doubtful signification, and were we only uncertain as to their meaning we ought to *give God the benefit of the doubt* and understand the word in a way to honor him, that is, in a limited sense, but when all but universal usage ascribes to *aiónion* limited duration, and the word *kolasin* is declared by all authorities to mean pruning, discipline, it is astonishing that a Christian teacher should be found to *imagine* that when both words are together, they can mean anything else than temporary punishment ending in reformation, especially in a discourse in which it is expressly declared that the complete fulfillment was in this life, and within a generation of the time when the prediction was uttered.

Therefore, (1) the fulfillment of the language in this life, (2) the meaning of *aiónion*, (3) and the meaning of *kolasis*, demonstrate that the penalty threatened in Matt. xxv:46, is a limited one. It is a threefold cord that human skill cannot break. Prof. Tayler Lewis thus translates Matt. xxv:46. "These shall go away into the punishment (the restraint, imprisonment,) of the world to come, and those into the life of the world to come." And he says *"that is all that we can etymologically or exegetically make of the word in this passage."*

Hence, also, the *zoen aiónion* (life eternal) is not endless, but is a condition resulting from a good character. The intent of the phrase is not to teach immortal happiness, nor does *kolasin aiónion* indicate endless punishment. Both phrases, regardless of duration refer to the limited results wronging or blessing others, extending possibly through Messiah's reign until "the end" (1 Cor. xv.). Both describe consequences of conduct to befall those consequences antedate the immortal state.

A Common Objection Noticed

"Then eternal life is not endless, for the same Greek adjective qualifies life and punishment." This does not follow, for the word is used in Greek in different senses in the same sentence; as Hab. iii:6. "And the *everlasting* mountains were scattered —his ways are *everlasting.*" Suppose we apply the popular argument here. The mountains and God must be of equal duration, for the same word is applied to both. Both are temporal or both are endless. But the mountains are expressly stated to be temporal —they "were scattered," —therefore God is not eternal. Or God is eternal and therefore the mountains must be. But they cannot be, for they were scattered. The argument does not hold water. The *aiónion* mountains are all to be destroyed. Hence *the word may denote both limited and unlimited duration in the same passage, the different meanings to be determined by the subject treated.*

But it may be said that this phrase "everlasting" or "eternal life" does not usually denote endless existence, but the life of the gospel, spiritual life, the Christian life, regardless of its duration. In more than fifty of the seventy-two times that the adjective occurs in the New Testament, it describes life. What is eternal life? Let the Scriptures answer. John iii:36, "He that believeth on the Son hath everlasting life." John v:24, "He that believeth on him that sent me hath everlasting life, and shall not come into condemnation, but IS PASSED from death unto life." John vi:47, "He that believeth on me hath everlasting life." So verse

54. John xvii:3, "THIS IS LIFE ETERNAL *to know thee,* the only true God, and Jesus Christ whom thou hast sent." Eternal life is the life of the gospel. Its duration depends on the possessor's fidelity. It is no less the *aiónion* life, if one abandon it in a month after acquiring it. It consists in knowing, loving and serving God. It is the Christian life, regardless of its duration. How often the good fall from grace. Believing, they have the *aiónion* life, but they lose it by apostasy. Notoriously it is not, in thousands of cases, endless. The life is of an indefinite length, so that the usage of the adjective in the New Testament is altogether in favor of giving the word the sense of limited duration. Hence Jesus does not say "he that believeth shall enjoy endless happiness," but "he *hath* everlasting life," and "*is passed* from death unto life."

It scarcely need here be proved that the *aiónion* life can be acquired and lost. Heb. vi:4, "For it is impossible for those who were once enlightened, and have tasted of the heavenly gift, and were made partakers of the holy Ghost, and have tasted the good word of God, and the powers of the world to come, if they shall fall away, to renew them again unto repentance: seeing they crucify to themselves the Son of God afresh, and put him to an open shame." A life that can thus be lost is not intrinsically endless.

That the adjective is thus consistently used to denote indefinite duration will appear from several illustrations, some of which we have already given. 2 Cor. iv:17, "A far more exceeding and *eternal* weight of glory," or, as the original reads, "exceeding an *aiónion* weight of glory excessively." Now eternal, endless cannot be exceeded, but *aiónion* can be, therefore *aiónion* is not eternal. Again, Rev. xiv:6, "The *everlasting* gospel." The gospel is good news. When all shall have learned its truths it will no longer be news. There will be no such thing as gospel extant. Faith will be fruition, hope lost in sight, and the *aiónion* gospel, like the *aiónion* covenant of the elder dispensation, will be abrogated, not destroyed, but fulfilled and passed away. Again, 2 Pet. i:11, "The *everlasting* kingdom of our Lord and Savior Jesus Christ." This kingdom is to be dissolved. Jesus is to surrender his dominion. 1 Cor. xv:24, "Then cometh the end, when he shall have delivered up the kingdom to God even the Father," etc. The everlasting kingdom of Christ will end.

The word may mean endless when applied to life, and not when applied to punishment, even in the same sentence, though we think duration is not considered so much as the intensity of joy or the sorrow in either case.

Biblical Words Denoting Endless Duration

But the Blessed Life has not been left dependent on so equivocal a word. The soul›s immortal and happy existence is taught in the New Testament, by words that in the Bible are never applied to anything that is of limited duration. They are applied to God and the soul's happy existence only. These words are *akataluton*, imperishable; *amarantos* and *amarantinos*, unfading; *aphtharto*, immortal, incorruptible; and *athanasian*, immortality. Let us quote some of the passages in which these words occur:

Heb. vii:15, 16, "And it is yet far more evident: for that after the similitude of Melchizedek there ariseth another priest, who is made, not after the law of a carnal commandment, but after the power of an *endless* (*akatalutos*, imperishable) life." 1 Pet. i:3, 4, "Blessed be the God and Father of our Lord Jesus Christ, which according to his abundant mercy, hath begotten us again unto a lively hope by the resurrection of Jesus Christ from the dead, to an inheritance *incorruptible*, (*aphtharton*,) and undefiled, and that *fadeth not* (*amaranton*) away." 1 Pet. v:4, "And when the chief Shepherd shall appear, ye shall receive a crown of glory that *fadeth not* (*amarantinos*) away." 1 Tim. i:17, "Now unto the King eternal, *immortal*, (*aphtharto*,) invisible, the only wise god, be honor and glory forever and ever, Amen." Rom. i:23, "And changed the glory of the *incorruptible* God into an image made like to corruptible man." 1 Cor. ix:25, "Now they do it to obtain a corruptible crown; but we an *incorruptible*." 1 Cor. xv:51-54, "Behold, I shew you a mystery; We shall not all sleep, but we shall be changed, in a moment, in the twinkling of an eye, at the last trump: for the trumpet shall sound, and the dead shall be raised *incorruptible*, (*aphthartoi*,) and we shall be changed. For this corruptible must put on *incorruption*, (*aphtharsian*,) and this mortal must put on *immortality* (*athanasian*).

So when this corruptible shall have put on *incorruption*, (*aphtharsian*,) and this mortal shall have put on *immortality*, (*athanasian*,) then shall be brought to pass the saying that is written, Death is swallowed up in victory." Rom. ii:7, "To them who by patient continuance in well doing seek for glory and honor and *immortality*, (*aphtharsia*,) eternal life." 1 Cor. xv:42, "So also is the resurrection of the dead. It is sown in corruption, it is raised in *incorruption* (*aphtharsia*)." See also verse 50, 2 Tim i:10, "Who brought life and *immortality* (*aphtharsian*) to light, through the gospel." 1 Tim. vi:16, "Who only hath *immortality* (*athanasian*)."

Now these words are applied to God and the souls happiness. They are words that in the Bible are never applied to punishment, or to anything perishable. They would have been affixed to punishment had the Bible intended to teach endless punishment. And certainly they show the error of those who declare that the indefinite word *aiónion* is all the word, or the strongest word in the Bible declarative of the endlessness of the life beyond the grave. A little more study of the subject would prevent such reckless statements and would show that the happy, endless life does not depend at all on the pet word of the partialist critics.

Did Jesus Employ the Popular Phraseology?

It is often remarked that as, according to Josephus, the Jews in our Savior's times believed in endless punishment, Jesus must have taught the same doctrine, as "he employed the terms the Jews used." But this is not true, as we have shown. Christ and his apostles did not employ the phraseology that the Jews used to describe this doctrine. As we have shown Philo used *athanaton* and *ateleuteton* meaning immortal, and interminable. He says *zoe apothneskonta aeikai tropon tina thanaton athanaton upomeinon kai ateleuteton*, "to live always dying, and to undergo an immortal and interminable death." He also employs *aidion*, but not *aiónion*. Josephus says: "They, the Pharisees, believe 'the souls of the bad are allotted *aidios eirgmos, to an eternal prison,* and punished with *adialeiptos timoria, eternal retribution.*" In describing the doctrine of the Essenes, Josephus says they believe "the souls of the bad are sent to a dark and tempestuous cavern, full of *adialeiptos timoria, incessant pun-*

ishment." But the phraseology of Jesus and the apostles *olethros aiónios* or *aióniou kriseos* "eternal chastisement," or "eternal condemnation." The Jews contemporary with Jesus call retribution *aidios*, or *adialeiptos timoria*, while the Savior calls it *aiónios krisis*, or *kolasis aiónios*, and the apostles *olethros aiónios, everlasting destruction*; and *puros aiónios, eternal fire*. Had Jesus and his apostles used the terms employed by the Jews to whom they spake, we should be compelled to admit that they taught the popular doctrine. See this point further elucidated at the end of this volume on the word *Aidios*. "To live always dying and undergo an endless death," is the language of "orthodox" pulpits, and of the Greek Jews, but our Savior and his apostles carefully avoided such horrible blasphemy as to charge God with being the author of so diabolical a cruelty.

Says a learned scholar: "*Aiónios* is a word of sparing occurrence among ancient classical Greek writers; nor is it by any means the common term employed by them to signify *eternal*. On the contrary, they much more frequently make use of *aidios, aei ón*, or some similar mode of speech, for this purpose.... To me it appears that the Seventy, by choosing *aiónios* to represent *olam*, testify that they did not understand the Hebrew word to signify *eternal*. Had they so understood it, they would certainly have translated it by some more decisive word; some term, which, like *aidios* is more commonly employed in Greek, to signify that which has neither beginning no end."

"Never Forgiveness —Eternal Damnation"
Matt. xii:32. "Whosoever speaketh against the Holy Ghost, it shall not be forgiven him, neither in this *world*, neither in the world to come." Parallel passages: Mark iii:29. "But he that shall blaspheme against the Holy Ghost hath never (*aióna*) forgiveness, but is in danger of eternal (*aiónion*) damnation." Luke xii:10. "And whosoever shall speak a word against the Son of man, it shall be forgiven him; but unto him that blasphemeth against the Holy Ghost it shall not be forgiven." Literally, "neither in this age nor the coming," that is, neither in the Mosaic, nor the Christian age or dispensation. but then, these ages will both end, and in the dispensation of the fullness of times, or ages, all are to be redeemed,

(Eph. i:10.) Mark iii:29 is the same as Matt. xii:32. The Greek differs slightly, and is rendered literally, "has not forgiveness to the age, but is liable to age-lasting judgment." The thought of the Savior is, that those who should attribute his good deeds to an evil spirit would be so hardened that his religion would have difficulty in affecting them. Endless damnation is not thought of, and cannot be extorted from the language.

In the New Testament the "end of the age," and "ages' is a common expression, referring to what has now passed. See Col. i:26, Heb. ix:26, Matt. xiii:39, 40, 49, xxiv:3. Says Locke "The nation of the Jews were the kingdom and people of God whilst the law stood. And this kingdom of God, under the Mosaic constitution was called *aión outos*, this age, or as it is commonly translated, this world. But the kingdom of God was to be under the Messiah, wherein the economy and constitution of the Jewish church, and the nation itself, that in opposition to Christ adhered to it, was to be laid aside, is in the New Testament called *aión mellon*, the world or age to come."

Another writer adds: "Why the times under the law, were called *kronoi aiónioi*, we may find reason in their jubilees, which were *aiónes*, "secula," or "ages," by which all the time under the law, was measured; and so *kronoi aiónioi*; is used, 2 Tim. i:9. Tit. i:2. And so *aiónes* are put for the times of the law, or the jubilees, Luke i:70, Acts iii:21, 1 Cor. ii:7, x:11, Eph. iii:9, Col. i:26, Heb. ix:26. And so God is called the rock of *aiónon*, of ages, Isa. xxvi:4, in the same sense that he is called the rock of Israel, Isa. xxx:29, i. e. the strength and support of the Jewish state;— for it is of the Jews the prophet here speaks. So Exod. xxi:6, *eis ton aióna* signifies not as we translate it, "forever," but "to the jubilee;" which will appear if we compare Lev. xxv:39-41, and Exod. xxi:2."

Pearce in his commentary, says "Rather, neither in this age, nor in the age to come: i. e., neither in this age when the law of Moses subsists, nor in that also, when the kingdom of heaven, which is at hand, shall succeed to it. The Greek *aión*, seems to signify age here, as it often does in the New Testament, (see chap. xiii:40; xxiv:3; Col. i:26; Eph. iii:5, 21.)

and according to its most proper signification. If this be so, then this age means the Jewish one, the age while their law subsisted and was in force; and the age to come (see Heb. vi:5; Eph. ii:7.) means that under the Christian dispensation."

Wakefield observes: "Age, *aióni; i. e.*, the Jewish dispensation which was then in being, or the Christian, which was going to be."

Clarke: "Though I follow the common translation, (Matt. xii:31, 32.) yet I am fully satisfied the meaning of the words is, neither in this dispensation, viz., the Jewish, nor in that which is to come, the Christian. *Olam ha-bo,* the world to come, is a constant phrase for the times of the Messiah, in the Jewish writers." See also Hammond, Rosenmuller, etc. Take Hebrews ix:26, as an example. "For then must he (Christ) often have suffered since the foundation of the world (*kosmos,* literal world) but now once *in the end of the world* (*aiónon,* age) hath he appeared to put away sin by the sacrifice of himself." What world was at its end when Christ appeared? Indubitably the Jewish age. The world or age to come (*aión*) must be the Christian dispensation, as in 1 Cor. x:11, where Paul says that upon him and his contemporaries "the ends of the world are come."

These passages state in strong language the heinous nature of the sin referred to. The age or world to come is not beyond the grave, but it is the Christian dispensation. It had a beginning eighteen centuries ago, and it will end when Jesus delivers the kingdom to God, the Father. (1 Cor. xv).

Everlasting Fire

Matt. xviii:8. "Wherefore if thy hand or thy foot offend thee, cut them off, and cast them from thee: it is better for thee to enter into life halt or maimed, rather than having two hands, or two feet, to be cast into everlasting fire." Matt. xxv:41 uses the same phraseology. "The *everlasting fire,* prepared for the Devil and his angels." Also Jude 7. "Even as Sodom and Gomorrah, and the cities about them in like manner, giving themselves over to fornication, and going after strange flesh, are set forth for an example, suffering the vengeance of eternal fire."

It is better to enter into the Christian life maimed, that is deprived of some social advantage comparable to an eye, foot, or hand, than to keep all worldly advantages, and suffer the penalty of rejecting Christ, typified by fire, is the meaning of Matt. xviii:8; and Jude 7 teaches that Sodom and Gomorrah are an example of eternal fire. But that fire has expired. That the fire referred to is not endless is shown by the use of the term in the Bible. "God is a consuming fire," (Heb. xii:29,) but it is a "Refiner's fire." (Mal. iii:2-3.) It consumes the evil and refines away the dross of error and sin. This corroborates the meaning we have shown to belong to the word expressive of the fire's duration. But whatever may be the purpose of the fire, it is not endless, it is *aiónian*. Benson well says: "The fire which consumed Sodom, &c., might be called eternal, as it burned till it had utterly consumed them, beyond the possibility of their being inhabited or rebuilt. But the word will have a yet more emphatical meaning, if (as several authors affirm) that fire continued to burn a long while."

Everlasting Destruction

2 Thess. i:9. "Who shall be punished with *everlasting* destruction from the presence of the Lord, and from the glory of his power."

Everlasting destruction, *olethron aiónion*, does not signify remediless ruin, but long banishment from God's presence. This is what sin does for the soul. *Olethros* is not annihilation, but desolation. It is found but four times in the New Testament. 1 Thess. v:3, 1 Cor. v:5, 1 Tim. vi:9. The passage in 1 Cor. shows us how it is used: "*deliver such a one unto Satan for the destruction of the flesh, that the spirit may be saved in the day of the Lord Jesus.*" The destruction here is not final —it is conditional to the saving of the spirit. Everlasting destruction is equivalent to prolonged desolation.

The Blackness of Darkness Forever

2 Pet. ii:17. "These are wells without water, clouds that are carried with a tempest; to whom the mist of darkness is reserved forever." Jude 13. "Raging waves of the sea, foaming out their own shame; wandering stars, to whom is reserved the blackness of darkness forever." "To

whom is always reserved the blackness of darkness," would be a correct paraphrase of this language. Those referred to are trees that bear no fruit, clouds that yield no water, foaming waves, stars that give no light. Endless duration was not thought of by either Peter or Jude. Indefinite duration, ages, is the utmost meaning of *eis aióna*, which is spurious in a 2 Peter ii:17, but genuine in Jude 13. The literal meaning is, for an age. Eternity cannot be extorted from the phrase.

Forever and Ever
Heb. vi:2. "The doctrine of the aionian, (*aiónion*) judgment." We make no special explanation of this passage. Whether the judgment of that age or the age to come, the Christian is meant, matters not. "The judgement of the age" is the full force of the phrase aionion judgment. Rev. xiv:11. "And the smoke of their torment ascendeth up *forever and ever*: and they have no rest day nor night, who worship the beast and his image, and whosoever receiveth the mark of his name." xix:3. "And her smoke rose up *forever and ever.*" xx:10. "And the devil that deceived them was cast into the lake of fire and brimstone, where the beast and the false prophet *are*, and shall be tormented day and night *forever and ever.*"

Attempts have been made to show that these [are - editor] reduplications, if no other forms of the word convey the idea of eternity. But the literal meaning of *aiónas aiónon*, in the first text above, is ages of ages, and of *tous aiónas ton aiónon*, in the other two, is the ages of the ages. It is perfectly manifest to the commonest mind that if one age is limited, no number can be unlimited. Ages of ages is an intense expression of long duration, and if the word *aión* should be eternity, "eternities of eternities" ought to be the translation, an expression too absurd to require comment. If *aión* means eternity, any number of reduplications would weaken it. But while ages of ages is proper enough, eternity of eternities would be ridiculous. On this phraseology Sir Isaac Newton says: "The ascending of the smoke of any burning thing *forever and ever*, is put for the continuation of a conquered people under the misery of perpetual subjection and slavery." The thought of eternal duration was not in the mind of Jesus or his apostles in any of these texts, but long duration, to be determined by the subject.

The Spirits in Prison

An illuminating side-light is thrown on this subject by commentators on 1 Pet. iii:18-20, in which Christ is said to have "preached unto the spirits in prison." Alford says our Lord "did preach salvation in fact, to the disembodied spirits, etc." Tayler Lewis "There was a work of Christ in Hades, he makes proclamation '*ekeruxen*' in Hades to those who are there in ward. This interpretation, which was almost universally adopted by the early Christian church, etc." Professor Huidekoper. "In the second and third centuries every branch and division of Christians believed that Christ preached to the departed." Dietelmairsays this doctrine "*in omni coetu Christiano creditum.*" Why preach salvation to souls whose doom was fixed for eternity? And how could Christians believe in that doctrine and at the same time give the aionian words the meaning of eternal duration?

Aion Means an Eon, Æon or Age

It is a pity that the noun (*aión*) has not always been rendered by the English word eon, or æon, and the adjective by eonian or aionion; then all confusion would have been avoided. Webster's Unabridged, defines it as meaning a space or period of time, an era, epoch, dispensation, or cycle, etc. He also gives it the sense of eternity, but no one could have misunderstood, had it been thus rendered. Suppose our translation read "What shall be the sign of thy coming, and of the end of the æon?" "The smoke of their torment shall ascend for æons of æons." "These shall go away into aionian chastisement, etc." The idea of eternity would not be found in the noun, nor of endless duration in the adjective, and the New Testament would be read as its authors intended.

Let the reader now recall the usage as we have presented it, and then reflect that all forms of the word are applied to punishment only fourteen times in the entire New Testament, and ask himself the question, Is it possible that so momentous a doctrine as this is only stated so small a number of times in divine revelation? If it has the sense of limited duration, this is consistent enough, for then it will be classed with the other terms that describe the Divine judgments. The fact that so many of those who speak or write never employ it at all, and that all of them together use it but fourteen times is a demonstration that He who has made known his will, and who would of all things have revealed so appalling a fate as endless woe, if he had it in preparation, has no such doom in store for immortal souls.

We now pass to corroborate these positions by consulting the views of those in the first centuries of the Christian Church, who obtained their opinions directly or indirectly from the apostles themselves.

Tayler Lewis

Prof. Tayler Lewis in the course of learned disquisitions on the meaning of the Olamic and Aionian words of the Bible, refers to the oldest version of the New Testament, the Syriac, or the Peshito, and tells us how these words are rendered in this first form of the New Testament: «So is it ever in the old Syriac version where the one rendering is still more unmistakably clear. These shall go into the pain of the *Olam* (*aión*) (the world to come), and these to the life of the *Olam* (*aión*) (the world to come)." He refers to Matt. xix:16; Mark x:17; Luke xviii:18; John iii:15; Acts xiii:46; 1 Tim. vi:12, in which *aiónios* is rendered *belonging to the olam*, or world to come.*Eternal life*, in our version, the words in Matt. xxv:46, are rendered in the Peshito "the life of the world to come."

We quote this not to endorse, but to show that one of the best of modern critics testifies that the earliest New Testament version did not employ endless as the meaning of the word. Of Prof. Lewis Dr. Beecher writes, "We are not to suppose that so eminent an Orthodox divine says these things in support of Universalism, a system which he decidedly and earnestly rejects."

The Apostles Creed

The Apostles' Creed is the earliest Christian formula. The idea of endless torment is not hinted. "I believe in God, the Father Almighty; and in Jesus Christ, his only begotten Son, our Lord, who was born of the Virgin Mary by the Holy Ghost, was crucified under Pontius Pilate, buried, rose from the dead on the third day, ascended to the heavens, and sits on the right hand of the Father; whence he will come, to judge the living and the dead: and in the Holy Spirit; the holy church; the remission of sins; and the resurrection of the body."

Ignatius

Our first reference to the patristic writers shall be to Ignatius (A. D. 115) who says the reward of piety "is incorruptibility and eternal life," "love incorruptible and perpetual life." Here the aionian life is strengthened by incorruptible," showing that the word *aiónion* alone was in his mind unequal to the task of expressing endless duration. He says, also, that Jesus "was manifested to the ages" (*tois aiósin*). Of course he intended to use no such ridiculous expression as "to the eternities."

Origen and Theodore of Mopsuestia

Origen used the expressions "*everlasting* fire" and "*everlasting* punishment" to express his idea of the duration of punishment. Yet he believed that in all cases sin and suffering would cease and be followed by salvation. He was the most learned man of his time, and his example proves that *aiónion* did not mean endless at the time he wrote, A. D. 200 —253. Dr. Beecher says "As an introduction to his system of theology, he states certain great facts as a creed believed by all the church. In these he states the doctrine of future retribution as *aiónion* life, and *aiónion* punishment, using the words of Christ. Now, if Origen understood *aiónion* as meaning strictly eternal, then to pursue such a course would involve him in gross and palpable self-contraction. But no one can hide the facts of the case. After setting forth the creed of the church as already stated, including *aiónion* punishment, he forthwith proceeds, with elaborate reasoning, again and again to prove the doctrine of universal restoration. The conclusion from these facts is obvious: Origen did not understand *aiónios* as meaning eternal, but rather as meaning pertaining to the world to come.... Two great facts stand out on the page of ecclesiastical history. One that the first system of Christian theology was composed and issued by Origen in the year 230 after Christ, of which a fundamental and essential element was the doctrine of the universal restoration of all fallen beings to their original holiness and union to God. The second is that after the lapse of a little more than three centuries, in the year 544, this doctrine was for the *first time condemned and anathematized* as heretical. This was done, not in the general council, but in a local council called by the Patriarch Mennos at Constantinople, by the order of Justinian. During all this long interval, the opinions of Origen and his various writings were an element of power in the whole Christian world. For a long time he stood high as the greatest luminary of the Christian world. He gave an impulse to the leading spirits of subsequent ages and was honored by them as their greatest benefactor. At last, after all his scholars were dead, in the remote age of Justinian, he was anathematized as a heretic of the worst kind. The same also was done with respect to Theodore of Mopsuestia, of the Antiochian school, who held the doctrine of universal restitution on a different basis. This, too, was done long after he was dead, in the year 553. From and after this point the doctrine of future eternal punishment reigned with undisputed sway during the middle ages that preceded the Reformation. What, then, was the state of facts as to the leading theological schools of the Christian world in the age of Origen and some centuries after? It was, in brief, this: There were at least six theological schools in the church at large. Of these six schools, one, and only one, was decidedly and earnestly in favor of the doctrine of future eternal punishment. One was in favor of the annihilation of the wicked. Two were in favor of the doctrine of universal restoration on the principles of Origen, and two in favor of universal restoration on the principles of Theodore of Mopsuestia.

"It is also true that the prominent defenders of the doctrine of universal restoration were decided believers in the divinity of Christ, in the trinity, in the incarnation and atonement, and in the great Christian doctrine of regeneration; and were, in piety, devotion, Christian activity and missionary enterprise, as well as in learning and intellectual power and attainments, inferior to none in the best ages of the church, and were greatly superior to those by whom, in after ages, they were condemned and anathematized.

"It is also true that the arguments by which they defended their views were never fairly stated and answered. Indeed, they were never stated at all. They may admit of a thorough answer and refutation, but even if so, they were not condemned and anathematized on any such grounds, but simply in obedience to the arbitrary mandates of Justinian, whose final arguments were deposition and banishment for those who refused to do his will.

Mosheim says of Origen: "Origen possessed every excellence that can adorn the Christian character; uncommon piety from his very childhood; astonishing devotedness to that most holy religion which he professed; unequaled perseverance in labors and toils for the advancement of Christianity; and elevation of soul which placed him above all ordinary desires or fears; a most permanent contempt of wealth, honor, pleasures, and of death itself; the purest trust in the Lord Jesus, for whose sake, when he was old and oppressed with ills of every kind, he patiently and perseveringly endured the severest sufferings.

It is not strange, therefore, that he was held in so high estimation, both while he lived and after death. Certainly if any man deserves to stand first in the catalogue of saints and martyrs, and to be annually held up as an example to Christians, this is the man, for, except the apostles of Jesus Christ and their companions, I know of no one, among all those enrolled and honored as saints, who excelled him in virtue and holiness."

How could universal salvation have been the prevailing doctrine in that age of the church unless the word applied to punishment in Matt. xxv:46 was understood by Christians to mean limited duration? *The fact that Origen and others taught an aionian punishment after death, and salvation beyond it,* DEMONSTRATES *that in Origen's time the word had not the meaning of endless, but did mean at that date, indefinite or limited duration.*

Eusebius
Eusebius (A. D. 300-25) describes the darkness preceding creation thus: "These for a long time had no limit," they continued "for a *long eternity:*" *dia polun aióna.* To say that darkness that *ended* with the creation endured for a long *eternity,* would be absurd.

Augustine
Augustine (A. D. 400-430) was the first known to argue that *aiónios* signified endless. He at first maintained that it always meant thus, but at length

abandoned that ground, and only claimed that it had that meaning sometimes. He "was very imperfectly acquainted with the Greek language."

Avitus

A. D. 410 Avitus brought to Spain, from Jerome, in Palestine, a translation of Origen, and taught that punishments are not endless; for "though they are called everlasting, yet that word in the original Greek does not, according to its etymology and frequent use, signify endless, but answers only to the duration of an age."

General Usage of the Fathers

In fact, every Universalist and every Annihilationist among the fathers of the early church is a standing witness testifying that the word was understood as we claim, in their day. Believers in the Bible, accepting its utterances implicitly as truth, how could they be Universalists or Annihilationists with the Greek Bible before them, and *aiónion* punishment taught there, unless they gave to the word thus used the meaning of limited duration?

The Emperor Justinian

The Emperor Justinian (A. D. 540), in calling the celebrated local council which assembled in 544, addressed his edict to Mennos, Patriarch of Constantinople, and elaborately argued against the doctrines he had determined should be condemned. He does not say, in defining the Catholic doctrine at that time "We believe in *aiónion* punishment," for that was just what the Universalist, Origen himself taught. Nor does he say, "The word *aiónion* has been misunderstood, it denotes endless duration," as he would have said had there been such a disagreement. But, writing in Greek with all the words of that copious speech from which to choose, he says, "The holy church of Christ teaches an endless *aiónios* (ATELEUTETOS *aiónios*) life to the righteous, and endless (*ateleutetos*) punishment to the wicked." *Aiónios* was not enough in his judgement to denote endless duration, and he employed *ateleutetos*. This demonstrates that even as late as A. D. 540 *aiónios* meant limited duration, and required an added word to impart to it the force of endless duration.

Believers in Annihilation and in Universal Salvation Applied the Word to Punishment.

Thus Ignatius, Polycarp, Hermas, Justin Martyr, Irenæus, Hyppolytus, Justinian, and others, (from A. D. 115 to A. D. 544) use the word *aiónion* to define punishment. And yet, some of these taught that decay out of conscious existence is the natural destiny of men, from which some only are saved by God's grace. Previous to this decay or extinction of being, they held that men experience *aiónion* punishment. The *aiónion* punishment is not extinction of being, for that was the soul's natural destiny. The punishment is not endless for it ceases. Let us illustrate: Justin Martyr says "Souls suffer *aiónion* punishment and die." The punishment is in the future world, but it concludes with extinction, and yet it is *aiónion*. A. D. 540, *aiónion* required *ateleutetos* prefixed to convey the idea of endless duration.

The First Six Centuries

Hence the word did not mean endless duration among the early Christians for about six centuries after Christ. To say that any one who contradicts these men is correct, and that they did not know the meaning of the word, is like saying that an Australian, twelve hundred years hence, will be better able to give an accurate definition of English words in common use to-day than we are ourselves. These ancients could not be mistaken, and the fact that they required qualifying words to give *aiónion* the sense of endless duration —that they used it to describe punishment when they believed in the annihilation of the wicked, or in their restoration subsequent to *aiónion* punishment, irrefragably demonstrates that the word had not the meaning of endless to them, and if not to them, then it must have been utterly destitute of it.

Therefore the uniform usage of these words by the early Church demonstrates that they signified temporal duration.

Thus it has appeared as the result of this discussion that

1. There is nothing in the Etymology of the word warranting the erroneous view of it.

2. The definitions of Lexicographers uniformly given not only allow but compel the view we have advocated.

3. Greek writers before and at the time the Septuagint was made, always gave the word the sense of limited duration.

4. Such is the general usage in the Old Testament.

5. The Jewish Greek writers at the time of Christ ascribed to it limited duration.

6. The New Testament thus employs it.

7. The Christian Fathers for centuries after Christ thus understood it. Hence it follows that the readers of the Bible are under the most imperative obligations to understand the word in all cases as denoting limited duration, unless the subject treated, or other qualifying words compel them to understand it differently. There is nothing in the Derivation, Lexicography or Usage of the word to warrant us in understanding it to convey the thought of endless duration.

If our positions are well taken the Bible does not teach the doctrine of endless torment, for it will be admitted that if this word ("Aionios" ed.) does not teach it, it cannot be found in the Bible.   J.W. Hanson

Ed. Now just what does the scripture teach concerning the doctrine of "eventual universal salvation?" Following as well, are inclusions from Hanson's

1875 book which closely follows historical Christian doctrine: *This author cannot endorse Hansen's other works, having not read them, but this one appears to be on target. Also let it be completely understood that this author does not endorse, nor support in any way whatsoever the Unitarian/Universalist doctrines of salvation, but consider them apostate to say the least Our belief in eventual universal salvation still demands the new birth experience through the shed blood of Jesus Christ who was none other than the third person of the Trinity, (God come in the flesh as the Savior of the world). Salvation by grace through faith, plus nothing minus nothing for all men! As well it must be said that in studying the Word of God we must all be very careful that we do not automatically come to doctrinal conclusions based on that which has previously been taught us. Rather though we need to accept what we read and find to be the literal meaning of the Greek/Hebrew manuscripts. Whenever the English translation is unclear or ambiguous it is essential to consult the original tongues and their correct definitions for the true meaning.*

Summary of Conclusions from Hanson's Book on Eventual Universal Salvation

A few of the many points established in the foregoing pages may here be named:

(1) During the First Century the primitive Christians did not dwell on matters of eschatology, but devoted their attention to apologetics; they were chiefly anxious to establish the fact of Christ's advent, and of its blessings to the world. Possibly the question of destiny was an open one, till Paganism and Judaism introduced erroneous ideas, when the New Testament doctrine of the ***apokatastasis*** (meaning: Eventual full restoration and salvation of all of the lost.) was asserted, and universal restoration became an accepted belief, as stated later by Clement and Origen, A.D. 180-230.

(2) The Catacombs give us the views of the unlearned, as Clement and Origen state the doctrine of scholars and teachers. Not a syllable is found hinting at the horrors of Augustinianism, but the inscription on every monument harmonizes with the Universalism of the early fathers.

(3) Clement declares that all punishment, however severe, is purificatory; that even the "torments of the damned" are curative. Origen explains even *Gehenna* as signifying limited and curative punishment, and both, as all the other ancient Universalists, declare that "everlasting" (*aionion*) punishment, is consonant with universal salvation. So that it is no proof that other primitive Christians who are less explicit as to the final result, taught endless punishment when they employ the same terms.

(4) Like our Lord and his Apostles, the primitive Christians avoided the words with which the Pagans and Jews defined endless punishment *aidios or adialeipton timoria* (endless torment), a doctrine the latter believed, and knew how to describe; but they, the early Christians, called punishment, as did our Lord, *kolasis aionios*, discipline, chastisement, of indefinite, limited duration.

(5) The early Christians taught that Christ preached the Gospel to the dead, and for that purpose descended into Hades. Many held that he released all who were in ward. This shows that repentance beyond the grave, perpetual probation, was then accepted, which precludes the modern error that the soul>s destiny is decided at death.

(6) Prayers for the dead were universal in the early church, which would be absurd, if their condition is unalterably fixed at the grave.

(7) The idea that false threats were necessary to keep the common people in check, and that the truth might be held esoterically, prevailed among the earlier Christians, so that there can be no doubt that many who seem to teach endless punishment, really held the broader views, as we know the most did, and preached terrors pedagogically.

(8) The first comparatively complete systematic statement of Christian doctrine ever given to the world was by Clement of Alexandria, A.D. 180, and universal salvation was one of the tenets.

(9) The first complete presentation of Christianity as a system was by Origen (A.D. 220) and universal salvation was explicitly contained in it.

(10) Universal salvation was the prevailing doctrine in Christendom as long as Greek, the language of the New Testament, was the language of Christendom.

(11) Universalism was generally believed in the best centuries, the first three, when Christians were most remarkable for simplicity, goodness and missionary zeal.

(12) Universalism was least known when Greek, the language of the New Testament was least known, and when Latin was the language of the Church in its darkest, most ignorant, and corrupt ages.

(13) Not a writer among those who describe the heresies of the first three hundred years intimates that Universalism was then a heresy, though it was believed by many, if not be a majority, and certainly by the greatest of the fathers.

(14) Not a single creed for five hundred years expresses any idea contrary to universal restoration, or in favor of endless punishment.

(15) With the exception of the arguments of Augustine (A.D. 420), there is not an argument known to have been framed against Universalism for at least four hundred years after Christ, by any of the ancient fathers.

(16) While the councils that assembled in various parts of Christendom, anathematized every kind of doctrine supposed to be heretical, no ecumenical council, for more than five hundred years, condemned Universalism, though it had been advocated in every century by the principal scholars and most revered saints.

(17) As late as A.D. 400, Jerome says «most people» (*plerique*). and Augustine said "very many" (*quam plurimi*), believed in Universalism, notwithstanding that the tremendous influence of Augustine, and the mighty power of the semi-pagan secular arm were arrayed against it.

(18) The principal ancient Universalists were Christian born and reared, and were among the most scholarly and saintly of all the ancient saints.

(19) The most celebrated of the earlier advocates of endless punishment were heathen born, and led corrupt lives in their youth. Tertullian one of the first, and Augustine, the greatest of them, confess to having been among the vilest.

(20) The first advocates of endless punishment, Minucius Felix, Tertullian and Augustine, were Latins, ignorant of Greek, and less competent to interpret the meaning of Greek Scriptures than were the Greek scholars.

(21) The first advocates of Universalism, after the Apostles, were Greeks, in whose mother-tongue the New Testament was written. They found their Universalism in the Greek Bible. Who should be correct, they or the Latins?

(22) The Greek Fathers announced the great truth of universal restoration in an age of darkness, sin and corruption. There was nothing to suggest it to them in the world>s literature or religion. It was wholly contrary to everything around them. Where else could they have found it, but where they say they did, in the Gospel?

(23) All ecclesiastical historians and the best Biblical critics and scholars agree to the prevalence of Universalism in the earlier centuries.

(24) From the days of Clement of Alexandria to those of Gregory of Nyssa and Theodore of Mopsuestia (A.D. 180-428), the great theologians and teachers, almost without exception, were Universalists. No equal number in the same centuries were comparable to them for learning and goodness.

(25) The first theological school in Christendom, that in Alexandria, taught Universalism for more than two hundred years.

(26) In all Christendom, from A.D. 170 to 430, there were six Christian schools. Of these four, the only strictly theological schools, taught Universalism, and but one endless punishment.

(27) The three earliest Gnostic sects, the Basilidians, the Carpocratians and the Valentinians (A.D. 117-132) are condemned by Christian

writers, and their heresies pointed out, but though they taught Universalism, that doctrine is never condemned by those who oppose them. Irenaeus condemned the errors of the Carpocratians, but does not reprehend their Universalism, though he ascribes the doctrine to them.

(28) The first defense of Christianity against Infidelity (Origen against Celsus) puts the defense on Universalistic grounds. Celsus charged the Christians› God with cruelty, because he punished with fire. Origen replied that God›s fire is curative; that he is a «Consuming Fire,» because he consumes sin and not the sinner.

(29) Origen, the chief representative of Universalism in the ancient centuries, was bitterly opposed and condemned for various heresies by ignorant and cruel fanatics. He was accused of opposing Episcopacy, believing in pre-existence, etc., but never was condemned for his Universalism. The very council that anathematized "Origenism" eulogized Gregory of Nyssa, who was explicitly a Universalist as was Origen. Lists of his errors are given by Methodius, Pamphilus and Eusebius, Marcellus, Eustathius and Jerome, but Universalism is not named by one of his opponents. Fancy a list of Ballou›s errors and his Universalism omitted; Hippolytus (A.D. 320) names thirty-two known heresies, but Universalism is not mentioned as among them. Epiphanius, "the hammer of heretics," describes eighty heresies, but he does not mention universal salvation, though Gregory of Nyssa, an outspoken Universalist, was, at the time he wrote, the most conspicuous figure in Christendom.

(30) Justinian, a half-pagan emperor, who attempted to have Universalism officially condemned, lived in the most corrupt epoch of the Christian centuries. He closed the theological schools, and demanded the condemnation of Universalism by law; but the doctrine was so prevalent in the church that the council refused to obey his edict to suppress it. Lecky says the age of Justinian was "the worst form civilization has assumed."

(31) The first clear and definite statement of human destiny by any Christian writer after the days of the Apostles, includes universal restora-

tion, and that doctrine was advocated by most of the greatest and best of the Christian Fathers for the first five hundred years of the Christian Era.

In one word, a careful study of the early history of the Christian religion, will show that the doctrine of universal restoration was least prevalent in the darkest, and prevailed most in the most enlightened, of the earliest centuries—that it was the prevailing doctrine in the Primitive Christian Church. J.W. Hanson.

False Doctrine of Endless Damnation Fathered Calvinism

Just supposing the heresy of endless (merciless) punishment to be true then it is no surprise that Augustine and Calvin came up with forced salvation for a few and forced damnation for those unfortunate enough to be overlooked or ignored by their damnationist god. They naturally concluded that God in His sovereignty (for secret reasons whatever), chose only a select few to be saved from endless damnation, and to consign the remaining majority of humanity of all ages to endless torment in the Lake of Fire. Since in Adam all are sinners and thus deserving of spiritual death and separation from God is absolutely true, but coupled with the false doctrine of E.D., there could be no other explanation as to why only the select/elect few are to be saved other than some (supposedly not yet revealed) hidden secret for their election.

Since man of course is a willing participant in sin which brings his fall and separation from God, and since God is the one who initiates salvation, then the false premise of E.D. forced them to conclude forced election to salvation for only a few must be true. Remember they already held universal Christian redemption to be a false conclusion.

That, also coupled with the fact that many thousands do die daily without ever even hearing the true plan of salvation, and that God in His sovereignty and holiness cannot be indicted with any wrong doing even if the lost are sent to Hell (which of course is true). Here as usual we have one heresy breeding another. Eternal/endless damnation fathering Augustinian/Calvinism, the hideous idea that God gives up on multitudes of lost souls, decides not to elect them (supposedly in eternity past) and thus forces them to be tormented in fire and brimstone for eternity!

Readers note: Since all of humanity who have not been regenerated by the Spirit of God are plainly termed as 'sinners,' the Word of God is clear that because God is upright and good, He will teach them the truth or the way of righteousness and salvation, with no condition to that promise. Psalm 25:8, "Good and upright is the Lord, therefore will He teach sinners in the way." Also we need to be aware of Psalm 21:4 which says, "He *(David)* asked life of thee and thou gavest it him, even length of days forever and ever." For those who are adamant that 'forever' means 'endless/everlasting' please consider this verse! What is it that God gave David in regards to what? Simple. God gave David 'length of days.' And then in response to what? In response to his heart's desire. (vs. 2). Then next, did God give David 'forever/endless physical life?' No! God gave David length of life 'forever and ever' plainly showing 'forever' in translation from the original tongue simply was 'continuous life or ages and ages of continuous life but certainly not endless life! Here again further proof that 'forever and ever' does not necessarily mean endless.

All of this makes Calvinism truly 'another gospel' and Christians should break fellowship with those holding such heresy. Calvinism as another gospel is not worthy of respect, nor should it be tolerated in our Christian institutions, colleges and churches. Calvinism claiming the gospel message is <u>not</u> that Jesus came to save all men, but that He came to save only the elect, or those secretly (for some secret reason issuing from God's sovereignty) elected to be called, chosen and washed in the blood of the Lamb, (thus consigning the remainder of humanity with no opportunity to be saved to burn endlessly in hellfire). Certainly a blasphemous conclusion that the Almighty would do such a thing, something myriads of times worse than what ISIS inflicts upon man. To accuse our blessed loving, compassionate Savior of being the creator of all of mankind, but then He is only willing to save a small percentage of them? Therefore He 'forces' the majority/remainder to be tormented in fire and brimstone for eternity, (because <u>'He'</u> does not elect them?) Satan the 'accuser of the brethren' thereby also being the 'accuser of God/

Christ' in a twisted perverted plan to 'force' the minority to be saved, while 'forcing' the majority to be mercilessly tormented in fire for eternity? Forced salvation and forced damnation on all of mankind is our Savior's gospel plan of redemption? Clearly Calvinism is a false satanic delusion parading as the true gospel of the Bible! It must be renounced by all bible believing Christians

CHAPTER NINE

SO WHO WINS THE GAME?

Who can deny that a continuing warfare exists between the forces of righteousness, and the forces of evil? That warfare has continued from before man's creation with the sin and fall of Satan, and will continue until the universe is perfected and sin is no more. Plainly the forces are headed by Jehovah on the one hand, and Satan on the other. No one will deny that. This being the case, and with this battle raging, who could possibly believe that Satan is going to be the ultimate victor and have his plan for man's destruction and alienation from God to reign supreme throughout eternity?

A very simple illustration can show that God indeed will ultimately reign supreme as complete and final victor over all sin, Hell and the grave. (It is well to add here that God cannot be said to "reign supremely throughout eternity" if Satan has won vast multitudes to his will for eternity in an eternal endless Hell/Lake of Fire... the will of God must and will overcome all evil, and be done in all men, and will totally defeat Satan's design for the ruination of man). Say for instance, God and Satan were to engage in a very serious game of chess. God makes His move and Satan his on and on...

The plain will of God in this game no doubt is to win and defeat the opposer. Now no matter how long this game were to play out, a day, week or years, it is only self evident that God would be the ultimate victor, and His will absolutely shall without doubt prevail over the opposition. Now it is very plain, that the will of God is perfect, it cannot be overcome and defeated by anyone at any time or any place! God's will is not that man should be tormented endlessly because of his ignorance, or his rebellion against the laws of God. His will is that all men should be saved and come to the knowledge of the truth. II Pet. 3:9.

If the Almighty has "…commanded all men everywhere to repent (Acts 17:30), then certainly that command must include 'ALL' men of all ages, of all nations. It can mean nothing else. The fact that millions die every century without finding true salvation in Christ Jesus, whether in ignorance or whatever, clearly shows that they must be included in the scope of this command. Plainly "all" means "all." Another point to consider is that truth must and will be embraced by all men one day. When that wicked rebellious man or woman has been stripped of their earthly existence, they can come to no other conclusion than that they were wrong in neglecting salvation.

Whether they lost out in being saved/born again in this life due to false religion, being deceived by Satan, or just plain willful ignorance is irrelevant since the first few seconds in the next life will irrefutably bring them to only one truth, namely that Jesus Christ is the only way of salvation, and they must yield their wicked hearts to Him. Forced salvation? No, because they will not need such force, but will (one day after the White Throne Judgment), gladly embrace free salvation since there can be no other way. In this life there are many 'ways' and many 'avenues' to pursue, many religions and cults to follow after, to believe or not to believe is as well an option, but then, in the next life, there is only one way, pain suffering and punishment for their sins, unto sorrow and repentance and the new birth into the family of God.

Some may say "Well why preach if all will be saved eventually?" The answer to that is simple, "Who could be so hard hearted as to refuse to rescue perishing souls from a burning house?" The horror that awaits the wicked lost after death cannot be fathomed. Remember, the last enemy to be destroyed is what? "DEATH." If "death" is to be destroyed then it cannot exist for anyone which plainly means that there can be no unsaved souls, "dead to God" and burning in Hell/Lake of Fire endlessly for eternity. God said it, I believe it, and that settles it!

It is important to remember here, that in this life, God often deals severely with the most hardened and wicked of sinners. They are often brought to repentance and salvation thru perhaps years of conviction, trials and deep afflictions. Often times they are subjected to deep pain and suffering, with the Holy Spirit forever convicting them of their waywardness, and then suddenly they yield to the call of the gospel and are born-again. John Newton, the wicked infidel, and slave trader, who was later converted and wrote many wonderful hymns such as "Amazing Grace" and "Glorious Things of Thee Are Spoken," was brought to God and salvation by a terrible storm he was in, and nearly lost his life.

Note as follows: When John was eleven, he went to sea with his father and made six voyages with him before the elder Newton retired. In 1744 John was impressed into service on a man-of-war, the H. M. S. Harwich. Finding conditions on board intolerable, he deserted but was soon recaptured and publicly flogged and demoted from midshipman to common seaman. Finally at his own request he was exchanged into service on a slave ship, which took him to the coast of Sierra Leone. He then became the servant of a slave trader and was brutally abused. Early in 1748 he was rescued by a sea captain who had known John's father. John Newton ultimately became captain of his own ship, one which plied the slave trade

Although he had had some early religious instruction from his mother, who had died when he was a child, he had long since given up any religious convictions. Then however, on a homeward voyage, while he was attempting to steer the ship through a violent storm, he experienced what he was to refer to later as his "great deliverance." He recorded in his journal that when all seemed lost and the ship would surely sink, he exclaimed, "Lord, have mercy upon us."

Later in his cabin he reflected on what he had said and began to believe that God had addressed him through the storm and that grace had begun to work for him. For the rest of his life he observed the anniversary of May 10, 1748 as the day of his conversion, a day of humiliation in which he subjected his will to a higher power. "Thro' many dangers, toils and snares, I have already come; 'tis grace has bro't me safe thus far, and grace will lead me home (The Story of John Newton by Al Rogers.)

No doubt countless conversions have occurred due to the unsaved being placed in extremely difficult and painful situations for long periods of time perhaps. Are not those painful experiences necessary, no doubt from the hand of God, in bringing those precious souls into the kingdom for whom Christ died? This author certainly thinks so. How much more, when man has scoffed and rejected the claims of Christ in this life as a libertarian or infidel etc, that being consigned to Hell's fires and torments/afflictions, on and on in the next, will he not be more than willing to bend his knee and admit his guilt?

The Bible certainly indicates such. "…EVERY knee shall bow…EVERY tongue shall confess that Jesus Christ is Lord to the Glory of God the Father…" Hell/the Lake of Fire can certainly be looked upon as God's deepest desire being executed upon man that he may be brought willingly into the Kingdom of Heaven. God certainly has no pleasure in the death of the wicked as scripture so clearly states, and no doubt He is grieved that such pain and affliction must be allotted to man in order to break men's stubborn will against His perfect will!

God having 'no pleasure in the death of the wicked' certainly is not because they die, since we all die, rather He 'has no pleasure' (Ez. 33:11), since that wicked soul must be placed in unutterable pain, suffering and anguish to humble and totally subdue his rebellion against the perfect will of God. For those souls to be placed in such conditions "endlessly and forever without end" would mean God's pleasure would/could never triumph over displeasure. Only the full pleasure of God in the salvation of all men can be acceptable to Him to whom the scripture says

"...will have all men to be saved and come to a knowledge of the truth," no matter how long the wicked must suffer in Hell/the Lake of Fire.

Yes the wrath of God is poured out upon the lost soul in Hell, but God has no pleasure in it. How can He? God's ultimate pleasure will one day come to full fruition with the salvation of that last lost soul. At that point, His displeasure will turn to pleasure for eternity for all men! It can be no other way! Is not the 'pleasure of God' fully realized in the death of Jesus on the cross for our sins and that God seeing the "travail of His soul" was satisfied? Isiah 53:11 For it to be said that God finds no pleasure in anything, anything at all, means that whatever He finds 'no pleasure' in, is outside of His will.

If that which is 'outside of His will' is to be left there for endless eternity, then that thing or condition whatever the case will have triumphed over the perfect will of God. No! Nothing, nor anything, outside of His pleasure will remain there endlessly for eternity, not even the damned in Hell/Lake of Fire. He "...has no pleasure in the death of the wicked..." and "...will have ALL men to be saved and come to a knowledge of the truth." Man's will cannot triumph over the will of God.

In thinking about the conditions in Hell, it comes to mind that no doubt there are degrees of suffering there. The scripture indicates such by saying in Revelation 20, that "...and every man was judged according to his works." Did not Jesus teach that "...by their fruits ye shall know them," does not the scripture plainly teach that "... faith without works is dead?" James 2:17, and as well the "fruit of the righteous is the tree of life." Prov. 11:30. The unsaved have nothing to offer God except their dead works, and outward righteousness which is as "filthy rags," which will be rejected and they will be judged according to.

The sinner's place and degree of suffering in the afterlife, will depend upon the degree of his wickedness in this one. Not only will they be judged according to their works, but the conditions of Hell will certainly be the opposite of conditions here on earth for them. Here they have comfort, food, water, rest and sleep, sunshine and fresh air (in this time of probation by undeserved grace), but since they have rejected God/Christ here, they lose His added physical blessings in the next life.

Nothing but pain, anguish, suffering and isolation from the physical blessings of this life. It is important to remember that the conditions in Hell are not identical for all lost souls. The scripture plainly indicates there is a "lowest Hell" and therefore if a 'lowest Hell' then no doubt there are different levels above the 'lowest.'

Psalm 86:13

> For great is thy mercy toward me and thou hast delivered my soul from the lowest Hell.

Deut. 32:22

> For a fire is kindled in mine anger, and shall burn unto the lowest Hell, and shall consume the earth with her increase, and set on fire the foundations of the mountains.

There is of course no doubt, as we have stated over and over again, that no unsaved, unregenerate person who *has* reached the age of accountability, will go to Heaven immediately after death. Absolutely none. The truly innocent babies and children who perish in this life of course will. David plainly said that his deceased baby would not "come to him, but that he would go to him." Calvin certainly did not think so. His idea was that some babies were elect unto salvation, and some were not. Those not elect unto salvation were hated by God as being unregenerate sinners and sent to Hell fire forever (endlessly so). The following is from his "Institutes of the Christian Religion, book 4, ch. 16-17. Quotation from "Calvinism-The Trojan Horse Within" by this author.

Readers note: Calvinism unwittingly brings the doctrine of the deity of Christ into question by inferring that Jesus lied by preaching a false warning, when He preached that one could go to hell forever if he did not repent and believe on Him! Why so? Simple, according to Calvinism no one is "in danger" of going to hell, the elect cannot possibly go there even if presently not saved since they will ultimately surely be saved (so why warn them?), and the non-elect must go to hell since there is no chance of them being saved since they cannot possibly be in "danger" of going there. To "be in danger of going to hell" clearly implies a possibility of not having to go there, which the "non-elect" do not have (according to Calvinism). Thus according to Calvin, no one is in danger of going to hell! To say that since we do not know who is elect and who is not, therefore we should preach such warning, still is to be preaching a false lying warning (if one believes Calvinism)! If our Savior preached a lie, then He sinned and obviously could not have been God! The fact Jesus did preach warnings about the possibility of one going to hell unless he repents, therefore proves Calvinism unwittingly brings the deity of Christ into disrepute. Isn't it amazing that so many Christian leaders, pastors etc, who are not Calvinists, do not regard Calvinism as a serious heresy or threat to Biblical Christianity?

Babies Not Justified are Hated by God

Quoting Calvin as follows. "In fine, if Christ speaks truly when he declares that he is life, we must necessarily be engrafted into him by whom we are delivered from the bondage of death. But "how?"… they *(ed. "they" being the ones opposed to infants being saved or lost according to election)* ask, are infants regenerated when not possessing a knowledge of either good or evil? We answer that the work of God, though beyond the reach of our capacity, is not therefore null. Moreover, infants who are to be saved (and that some are saved at this age is certain) must without question be previously regenerated by the Lord. For if they bring innate corruption with them from their mothers womb, they must be purified before they can be admitted in the kingdom of God into which shall not enter anything that defiles (Rev. 21:27).

If they are born sinners as David and Paul affirm, they must either remain unaccepted and hated by God or be justified. And why do we ask more when the Judge himself publicly declares that "except a man be born again he cannot see the kingdom of God" John.3:3.

A casual reading of Ps. 88:10 appears to contradict the idea that there will be post mortem salvation after enlightenment in Sheol/Hades. It says: "Wilt thou shew wonders to the dead? Shall the dead arise and praise thee?" No, there is no contradiction here. First it must be remembered that the scripture is a divinely inspired record of all events. This Psalm is the prayer of David accurately recorded. David is simply pointing out that God does not show wonders to those dead bodies in the graves. He as well asks will those dead bodies get out of the graves and praise God.

He is not denying the resurrection of the dead at all. Daniel taught it, as well Jesus taught it, and the New Testament gives further light on it in I Cor., II Thess, and Revelation etc. Getting back to the subject of levels in Hell and conditions there as varying in degree. No doubt those who die unsaved, but with lesser defilement or sins, will be there suffering, but only temporarily so and too much lesser degree than those who go to the lower levels of Hell.

The Last Enemy "Death" is Totally Defeated by Our Savior Who Ultimately Liberates Those Separated from God!

The last enemy that shall be destroyed is death" (I Cor. 15:26). Who can deny that the Word of God accurately gives us the final enemy, which our Lord must and will conquer? The scripture is plain and cannot be broken. Are not those unsaved souls who have perished and entered Hell/the Lake of Fire considered "separated from God by their sins? Are they not considered to be "dead in trespasses and in sins?" Who can deny that? J. Preston Eby gives an interesting explanation of the "death of death" as being when Rev. 20 tells us that "…death and Hell were cast into the Lake of Fire, this is the second death." Quoting Eby:

> Rev. 20:14 God tells us exactly what the SECOND DEATH is. "And death and Hell were cast into the lake of fire. THIS IS THE SECOND DEATH." Now let me make this a little plainer. Definitions of men can be given backward. For instance, the definition, "An island is a tract of land completely surrounded by water," can be given thus: "A tract of land completely surrounded by water is an island." This is but another way of stating the same fact. It does not, in any way, change the meaning. Now let us try this on the definition of the second death. The Bible states it thus: "Death and Hell were cast into the lake of fire. THIS IS the second death." Now let us turn

this around for clarity. "The second death IS death and Hell cast into the lake of fire." Therefore we have exactly the same meaning either way it is stated.

What is the second death? It is the first death and Hell cast into the lake of fire! This fact is very IMPORTANT. The second death is not merely the lake of fire. The second death is not men being tortured forever in the lake of fire. The Holy Spirit has made it very simple and plain. The second death is the first death and Hell CAST INTO THE LAKE OF FIRE. That is the Holy Spirit's definition, not mine. Can we now open the eyes of our understanding to see that everything cast into the lake of fire pertains to DEATH? Death itself is cast into the lake of fire. Hell, the realm of the dead, is cast into the lake of fire. And those whose names are not written in the Book of Life, those who are dead, in trespasses and in sins, who inhabit Hell, are cast into the lake of fire. That is the end of death and Hell and sin, for God shall destroy death in the lake of fire, He shall burn up Hell in the lake of fire, and He shall consume sin and rebellion in the lake of fire.

How I long to see the end of sin and death and Hell! The time is coming, praise His name! when God's Kingdom shall be All in All, and there shall be neither sin, nor sinners, nor death, nor Hell. It is clear that God does not destroy men in the lake of fire, nowhere does it say that, for that would be a contradiction of terms. How can you destroy death by creating death? How can you abolish death by bringing men under the power of eternal death from which there is no escape? Oh, no, it is not men who are destroyed in the lake of fire - it is SIN and DEATH and HELL that are destroyed. "And the last enemy that shall be destroyed is death" (I Cor. 15:26). Thus, the lake of fire is nothing more nor less than THE DEATH OF DEATH! *(Ed. Note here, Eby is not saying here that the new birth and the blood of Jesus is not necessary to salvation, but rather that*

> *sin will be permanently defeated/put down/destroyed in the lives of those so unfortunate to be punished by going to this lake of fire.)*

One possible disagreement with Eby here is that he seems to define 'death' as merely 'death' and the condition thereof, when it seems apparent that the scripture here indicates that 'death' refers to the physical body in the grave. Now if the 'condition' is thrown into the Lake of Fire and destroyed, then that could be a possible rendering, however the physical resurrection of the body is plainly shown here. None the less, Eby is a brilliant scholar.

Verses Commonly Used to Uphold Endless Punishment in Church Constitutions

Matthew 25:41-46; Mark 9:43-48; Luke 16:19-26; II Thessalonians 1:7-9; Jude 6-7; Revelation 20:11-15.

Matt.25: 41-46. That the punishment is eternal/endless in its duration is of course without merit (Greek "Aionios" not "Aidios" as previously discussed), but that the punishment is eternal in its effects, and as well the fire experienced by the wicked is fire that ***cannot*** be extinguished (i.e. as opposite of fire as we presently know it, and it cannot be extinguished until it's purpose is fullfilled) is the literal rendering here. Those going into everlasting punishment are not going into endless (Aidios) punishment as most think. The original Greek reigns.

Mark 9:43-48. Here going into Hell where the worm dieth not and the fire is not quenched simply shows that in Hell after death the fire is not a quenchable fire but that it burns on and on. Second that those who go to Hell indeed suffer there for their sins without dying as they would in this world under such a fiery state. Simply spoken, the wicked are not annihilated there, but rather live on and on and on, forever and forever, or for ages and ages (Aionios and Aionios, not Aidios and Aidios or endlessly). The original Greek reigns.

Luke 16-19-26. Indeed here is irrefutable proof that in Hell unsaved/unregenerate people are punished for their sins in unquenchable fire, and are consciously suffering on and on, deservedly so! It is well to remember here that all Christians who believe in "eternal/endless suffering in Hell" *do not believe* that Hell itself is "endless," since the scriptures are plain that Hell is emptied at the beginning of the final white throne judgment in Rev. 20! The original Greek reigns.

II Thess. 1:7-9. I Tim. 6:8 tell us that "…drown men in destruction and perdition…" This same word "destruction" in the Greek, is the same as used in II Thess. and means (Strongs 3539 "Olethros") "destruction, ruin, punishment, death". "Aionios Olethros" certainly does not mean "eternal/endless punishment or annihilation!" It simply means as shown previously, "punishment on and on for an undetermined period of time." Certainly not "Aidios" or endless punishment. Where in the Word of God does the Greek (or Hebrew for that matter) teach that punishment is endless in its application? Absolutely nowhere! The original Greek reigns.

Jude 6-7. In verse 6 we notice that the "chains" are called "everlasting ("Aidios" not "Aionios") chains." This simply shows that the fallen angels are in chains that are endless in their restraint capabilities, and not in like fallible chains made by man. The angels are not "restrained endlessly for eternity!" That this is NOT the meaning here is clarified by the simple statement in this verse that they are "…reserved…unto the judgment of the great day." One day they will be taken out of those endlessly powerful chains and stand the judgment bar of God. Then further, of Sodom and Gomorrah it is said in verse 7, "…suffering the vengeance of eternal fire…"

Now when did Sodom and Gomorrah suffer this vengeance? *In time*, and at the destruction of fire from heaven at the hand of a righteous God! The "eternal fire" that consumed those two cities did indeed "burn on and on" no one knows for how long the fires raged there. The fires were indeed fires of judgment for sin and wickedness and they were indeed "Aionios" (not "Aidios/endless) everlasting fires, but fires that had an ending in their judgment. The original Greek reigns.

Rev. 20-11-15. The Lake of Fire here is the same Lake of Fire as found in Rev. 19:20, where plainly the Beast and the False Prophet are cast into, yea a "*physical* lake of fire." It is the same place of punishment in fiery brimstone in Rev. 14:10-11, where those who received the mark of the beast earlier were cast. Yes they are plainly "alive" and do not cease to live and since the powers of death were suspended (Rev. 9:6, "…and in those days shall men seek death and shall not find it, and shall desire to die, and death shall flee from them.").

As stated earlier, they are therefore in a place of living Hell as retribution for their sins. The same fate, which befell Satan, the beast, and the false prophet, is seen to befall those in Rev. 20:12 at the second resurrection. The unsaved dead are raised there and when judged according to their works, are cast into the place of torment/affliction/punishment, to be punished "day and night (which indicates time and not eternity) on and on forever and ever or "Aionios and Aionios (undetermined period of time but not "Aidios" for eternity) the length of time clearly according to the degree of their evil works.

Remember they were judged "according to their works." Lastly it is called the "second death" because it is the second time the unsaved are separated from God. The first is at death in this life when they die and are consigned to Hell thus being separated from God, the second death takes place here when they are again made alive on earth (resurrected), judged, and cast into the Lake of Fire again separated from God. Again the original Greek reigns.

Certainly the above scriptures in *English* do seem to teach "endless/never ending punishment," but the Greek is clearly master of the truth. **The Holy Scriptures in the original language do not support it.**

Is it any wonder that Calvinism was so easily birthed and then came to enslave the majority of Christendom under Augustinianism/Calvinistic theology due to the slanderous doctrine of Unconditional Election (supposedly glorifying the sovereignty of God)?! The false perception that endless destiny is/was fixed before or at death, bonds these three doctrines (Calvinism/Unconditional Election/Sovereignty of God) into one unholy triune doctrine. As well this triune doctrine seems to answer the problematic fact that many millions upon millions have died and continue to die without ever having a chance to accept or reject a message they've never heard *(ed. but will supposedly/falsely be tormented accordingly for endless eternity)*.

Finally, it is important to say here that Augustinian theology unfortunately may be here to stay until the return of Jesus. Reason being that those who are able to recover from this divisive snare may well be terrified or frightened to "come out" and admit such to their parishioners or peers. Imagine a pastor of a large church who becomes enlightened in this matter, and begins preaching it to his congregation. Immediately, he would surely be terminated by his church due to the false concepts Augustinian theology breeds concerning the doctrine of universal salvation. Most people equate the doctrine of eventual universal salvation with Unitarianism a very damnable heresy.

Also as well any good born again Christian (who regularly fellowships in the average evangelical churches) who rediscovers this Biblical doctrine and takes a stand on it no doubt will be instantly broken fellowship with, and probably not be allowed to attend church services there. Sad, but no doubt true. What is the answer? Stand firm on the Word of God, and refuse to compromise the truth no matter who may oppose you!

The Damnationist Doctrine Robbing the Saints...
Yes indeed, robbing so many precious grieving saints of hope for their loved ones who have died and gone into the next world unsaved and unregenerate. How many mothers and fathers have wept, grieved, and been thoroughly devastated by the untimely death of a son or daughter who to all appearances died lost and undone. To say that they will heal

eventually and accept that fate is but to sidestep the fact that a mothers or fathers love for their children is and was meant to last for eternity.

God never intended for a parent to cease loving their children, saved or lost. Yea rather to pray for that wayward one and seek for their salvation for as long as it may take. Yes the damnationist doctrine has robbed them of the peace and delight to know that one day, no matter how long it may take, that loved child or loved one who died lost one day will walk the streets of gold with them. The hope of this author, is that by reading the truth in this booklet, the damnationist will come to see the glorious truth of eventual universal salvation for all. Lord Jesus, let the scales fall from their eyes, to the full abandonment of that hideous doctrine of endless damnation, and the supposed eternal dualistic universe with endless suffering for the lost in Hell-fire, because a defeated Jehovah was unable to win them from Satan.

Away with the doctrine of endless damnation. The Biblical Hell/Lake of Fire is literally real, and it is a place of controlled/remedial/correction (no not a purgatory) unto eventual salvation. On the other hand the traditional Hell/Lake of Fire is an imaginative eternal torture chamber created by a defeated sadistic god, unable with his unlimited power and resources to woe and win all of mankind to himself, thus allowing Satan to win and eternally damn the majority of humanity.(The Bible teaches this? Not hardly).

An Augustinian Damnationist Attempts to Answer Why an Eternal Hell/Lake Of Fire

Damnationist: Yes, I can explain why God has created an endless Hell/Lake of Fire. The wicked need to be severely punished and taught a lesson they will never forget!

Christian Universalist: Oh? To punish and 'teach' them a lesson? Now, 'teach' infers 'learning.' So you admit that the unsaved in this life can die in ignorance to the truths set forth in the Word of God, yea often willingly ignoring warnings and pleadings to mend their evil ways. So, they need to be 'taught' a lesson? And as well when they go to Hell they will no doubt begin 'learning?'

Damnationist: Yes!

Christian Universalist: I am fully in agreement with you that they need to be severely punished to 'learn' or be 'taught a lesson. In other words they need to be 'educated' and is not an education meant to bring forth a better end for the person who is being 'educated' or 'taught' is that not correct?

Damnationist: Well, yes and no. 'Yes' they need to be 'taught a lesson' but 'No' since then it will be too late to have a better end since they will be in Hell or the Lake of Fire forever thereafter. They can have no 'better end' since they are in Hell/Lake of Fire forever.

Christian Universalist: We are agreed that 'teaching' is always beneficial. Just what 'benefit' will they receive by being tormented/afflicted with smoke, fire and brimstone if it is indeed for eternity? You are saying that the wicked are going to be 'taught a lesson' which will benefit them for eternity while they suffer endlessly in Hell fire? Now, just what is the benefit they will have received or gained while suffering endlessly for eternity?

Damnationist: Well, they will then know that they were wrong by ignoring God's plan of redemption, that will be the lesson taught and the benefit received.

Christian Universalist: Yes, I do agree! So then once the sinner has gained such knowledge in Hell by being 'taught' by experience, he certainly has improved in a positive way, has he not? I.e. has he not gone from being in sin, ignorance and rebellion while alive, to being given an irrefutable 'education' as to his error and wickedness after death, and as well is he not totally subdued behind the gates and chains of Hell?

Damnationist: Well, yes I suppose so.

Christian Universalist: Do you suppose that when sinners stand before the judgment bar of God after death, that they will be able to show God to be wrong or vice versa? Of course you agree that they will be forced to agree with their damnation is that not correct?

Damnationist: Yes, absolutely they will agree, fully so! They will have to. They cannot prove God wrong.

Christian Universalist: So, you must agree that this sinner has had a 'good' thing happen to him since he has 'improved' after death due to his being 'taught' these lessons and has been forced to cease his sinful living do you not? In other words, if a wicked sinner suddenly changes his mind about God and agrees with the Lord as to his damnation, ceases to live in sin, then could it not be said that in going to Hell/Lake of Fire, he certainly has 'improved' or had a 'good or beneficial' thing happen to him?

Damnationist: Well, when you put it like that you are right, but they are still in Hell/Lake of Fire forever.

Christian Universalist: So it could be said that mental confusion and acts of degeneracy stop at the gates of Hell and education begins? Maybe like reeducation about God and sin 101?

Damnationist: Yes, they will stop their acts of wickedness and be 'taught' and forced to admit/submit to the truth no doubt.

Christian Universalist: So since God/Jesus created Hell and the conditions therein, and these conditions have begun improvement in the sinner, are we to believe that God has 'given up on them' or has just begun to 'educate them?'

Damnationist: Well, yes they have begun an education, there is no doubt, but it is too late.

Christian Universalist: Well now, if God has the wicked in Hell to 'teach' them a lesson they'll never forget, and as well give them irrefutable revelation of Himself and His justice, then is that a good thing God does, or is it an evil thing He does?

Damnationist: O.K. God cannot do evil or bad ever, so I must admit what God does to the wicked in Hell is a good thing. No doubt about that, but it is still too late.

Christian Universalist: Yes too late to live their life over and do what is right, but why should God 'reeducate' them with irrefutable truth about Himself if He is totally giving up on them? I thought that you damnationists believed that Hell/Lake of Fire is the place people go who are hopeless? You admit that they 'begin' to improve by having irrefutable revelation forced on them, and as well are being 'taught' by being in Hell that they shouldn't have been involved in sin. That being the case, and I agree with that summation except the 'hopeless' part, but then you have God doing something good for the unsaved in Hell by 'teaching and educating' them which is not 'bad' but a 'good' thing! Right?

Damnationist: Yes that is a good thing.

Christian Universalist: So, God is doing something 'good' for the wicked in Hell and if that which He does is indeed 'good' then no doubt the sinner is improved thereby.

Damnationist: Yes, I believe it is good that God does that for the sinner in Hell so he will be forever taught those truths he rejected while alive on earth. I guess he has then improved.

Christian Universalist: So let's see, God will do something good for the wicked in Hell, when that good thing He does for them does indeed improve them significantly, i.e. attitude adjustment. But He does it knowing He will continue tormenting them endlessly in fire and brimstone despite their improvement? So He improves them so they will fully understand why He is going to torment them endlessly eternally? Is not that a sadistic charge against the All Mighty?

Damnationist: Yes their improvement will help them better understand the justice in their endless eternal damnation. A sadistic charge? For God to teach someone truth in order to better justify why He is going to torment them for eternity in fire does sound sadistic, but God cannot be charged with that, He can do no wrong.

Christian Universalist: Do you suppose that if Sodom and Gomorrah were to be raised from the grave death and Hell that they would be happy to repent of their evil deeds? As well do you think they have now realized their wickedness against God?

Damnationist: Yes absolutely so. If they were given a second chance to live again, they no doubt would not engage in the sins they were committing, but it is too late.

Christian Universalist: So you admit that punishment in Hell/Lake of Fire does do some good no matter how small?

Damnationist: Yes I have no doubt it does but it is still too late.

Christian Universalist: Now, if your son or daughter were to die unsaved and go to Hell, you say that would be a bad thing for you and them, but since God would be educating them there, then He would be doing something good for them. Right?

Damnationists: Possibly so, but their fate is sealed for eternity.

Christian Universalist: We'll look at the 'fate is sealed for eternity' in just a moment but for now a few more questions. Next question is, if God does something good, then couldn't you say that he gladly does it? In other words, If God does something good, then He certainly could not be unhappy or displeased that He is doing it, but glad instead. Correct?

Damnationist: Yes of course.

Christian Universalist: Then you agree that it is a good thing God created Hell/Lake of Fire and put the wicked there, and in so doing such a good thing, it is easy as well to say He did it gladly. Correct?

Chapter Nine | So Who Wins the Game?

Damnationist: Yes, I suppose so. If God putting the wicked/lost in Hellfire forever was a bad thing, then He could not be said to be a good God. God cannot do bad.

Christian Universalist: So you teach the ultimate end of being in Hell is being there for eternity. If you are correct and that is the case then going to Hell/Lake of Fire would be a bad thing for anyone. Correct?

Damnationist: Yes it would I suppose, that is a terrible fate for anyone, to be totally abandoned and given up on and tormented in fire and brimstone for eternity. I guess you are right, that would not be a good thing by God doing so.

Christian Universalist: As well, would it not be true that if a good God put someone in Hell/Lake of Fire for eternity that he could not have done it 'gladly'? Either He was a 'bad' God gladly doing a sadistic thing, or a good God gladly doing a good thing which would eventually have a happy ending. Do not the scriptures teach that the 'goodness of God leadeth thee to repentance?'

If your son or daughter were to die lost, and God therefore puts them in Hell for eternity, would that not be a bad thing, and if a bad thing then it could be said that God gladly did a bad thing with a bad end since He issues the final judgment decree supposedly for eternity.

Damnationist: Yes that would be bad to have my children wind up in Hell/Lake of Fire forever.

Christian Universalist: if say an atheist begins to believe in the existence of God in this life, then they are improving so some degree in their beliefs which may eventually lead to their salvation, so could it not be said that an atheist in Hell who begins to believe in God, had begun to 'improve' there as well?

Damnationist: Yes I suppose so, but they are still in Hell.

Christian Universalist: So as well when God sends the wicked/atheist etc. to Hell/Lake of Fire and they begin to believe in the existence of

God and as well they agree that their punishment is due and just, could it not be said that such is good, that God has done a good thing, and that He has gladly done it?

Damnationist: Yes it is a good thing the wicked are sent to Hell, they certainly deserve it.

Christian Universalist: As well I fully agree. So if a good God does a good thing, then He gladly does it and whatever a good God does must have a favorable ending! So do you not agree that a good God cannot do a good thing if the end thereof is going to be bad and say maim someone (with fire and brimstone) for eternity?

Damnationist: Yes I suppose so.

Christian Universalist: Is not God a God of perfect justice, and does He not apply it evenly and fairly to all?

Damnationist: Yes of course.

Christian Universalist: Would it be just and righteous for say a judge or court to permanently maim or disfigure a thief by having his hand cut off for say stealing a pack of cigarettes?

Damnationist: Of course not!

Christian Universalist: Then what about doing the same thing to say a 12-16 year old boy or girl?

Damnationist: Of course not.

Christian Universalist: Does not our own sense of fair justice tell us that such would be a perversion of justice?

Damnationist: Yes of course.

Christian Universalist: Then would it be justice for God to permanently maim and disfigure a soul for eternity by burning them with fire and brimstone endlessly forever despite the fact they have been enlightened with irrefutable revelation after death? Also couldn't it be said that therefore such endless torment in liquid fire and brimstone would not nor could be gladly done by a good God?

Damnationist: Yes that would seem to be correct but the Bible says the wicked will be tormented in fire and brimstone for eternity.

Christian Universalist: Now where in God's Word does it say the wicked will be in Hell/Lake of Fire for eternity?

Damnationist: God's Word, the King James 1611 version which is the infallible Word of God, tells us that the wicked will be tormented in fire and brimstone forever and forever in Revelation. That account is the Lake of Fire in Revelation 14, and then those in Revelation 20 who are cast there as well will no doubt have the same sentence "forever and forever." I believe God's Word is infallibly true. If the 1611 is in error then we do not have the Word of God!

Christian Universalist: I am aware of the following facts which you cannot dispute. 1. The K.J.V. 1611 is a translation of the original languages in which the Word of God was written in. 2. No *translation* can ever be said to be given under divine inspiration, equal to the way the original autographs were given under direct and perfect inspiration of the Holy Spirit (i.e. literally 'God breathed'). So therefore a translation done by fallible men is only as accurate as it is accurately translated by them. 3. Jesus never used the word "endless" in the original languages relating to duration of punishment in Hell/Lake of Fire. He did use the word for "continual" or "continuous" (Gk. aionios) which in any language does not mean "endless" (Gk. aidios). 4. The Word of God plainly says that "All Israel shall be saved" (Romans 11:26) and "all" means "all." As well scripture plainly teaches that every knee shall bow and every tongue confess that Jesus Christ is Lord to the glory of God the Father. 5. The English words, "eternal, everlasting, eternity" just happen to be words coined in the 13th century and have no equivalents in the Greek. 6. "Continuous" (aionios) in the Greek was/is (erroneously so) translated "Eternal" (English for 'endless') in the K.J.V. 7. "Continuous" and "Endless" *do not mean the same thing in any language.* A fact which no one can deny. 8. Revelation

22 irrefutably states that the old earth, heaven, and all the former things, which naturally includes the Lake of Fire, *pass away and are no more.* 9. And lastly, the last enemy to be destroyed is "Death" (remember, 'death' encompasses all aspects of death, both physical and spiritual) or separation from God by sin, and that would naturally include all of humanity. Adam died two ways. The day he disobeyed God he died spiritually, and as well eventually died physically, and when Revelation 22 is fulfilled physical and/or spiritual death will be no more. No more, means no more for anyone! God cannot be defeated, not willing that any should perish, but that all should come to repentance. Sad it is, the god of damnationism is a defeated god who was only able to win a small percentage of humanity to himself, while Satan was/is able to win the majority to himself. The God of universal salvation however totally defeats Satan, sin, death Hell and the grave and ultimately wins all to Himself losing none, and is ultimately shown to be the all powerful, all sufficient blessed Savior of the world! If the god of damnationism is the true God, then He as God can speak the *wicked out of existence* just as easily as He spoke them *into existence* at their conception. By that solution He could not be charged with sadistically burning them in fire and brimstone for eternity hearing their screams and cries for mercy endlessly forever. As well also He could not be said to be punishing finite sins with infinite punishment which is gross violation of true justice. Why not take a disobedient dog, and ignite him in gasoline daily year after year with no mercy!? Why not do the same to wicked criminals in prison continually day after day the rest of their lives with no mercy disregarding their screams of pain and suffering until they finally die? Oh no that would be sadistic and cruel, but disobedient/ignorant man must be treated worse than that dog or criminal by some monster god after death by being unmercifully soaked in fire and brimstone for eternity? Is that the kind of god you serve??? No doubt there is fire, pain and suffering in different levels of the Biblical Hell. However though, that punishment will be meted out according to works (which were only temporary in nature). As well that punishment will be continuous, measured, remedial and corrective, but it will not be endless!

Damnationist: Well, I still believe that God's Word is infallibly and perfectly preserved in the A.V. 1611, and God has used the English language to preserve His Word. All I need is the 1611, an English dictionary and I can understand any doctrine without having to go to the Greek etc. I believe the A.V. is superior to the Greek/Hebrew etc. manuscripts from which it was translated.

Christian Universalist: So then the world did not have the infallible Word of God until 1611, meaning that for 1600 years or so, the gates of Hell prevailed against the church defeating it, and thereby meaning billions died and went to Hell because they did not have the 1611 A.V.? Well I believe Jesus was correct when He said the gates of Hell *would not* prevail against the church. I for one do not believe the gates of Hell prevailed against the church for 1600 years until the K.J.V. 1611 came along. Your ignorance of the truth is deplorable and inexcusable, and you have a total lack of education in the preservation of God's Holy Word. Also you damnationists need to realize that the only possible reason for God to inflict endless pain and suffering in Hell fire and brimstone on anyone, is if He were a god of sadism, and had totally given up in defeat against the powers of Satan in attempting to win those lost souls to Christ. To inflict such horrific pain and suffering on lost souls for eternity *not to **teach any lesson*** to them, could only be due to God supposedly being a sadistic God who delights in inflicting pain and suffering *for no reason*. Evidently your god is that type god, mine certainly is not.

Damnationist: I believe God has ordained that the English language is to be the language in which His word is translated into for the entire world. Since God's word is pure like pure gold and silver it must be preserved for us today and I believe it is so in the English language. Psalm 12:6-8 says, "The words of the Lord are pure words, like silver tried in a furnace of earth, purified seven times..." and also Psalm 119:89, "Forever O Lord, thy word is settled in heaven..." So we have the pure word of God in our language, the English language!

Christian Universalist: You need to remember the curse placed on those who distort, change, or pervert God's word! Revelation 22:19 warns against adding or taking away from God's word. It says, "If any man shall take away from the words of the book of this prophecy, God shall take away his part out of the book of life, and out of the holy city, and from the things which are written in this book." You damnationists have bought into the false heretical teaching that 'aionios' Greek, (continuous/on and on or ages and ages) is the same equivalent as 'aidios' Greek (endless). You ignore that fact and also the fact that never did our Savior or His disciples teach 'endless' punishment, yea only 'continuous/indefinite length' punishment!! You pervert God's word by denying that "...ALL Israel shall be saved," or that "...Jesus is the Savior of ALL men," or that "...EVERY KNEE shall bow and EVERY TONGUE shall confess, "...or that "...God is not willing that any should perish!" You deny where the Word of God plainly says that the '...former things pass away...' which includes the Lake of Fire, the original heavens and the earth and all therein. Denial, denial, denial of God's word in the original languages, and seeking to deify the English translation.

Damnationist: You insist on correcting God's infallible Word. You must not believe the Bible is God's holy word. I am not a 'Bible corrector like you are, I am a Bible believer.'

Christian Universalist: If you are a true Bible believer then you must believe that God gave us His sacred, infallible word in the Greek/Hebrew languages, *not* the English. I therefore challenge you to prove God gave us His infallible word in the English, and that you cannot do, so your argument is false. As well, it is a fact that 'endless' and 'continuous or ages and ages' are not the same equivalents, and that is true in any language. By following unclear English translation *you* are the one subverting the word of God by forcing it to say that which it does not! By following the perversion of God's word by Augustine, you are the one who in reality is a Bible corrector and I am the one who is the Bible believer! Let me ask you this. Do you believe that all Jews who have denied Jesus is their Messiah over the centuries will be in Hell fire and brimstone for eternity?

Damnationist: Absolutely! Every Jew or Israelite who died without accepting Jesus as his Messiah is going to burn in Hell/Lake of Fire for eternity. They cannot ever be saved without accepting Jesus! That is the same with the Gentiles!

Christian Universalist: It is true that no one can be saved without accepting Jesus as Lord, but you deny the truth of Romans 11:26 and Isaiah 45:22-25 which says "...*ALL* Israel **shall be saved.**" *You* change God's word by saying "Only **some** of Israel shall be saved!" Now that makes you a Bible corrector and I the Bible believer! Another place you 'correct' the Word of God is where you are claiming that "ALL" does not mean "ALL."Romans 3, vss. 12, 15, 18-19. "Wherefore as by one man sin entered into the world, and death by sin, and so death passed upon *all* men for that *all* have sinned, But not as the offence, so also is the free gift. For if through the offence of one *many* be dead, much more the grace of God and the gift by grace which is by one man, Jesus Christ, hath abounded unto *many*. Therefore as by the offence of one judgment came upon *all* men to condemnation even so by the righteousness of one the free gift came upon *all* men unto justification of life. For as by one man's disobedience *many* were made sinners, so by the obedience of one shall *many* be made righteous." It is clear here that 'all' and 'many' in this case are synonymous so it could be paraphrased as follows: (Romans 5:18-19), "Therefore as by the offence of one judgment came upon all men to condemnation, even so by the righteousness of one, the free gift came upon all men unto justification of life. For as by one man all were made sinners, so by the obedience of one, shall all be made righteous." So by saying that most of humanity will burn in Hell-fire and brimstone for eternity you are the one changing the Word of God not I! You therefore are the Bible corrector, and I the Bible believer.

Reader note: J.W. Hanson wrote: "When our Lord spoke, the doctrine of unending torment was believed by many of those who listened to his words and they stated it in terms and employed others, entirely differently, in describing the duration of punishment, from the terms afterward used by those who taught universal salvation and annihilation, and so gave to the terms in question the sense of unlimited duration. For example the Pharisees according to Josephus, regarded the penalty of sin as torment without end, and they stated the doctrine in unambiguous terms. They called it *eirgmos aidios* (eternal imprisonment) and *timorion adialeipton* (endless torment), while our Lord called the punishment of sin *aionion kolasin* (age-long chastisement*). " At this point, the reader of this book should now see the need for the K.J.V. etc., to be thoroughly revised in regards to the unclear translation of the terms 'eternal, everlasting, forever, and eternity. Such a thorough revision is long overdue.*

Our Lord Taught Only a Few Would Be Saved!?

Sadly our Damnationist friends cannot move beyond the simple warnings our Savior gave in His teachings that only a few would be saved, few would be called and only a few chosen. The following scriptures show such (etc).

Luke 13:23-24

"...Lord are there few that shall be saved?" Jesus said..."Strive to enter the strait gate for many I say unto you will seek to enter in, and shall not be able..."

Matthew 20:16

"So the last shall be first and the first last, for many are called but few chosen."

Of course naturally they ask the question of how possibly could U.C.R. fit into these verses? The answer is simple. It must be realized that the Bible, the Word of God which we use today, was recorded for all of the centuries leading up to the beginning of the Day of the Lord and the translation of the church called the rapture. It is our guide book and inspired truth which will find its usefulness exhausted maybe sometime before or on into the millennium. During the millennium we will not need the Bible to guide us since we will be in the literal presence of our Savior. He will rule and reign here on earth in person with a rod of iron. It follows therefore that of course during all the ages up to and including the millennium, only a small minority will be saved. During these ages God's people have evangelized the world as best they could, with of course much satanic opposition from the world the flesh and the Devil. Jesus making these statements simply was forecasting the fact that the majority of people living during this time (the time the scriptures are of the utmost importance to the church) would *not* be saved. Thankfully the Word of God gives the final picture after the White Throne Judgment, "…every knee shall (*finally ed.*) bow and every tongue shall confess that Jesus Christ is Lord to the glory of God the Father…" So in the end, there is no contradiction to what Jesus taught when He was here. He was simply referring to all the ages up to and maybe including the millennium.

Sadly, Damnationists Do Not Really 'Know' the Real Jesus, The Jesus of the Bible

Oh, yes! Of course there is no doubt that many of those whom we term as 'damnationists' are truly born again, blood washed wonderful saints of God! It is so sad though that the 'biblical Jesus' the true Savior of the world is looked upon by them as one who indeed loves all peoples of all generations, that is so long as they are alive. However, if they die without receiving Him in the full pardon of sins, then His love for them suddenly ends, and He in unmitigated wrath and anger supposedly consigns them to a fiery inferno to be mercilessly tortured in fire and brimstone for endless eternity (yes by Him-Jesus, since He designed the Lake of Fire and the conditions therein). As well, sad it is that their churches sing God/Christ honoring music, and bring magnificent adoration to His name by sermon and Sunday school lessons, honoring His holy name. Then on the other hand He is portrayed by these same services (unwittingly of course and in ignorance) as to being a sadist god who gives up in frustration on all who die lost, and mercilessly torments them in fire and brimstone for endless eternity. So in the final analysis, damnationists do not really know, nor can they truly deeply appreciate the biblical Jesus and bring the true honor and adoration to Him He really deserves. Then lastly, the worse part of having this false perception of Christ is how much God/Christ and of course the Spirit of God must be grieved, offended and insulted by such hateful doctrine. God help the church to see this truth.

The Doctrine of Endless Damnation Creates a Cruel and Revengeful Spirit — Illustrated From History.

Most shocking of all, the doctrine of merciless endless torment in hell fire/brimstone (which is/was held as the gospel truth in past history by the Roman Church), bred the worst of sadistic persecutions which were inflicted upon those outside of her folds. In years past, this author for one could not fathom the depravity of, nor the reason for the inquisitions by the Roman Church, which were inflicted on all multitudes she deemed as heretics. In 1855, Dr. Thomas B. Thayer wrote the following shocking historical facts concerning this. *(Ed. Note: It is only fair for this author to remind the reader that while we quote Dr. Thayer, we are of course in disagreement with his theology concerning the Fatherhood of God, and brotherhood of men, and his seeming downplaying of the righteous wrath of God upon the wicked. Plainly speaking we do not accept his type of Universal theology. None the less, his article vividly portrays the hideous fruit of the doctrine of endless damnation which is still very relevant).* We quote as follows:

It matters not by what name a man is called, whether Pagan, Jew, or Christian; nor matters it at all where the lot of life has fallen to him, whether in a land over which broods the night of heathenism, or on which rests the radiant light of the Gospel. He is still a man, though a Christian; he is born, lives, and dies; he thinks and feels, hopes and fears, rejoices and sorrows, after the manner of all other men. Hence, if the Christian believe in a cruel religion, believe in it with all his heart, it will make him cruel; it will certainly harden his heart. If he believe in and worship a God of a merciless and ferocious character, this will eventually be, visibly or invisibly, his own character. If he believes the God of the Bible hates any portion of mankind, or regards them with any dislike or displeasure, he also will come to hate them, and to entertain towards them the same feelings which he supposes reside in the bosom of God. If he believe that God will, in expression of those feelings, or for any reason, devote them to flame and torture hereafter, it is natural and necessary that he should infer it would be, for the same reason, acceptable to God that he should devote them to flame and torture here. And if the degree of civilization and the condition of society shall permit; or, in other words, if no power from without prevent, he will assuredly do this, as a most acceptable offering to Heaven; and to the utmost of his power will conform to what he believes to be the disposition and wishes of God in this respect.

And this is not said without ample means for proving the correctness of the statement. The history of Christianity, so called, in all ages and among every people, and in every form which it has taken, will abundantly establish the truth of the position, that the temper and practice of a people is determined by the spirit of their religion and their gods.It is not necessary to enter into a labored description of the doctrines of the Christian church in the days of its darkness and corruption, nor of the awful and revolting views entertained of God, of His disposition towards man, of His government, laws and punishments. It is enough that Paganism in its worst forms has never surpassed, if it has equaled, the savage and terrible descriptions which have been given by Christians of their God. The character ascribed to Him; the dreadful wrath and vengeance with which He is moved; the cold and malignant purpose of creation in regard to millions of souls; the stern severity and gloom of His government; the horrible and never-ceasing tortures which He *(Ed. Supposedly)* will inflict on His helpless children - all this, and much more of like character, defies the power of language to set it forth in its true light, or to present it in a manner adequate to its shocking and revolting reality. I give a single example:

Dr. Benson, an eminent English minister, in a sermon on "The Future Misery of the Wicked," says, "God is present in hell, in his infinite justice and almighty wrath, as an unfathomable sea of liquid fire, where the wicked must drink in everlasting torture. The presence of God in his vengeance scatters darkness and woe through the dreary regions of misery. As heaven would be no heaven if God did not there manifest his love, so hell would be no hell if God did not there display his wrath. It is the presence and agency of God which gives everything virtue and efficacy, without which there can be no life, no sensibility, no power." He then adds, "God is, therefore, himself present in hell, to see the punishment of these rebels against his government, that it may be adequate to the infinity of their guilt: his fiery indignation kindles, and his incensed fury feeds the flame of their torment, while his powerful presence and operation maintain their being, and render all their powers most acutely sensible; thus setting the keenest edge upon their pain, and making it cut most intolerably deep. He will exert all his divine attributes to make them as wretched as the capacity of their nature will admit." After this he goes on to describe the duration of this work of God, and calls to his aid all the stars, sand, and drops of water, and makes each one tell a million of ages; and when all those ages have rolled away, he goes over the same number again, and again, and so on forever.

Yet, Christians have believed all this; have believed that God is the enemy of the sinner and unbeliever; that He regards with a fierce displeasure those of a wrong faith or a wrong life; that heretics and the impenitent are an abomination in His sight; and that upon these wretched victims the vials of His wrath will finally be broken, and overwhelm them in endless and irretrievable ruin. As remarked, it will not need that we should give a lengthened or labored review of this point. A more important question is that which regards the influence of this savage creed upon the believer. To this let us give some attention, and we shall find, what we may expect, that its tendency in all ages, when believed in right earnest, has been to harden the heart, to brutalize the affections, and render those receiving it, under any of its forms, cruel, and ferocious in disposition, and, so far as circumstances would allow, in practice.

Take as a worthy example the celebrated passage of Tertullian, already quoted: "How shall I admire, how laugh, how rejoice, how exult, when I behold so many kings and false gods, together with Jove himself, groaning in the lowest abyss of darkness! so many magistrates who persecuted the name of the Lord, liquefying in fiercer flames than they ever kindled against Christians; so many sage philosophers, with their deluded scholars, blushing in raging fire!" Without doubt, Tertullian was of a fierce and bitter spirit, independently of his religious faith; but this fiery ebullition of hate and ferocity serves to show how perfectly fitted that faith was to add fuel to the flame, and what an ample field and congenial scenes it furnished for his savage nature to revel in. Under the influence of such a belief, his wild temper gathered new vigor, his revengeful feelings were cultivated and strengthened to a frightful degree, till at last he comes to rejoice and exult in the agonies of the damned with a relish that a devil might envy. One cannot but see that it only needed the power to have engaged this ferocious man in the work of torture on earth, the prospect of which in hell he contemplated with such fiendish delight.

A further illustration may be found in the crusades against the Albigenses in the thirteenth century, one of the darkest and bloodiest pages in the history of any religion, Christian or Pagan. The sacrifices of the Goth and Mexican, and the revolting cruelties of the Polynesian and the negro of Dahomy, are scarcely equal to the savage butcheries and the shocking barbarities inflicted by the Catholic crusader, in the name of his God, upon this gentle and virtuous people. No passage in the history of man is more to the purpose of our argument, or more conclusive of the direct influence of religious faith upon the temper and character, than that in which are recorded the persecutions and sufferings of these unhappy reformers. Throughout the whole of this merciless crusade, and amid all its scenes of burning and desolation, of murder and torture, the cry of the ruthless priest was heard, "It is for the glory of God!" And the brutal multitude, believing that they were doing God a service, and securing their own salvation by the slaughter of heretics, rushed forward to the bloody work with the ferocity of tigers and the joy of a Tertullian.

Sismondi says, speaking of the deliberate savageness of the monks who occupied the pulpits, and urged on the people to this diabolical work, they "showed how every vice might be expiated by crime; how remorse might be expelled by the flames of their piles; how the soul, polluted with every shameful passion, might become pure and spotless by bathing in the blood of heretics. By continuing to preach the crusade, they impelled, each year, waves of new fanatics upon those miserable provinces; and they compelled their chiefs to recommence the war, in order to profit by the fervor of those who still demanded human victims, and required blood to effect their salvation." They represented this inoffensive people as the outcasts of the human race, and the especial objects of divine hatred and vengeance; and no devotional exercise, no prayer or praise, no act of charity or mercy, was half so acceptable to God as the murder of a heretic.

"The more zealous, therefore, the multitude were for the glory of God, the more ardently they labored for the destruction of heretics, the better Christians they thought themselves. And if at any time they felt a movement of pity or terror, whilst assisting at their punishment, they thought it a revolt of the flesh, which they confessed at the tribunal of penitence; nor could they get quit of their remorse till their priests had given them absolution." "Amongst them all not a heart could be found accessible to pity. Equally inspired by fanaticism and the love of war, they believed that the sure way to salvation was through the field of carnage. Seven bishops, who followed the army, had blessed their standards and their arms, and would be engaged in prayer for them while they were attacking the heretics. Thus did they advance, indifferent whether to victory or martyrdom, certain that either would issue in the reward which God himself had destined for them."

And most frightfully did they do the work of religious butchery and cruelty. Like the Scandinavian pirates, wherever they went they desolated with fire and sword, sparing neither age, nor sex, nor condition. They even wreaked their furious vengeance on inanimate objects, destroying houses, trees, vines, and every useful thing they could reach, leaving all behind a wide and blackened waste, marked by smoldering and smoking ruins, and the dead and putrefying bodies of murdered men, women, and children. At the taking of Beziers the wretched sufferers fled to the churches for protection, but their savage enemies slaughtered them on the very altars, and filled the sanctuaries with their mangled bodies. And when the last living creature within the walls had been slain, and the houses plundered, the crusaders set fire to the city in all directions at once, and so made of it one huge funeral pile. Not a soul was left alive, nor a house left standing! During the slaughter one of the knights inquired of a fierce priest how they should distinguish between Catholics and heretics.

"Kill them all!" was his reply, *"the Lord will know his own."* In this one affair from twenty to thirty thousand human beings perished, because the religion of their butchers assured them that such bloody sacrifices would be acceptable to God.

But the priests and crusaders were not content with simple murder. It was often preceded by the most exquisite cruelties. De Montfort on one occasion seized a hundred prisoners, cut off their noses, tore out their eyes, and sent them with a one-eyed man as a guide to the neighboring castles to announce to the inhabitants what they might expect when taken. And often, as matter of amusement, so hardened had they become, they subjected their victims to the most dreadful tortures, and rejoiced in their wild cries of agony, and manifested the highest delight at the writhings and contortions of the dying wretches. So perfectly fiendish had these fanatics grown through the influence of their religious belief! And what can more clearly show the connection between faith and practice, or more conclusively demonstrate the truth that the worshipper will be like his god, than the revolting barbarities inflicted upon these humble and innocent people, on the ground that they were hated of the Deity, and devoted by Him to the flames and torments of an endless hell! Verily, the Christian is but a man, and that which makes the Pagan ferocious and blood-thirsty will produce the same effect upon him.

The massacre of St. Bartholomew is another terrible proof of the power of religious faith to convert man into a fiend. As a single exhibition of slaughter and cruelty in the name of God and religion, this is perhaps the most monstrous, and on a more fearful scale, than any before or since. Probably thirty or forty thousand victims perished in Paris and in the provinces in this one butchery! And it would be almost impossible to describe the variety of forms in murder, or to give a catalogue of the cruelties practiced. Even children of ten or twelve years engaged in the work of blood, and were seen cutting the throats of heretic infants! But what is the most impious of all is the manner in which the news of this massacre was received at Rome by the Church and its head. The courier was welcomed with lively transports, and received a large reward for his joyful news. The pope and his cardinals marched in solemn procession to the church of St. Mark to acknowledge the special providence; high mass was celebrated; and a jubilee was published, that the whole Christian world might return thanks to God (!) for this destruction of the enemies of the church in France. In the evening, the cannon of castle St. Angelo were fired, and the whole city illuminated with bonfires, in expression of the general joy for this dreadful slaughter. 2

And when we remember that all this was done in the name of Christianity and the church, that it was deemed a grateful offering to God, who, it is supposed, hates heretics, and will give them over to torments infinitely greater than these, and endless, we shudder to think how terrible an engine is superstition, and how nearly it has turned the Christian church into a slaughter-house! Truly, one has well said: "The ancient Roman theater, with its mere sprinkling of blood, and its momentary pangs and shrieks, quite fades if brought into comparison with that Coliseum of Papal cruelty, in which not a hundred or two of victims, but myriads of people - yes, nations entire - have been gorged!" To complete the picture of depravity and cruelty, and confirm the argument for the influence of religion on the heart and life, we need only refer to that thrice-accursed institution, the INQUISITION! In this was concentrated all that was monstrous and revolting. It were impossible to put into words sufficiently expressive the abominable principles upon which its ministers proceeded in their persecutions, or the cold, deliberate, malignant ferocity with which they tortured their miserable victims. Every species of torment was invented that the united talents of the inquisitors could devise; and the protracting of life under the most excruciating agonies, so that the poor wretch might endure to the last degree, was reduced to a perfect system. The annals of Pagan sacrifice, with all its horrors, furnish no parallel to the atrocities of the Romish Inquisition. 4 The blackest and bloodiest page in the history of superstition is that which bears the record of inquisitorial bigotry and ferocity. One would think that even hell itself might applaud the refinement of cruelty, were not the devils kept silent through envy of the superior skill and savageness of their earthly rivals.

But this terrible influence was not confined to the priests of this religion; the cruel and ferocious spirit of it was diffused abroad among all its believers; and its pestilential breath spread over the whole social life of the people. Informers were encouraged, heretics were hunted, private hatred took its revenge, and the most malignant passions of the corrupt heart were roused into action in the service of God and the church. Even the tenderest ties of affection, and the holiest relations of life, were crushed beneath the iron heel of religious zeal. Husbands betrayed their wives, and parents their children, and sisters their brothers, and gave them up to the cruelties of the holy office, and to the flames of the auto-da-fe; and, so doing, congratulated themselves upon their fidelity to God, measured by their triumph over the loveliest attributes of humanity. 5 So mighty, in this case also, was the power of a savage religion to crush every kindly feeling, every emotion of love and pity, and to train its followers to cruelty and blood.

But this influence is not confined to Catholics beliefs; it is found wherever the doctrines of which it is the offspring are found. The history of Calvin and Servetus *(Ed. Calvin was responsible for the murder of Servetus, a so called heretic whom Calvin hated and condemned)* who was a brilliant scholar of his day in many fields shows the same savage faith, having the power, doing the same infernal work. And the history of the Puritans of our own land, of the Dissenters of England, of the Covenanters of Scotland, of the Jews everywhere, discovers also the same faith; shorn of its power, to be sure, by the progress of society and civil institutions, but, with a change of circumstances, ready at any time to seize the dagger or the torch, and spring forth to the work of death. Reluctant as we may be to admit it, we cannot blind ourselves to these facts. The cruel butcheries of the past, the dungeon, the rack, the fagot, the bloody scourge falling upon the back of the meekly suffering Quaker, the cry of agony, the unheeded prayer for mercy - all these in the past; - and the exceeding bitterness, the fierce clamor and unblushing falsehoods of controversy in the present; the refusal of the common courtesies of life, or the stern hate that often lurks beneath outward civility; the malignant sneer at the labors of those who seek to unfold the truth of God's saving love for all; the half exultation at any seeming proof of the final triumph of evil and the ceaseless torments of the wicked; the hardness of heart with which this result is sometimes contemplated, and the indifference with which one sect devotes another to this awful doom - all these show clearly that the Christian is subject to the same law which governs other men; show with a painful distinctness that, so far as the refining influences of literature and civilization would permit, the belief in a ferocious god and an endless hell have done their legitimate work upon his heart. Like the Aztec of America, and the Norseman of Europe, he has partaken of the spirit of his deity, and, supposing it a duty and a most acceptable service, he begins, so far as he can in this world, the work of torment which he believes his unforgiving god will make infinite and endless in the next.Queen Mary of England was right when, as Bp. Burnet says, she defended her bloody persecutions by appealing to the supposed example of the Deity: "As the souls of heretics are hereafter to be eternally burning in hell, there can be nothing more proper than for me to imitate the divine vengeance by burning them on earth." This is legitimate and logical reasoning, and exhibits the natural fruits of the doctrine.

If, then, we would make mankind what they should be, we must begin with the object of their worship; we must first make their religion what it should be. We must cast out from the holy place all the dark and ferocious superstitions of the past and the present, whether Pagan or Christian, and in the place of these set up, in all its divine beauty and simplicity, the merciful and loving religion of Jesus Christ. The views which this unfolds of God the Father, of His government and its final issues, can alone be favorable to the spiritual progress of humanity, can alone form the heart of man to gentleness and goodness, and recreate it in the image of heaven. "National religions," says a celebrated German, "will not become the friends of virtue and happiness until they teach that the Deity is not only an inconceivably powerful, but also an inconceivably wise and good being; that for this reason He gives way neither to anger nor revenge, and never punishes capriciously; that we owe to His favor alone all the good that we possess and enjoy; that even our sufferings contribute to our highest good, and death is a bitter but salutary change; in fine, that the sacrifice most acceptable to God consists in a mind that seeks for truth, and a pure heart. Religions which announce these exalted truths offer to man the strongest preservatives from vice, and the strongest motives to virtue, exalt and ennoble his joys, console and guide him in all kinds of misfortunes, and inspire him with forbearance, patience, and active benevolence towards his brethren." Even so; let this be the religion of the nations, and soon the world shall be getting forward toward heaven. And it was to reveal these truths, and to bring them near to the heart of humanity, that Jesus gave His life, and labored with all the earnestness of His loving heart.

Let this, then, be the religion of the Christian, and he will be a Christian indeed. Let him believe in God as the parent of all, as the dispenser of life and good to all; let him see Him as Christ saw Him, clothed in robes of light and mercy, and he will love as Christ loved, and, so far as he may, will live as Christ lived. Let him believe that God always blesses, and he will not dare, he will not wish, to curse whom God hath blessed. Let him believe that God never hates, is never angry; and, that he may be like Him, and approved of Him, he will diligently seek to expel all hatred and passion from his own heart. Let him believe that all men are brethren, journeying homeward to the presence of the Father, where, delivered from all evil, we shall be as the angels; and that it is the earnest entreaty of this Father that we should not fall out by the way, but bear each other's burdens, and love one another as He loves us, loves the world: let these be the Christian's views of God, and he shall indeed be born again from above. Let this be the religion of the nations, and "Earth shall be paradise again, and man, O God, thine image here. End of quote.

The Wrath Anger and Displeasure of God As Viewed From the Generic Universalist vs. the Christian Universalist

Thayer's brilliant expose that the devastating effect the hideous doctrine of endless damnation has wrought unimaginable pain and suffering upon humanity, makes it very clear that both camps are doctrinally diametrically opposed on the wrath, anger and displeasure of God upon humanity. The basic difference is that Thayer seems to be a generic Universalist. He seems to down play the plain biblical teaching that God is indeed or can be a God of wrath, anger and displeasure, and often executes that wrath by bringing severe pain and suffering to the wicked in this life, or in consigning them to Hell/Lake of Fire in the next. The problem (with generic Universalists) is that they do not understand that these attributes of God/Christ are exercised, not to unjustifiably torment man for eternity, but rather to bring him to humility, submission and holy reverence, with an end view of bringing him to repentance, the new birth and salvation! They evidently feel that to admit to these attributes of God is to portray a God void of sympathy compassion and love. Actually on the contrary, the backside, of these attributes is compassion and love demonstrated. All of God's attributes are attributes of virtue and honor, which in themselves are exercised in love to bring wicked man to his knees in faith and repentance.

Years ago, I as a dyed in the wool damnationist, was impressed with a message from the Lord to my heart. While I usually highly doubt many who say "The Lord said to me…" (not that God cannot speak to us in His own way), I distinctly was impressed with the message from the Lord to my heart that, "You do not know the spirit you are of…" Of course at the time, I had no idea what such message meant. Then again visiting a sister church, I was approached by a good brother who asked me (regarding the other church I normally attended), "Oh you are attending that hellfire brimstone church?" Both times I had no clue what inference was meant by these comments. Especially the second since both churches were damnationist type churches. Then several years later, the thought came to my heart, "How can anyone believe in universal redemption, that all are going to ultimately to be saved one day." Contemplating this last thought, I began to search 'universal redemption" on the different web sites, and gradually began to see biblical facts I could not refute about universal redemption. Thus studying and writing over the next 4 years or so, I found solid biblical facts, to see the truth of universal Christian redemption, and as a result this book. Thank God!

The Roman Catholic Church and Her False Claim That God Granted Her Authority to Forgive Sin Examined

Little wonder is it that when a church considers itself and its leaders so honored by Almighty God to have the power and authority to forgive sins, (a privilege/position only owned by God Himself) that it assumes absolute spiritual authority over every person on earth! That the Roman Church claims the infallibility of the Pope is no new revelation. Wikepedia tells us: *Papal infallibility Papal infallibility is a dogma of the Roman Catholic Church which states that, in virtue of the promise of Jesus to Peter, the pope when appealing to his highest authority is preserved from the possibility of error on doctrine "initially given to the apostolic Church and handed down in Scripture and tradition".* (Wikepedia)

Thus when over the many centuries the Popes commanded 'Death to the Protestant Heretics' in Europe etc., and millions of poor souls were slaughtered by sword, inquisition, hanging, poison etc, while the Roman church (fully participating) considered the Popes blameless at that savage butchery. Also that false assumption seems to give the Papacy the right to destroy all Protestants, non Catholics etc., who refuse to join her ranks. Certainly when ever/where ever in past centuries she comes into absolute control of the government, she suddenly will not peacefully co-exist with those of other faiths. Those poor souls suddenly find themselves persecuted, hounded, attacked, put to the fire/ guillotine, noose or sword! Thankfully, America was founded by non-

Catholic Protestant type settlers, who were willing to give religious freedom to all people of any religion. That is what our wonderful constitution demands. Therefore today, Roman Catholics are forced to dwell in peace and security, and are free to worship at they please.

Does the Roman Catholic Church Have Power Through Her Priests To Forgive Sins?

For centuries the Roman Church has claimed the power to forgive sins through her priests. She proudly goes to the scriptures to point out John 20:25 as her (supposed) proof text. As well she goes to Matthew 16:13-19 in attempt to show that our Lord Jesus built his church and commissioned it upon the Apostle Peter (whom they claim was the first Pope). Scholars point out that there was/is no historical evidence that the Apostle Peter was ever in Rome. We should add if our memory serves us, that in Rome there certainly was a pagan follower/leader in a certain Babylonian cult in the time of Christ named Peter, but certainly not the Apostle Peter.

Historian Alexander Hislop, who authored 'The Two Babylons' proves that same cult which had confession, the priest craft, worship of Semarimas the supposed virgin goddess/god and her supposedly virgin born son Nimrod etc, eventually morphed into a so called 'Christian religion adopting some of the beliefs of the early Christian church. The true early Christian church because of her popularity surrounding our Lord caused that Babylonian cult to fear its own demise. So, it quickly adopted the main tenants of the true Christian church. Of course her plan of salvation was/is based on the works system of merit and eventually became what the Catholic Church is today, a false system of worship with Mariolatry at its heart. The simple fact that the roots of the Roman Catholic Church can be traced to the Babylonian system of worship instituted and founded by Nimrod and his mother Semaramis, which could possibly endorse their claim of being the oldest religion in the world. (I.e. 'religion' created and instituted by man, which true Christianity is not.)

Revelation 17-18 clearly describes that Babylonian religious system, which is built upon seven mountains, and as well reveals her destruction close to the return of Christ. Rome is the only city in the world built on seven mountains which today is the headquarters for the Church of Rome.)

Matthew 16:13-19

When Jesus came into the coasts of Caesarea Philippi He asked His disciples saying, Whom do men say that I the Son of man am? And they said, Some say that thou art John the Baptist, some Elias, and others, Jeremias, or one of the prophets. He saith unto them, But whom say ye that I am? And Simon Peter answered and said, Thou art the Christ the Son of the living God. And Jesus answered and said unto him, Blessed art thou Simon Barjona for flesh and blood hath not revealed it unto thee but my Father which is in heaven. And I say also unto thee that thou art Peter and upon this rock I will build my church and the gates of Hell shall not prevail against it. And I will give unto thee the keys of the kingdom of heaven: and whatsoever thou shalt bind on earth shall be bound in heaven: and whatsoever thou shalt loose on earth shall be loosed in Heaven. Then charged He his disciples that they should tell no man that He was Jesus the Christ.

First it must be said that to make such a claim, (that our Lord gave the Apostles the power to forgive sin in these verses) is truly a great stretch away from the truth. The Apostle Peter was a sinful man, who later betrayed our Lord Jesus and left his side denying Him. That the 'church' is the 'ekklesia' or the 'called out assembly of what and who? Certainly not Peter, since even his name (and later character failure) contradicts the idea the church would be 'built' on him since his name 'Peter' in Greek is 'pebble or small stone.' Our Lord plainly said 'Upon this **rock**...' actually referring to the explanatory explanation that it was the declaration '<u>Thou art the Christ the Son of the living God</u>. Yes, Yeshua/Jesus is/was the <u>Rock</u> the church would be built on, and not the apostle Peter.

1 Corinthians 10:1-3 & 4

"...how our fathers were under the cloud...and did all drink the same spiritual drink: for they drank of that spiritual Rock that followed them and that Rock was Christ."

I.e. The church was/is to be built on the Lord Jesus who was God come in the flesh and not Peter. Next we need to look carefully at John 20:23

John 20:21-23
"THEN SAID JESUS TO THEM AGAIN, PEACE TO YOU, AS MY FATHER HATH SENT ME, EVEN SO I SEND YOU. AND WHEN HE HAD SAID THIS, HE BREATHED ON THEM AND SAID UNTO THEM, RECEIVE YE THE HOLY GHOST. WHOSOEVER SINS YE REMIT THEY ARE REMITTED TO THEM, AND WHOSOEVER SINS YE RETAIN THEY ARE RETAINED."

These verses have been so misapplied, and so misinterpreted over the centuries that much damage has been done to the cause of Christ, and the furtherance of the Gospel message. For the fundamentalist evangelical, these verses are merely our Lord commissioning the disciples to understand that the gospel message they would be preaching would result in the forgiveness of sins in their listeners. Of course we cannot disagree with that application of these verses in generality. We do know when the gospel is preached and people respond to the invitation in true repentance and faith, that they become born again believers, and note, they become born again, born into the family of God by the Holy Spirit, the Spirit of God. "That which is born of the flesh is flesh and that which is born of the Spirit, is Spirit..." and "The wind bloweth where it listeth and thou hearest the sound there of but canst not tell whence it cometh or where it goeth, so is every one that is born of the Spirit. John 3:6-8. KJV. First, in order to clearly understand the John 20 verse, one Biblical absolute doctrine which no one should dispute is that...

God and Only God Alone Can Forgive Our Sins!
Mark 2:7, "Why doth this man (Yeshua/Jesus) thus speak

blasphemies? Who can forgive sins but God only?"(**Reader note: Yes Yeshua was God come in the flesh despite what the Pharisees believed about Him**).

Isaiah 43:25, "I, even I am he that blotteth out thy transgressions for my own sake, and will not remember thy sins."

Upon a casual reading of the above verse (23), no doubt the average reader seems to be led to believe that Yeshua/Jesus is giving his disciples the power to forgive (remit or retain) sin. For this reason the Church of Rome has stalwartly maintained that she bestows upon her priests, the power to forgive men's sins in the confessional booth, through apostolic succession. In reality though, that is further from the truth as can be. Unfortunately for this misunderstanding, the confessional booth has been used over centuries by unscrupulous clergy for controlling the masses, especially political figures and leaders, by what is commonly called blackmail. So the question looms, "Well just what then are these verses teaching?" In answering that, we must first again, emphasize that only God and God alone can forgive sin! That in itself is the key to unlock the true meaning of these verses. Before giving what can only be the true teaching of this verse it must be remembered that our God, is a triune God, one God in three persons, three distinct and separate personalities, three in one or one in three, the Trinity. Now the scriptures are clear that the Godhead is in close collusion with each other. In Genesis chapter one, God said, "Let us make man in our image." Clear collusion (some may say 'consultation') among members of the God head. Then later Genesis 11:6-7 we find God saying, "Let us go down...and there confound their language etc." Again clear collusion/consultation between members of the Triune Godhead. Now to explain the real truth found in the John 20 verses. What is clear in these verses is not our Lord Yeshua/Jesus giving the apostles the right to forgive sin in the stead of God, but rather *a monumental breath taking revelation of huge importance to Bible scholars everywhere!*

Our Savior (in anticipation of the coming of the Spirit of God on the day of Pentecost was COMMISSIONING the Holy Spirit to cancel sin under the preaching of the gospel by these same apostles and disciples of Christ whom he was also commissioning to carry the word of reconciliation! I.e. First, our lord was supplying his sacrificial death as an offering for the sins of the world, secondly He was commissioning the disciples to carry that message to the unsaved world, and thirdly was commissioning the Spirit of God to wash the sins of the repentant away and by the power of the Holy Spirit birth them into the family of God.

Certainly it is argued by the Church of Rome, that , "Well our Lord was speaking **to the disciples** when He made this declaration, so then it has to be **to them** that the power to forgive sins must have been given, so God does give our clergy/men of God the power to forgive sins.' Our answer to this objection is found in Matthew 16:23 when our Lord Yeshua rebuked Satan by directing the rebuke to Peter. Peter was not the one guilty of originating the demeaning insult to Jesus when he said as follows:

Matthew 16:22
Then Peter took him and began to rebuke him saying, Be it far from thee Lord this shall not be unto thee.

Clearly 'Satan' was the one who instigated and influenced the thinking of Peter, so though our Lord aimed His rebuke at Peter it was clearly intended for Satan, by "Get thee behind me Satan, thou art an offence unto me, for thou savors not the things that be of God, but those that be of men.

As far as this author knows, this (Jn.20) 'commissioning of the Spirit of God' to forgive/regenerate/save the repentant soul, is one of the few places recorded in the pages in God's word, that one member of the Trinity can be found addressing another member to an action beneficial to man's eternal salvation.

If the Roman Catholic Church were correct in its interpretation of verse 23 then salvation to be obtained by any person would necessarily have to come directly from one of the proclamations/edicts/or blessings from her priests or clergy. Meaning simply that no one could find eternal salvation outside of that church. (In the Church of Rome the 1500 Council of Trent still stands proclaiming that there is absolutely no salvation outside of her folds, thus (supposedly) damning all non Catholics to eternal damnation.)

Of course we are aware that in recent years there has been attempts by the Church of Rome to somewhat modify this position for the 'heathen.') This author myself, experienced the new birth and regeneration in the living room of a Bible study group, without the presence of 'clergy.' Some have found Christ kneeling by their bedside at night, I have led souls to Christ over the telephone, some have been saved/born again driving on the highway, kneeling in a corn field, etc and etc.

So here in these verses, in anticipation of the Day of Pentecost and the descent of the Holy Spirit into the world our Lord was giving His plan of action for the Holy Spirit. I.e. the commissioning of the coming work of the Spirit of God. Remember that the Holy Spirit was coming to convict the world of sin, righteousness, and judgment, and would come to indwell all believers, yea to 'birth' souls into the family of God and as well to make their bodies vessels or yea temples of the Spirit of God! One very essential Biblical fact must be considered and that is...

Protecting the Purity of the Gospel Message
One very important issue that comes to mind in dealing with the subject of the preaching of the gospel is that most Christians have but little idea about the implications of denominational doctrinal differences in the gospel message. It is very plain that the gospel message between different denominations more often than not is very contradictory to each other. The Baptists, Church of Christ, Mormons, Watchtower, Roman Catholic (don't forget the Calvinists etc.) all preach a different gospel

message. To the Baptists salvation is strictly by grace thru faith, plus nothing minus nothing. To the Church of Christ water baptism is essential to regeneration and salvation, i.e. 1. Hear the Gospel. 2. Believe the Gospel. 3.Repent. 4. Confess. 5. Be baptized (by their minister.) To the Mormons salvation is found only in and through joining and being faithful to that organization. Works are an essential element in that group to obtain and keep salvation. To the Watchtower again salvation is obtained by joining their group, and being faithful to their doctrine till death. To the Roman Catholic no one can say they are 'saved' until after death, and that baptism into the church, being faithful to the sacraments of the church, mass, confession etc will ultimately bring one into heaven after death (of course after a stint in purgatory to purge venial or small sins away). No one according to them can say they are 'saved' or 'born again' until after death. Then lastly the Calvinists who deny the gospel is for everyone except the 'frozen chosen' and teach the heresy of forced salvation of a few, and forced merciless eternal/endless torture in the Lake of Fire for eternity for the majority. According to the Calvinists, God, supposedly in His majestic sovereignty, (with no mercy), simply refused to elect/force the majority to be saved. Calvinists claim this idiocy glorifies God! So just how important is the gospel message, and what is the 'purity element' we are mentioning. The apostle Paul made it very clear just how important the gospel is and exactly what it consists of.

1 Corinthians 15:1-4

"...I declare unto you the gospel...by which ye are saved...for I delivered unto you ...that Christ died for our sins...that he was buried...and that he rose again the third day..."

Clearly the gospel is the death, burial and resurrection of Christ, but how important is that message in its purity?

Romans 1:16

"...For I am not ashamed of the gospel of Christ for it is the power of God unto salvation to everyone that believeth (salvation by faith in Christ or Eph. 2:8-9) to the Jew first and also to the Greek."

Clearly we can see that the gospel and what man does with it, makes the difference whether he is saved and goes to heaven, or is damned to judgment in Hell and later the Lake of Fire! So the gospel message and faith (to everyone that *believeth*) in the risen Savior brings the lost to instant/present salvation. Paul made it crystal clear that baptism was not part of the gospel or the gospel message bringing salvation.

1 Corinthians 1:14-17
"I thank God that I baptized none of you but Crispus and Gaius...for Christ sent me not to baptize but to preach the gospel..."

At this point we must ask, "How can the gospel message become impure/tainted or corrupted? To which the answer is simple, 'By adding to or taking away from it.' Simply speaking, if a minister etc. adds one single thing to the gospel, such as 'works/baptism/church membership/penance/indulgence/enduring to the end' or any other thing telling someone that's what is essential for him to do to be saved, then he effectively shuts the door of heaven up to that lost soul by corrupting the gospel. Once a person comes to believe that to be saved is Jesus plus works, or Jesus plus baptism, etc. then his faith is corrupted and God cannot honor corrupted faith, i.e. faith that is fully persuaded that what God has promised He is also able to perform. God cannot and will not honor the preaching of a perverted gospel, nor will He 'birth' into His family that seeking sinner seeing that his faith is not fully persuaded that salvation is by the Lord Jesus Christ, plus nothing minus nothing!

Romans 4:3-5 &20-25
"For what saith the scripture? Abraham believed God, and it was counted unto him for righteousness...but to him that worketh not but believeth on him that justifieth the ungodly his faith is counted for righteousness...He staggered not at the promise of God through unbelief but was strong in faith giv-

ing glory to God: and Being fully persuaded that what he had promised he was able also to perform and therefore it was imputed to him for righteousness. Now it was not written for his sake alone that it was imputed to him, but for us also to whom it shall be imputed if we believe on him that raised up Jesus our Lord from the dead, who was delivered for our offences and was raised again for our justification.

Sadly preachers/teachers of perverted gospels, gospels that are added to or taken away from, thereby corrupt the faith of lost souls and prevent them from coming to Jesus not being 'fully persuaded' and send them to judgment in Hell and later the Lake of Fire! That is the reason that Paul warned the early church that anyone who preaches a false gospel is cursed by God.

Galatians 1:6-9

"I marvel that ye are so soon removed from him …to another gospel…which is not another…but some would pervert the gospel of Christ..if any preach any other gospel than I preached to you let him be cursed…If any man preach any other gospel unto you …let him be accursed."

Lastly to show our Saviors displeasure toward those who would dare pervert the way of salvation by adding to or taking away from the pure gospel message we only need to quote…

Matthew 23:13

"Woe unto you, scribes and Pharisees, hypocrites! For ye shut up the kingdom of heaven against men for ye neither go in yourselves, neither suffer ye them that are entering to go in."

So…whenever someone corrupts/distorts/changes/adds to/takes away from the simple gospel message which is the power of God unto salvation, he necessarily is stumbling parishioners/seeking souls toward being totally disqualified (if you will) to receive the Holy Spirit and forgiveness of sins and the new birth into the family of God! Again, just what is the gospel which is the power of God unto salvation? It is exercising simple faith and repentance in the finished work of Christ, in His death burial and resurrection receiving Him as God and Savior to become born again, plus nothing, and minus nothing. Truly "The just shall live by faith." End.

Please go to our web site universalchristiancurba.com to find our new books on theology including: "The Death of Endless Damnation" which proves eventual universal salvation of all souls, "Abraham the Trinity and Lot Exonerated" proving Genesis 18 clearly presents the Triune God appearing to Abraham, and then two of the Trinity appear to Lot. As well the Bible in these chapters fully exonerates Lot, "The Infamous Rapture Conflict Settled" which proves the post-trib pre-wrath rapture of the church, and "Calvinism the Trojan Horse Within" which exposes Calvinists as (apostates) those we must break fellowship with.

CHAPTER TEN

CONCLUSION

Jesus didn't preach the gospel so the majority of people would burn in Hell/the lake of fire for eternity. Jn. 4:42... "...this one is indeed the Savior of the world."

Jesus in Jn.6:33 is the 'bread' which gives life to the 'world.'

Jesus was God come to reconcile the world to himself, not just a small minority. Universal salvation eventually comes to all. II Cor. 5:19-21 tells us He gave us the ministry of reconciliation and we are to tell everyone that God was in Christ restoring the world unto himself!

Jesus is the Good Shepherd sent to find the lost sheep of the house of Israel. No doubt that He will find every one without exception and bring them into the fold. Lk. 15:4 tells us that Jesus the good shepherd who leaves the 99 in open pasture, and goes after the one lost sheep until He finds it. He has come to seek and save that which is lost. Lk. 19:10, and Matt. 18:11-14.

Jesus came to destroy the works of the devil. Heb. 2:14 tells us that Jesus renders death powerless and destroys the works of the devil. See also I Jn. 3:8. Now if death is to be destroyed then the final lake of fire certainly does not lead to endless death, but yea rather to bended knee and confession unto salvation. "Wherefore God also hath highly exalted Him and given Him a name which is above every name, that at the name of Jesus every knee shall bow (things) in heaven, in (things) earth, and (things) under the earth that every tongue shall confess that Jesus Christ is Lord to the glory of God the father." Phil. 2:9-11 (Here plainly the A.V. is misleading and fails to give a clear indication that 'people' are meant so keep in mind and remember that the unwarranted word 'things' is italicized-not in the Greek so omit)

In closing, the disastrous fruits of the false teaching of endless punishment/damnation have been polluting mankind's concept of Almighty God from the time it was introduced in the early centuries of the church. It has bred atheism in every century, reason being that atheists/unsaved naturally find it easy to reject an all-powerful infinite God, who could/would inflict pain for eternity, as a never-ending punishment for finite sins. The 'Augustinian God' of endless damnation, which the fundamentalists have come to embrace as the true God, is presented to the unsaved world as the true God of Christianity.

That being the case, atheists feel quite comfortable in rejecting such a God! And we may add, rightly so. Infinite punishment for finite sins? Not hardly! Never ending pain can have absolutely no purpose, and could only reflect a viscous vindictive God, who is sadistic, cruel, and unjust in his dealings with man. To say that God is going to torment a soul endlessly for eternity, is to say that God is willing to extend endless anger and wrath on that soul forever endlessly. The scripture is plain that "…The Lord is merciful and gracious, slow to anger, and plenteous in mercy. He will not always chide, neither will He keep His anger forever." Psalm 103:8.

To say that 'man' is the one responsible for his eternal/endless damnation, and not 'God' seems to be palatable enough, except one must remember that All Mighty God is the one who designed and made the place called Hell, along with the duration of man's punishment and as well the degree thereof. Once a man dies, is judged and enters the fires of Hell, he is instantly convinced of his errors and wickedness. Therefore only limited duration of punishment is needed according to their works (wickedness) as Revelation 20 plainly states. Further the doctrine of endless damnation has turned away and deeply offended the Jewish community by inferring that all of their Jewish ancestors are burning in Hell fire for endless eternity since they did not accept Jesus as their Messiah.

The fundamentalists who hold to endless damnation have convinced many myriads of thousands that the Bible teaches endless damnation, and thus have turned many unsaved souls away to false religions and cults. Such teaching as well enforces the mistaken idea that there is an unpardonable sin. Jesus simply taught the blasphemy against the Holy Spirit was indeed a grave sin which was one which would be held against the person who commits it during several ages of judgment, or "…in this world (age) and the world (age) to come."

The Psalmist is clear in many places that the mercy of the Lord endureth forever. Finally, consider the many, many families who have lost a wayward son or daughter etc, and if it was apparent they died in a non-repentant state, and just think of the terrible devastating anguish this false doctrine brings upon them. They, (the families) being taught that death fixes the eternal destiny of a lost soul, are forced to believe that their loved one, is now suffering in Hell-fire endlessly, except long enough to be judged at the Great White Throne Judgment, and then cast permanently into a lake of fire to again be tormented endlessly forever! Consider precious children who are raised thinking that God is one who will force the unsaved into a fiery Hell/lake of fire to be endlessly tortured with pain and suffering!

No doubt when the invitation is given to be saved from such suffering, little children cannot help but attempt to 'come to Jesus' to escape such a terrible fate. Now that is a real problem, since 'escaping such a fate' is not the reason Jesus came to save us, He came to save us from our sins and to reconcile us to God, not to save us from going to Hell 'endlessly forever!'

The bottom line therefore is no doubt that many many children are raised with a false profession of faith in Christ by seeking to be delivered from Hell, rather than to be convicted of their sins and seek deliverance and salvation from the same! This author wonders how many precious children are raised with a false profession of faith, thinking they are saved because they went to the altar, then have gone through life, died and were lost anyway!? Then also there are children who no doubt sit under the 'endless damnation of Hell-fire brimstone preaching and become paralyzed with fear of such a God.

My aunt was one such person. She died unsaved as far as I know. My great grandfather preached endless Hell-fire damnation as she sat traumatized under his ministry (when just a little girl), and as a result totally rejected God and Christ. I often witnessed to her, but her fear with such a concept of God was so predominate that she closed her mind to any idea of coming to Christ. Eventually she became senile and died in a nursing home in her 90's no doubt to all appearances, unsaved having never been born again.

Amazing, that the fundamentalists (damnationists) who teach endless damnation/Hell fire on one hand, present Jesus as the all loving, kind and compassionate caring Savior who willingly and unselfishly laid down His life for ALL. Then on the other hand they teach that this same Jesus (who has all power) will fail in reaching the majority of humanity, and therefore desire to torment them (without compassion) for endless eternity, in fire and brimstone because He couldn't reach them and they didn't accept Him!

The message then becomes Jesus as saying, "Come to me and I will give you free salvation, and if you don't accept me I will be vindictive to the utmost in my dealings with you by putting you in eternal endless torment in a lake of hell-fire and brimstone!" This is the Jesus of the Bible? Absolutely not! Then what about those who have never heard, or those who have been deceived by Satan in a false religion and have perished? Are we to believe that Jesus lines them up on the other side of death, reads them the endless damnation act and sends them screaming into the endless fires of eternal damnation? I think not.

There is no doubt that these will go to Sheol/Hades, that place of suffering <u>to whatever degree they deserve</u>. But rest assured immediately after death, they will instantly see the irrefutable revelation of just who Jesus Christ really is and how much He loved them! The Jesus of the Bible shows infinite love and concern to the lost and dying by promising never to give over to loosing one soul to sin's degradation, even though that soul has died unrepentant.

No doubt after death, and being sent to Hell under the wrath of God, that lost and damned (judged) soul finds so many lessons by suffering in the regions of the damned, so that one day he is truly able willingly and sincerely to bend those knees to Jesus and thank Him for such terrible chastisement/punishment! Yes, punishment under the wrath and anger of Almighty God on the one hand, but on the other punishment done in love with the view of working true repentance with free endless salvation!

Now THAT is the Jesus of John 3:16, one who gives Himself for our salvation, that we would not perish, or as dying unsaved we would not remain in an endless Hell but certainly and eventually come to endless salvation. It needs to be reemphasized here that Sheol/Hades the underworld place of departed spirits, was recognized as such a place starting of course in the Old Testament, and then was spoken of by Jesus in the New. That this place is now only inhabited by the un-regenerate is of course without dispute, since for the saint "To be absent from the body is to be present with the Lord."

What is disputed is that this place is not strictly an environment of burning fiery torment, a place which only serves to torment/punish all who are therein. No! The fact is that parts, levels, or areas of this place do serve as such terrible infernos of pain and suffering for the wicked, but other levels/areas are not! An illustration of being in a country in prison under the sentence of hard labor serves to show such.

To say a person is in that country confined to hard labor, is not to say that all who do go to that country are going to a place of hard labor. It's as simple as that. Those dying in ignorance and with much innocence especially young people/children etc, will be no doubt be dealt with accordingly and fairly so. Eventually they will be regenerated, and no, Sheol/Hades is not akin or a place which can be called purgatory, as only the blood of Jesus can wash away sins.

So which God is yours? One who designed an endless place of torment to inflict unimaginable pain for endless eternity as payback for not accepting Jesus, or one who did so as a place to measure out remedial correction and punishment to bring one to redemption and repentance in Christ Jesus?

Scriptures Teaching Eventual Universal Salvation

1) 1Tim 2:4 God will have all to be saved. (KJV) Can His will be thwarted?

2) 1Tim 2:4 God desires all to come to the knowledge of truth Will His desire come to pass?

3) 1Tim 2:6 Salvation of all is testified in due time Are we judging God before due time?

4) Jn 12:47 Jesus came to save all Will He succeed?

5) Eph 1:11 God works all after the counsel of His will Can your will overcome His?

6) Jn 4:42 Jesus is Savior of the world Can He be Savior of all without saving all?

7) 1Jn 4:14 Jesus is Savior of the world Why don't we believe it?

8) Jn 12:32 Jesus will draw all mankind unto Himself To save only a few?

9) Col 1:16 By Him all were created Will He lose a part of His creation?

10) Rm 5:15-21 In Adam all condemned, in Christ all live The same all?

11) 1Cor 15:22 In Adam all die, in Christ all live Again, the same all?

12) Eph 1:10 All come into Him at the fulness of times Are you getting tired of seeing the word, all?

13) Phl 2:9-11 Every tongue shall confess Jesus is Lord Will not the Holy Spirit be given to everyone?

14) 1 Cor 12:3 All cannot confess except by Holy Spirit

15) Rm 11:26 All Israel will be saved But most Jews don't believe yet!

16) Acts 3:20,21 Restitution of all All only means a few?

17) Luke 2:10 Jesus will be joy to all people Is there joy is "Hell"?

18) Heb 8:11,12 All will know God How long, O Lord?

19) Eph 2:7 His grace shown in the ages to come Have we judged Him before the time?

20) Titus 2:11 Grace has appeared to all Experientially or prophetically?

21) Rm 8:19-21 Creation set at liberty How much of creation?

22) Col 1:20 All reconciled unto God There's that word "all" again.

23) 1Cor 4:5 All will have praise of God What for?

24) Jms 5:11 End of the Lord is full of mercy Is "endless Hell/lake of fire" mercy?

25) Rev 15:4 All nations worship when God's judgments are seen Endless torment is merciful judgment?

26) Rm 11:32 All subject to unbelief, mercy on all All?

27) Rm 11:36 All out of, through, and into Him All into Him?

28) Eph 4:10 Jesus will fill all things Including "Hell?"

29) Rev. 5:13 All creation seen praising God?

30) 1Cor 15:28 God will be all in all What does that mean?

31) Rev 21:4,5 No more tears, all things made new "All" made new?

32) Jn 5:25 All dead who hear will live How many will hear?

33) Jn 5:28 All in the grave will hear & come forth All not equally dealt with?

34) 1 Cor 3:15 All saved, so as by fire All not equally dealt with?

35) Mk 9:49 Everyone shall be salted with fire Including you?

36) Rm 11:15 Reconciliation of the world

37) 2Cor 5:15 Jesus died for all Did He die in vain for some?

38) Jn 8:29 Jesus always does what pleases His Father What pleases the Father? (1Tim 2:4)

39) Heb 1:2 Jesus is Heir of all things Does "things" include people?

40) Jn 17:2 Jesus gives eternal life to all that His Father gave Him How many did the Father give Him?

41) Jn 3:35 The Father gave Him all things (Repeated for emphasis) Study the word "things" in the Greek.

42) 1 Tim 4:9-11 Jesus is Savior of all! Jesus is Savior of all!

43) Heb. 7:25 Jesus is able to save to the uttermost "Uttermost" only for a few?

44) 1Cor 15:26 Last enemy, death, will be destroyed Including "lake of fire" which is "second death?"

45) Is 46:10 God will do all His pleasure Does Old Testament agree with the New?

46) Gen 12:3 All families of the earth will be blessed All means all

Chapter Ten | Conclusion

47) Dan 4:35 God's will done in heaven and earth What can defeat His will?

48) Ps 66:3,4 Enemies will submit to God Can any stay rebellious in "Hell?"

49) Ps 90:3 God turns man to destruction, then says return How can one return from "destruction?"

50) Is 25:7 Will destroy veil spread over all nations All nations?

51) Deut 32:39 He kills and makes alive Kills to bring life?

52) Ps 33:15 God fashions all hearts "All" hearts, including men like "Hitler?"

53) Prv 16:9 Man devises, God directs his steps What about "free will?"

54) Prv 19:21 Man devises, but God's counsel stands So much for "free will."

55) La 3:31,32 God will not cast off forever Why does He cast off in the first place? (1 Cor 11)

56) Is 2:2 All nations shall flow to the Lord's house "All" nations?

57) Ps 86:9 All nations will worship Him "All" nations!

58) Is 45:23 All descendants of Israel justified Including the wicked ones?

59) Ps 138:4 All kings will praise God

60) Ps 65:2-4 All flesh will come to God

61) Ps 72:18 God only does wondrous things

62) Is 19:14,15 Egypt & Assyria will be restored

63) Ezk 16:55 Sodom will be restored to former estate Sounds impossible?

64) Jer 32:17 Nothing is too difficult for Him Nothing? Not even the salvation of all!

65) Ps 22:27 All ends of the earth will turn to Him For what purpose?

66) Ps 22:27 All families will worship before Him Praise His name!

67) Ps 145:9 He is good to all Including your worst enemies.

68) Ps 145:9 His mercies are over all his works

69) Ps 145:14 He raises all who fall Who hasn't fallen in sin?

70) Ps 145:10 All His works will praise Him For "endless torment?"

71) Is 25:6 Lord makes a feast for all people And ALL are invited.

72) Jer 32:35 Never entered His mind to endlessly torture with fire This came from man's mind.

73) Jn 6:44 No one can come to Him unless He draws them You can't "chose" to follow Him.

74) Jn 12:32 I will draw all mankind unto Myself Amen!!!

75) Ps 135:6 God does what pleases Him. It pleases Him to save all that He might be all in all Also… Jesus didn't preach the gospel so the majority of people would burn in Hell/the lake of fire for eternity. Jn. 4:42… "…this one is indeed the Savior of the world." Jesus in Jn.6:33 is the 'bread' which gives life to the 'world.'

Reasons Damnationists Reject and Fear the Doctrine of Universal Reconciliation

Amazing it is that the damnationists usually flee this biblical doctrine, and even instantly refuse to consider any scripture or doctrinal argument in its favor. As well they usually will break fellowship with a good brother or sister who stands firm in their conviction that all will eventually find forgiveness and salvation in Christ Jesus. The following reasons will maybe answer why.

1. Damnationists are usually thoroughly brainwashed into equating the (1611 K.J.V.) words, everlasting, eternal, forever in the English

with the word 'endless.' They have been fully deceived into believing this lie.

2. They usually hang this lie on the one verse of scripture, which says "It is appointed unto man once to die, and after this the judgment" as if this is the only verse in scripture which addresses the issue.

3. To them the idea of post mortem salvation would encourage the unsaved to neglect salvation and delight in profligacy, wantonness and riotous living during their lifetime. (Forget the work of the Holy Spirit in convicting men of sin and bringing them to Jesus).

4. They have been convinced that death is the point at which a person's eternal endless destiny is fixed, even though there is no scripture which supports such an idea as that.

5. They place 100% of the blame for someone going to Hell on that persons head, despite the fact that many factors can be pointed to which influence one's choice or rejection of Christ. Such factors as, ignorance due to not being reached with the gospel before death, being raised in a heathen environment and never hearing the gospel, being totally indoctrinated in a false religion or philosophy, or being enslaved by the power of sin and therefore not wanting to repent, and as well being stumbled by someone else into Hell.

6. They are perhaps in total ignorance of the underlying Greek/Hebrew which contradicts their views, and as well they may be of the "Ruckman" heresy concerning the A.V. that the K.J.V 1611 is superior to any Greek/Hebrew manuscript, and is in no need of further clarification by the original languages.

7. They deeply fear losing fellowship and yea even fear persecution from their local churches over the issue should they begin to question or study these doctrines.

8. They adamantly point to Luke chapter 16 as final destiny for the unsaved after death, but fail to consider in the last chapter in Revelation that all former things 'pass away.'

9. They equate universal Christian restoration/reconciliation to the deadly heresy of Universal/Unitarianism.

Indeed all of this does beg the question to be answered, "Is there any hope for the church to wake up to this sacred doctrine of universal reconciliation before Jesus returns?" Our answer, "If we expose the church to it and are faithful in promoting it, despite persecution maybe there is."

Questions Damnationists Cannot Resolve!

(Is It Any Wonder?)

1. Why cannot damnationists understand there is no justice for countless souls to perish without ever having heard the true plan of salvation, and then be consigned to endless eternal torment in the Lake of Fire?

2. Why cannot damnationists understand that the word 'forever' *may or may not* mean endless, but as well can easily denote 'continuous indefinite,' not necessarily 'endless' duration? (In the English such can be the case).

3. Why cannot damnationists understand the words eternal/everlasting/eternity in the K.J.V. (English words coined in English, 1300 a.d. *see "On Line Etymology"*) didn't have the fixed meaning of 'endless' but rather 'continuous or ages and ages in the original Greek.

4. Why cannot damnationists understand 'endless (aidios *Gk.*)' and 'continuous (aionios *Gk.*)' are words in any language which don't mean the same thing unless used together?

Chapter Ten | Conclusion

5. Why do damnationists exalt the modern definitions of English words, from English dictionaries to reign above the true irrefutable meanings of the Greek/Hebrew scriptures?

6. Why don't damnationists understand that God does not give infinite punishment for finite/temporal sins? At the Lake of Fire men are judged 'according to their works,' (which were temporal) i.e. temporary punishment for temporal sins, that is justice!

7. Why don't damnationists understand that God does not sadistically torment/afflict souls for eternity simply to see them suffer, but rather 'punishes' them with a view of bringing them to sorrow/remorse/repentance/and eventual knee bowing confession unto salvation?

8. Why don't the damnationists understand that Hell/Lake of Fire is not to torture the wicked lost, but rather is a place of judgment unto correction? Is the God of Christianity a sadist? I.e. why don't they understand the Hell of tradition is hopeless and eternal/endless, while the Hell of the Scripture like every judgment of God is corrective, remedial, and restorative?

9. Why don't damnationists understand that Augustinian influence radically and tragically changed the true simple meanings of these few Greek/Hebrew words, and as a result caused nearly all modern post 1500's lexicons and dictionaries, including Strongs etc., to redefine them (rock solid original Biblical words) to have many or a variety of meanings?

10. Why don't damnationists understand the last chapter of the Bible says 'the former things' which naturally includes the Lake of Fire the old heaven and earth *pass away* (are dissolved) and thereafter God creates a new heaven and earth with *no more death*?

11. Why don't damnationists understand that the last enemy to be destroyed is death, and death and the dead in the Lake of Fire are cer-

tainly separated from God therefore cannot endure in such a state for eternity?

12. Why don't damnationists believe that Jesus is *not* willing that any should perish but that *all* should come to repentance? Does not 'all' mean 'all'??

Why??
The Simplicity of Eventual Universal Salvation

1. It has been clearly shown that ALL men, all of humanity are born sinners. "All have sinned."

2. The scripture is abundantly clear that Jesus died for all sinners. "He is the Savior of all men especially them that believe." None excluded here. None can deny this.

3. If Jesus died for all men, then all men must be afforded a valid opportunity to hear, believe and repent, otherwise God could not be fair and just in His dealings with man! The question therefore is, would God provide the means of salvation for all men, only to make it available to some, allowing others to perish in the Lake of Fire forever for eternity without access to the same. To say that is justice is blasphemy against God.

4. "Infinite endless pain and suffering in return for finite sins cannot be just in the scales of God's just dealings with man.

5. After death, all men are irrevocably forced to meet God, and are therefore forced to give ascent to all the Biblical truths which they may have failed to do so while alive, whether by ignorance, deceit by Satan, or by simple procrastination.

6. As well these who neglect or fail to receive salvation while in this life ultimately will be punished for their sins and rebellion against the Lord.

7. The scripture is abundantly clear that God has "no pleasure" in the death of the wicked, and that He is not willing that any should perish, but that ALL men should come to a knowledge of the truth. ALL therefore will have access to the truth of redemption if not in this life, then in the next.

8. Punishing a man according to the degree of his sins is indeed just, as scripture plainly says the wicked are "…judged according to their works." Never does Rev. 20 say man will be punished endlessly for eternity. That is falsely read into the text.

9. The scripture is irrefutably clear that all who die in sin, and die as guilty sinners without being born again, will stand the Great White Throne Judgment and be punished in the Lake of Fire, the crucible which burns away the dross of rebellion and attitude of wickedness unto total submission unto repentance on bended knees before the throne of Almighty God.

10. Finally, at the end of such judgment every knee shall bow, and every tongue shall confess that Jesus Christ is Lord to the Glory of God the Father. Romans 10:13 explains the result of such bended knee and confession. "That if thou shalt confess with thy mouth the Lord Jesus, and believe in thine heart that God hath raised Him from the dead, Thou Shalt Be Saved! What is the LAST enemy that shall be destroyed by our Savior? "DEATH" whether death by separation of body from spirit, or death by separation from God by sin!

11. There are only three possible plans of redemption for mankind. First, Calvinism, or forced damnation and forced salvation. Secondly the Fundamentalist Damnationists idea that God will lose the majority of mankind who will be damned/lost endlessly forever. Thirdly, Eventual Universal Reconciliation where our Lord and Savior Jesus Christ will have final victory over Satan, sin, Hell, death and the grave, thus bringing salvation to all mankind!

The Doctrine of Endless Damnation Breeds...

The false doctrine of endless/eternal punishment breeds not only atheism and agnosticism but also can easily cause a rejection of the fundamental Biblical doctrine of salvation by grace through faith. The unsaved can easily refuse to accept a god who gives infinite punishment for finite sins, or a god who has designed Hell to be a place of sadistic endless punishment for the ignorant, unlearned, or those never exposed to the saving gospel of the Bible, much less for those who have been deceived in the false religions in which they were raised.

The gospel of Christ thus becomes 'tainted' and 'tarnished' along with becoming another gospel! How so one asks? Simple, the true gospel is that Jesus came to die for all sinners, to save all sinners to the exclusion of none, and that He will succeed in doing just that. Anything less would not be the true gospel or good news of the gospel. Thus the doctrine of endless punishment taints the gospel of good news of salvation for all men, to becoming good news that only a small handful will be saved, thus becoming 'another gospel.'

Interesting it is, and very correct as well, once any unregenerate/unsaved person buys into endless/eternal damnationism, then he or she is more easily persuaded of the following:

1. Atheism. Reason being no rational person could honestly believe that a God of true justice and mercy, who as well is all powerful, would endlessly torment souls in fire and brimstone for eternity as payback for refusing to bow to His will and be subject to His laws in a short lifetime. As well all people everywhere see that myriads of non Christian people live and die each and every day, people who are perhaps deceived and totally indoctrinated in false religions and or ignorance.

   Is it any wonder infidels such as Bob Ingersol and Madylyn Murray O'Hair despised and ridiculed damnationist type Christianity? In one of Ingersol's speeches he said, "Christianity has such a contemptible opinion of human nature that it does not believe a man can tell the truth unless frightened by a belief in God. No lower opinion of the human race has ever been expressed." Again he also proclaimed, "The doctrine of eternal punishment is in perfect harmony with the savagery of the men who made the orthodox creeds. It is in harmony with torture, with being flaying alive, and with burnings.

The men who burned their fellow-men for a moment, believed that God would burn his enemies forever. — *Robert Green Ingersoll, "Crumbling Creeds" (Ed. No doubt Ingersol and O'Hair are suffering in Hell today and will continue to be there until the Great White Throne Judgment at which time they will justly be judged according to their works).*

2. Agnosticism. The unsaved can easily see that the majority of different Christian faiths, hold to endless damnationisim, and as well are fully aware of the terms everlasting, eternal, forever and endless etc., in the K.J.V. In considering such, many unsaved become confused how such could be in the light of the scripture which clearly teaches that God is a God of justice, love and mercy. Therefore such a contradiction of thought how God could give infinite punishment for finite sins, drives them just to say, 'Well I just don't know if there is such a supreme being or not.'

3. Annihilationism. For those unsaved who do intellectually hold to endless damnationism, it becomes easy to believe that a God of love and mercy could not possibly mete out endless pain and suffering for eternity to those who die unregenerate/unrepentant. Their thinking becomes the false premise that 'wrath gives way to mercy.' Therefore the terms everlasting/eternal death easily become endless annihilation.

(The real truth here is that God's mercy is as endless as He is, and is still constant even while His wrath may be exercised against the wicked. i.e. True it is, the wrath of God is administered upon the wicked but is superintended by His mercy, which in reality eventually does lead to universal Christian redemption.) No doubt this has given rise to the Watchtower, Seventh Day Adventists and others who hold to this false doctrine of annihilation.

4. Calvinism. Here again, the fact that so many billions have died having been non-Christian etc., does lead many to become Calvinists who also firmly believe in endless damnationism. The thought here is, 'Since death fixes the state of eternity for the non-Christian (which of course is false) and so many die without Christ, and since God is a God of justice He must have some unknown secret for bringing such a small minority to salvation, while endlessly damning the majority. Naturally it follows to these people attracted by Calvinism, that since the Bible does speak of election, then those who have fixed fates of endless punishment must not have been elected. Here again damnationism has bred the false doctrine of Calvinism.

5. Unitarianism. This deadly heresy is easily bred due to an *overemphasis* on the love of God for all, and a *figurative interpretation* of the Bible since there is such a *seeming* contradiction in scripture regarding God's love for the wicked lost, Jn. 3:16 etc., as opposed to the 'everlasting/endless suffering' indicated in what Jesus supposedly said and taught about Hell, (at least according to mistranslated 'Aionios' etc.). Remember Jesus our Lord actually taught 'continuous' or 'ages and ages' of suffering, but not 'aidios' or endless suffering in Hell fire. Here again damnationism is responsible for breeding Unitarianism.

6. Hopelessness. One asks, 'Hopelessness in what regards? Very simple. How many Christian parents, husbands and wives, have lost a wayward rebellious child (etc.) to an early death, only to be taught the damnationist doctrine that destiny is determined at death, or the old saying, 'As a tree falls so shall it be.' What horrible mental pain and anguish they are in to believe that precious loved one is now going to be consciously tormented in fire and brimstone endlessly for eternity?

How devastating to sit in a funeral where the damnationist pastor can only piously say, 'We commit this soul to your keeping Lord and to your will,' while really believing that deceased lost teen etc., is now going to be forever tormented in fire and brimstone. Yea he can offer no comfort to the parents at all. All of this grief especially in the light of I Cor. 15:22, 25-26. Vs. 25, "For as in Adam all die, so also in Christ shall all be made alive." Now how many are/were born in Adam? "All" which is to the exclusion to none! I.e. 'all' are lost in Adam! Then next, how many are made alive in Christ? "All" which is again to the exclusion of none! I.e. 'all' are saved in Christ!

Then verses 25-26, "For He must reign until He has put all enemies under His feet. The last enemy that shall be destroyed is death." Now is not death an enemy of all including the unsaved? Plain it is that after he reigns for 1000 years, once the second death is completed (in which all unsaved will be judged according to their works, and be partakers of), that there will be no more death ever again for all eternity. Rev. 21:4, "...there shall be no more death...neither pain neither sorrow nor crying, neither shall there be any more pain for the former things shall pass away."

How plain it is to see that in Hell/Lake of Fire these things will cease to be once punishment for the unsaved is complete, and their salvation is secured on bended knee and confession unto salvation. "Every knee shall bow, and every tongue shall confess that Jesus is Lord to the glory of God the Father."

Years ago, I was witnessing to an agnostic neighbor who was considerably senior in years. I pressed upon him the importance of receiving Jesus as his personal Savior, and the peril he faced after death of endless damnation in Hell fire. (At that time I was a dyed in the wool damnationist). His attitude was very cavalier, as I asked him what he was going to do when he died if the Bible was right and he was wrong and God consigned him to Hell for eternity. He simply answered, "Well in that case I guess I'll just have to make the best of it." Stunned, and lost for words I could say no more. Here no doubt was a lost soul who had been exposed to the false doctrine of endless damnation and thus was unable to come to Christ.

Here again, naturally it was too much for him to believe that there could be a real God since the one he was taught exists gives sadistically inflicted endless punishment in fire and brimstone for eternity. Therefore due to that heresy, he simply lapsed into disbelief and from what I know, he died in that condition. It becomes easy to understand, that had he had a correct concept of God, he could have been led to true repentance and salvation. The following verse clearly indicates that the fear of God and His tormenting souls in Hell-fire/brimstone for endless eternity is not the basis for man coming to repentance and salvation, since such fear cannot bring true repentance and conversion.

Romans 2:4
> "Or despises thou the riches of His goodness and forbearance and longsuffering, not knowing that the goodness of God leadeth thee to repentance."

Sad it is that so many ministers have the attitude to "...hold them over Hell and roast them" in regards to bringing lost souls to the Lord. May the Lord deliver us from such false notions as this.

Steps in Converting from Augustinian/Romish Doctrine of Endless Damnation to Universal Christian Redemption

Never would this author have believed that in his latter years would he be converted to the doctrine of universal Christian redemption. Interesting it is that Jesus had to '...open the eyes of their *(His disciples/followers)* understanding...' in regards to the fact of His resurrection and all that the scriptures had to say concerning such. My spiritual eyes needed opening as well. Certainly, since I had been exposed to nothing but the doctrine of endless damnation and the contemporary meanings of 'forever, eternal, everlasting etc,' how could I (or anyone else for that fact) come to any different conclusion? Following are the simple steps I went through in coming to the truth.

1. Being raised in the traditional endless/damnationist movement, it was a simple matter of accepting the interpretations of others in regards to the A.V. and other versions, concerning the terms everlasting, eternal, forever, etc. That coupled with the full understanding that God was indeed fair, just, and would treat all men fairly in regards to bringing them the Word of God and salvation should He see they were open to such. Thus the doctrine of endless damnation was indeed plausible, and as well it certainly did produce very strong soul winning evangelistic efforts, especially in believing that any man could drop into Hell any minute, and thus be there endlessly eternally.

2. Being fully aware of the heresy of 'Unitarianism' the false doctrine which says as long as one believes in 'a' supreme god of some sort that it did not matter, and one need not worry about going into Hell fire after death. Thus according to them all would be saved and go to heaven. This awareness and justified aversion of Unitarianism completely blinded this author to even remotely considering U.C.R.

3. Being fully aware that many of those who hold to universal redemption were not of the Unitarian persuasion, the question suddenly came to mind on just how could these good people who believe the Bible, but reject Unitarianism, possibly come to believe in universal redemption. This question of curiosity led me to begin to look at their arguments, to try to understand how they could come to such a seemingly false position.

4. Since I have always been very interested in refuting error, and winning men to Christ, I felt compelled to look into the interpretations/explanations these universalists used on their side to give credence to their doctrine.

5. As I began to search out these arguments in web site after site, suddenly many of these arguments based on the Word of God began to uphold their position. Since the Bible is, at least to this author, the final word on any subject of controversy, I found my basic theological foundation shaken somewhat and thereby challenged to accept some of their scriptures supporting their position. Of course I was still unconvinced yet.

6. The biggest hurdle of course was in the A.V. which I have used for over 50 years and the terms everlasting, eternal, eternity, forever etc. contained therein. I had totally misunderstood these words, thinking that they were properly translated from the original languages into the English. Then as well, it was at the time quite unfathomable that for so many centuries that the church could be so misled on such an important matter. Now however, understanding that Satan is the god of this world and the false accuser/slanderer of man and God, it appears that anything man attempts to do can be flawed, and subject to serious misunderstanding. So with the translation of the Holy Scriptures by fallible man.

7. Of course with my basic belief that 'truth will stand examination' I was eager and willing to converse with my brethren on the subject to see if the Universal Christian Doctrinal position would find any favor in their eyes. Most of those whom I conversed with simply made statements such as, "Well I just don't believe that and never have. And as far as the original languages on the subject I am not a scholar enough to comment on that as well." I sent out dozens and dozens of copies of this book to scholars and theological professors in Christian institutions.

   I asked them to review and give some simple refutation of the U.C.R. position as contained in this book, and as well explained that this book would *not* be published if they could bring some basic Biblical discredit to it. I was amazed that not one of these Christian scholars and leaders, who of course were of the damnationist movement, would give any comment at all on the book. Of course at the publication of this book, now it seems that no one would or could refute it, so it goes to press.

8. I will admit, that coming out and taking a public stand on this subject has been very difficult indeed. The biggest hindrance to coming out on this position, is that no doubt many of my pastor/minister brethren will break fellowship with me, and it is with great sadness I will lose their fellowship and friendship over the matter. No doubt they will class me with the apostate Unitarians.

9. No matter what losses this author will experience over taking this new/old Biblical position, it must be done that our Savior is not to be continued to be looked upon as a sadist God, inflicting endless eternal punishment on those who die without Biblical salvation.

10. It is this authors firm belief that this book, perhaps could be the turning point in bringing the evangelical church into deeper, richer harmony with our Lord Jesus Christ, and prepare her for the coming marriage supper of the Lamb with His bride the church.

Reflecting on what I was theologically as a damnationist, and now what my position is on U.C.R. I am absolutely aghast that I could have slandered my blessed, loving, compassionate Savior by preaching and holding such a corrupt theological perception as the Romish/Augustinian false doctrine of endless punishment. Of course the question is asked, 'Do you still have the same burden for lost souls now that you are of the U.C.R. position.' To which I answer, 'Yes of course, but now it is tempered, and I have much more patience in attempting to reach the seemingly incorrigible type lost souls.'

As well I notice that the radical fear that I may send someone to an endless Hell by not witnessing to him is gone, praise God. Actually, as a damnationist one can come to no other conclusion. My great fear now for the lost is the same as say a firefighter seeking to save someone in a fire from death, pain and suffering. Also as well there is the deep fear of someone continuing in sin and depravity, ruining their lives (and the lives of others) in sin, disease, shame and suffering by not coming to Christ, and of course in them going for ages and ages to that terrible place of suffering and pain 'Hell,' and later the Lake of Fire! Lastly, as a damnationist I am now shocked at the sadistic thirst I had at times, relishing and rejoicing in the thought that the unrepentant wicked unsaved would be cast into fire and brimstone for eternity!

Yes, glad indeed that they would be tormented eternally! Now the truth is, being 'glad' a man goes to Hell/Lake of Fire can only be righteous if one is 'glad' that the truly justified pain and suffering is going to bring the sinner to a better end. What better end? Simple, the end being humility and remorse, and finally being brought to total submission on bent knee with confession unto salvation. My 'gladness' therefore as a damnationist was indeed sadism, nothing more and nothing less.

Why Not Include All/Any Sadism in Hell?

Damnationists readily agree that our Lord Jesus has created Hell/LOF to torment the unsaved for eternity in liquid fire and brimstone. This author then asks why shouldn't Jesus have used needles and pins to say pierce the eyes and under the fingernails of the lost wicked continually for eternity? Why should he not have created torture racks or any other hideous form of torture such as flesh tearing/eating beasts, angels with slashing swords all bringing constant unbearable pain and suffering on the unsaved, or to forever splash some flammable liquid (like gasoline) on them and set them ablaze when the fire dies down? This is what Jesus could have given to the unfortunate victims of His supposed endless torture in the place called Hell?

'Oh!' The damnationists say, 'Such would be to sadistic for Jesus to have done,' but then they promote and extol Him as the creator of Hell/LOF to mercilessly soak people in liquid fire and brimstone for eternity as payback for not accepting Him due to their rebellion and or ignorance! We shudder at the hideous acts of barbarism the ISIS terrorists inflict on people, but their acts of unutterable pain and suffering come to an end when their victim dies, but the damnationists 'Jesus' supposedly immerses those who reject Him in liquid fire and brimstone and mercilessly torments them day and night for all of eternity! Sorry but the Word of God contains no such a sadistic Lord and Savior Jesus Christ.

You Must Be a Greek Scholar?

Must we as Christians, be Greek scholars in order to study the English in the light of the original languages to be proficient in Biblical truth? That is absolutely not true. The 'scholars' who promote the heresy of endless damnation piously tout such nonsense. We ask them a simple question. Do they understand exactly how an automatic transmission works before they use it? What about electricity? What about their cell phones or computers or any other devise they use daily? Cannot someone successfully use an automatic transmission going from one place to another without understanding exactly how it works?

Suppose there were a law restricting anyone from using anything unless they understood everything possible to know about it? Utter nonsense you say? Yes we agree, but why shouldn't the same apply to we who are not scholars in the original languages as we seek truth from God's word? Are there not scholars who have settled these issues for us to understand? While the author of this book does not claim to be a scholar in the original languages, he certainly has based the Biblical doctrine of universal Christian redemption on the Word of God in the original languages, and as clearly reflected in the English translations thereof.

Good men who do know the original languages such as Dr. J.W. Hanson, have readily upheld and exonerated this Biblical doctrine with incontrovertible exegesis and logic!

So in the final analysis, having covered all of our bases, please allow me to ask you the reader the following question: Just who is going to define the word 'aionios?'

1. The Webster dictionary? The original meaning of 'aionios' is determined by an English dictionary? So that 'aionios' means, eternal, perpetual, forever, endless etc. etc.???

2. By Strong's concordance which clearly gives ways the translators determined just what English word should best represent 'aionios?' World, age, eternal, forever, endless etc.?

3. By Augustine and Calvin (or the Latin the 'sacred' language of the Roman Catholic Church), knowing they held to the heathen/pagan doctrine of endless merciless punishment by a sadistic god and demanded 'aionios' to be translated as eternal/endless?

4. By all of the above?

5. Or by none other than our Savior, the Word of God which became flesh and dwelt among us?

This author for one, will choose only number five as the final authority for the true and only meaning for 'aionios' and Jesus certainly did not indicate that it meant endless duration, but rather 'quality' of continuous life when receiving the new birth into the family of God. Notice what Jesus said in John 17:3.

"And this is life eternal _that they might know thee_, the only true God and Jesus Christ whom thou hast sent."

Clearly this hotly debated word does not mean 'endless' but rather denotes the 'quality' of life one comes into when they embrace Biblical salvation in Christ Jesus our Lord.

Reader note: 2/09/15. The world was shocked beyond belief recently when the Jordanian pilot was put in a cage and burned alive by ISIS militants. He was a true

Muslim and no doubt not a born again Christian. So the eternal damnation torment in fire and brimstone doctrine would have us believe that Jesus our Savior, after this pilots hideous death, puts him in a cage called Hell/Sheol and soaks him in fire and brimstone, burning him alive forever for eternity without mercy?! ISIS in such a case is shown to be merciful to end the pilot's physical torment in this life only to have Jesus continuing his suffering in fire and brimstone for all eternity??? This is our compassionate Savior who wept over lost Jerusalem but one who supposedly burns the unsaved in liquid fire for eternity? Temporal remedial punishment yes, eternal/never ending punishment no. One last note here. In some countries of the world criminals are punished strangely and by what we consider as cruel and unjust punishment. Cruel and unjust punishment in our American society and judicial system is rightly scorned and rejected. Say to cut a man's hand off for stealing a pack of cigarettes, to throw a gay man off a roof top to kill him or surgically remove his sex organs, or to put a man to the guillotine or saw his head off as ISIS is doing we look upon as cruel and unusual and unusual punishment do we not? So why should we believe that God/Jesus places the unsaved who have perhaps only lived 10-70+ years or so in a liquid lake of fire and brimstone and burn/scald them head to toe for endless eternity, thereby giving them infinite punishment for finite sins?? This is the conclusion of the corrupt doctrine of Augustinianism by which the Christian church has been polluted. God save us from this hideous indictment of God/Jesus our blessed compassionate Savior who will have all men be saved and come to a knowledge of the truth.

Lastly the Old Testament Plainly Teaches...

"All the ends of the earth shall remember and turn to the Lord; and all the families of the nations shall worship before him." (Psalm 22: 27)

"All your works shall give thanks to you, O Lord ... You open your hand, satisfying the desire of every living thing. The Lord is just in all his ways and kind in all his doings. ... My mouth will speak the praise of the Lord, and all flesh will bless his holy name forever and ever." (Psalm 145: 10, 16-17, 21)

"On this mountain the Lord of hosts will make for all peoples a feast of rich food, a feast of well-aged wines ... And he will destroy on this mountain the shroud that is cast over all peoples, the sheet that is spread over all nations; he will swallow up death forever. Then the Lord God will wipe away the tears from all faces, and the disgrace of his people he will take away from all the earth." (Isa. 26:6-8)

"By myself I have sworn, from my mouth has gone forth in righteousness a word that shall not return: 'To me every knee shall bow, every tongue shall swear.' " (Isa. 45:23)

"From new moon to new moon, and from sabbath to sabbath, all flesh shall come to worship before me, says the Lord." (Isa. 66:23)

"For from the rising of the sun to the setting my name is great among the nations, and in every place incense is offered to my name, and a pure offering, for my name is great among the nations." (Mal. 1:11)

The Final Question...

The final question is then, 'does the god of endless damnationism exist?' The answer is an emphatic yes! He exists as a pagan false god who ultimately gives up in defeat and frustration not being able to reach woo and win all of mankind to salvation. Then His son (supposedly the Lord Jesus Christ the promised messiah) is a sadist WHO BURNS and torments the lost with fire and brimstone endlessly for all of eternity because they reject him. Such an imaginative 'god' is not worthy of love! No doubt satan laughs at those who ignorantly worship such a god, an impotent sadist god who doesn't really exist. Is this false god going to give the judgment of infinite punishment in fire and brimstone for eterntiy to men who have had only maybe 100 years or less on earth, men exposed to and trained up in a false religious culture of nefarious and false doctrine? Men whom the church was unable to reach with the gospel in this lifetime (and let no one claim the church reaches all men with the gospel in any generation)?

On the other hand we Praise God for the true Lord and Savior Jesus Christ, the true God who is the ultimate victor over sin, Hell and the grave, one who is not willing that any should perish but that all should come to KNOW and receive the truth. This Biblical Jesus will thus universally woo and win all of mankind to Himself. He and He alone is the only true just and merciful God of the universe. He and He alone is truly

EPILOGUE

Why Witness to the Lost Since All Will Ultimately Be Saved Anyway?

The above disgraceful false and yea fairly blasphemous-anti Christ accusation has been spoken to this author in respect to this book and the doctrine of universal Christian salvation. This sentiment is usually spoken from the lips of those who have no real heart for winning the lost to Christ, and who don't really care about the true peril the unsaved face on a daily basis. Suppose that my neighbors are born again Christians, a fine family of good godly parents and children.

Suppose one dark night an intruder sets their house on fire while they sleep. Then say, I see what is happening and yawning, say "Well it's late and I am in for the night, and as well they are saved and will certainly be in heaven shortly, enjoying the beauties of heaven seeing their dearly departed families." Anyone with an ounce of sense would rightly argue, "Your neighbors are about to be mercilessly murdered, and you are going to stand by and do nothing? How wicked of you! You have become compliant in their execution and murder." They would be exactly right. Then another scenario, say the same family was not saved, not born again, and someone was quietly in the middle of the night setting their house ablaze. So I seeing it say, "Well they are unsaved and will go to Hell and later the Lake of fire, but they will be saved in the end anyway, so I won't get involved."

How bad is that in being compliant in watching people be murdered while I do nothing? Consider first the horrible pain, fear and suffering they experience while the raging fire burns their lungs, their flesh and snuffs their life out, parents and children alike. Consider that after their death they will be sent by the Lord as lost souls to dwell in a literal Hell, and later be judged and punished according to their works in the Lake of Fire. Now who in their right mind would want that to happen to any human being saved or lost? The first murderer said, "Am I my brother's keeper?" Then also the scriptures say, "Thou shalt love thy neighbor as thyself." Certainly we are our neighbor's keeper. Certainly we are to rescue the perishing, and possibly turning a lost soul or souls away from a ruined life of sin, into a healthy godly, Christ like life, and thereby glorifying our blessed Savior who indeed died for sinners. It is well to remember Jude 23.

Jude 23

And …others save with fear, pulling them out of the fire, hating even the garment spotted by the flesh.

So we are to believe that the unsaved dying in their sins deserve to 'burn in hell fire and brimstone and later the lake of fire for eternity?

The damnationists (those who believe the lost are going to be tormented in Hell fire for eternity with no mercy from God or Christ), are quick to say, "Well they chose to reject Jesus and so are really the ones choosing to spend eternity in the Lake of Fire." To this we must say the following:

1. No human has ever chosen to be tormented in Hell fire for eternity. No human would do such a thing making such a choice, or ever would whether he believed in that evil doctrine or not.

2. Our Lord it plainly says in Revelation 4:11, has **pleasure** in everything He created, whether in heaven or earth. The incontrovertible truth is that Jesus/Yeshua a. Created the place called Hell/Sheol the place of the departed unsaved spirits, and b. He also necessarily created the conditions therein for those going there! Now it is plain from the scriptures and has already been pointed out in this book,

Epilogue

that the scriptures teach there are levels of Hell/Sheol, and as well the conditions therein are not the same at all levels, else there would be no 'levels.' I.e. not everyone going to Sheol/Hades after death as an unsaved person, will have the same level of pain and suffering, and as well the upper levels no doubt have little or no 'fiery torment to those not worthy of such. Our God is a merciful God and will not **undeservedly** inflict pain and suffering on anyone, whether in this life or the next.

3. True, Sheol is not heaven, but it is still awaiting place for those souls to eventually stand the White Throne Judgment, which no born again Christian will have to face. After the White Throne Judgment and those resurrected lost souls from the dead are punished "according to their WORKS" (not infinite punishment for finite sins), when that punishment is completed, they will gladly bend their knees and embrace the Savior giving confession unto salvation the new birth, and therefore the right to enter the new Heaven and Earth! So...the damnationist has a real problem with this verse 11. The word 'pleasure.' There are only two possibilities that our Savior would have 'pleasure' in that place He indeed created. First possibility, according to the damnationist, He has pleasure that the lost souls in Hell/Lake of Fire are in excruciating pain and suffering for eternity for rejecting Him. That not only makes Him happy they are suffering for eternity (if the damnationists are right), but that He is rewarding them infinite punishment for finite sins, and as well makes Him a sadist, as one who inflicts pain and suffering on people and enjoys doing so. Or the second possiblility... as the position of this book, is that yes He does have pleasure in the place He designed, but for a different reason. His pleasure is really pleasure that the suffering the lost will experience in Hell/Lake of Fire, will ultimately bring humility, submission and repentance and then the glorious new birth immediately after they end their suffering in the

Lake of Fire. Yes this is the second death, and the fact is that 'death cancels death' since our Lord destroys that as His last enemy.

1 Corinthians 15:25-26
> For He must reign till He hath put all enemies under His feet.
> The last enemy that shall be destroyed is death.

Again, we must emphasize the fact that the damnationist believes that the unsaved lost will experience 'eternal never ending death' and tormenting pain for all of eternity as pay back for not accepting Jesus as Lord Savior and God. This 'eternal never ending death' actually is totally contrary and contradicts the scriptures which are plain that after the new heavens and earth 'death and pain will be no more!

Revelation 21:4
> And God shall wipe away all tears from their eyes and there shall be **no more death,** neither sorrow, nor crying **neither shall there be any more pain** for the former things shall pass away.

May the reader of this book, please seriously consider your personal relationship with the Lord. It is so important to understand that all of us, are either in a state of salvation, having been born again at some point in our life, or we are lost and without Christ, and may not even fully realize our true condition. Following are simple steps to secure your immediate salvation, providing you are sincere and honest before God.

1. First it must be realized that true salvation does not reside in any church, church institution, or ordinance. Salvation is only found in the Savior, the Lord Jesus Christ. He and He alone is the Savior of the world, and in Him and in Him alone is there salvation. Good works, church membership, prayers, church ordinances, or whatever cannot bring salvation, nor even help bring salvation to a lost soul. The angel told Mary, "Thou shalt call His name Jesus for He shall

save His people from their sins." Jesus also said, "Him that cometh to me I will in no wise cast out..." John 6:37, and Matt. 1:21.

2. All without exception who are truly born of God, and are born into His family by the new birth, have the Holy Spirit indwelling in their body. "Know ye not that your body is the temple of God and the Spirit of God dwelleth in you..." The scripture is plain as well, "If any man has not the Spirit of God he is none of His for the Spirit of God dwelleth in him." If you do not positively know that the Holy Spirit dwells in you then you are not saved nor are you a child of God. I Jn. 3:24, 4:13, 5:10. Also Romans 8:9. I Cor. 6:19.

3. Simply admit that you are a sinner, as we all are, and that Jesus died to save you from your sins. Romans 10:13 says, "For whosoever shall call upon the name of the Lord shall be saved." Then pray the sinner's prayer or one amounting to the same thing and God/Jesus will save you now! Pray as follows

Sinners Prayer

Dear Lord Jesus. I know that I am a sinner and need to be saved. I know you are God the Son and came to die for my sins so I am asking you to come into my heart and save me, and please wash all my sins away in your precious blood. I do hereby accept you as my God and Savior and by your strength will live the rest of my life for you.

Dear Holy Spirit. I ask you to come into my heart, and wash away all my sins in the blood of Jesus Christ. I know He died for my sins and do hereby accept Him as my Savior and King. Please come to live in my body making it the temple of God for the rest of my life. I ask you to come into my body, soul and spirit to save me forever more.

Dear Father in Heaven. Thank you for sending Jesus to die for my sins. I do hereby accept Jesus your son as my personal Savior and Lord. Thank you for receiving me into your family for eternity. I give my life to you from this day onward. In the name of Jesus Christ I pray. Amen.

Readers note: Just how far has today's Christian perception of the Biblical Jesus been perverted and distorted? It takes only a look at characterizations of our blessed Lord by artists and the doctrinal positions of the damnationists. We see shameful pictures of a shaggy long haired bearded man hanging on walls and adorning Christian literature. Shameful pictures they are since the scriptures plainly teach that it is a shame for a man to have long hair! (I Cor. 11:14). Paul taught the church at Corinth (under the inspiration of the Spirit of God), that "... for it is a shame for a man to have long hair." Jesus is therefore seen to be an effeminate looking man, one who ignores the very scriptures which He as also a member of the Trinity gave under divine inspiration through the Holy Spirit! For Jesus to have violated God's very plain command for a man to not be effeminate would have made Him to have sinned in the way He wore His hair. While Jesus probably had a beard, rest assured it was trimmed and neat, and His hair was short, not long. Then in the doctrine of the damnationists, He is made to be a sadist since all who disagree with Him will ultimately be sent to endless torture in fire and brimstone, in a place He engineered and designed, and in a place which is supposedly run by Him. Then lastly He is portrayed by their doctrine to have pleasure in the death of the wicked since He supposedly wants to endlessly torment/torture the unsaved forever endlessly after death! Now that certainly is not the Biblical Jesus!

Work Sheet References for Defeating Damnationists, Watchtower/Seventh Day Adventists, Annihilationists and Calvinist Doctrinal Positions

1. **A Debate Between Damnationist and Christian Universalist.** A Damnationist and a Christian Universalist debate use of 'eternal.' Pages 145.

2. **Aion the Time Greek Word and Root.** 'Aion' root for 'Aionios' is a 'time' word unless modified to a different understanding. Page 85. See also top page 126.

3. **Aionios and Aidios Two Different Words.** 'Aionios and Aidios' strictly defined and are not the same words, and do not mean the same thing. Chapter 3, page 79 and on. Also page 83 third ppg. Greek for 'endless' defined.

Epilogue

4. **Aionios and English Equivalants.** English equivalents to 'aionios' in the Greek. Page Bottom of page 137.

5. **Aionios Wrongly Translated Differently K.J.V.** 'Aionios' and incorrect translations in K.J.V. pages 96-99. Page 104.

6. **All Israel Shall Be Saved, No Exceptions.** Israel (every seed) shall be saved. Page 156.

7. **A.T. Robertson and A.B. Bruce Correct Matt. 25:46.** A.T. Robertson and A.B. Bruce Greek scholars verify perversion of Matthew 25:46. Page 107-109, and 117.

8. **Baptizo and Aionios in K.J.V.** 'Baptizo and Aionios' unclear trans... Page 140-141.

9. **Calvinists and the Non-Elect??** For Calvinists: No such thing as someone being 'non-elect.' Page 51-52.

10. **Christian Universalist and Damnationist Debate Eternal in the K.J.V.** Christian Universalist and Damnationist debate eternal damnation K.J.V. Pages 288-299.

11. **Damnationist Doctrine Discourages the Death Penalty.** The death penalty discouraged by endless damnationists. Page 173.

12. **Death is Annihilation?** *If* death is 'annihilation no problem since Jesus cancels, reverses, does away with such making the condition opposite of what Watchtower/etc. claim death is, which is 'annihilation or ceasing to exist,' (or separation from God as the Damnationists teach). This clearly means that ALL of humanity will 'not cease to be' or 'will not be separated from God forever.' Page 102-106.

13. **Damnationists Unwittningly Adding to Gods Word.** Damnationists unwittingly adding to God's word. Page 219.

14. **Elect Only are Drawn/Come to Jesus?** Jesus said He would draw ALL men unto Himself, God cannot fail to draw all to salvation in Christ. John 12:32

15. **Eternal/Everlasting Added.** 'Eternal/forever/everlasting/eternity' added to English language in 1300's. Pages 119-121.

16. **Eternal/Everlasting Improperly Drawn.** The words 'eternal, forever, eternity' shown to be improperly drawn from 'aionios.' See 'In A Nutshell' page xli.

17. **Eternal Life and Everyone Has It?** Everyone has eternal life!?? Page 143-144.

18. **Every Knee Shall Bow.** Every knee shall bow, and every tongue shall confess...Isaiah 45:21-25, Romans 14:9-11, Philippians 2:9-11.

19. **Four Gods of Modern Christianity.** The four 'Gods' of modern day Christianity. Page 122.

20. **Hell, Grave, and Pit Mean the Same?** 'Hell,' 'grave' and 'pit' from the Greek point of view, not the same. Page 10-12. 'Gehenna' the Jerusalem garbage dump and its parallel to 'Hell' pages 13-15, also page 17-18 and points 3, 4, 5. Also chastening children and delivering them from 'sheol.' (Certainly not the grave or pit.) Proverbs 13:24; 22:15; 23:13,14 page 74.

21. **Hell is Endless?** 'Hell' a place of endless torment or punishment? Page 41-45.

22. **Hell is the Grave?** 'Hell' is the 'grave?' Page 31-36. ('Sheol' translated 65 times as 'Hell,' 'grave' and 'pit.') The English determines the Greek meaning or vice versa?!

23. **Hell/Lake of Fire the Refiners Fire Not Gods Torture Chamber.** 'The Refiners Fire" Page 172 bottom.

24. **Hitler and the Jesus of the Damnationists Paralell.** Hitler and the 'Damnationists Jesus' parallels. Page 153.

25. **In Adam All Die, in Christ All are Made Alive, All Means All!** In Adam all die, in Christ all made alive, all means ALL. I Cor. 15:22. Page 197.

26. **Jesus Made False Claim of Severity of Judgment?** Severity of punishment shown by Jesus must mean something or nothing! Page 17 (and points following).

27. **Jesus Taught Aidios/Endless Punishment?** Jesus never taught 'aidios' or 'endless' punishment. Page 77-83.

28. **John 3:16 and the Truth It Teaches.** John 3:16 clarified. Page 135.

29. **Jude 14 and Jesus Comes to Convince Not Torture.** Jude 14 Jesus comes not to endlessly torment lost souls, but 'convince' them. Page 182 & 207 pg.2.

30. **J.W. Hanson Greek Scholar and Aionios.** J.W. Hanson Greek scholar. Pages 223-274.

31. **Lake of Fire Ceases to Be.** The Lake of Fire ceases to exist after it's purpose of punishing according to works is fulfilled according to Revelation 20 and shown to cease to exist in chapter 21:4. The damnationists add to God's Word by saying that the Lake of Fire will continue for eternity. No such scripture exists! Pages 26-29 and page 133 bottom page following.

32. **Lake of Fire Destroys Death.** The Lake of Fire destroys (cancels) death, it does not produce it. Points 6 and 7 page 22.

33. **L.I.D. and E.d. Examples in K.J.V.** L.I.D and E.D. examples. Page 123-125.

34. **Lake of Fire to Torment Souls Eternally/Endlessly?** Nowhere scripture states that the Lake of Fire torments people eternally/endlessly. Page 23, point 10 and following. Also Preston Eby pages 54-67. (No endless torture for millions). Also pages 127-135.

35. **Luke 12:47-48 Teaches Endless Damnation? No!** Page 157.

36. **Many Scriptures Teach Universal Salvation!** Scriptures teaching universal salvation pages 318-322.

37. **Mark 9:43-48 Teaches Endless Torment?** Mark 9:43-48 teaches endless damnation? "...if thy hand offend thee cut it off...two hands cast into Hell fire where the worm dieth not and the fire is not quenched etc..." Page 141-143.

38. **Matthew 25:46 Incorrect Translation.** Matthew 25:46. Page 107 on.

39. **Mercy of God Ends After White Throne?** God has no pleasure in the death of the wicked Ez. 38:11, and His mercy is without ending Psalm 106:7. All will be saved. Ps. 145:9, "The Lord is good to all and His tender mercies are over all His works."

40. **New Heavens and Earth Containing Continuing Eternal Pain and Suffering Endlessly/Forever?** No! There will be no more pain, sorrow or death in the new heavens and earth. Death will be swallowed up in victory. I Corinthians 15:25-26, and 54-55.

41. **Old Testament Plainly Teaches U.C.R.** Page 339.

42. **One Lord/God and Savior Not Two.** Jesus our Lord is known as 'God and Savior.' I Jn. 5:20 and Jude 25. Acts 20:28. See also Isaiah 43:10 and 21-25, and Jn. 1:1 and verse 14.

43. **Origin of Endless Punishment in Jesus Day.** Origin of 'endless punishment' in Jesus' day. Page 37.

44. **Red Hot Coals in the Eyes of a Dog and False Watchtower Claim.** J.W.'s and being cast forever into Hell-fire same as red hot coals in eyes of dog. Point 2 of page 15.

45. **Revelation 14:10-11 and Forever Means Endless??** Revelation 14:10-11, "...and he shall be tormented with fire and brimstone in the presence of the holy angels, and in the presence of the Lamb. And the smoke of their torment ascendeth up forever and ever:

and they have no rest day nor night, who worship the beast and his image and whosoever receiveth the mark of his name." This is not speaking of endless torment, but rather limited/undetermined 'time' (aion/aionios) punishment. Page 86. See also page 127 Eby comments.

46. **Revelation 21:4.** Revelation 21:4 the Lake of Fire and all former things pass away. Page 180.

47. **Rich Man and Lazarus Luke 16.** Luke chapter 16. Bottom page 91.

48. **Romans 5 Teaches Universal Christian Redemption.** Romans 5 examined on pages 5-10 proves that '...all are sinners' and that since Christ died for 'all' then 'all will find righteousness in Christ.

49. **Soul and Spirit is the Body?** The 'soul/spirit' is not the 'body.' Page 45-48.

50. **Strong and His Failure.** Strong's failure to properly define the Greek in many cases. Pages 83-86.

51. **The Last Enemy To Be Destroyed is Death.** The last enemy 'death' is cast into the Lake of Fire. Eby comments bottom page 282.

52. **The Tale of Three Kingdoms.** The "Tale of Three Kingdoms." Page 174-179.

53. **Unpardonable Sin? No!** No permanently unpardonable sin, but yes unpardonable for two ages. Page 99-100.

54. **Unquenchable Fire is Endless Fire?** Unquenchable fire is endless fire? (Eby) Page 193.

55. **White Throne Endless Torment Judgment?** Lost souls at the Great White Throne judgment are not judged 'eternally' but rather 'according to their works.' Revelation 20:12-13. Pages 130-134.

56. **White Throne Judgment for Only Unsaved?** Proving not all are unsaved at the White Throne Judgment as most Damnationists claim. Page 70 and on.

57. **Yes the God of Endless Damnation Does Exist!** Does the God of endless damnation exist? Yes indeed! Page 340.

58. **Yes, Break Fellowship With All Calvinists.** Page 273. Calvinism is a subtle satanic attack upon the Deity of Christ. Page 280.

59. **Yes the Doctrine of Endless Damnation Breeds and Has Bred the Worst Cruelty Shown by History.** Pages 301-311.

Epilogue

The Death of Endless Damnation

THE 'CHRISTIAN CHURCH' IN DISSARAY-2018

2018 sadly finds the "Christian Church" in a sad state of disarray. On the one hand, many churches/denominations vociferously claim to believe the absolute authority of the Holy Scriptures, but are at odds one with another on doctrinal issues. On the other hand many have watered down doctrinal positions, and don't take much of a stand on any Biblical truth. It could be said they stand for nothing and fall for everything. If ever the professing church were able to come together, the true Christian born again type that is, we would see real revival sweep our land. Below are a few very divisive issues which no doubt quench the working of the Spirit of God.

1. Calvinism, or double predestination, where God supposedly forces (they use the word 'elects') only a select few to be saved, and then consigns (doesn't elect yes forces) the majority of humanity to be tormented in fire and brimstone for eternity, only because He supposedly for some secret reason decides (according to His sovereignty) not to save them. In reality, Calvinism is an attack on the deity of Christ by inferring He lied when He preached to the multitudes that "any" of them could be saved, while really knowing He only elected a certain few to be saved. The apostate Calvinist message therefore is: "If you are elect you will be saved, otherwise don't worry about it as only time will tell if God elected you or not."

2. Damnationism. Those traditional Baptists and most others of the Christian faith holding to the doctrine of endless torment in hellfire and brimstone for eternity for those who were not reached with the saving gospel of Christ before they died. According to damnationists it doesn't matter whether the lost ever had a chance to be saved, that they can justifiably be eternally damned by a gospel they never had a chance to reject. They accept the false reasoning that 'aionios' (Greek for continuous/indefinite duration/ages and ages) can only mean 'endless.' Admittedly aionios can mean endless *if modified* to mean such, (as it is in John 3:16 i.e. 'shall have everlasting/aionios life <u>in Christ</u> *the modifier*) but normally it is a 'time word.' It means indefinite duration or temporary and will end as in 'everlasting mountains' or where the servant will serve his master 'forever' when his ear is pierced with the awl etc.

3. The health/wealth/prosperity type ministries. If you are not healthy and wealthy it is only because you don't have the faith to overcome health and financial problems. Of course they want you to give to their ministries to have financial prosperity and good health. Paul had some health problems until the end, and as well there were many poor needy Christians in the early church such as widows etc, and the church was to help provide for them, not condemn them for some lack of faith.

4. King James onlyism, making the 1611 A.V. (as a translation) an idol equal to the original autographs, and supposedly superior to any existing Hebrew/Greek manuscripts. Also known as Ruckmanism.

5. So called 'divine healers' who would never darken the door of a hospital to use their so called healing powers. Yes God can and does heal at times, but no one has the absolute Biblical gift of healing today where the dead are raised, and the stone blind are made to see etc.

6. Baptismal regeneration or 'water salvation.' The false idea that baptism brings salvation and the new birth, and/or no one can be saved without being baptized.

7. Conditional salvation or a salvation one can lose if he or she becomes unfaithful to the Lord.

8. Charismaticism, or the false doctrine that 'speaking in tongues' is a gift for today, when the only true Biblical 'gift of tongues' is the gift to speak in another language without first formally or informally learning it. To those who claim they speak in some heavenly language, or an angelic language, the Word of God says we are *not* to speak in an *'unknown'* language (I Cor. 14:9) nor are to speak words which Paul said (as when he was caught up to the third heaven and heard such II Cor. 12:4) are *not* lawful to utter. Some false teachers say one must speak in tongues as evidence that they are saved and have the Spirit of God.

9. Unisexism. The flourishing unisex society in (dress and conduct) creeping into the church. God doesn't care about dress code for Christians? A unisex society is becoming welcome in the churches with effeminate long haired men and with women dressing as men! Two people walking down the street together holding hands, indistinguishable from which sex they are. Some so called Christian churches performing gay weddings!? Two cities in the Bible were incinerated with fire and brimstone from God out of heaven, because they were unisexual sodomites. No! God does care, and His word plainly says so. Deut. 22:5, The woman shall not wear that which pertaineth to a man, neither shall a man put on a woman's garment, for all that do so are an abomination unto the Lord thy God." (Cross dressing). If men wore women's dresses and skirts to church, like say skirts tailored for men with a fly and hip pocket for his wallet, they would be scorned. Certainly a double standard with women wearing pants to church. Some who will defy the Word of God on this matter probably say, "Well that is an Old Tes-

tament standard only." Today men are fortunately not drifting to women's dresses and skirts (yet) but many women more and more are seeking to defeminise and dress as close to men as they can. (Are the 10 Commandments O.T. standards only?). One day men and women (especially those married) may realize that the more opposite they dress from each other, the more attraction (and happiness) will be precipitated drawing them closer together. Is it any wonder men lose interest in their masculine/defeminized wives, and their children have same sex attraction problems? (Naturally the ungodly/unsaved mock those who uphold the Word of God and its forbidding same sex attractions and sexual activity.)

10. Deconstruction of the local church slowly replacing it by internet and television. Only one question needs to be asked here. "If internet and television did not exist, by what percent would church attendance and fellowship "not" increase? Zero Percent? No doubt it would dramatically increase! Sadly many Christians are not responsible enough to fully stand behind their local church, but would rather opt out to enjoy the luxury of their living rooms, coffee and television set, with their television 'pastor' bringing them a universalist/non conflicting palatable/pacifist message. While there are some very good solidly biblical programs on television or internet, many are of the health wealth prosperity, positive only/never negative ministries, happy to take viewers tithes and offerings which should go to the local church. The value of the local church pastor can be seen when those supporting the television ministries need a biblical marriage counselor, a pastor to officiate a wedding or funeral, or one to visit them or their loved ones in the hospital. They should try calling their television 'pastor' to come to their aid, or ask them for financial assistance! The scriptures tell us "Not forsaking the assembling of ourselves together as the manner of some is."

11. Electronic/emotional sabotage disrupting/destroying the family unit. How so? Simple. Husbands and/or wives can very easily

establish romantic/emotional relationships on the internet. This generally results in adultery, court battles, bitter divorce, devastated uprooted children and then a family unit decimated and out of church. While the old saying is true, "The grass looks greener on the other side of the fence," more often than not there is a devastatingly high price by going there.

12. Women 'pastors' violating the sacred scriptures for a woman not to teach or usurp authority over the man but to learn in silence etc. See Timothy. Many women readily shedding their femininity dressing as men with short hair and pants, preaching and teaching to 'mixed' (men women and children) congregations. No doubt women can be scriptural and 'teach' other women and children, but not men. Most men are not attracted to a defeminized wife, and suddenly his 'manly' wife wonders why their romance has disappeared and she is soon facing divorce proceedings, with her husband taken aback by some "sweet and very feminine young thing."

13. Pastors seeking to build up their congregations by conforming to worldly unspiritual heavy metal 'rock and roll so called gospel music.' Lowering their standards of dress and conduct for members so as not to 'offend' and drive someone off, or not to attract new members (no matter what the cost). As well these pastors are not teaching/leading in personal soul winning and evangelism, thinking lowering standards will draw more people. (Plainly attempting to build a large congregation of worldly 'Christianized' lost souls). Worse of all, Pastors/Christian ministers gaining fabulous wealth from 'ministering to the needs of the flock.' In 11 Kings, Elisha refused to be 'paid' for his services of seeing Naaman the Syrian leper healed. His servant Gehazi saw his refusal to accept the gold etc from Naaman and followed him a good distance away from Elijah's presence and then begged the gold etc. Of course Naamam happily gave Gehazi the wealth he wanted, but when Elisha found out, he cursed him with leprosy the rest of his life. A pastor being fed, clothed and sheltered, is a far cry from him amassing great

wealth and fortune from his ministry to God's people as so many of today's televangelist ministers. Jesus didn't own a stone to lay His blessed head on, a far cry from pastors amassing wealth today. (Gehazi wealth).

14. Then there is very serious departure from the only gospel for salvation by the late Billy Graham. *(Graham's early ministry however was very fruitful thankfully winning many to Christ).*

Billy Graham's Apostasy Unfolds In 1978

(We quote as following from carm.org:) As indelicate as it might be to ask, is Mr. Graham's error the result of old age; or is this error something that he has taught before? Consider the following spoken by Graham in 1978:

> "I used to play God, but I can't do that anymore. I used to believe that pagans in far-off countries were lost – were going to hell – if they did not have the gospel of Jesus Christ preached to them. I no longer believe that. I believe that there are other ways of recognizing the existence of God – through nature, for instance – and plenty of other opportunities, therefore, of saying "yes" to God."

> (James Michael Beam, "I can't play God anymore." McCall's (January 1978): 158, as cited in a pdf by Kurt A. Edwards in a dissertation for doctor of philosophy at the Bowling Green State University. Pages 65-66.) Clearly Graham taught heresy in 1978. Pagans without the gospel are not saved. We do not find God through nature - which is why we have the Scriptures and the preaching of the Gospel. Billy Graham's sentiment is worldly and not biblical. It is a shame that he began teaching this false doctrine.

And Then... Graham's Further Admission of Apostasy to Bob Schuler Pastor of the Crystal Cathedral 1997 Interview

BOB SCHULER: Tell me what you think of the future of Christianity.

Billy Graham: Well Christianity and being a true believer I think there is the body of Christ which COMES FROM ALL THE CHRISTIAN GROUPS AROUND THE WORLD OR OUTSIDE OF THE CHRISTIAN GROUP. I think that everybody that loves Christ or knows Christ whether they be conscious of it or not, they are members of the body of Christ. I don't think we're going to see a great sweeping revival that will turn the whole world to Christ at any time. I think that James the apostle answered that at the first Council at Jerusalem when he said that God's purpose for this age was to call out a people for His name and that is what God is doing today. He's calling people out of the world for His name whether they come from the Muslim world or the Buddhist world or the Christian world of the non believing world they are members of the body of Christ because they've been called by God. THEY MAY NOT EVEN KNOW THE NAME OF JESUS BUT THEY KNOW IN THEIR HEART THEY NEED SOMETHING THEY DON'T HAVE AND THEY TURN TO THE ONLY LIGHT THEY HAVE AND I THINK THEY ARE SAVED AND THAT THEY'RE GOING TO BE WITH US IN HEAVEN.

BOB SCHULER: This is fantastic to hear you say that there is wideness in God's mercy.

Foot note: If you the reader agree with this false theology, you disagree with Jesus. Jesus said, "I am the door, by ME if any man enter in he shall be saved..." and also "...if any man climb up any other way the same is a thief and a robber." Also, "For there is one God and *one* mediator between God and man *(not two or many ways as above,ed.)* the man Christ Jesus," and finally "Neither is there salvation in any other, for there is none other name under heaven given among men whereby we must be saved." Tim. 2:5, John 10:9, 10:1, Acts 4:12. Sad that we have a fast developing corrupted church mentality allowing us to exegete our own personal theology, contrary to the Word of the Lord. Romans 16:17 clearly tells us to "... mark them which cause divisions and offences contrary to the doctrine which ye have learned, and avoid them." So it is not a serious matter when Graham has clearly contradicted Jesus?

Foot note: One more minister has come to mind, who has fallen to apostasy, and that is the Dr. Jack Van Impe. Impe has come to embrace the Church of Rome as being a credible source of truth. One needs only to read the historical birth of this system in the "Two Babylons" by Alexander Hislop. Hislop accurately traces Catholicism back through the time of Christ to Nimrod and his formulation of the false Babylonian system of worship, which was prevalent during the time of Christ. Because embryonic Christianity in the first century was such a formidable contester for the hearts of the people, in order to prosper, that pagan Babylonian system had to morph into a counter but also (still) false system of worship embracing Jesus as their God also. It must be remembered that Nimrod was supposed to be worshipped as the supposedly virgin born son of the infamous lady Semarimus, (virgin born in the sense of no 'earthly' father) who was touted as the queen of heaven. Supposedly, a spirit of the god(s) overshadowed her and she conceived giving birth to Nimrod. Eventually Nimrod married his mother so he not only was the son but the father as well and king. Thus the priesthood, prayers for the dead, confession to the priest, salvation by good works, a virgin birth bringing a god/son into the world to be worshipped etc, all had already become ingrained into the Babylonian false system of worship by first century a.d. (As well this pagan system of worship also held to the doctrine of eternal/endless torment after death to those outside her folds.) Revelation tells us that this system of worship was called "Mystery Babylon mother of harlots" and her location is given as being on seven hills/mountains, which is where Rome is located. See Revelation 17:9 and chapter 18. During the great tribulation she will be destroyed by the forces of the 10 kings under the leadership of the anti-Christ. Quoting from carm.org, quoting Van Impe: He (Van Impe) excitedly exclaims, "You Catholic people listen to your priests... Thank God for these Catholic leaders, The Catholic doctrine is right on!" Then according to TBN's Jack Van Impe (program) he says the Vatican's doctrines are wonderfully correct. He says, "I believe this book," Van Impe tells the audience holding high the New Catholic Catechism." "The Catholic doctrines are right on," he adds.

Who turned Van Impe around to the Papacy's way of thinking? Why, it was the Pope himself Van Impe reveals:*"Pope John Paul II has given me real direction in my life." "He is a giant of the faith,"*says Van Impe.

In an article for the October-December 1995 issue of Foundation Magazine Van Impe offered praise to Pope John Paul II and praise for the Pope's plan for unity among all "Christians" and the establishment of a "world church." John Paul II, whom evangelicals like Van Impe have praised, trusted Mary instead of Christ for his eternal destiny. In a

February 1980 addendum to his Last Will and Testament of March 6, 1979, John Paul II entrusted "that decisive moment [of death] to the Mother of Christ and of the Church [and] of my hope. In life and in death, Totus Tuus [totally yours] through the Immaculate." Embroidered inside all of his robes was the phrase, Totus tuus sum Maria, "Mary I am all yours." His Apostolic Letter of Oct. 16, 2002, ended with these words:

"O Blessed Rosary of Mary, sweet chain which unites us to God, bond of love which unites us to the angels, tower of salvation against the assaults of Hell, safe port in our universal shipwreck, we will never abandon you. You will be our comfort in the hour of death: yours our final kiss as life ebbs away. And the last word from our lips will be your sweet name, O Queen of the Rosary of Pompei, O dearest Mother, O Refuge of Sinners, O Sovereign Consoler of the Afflicted."

Instead of obeying Jude's command to "earnestly contend for the faith once delivered to the saints," Van Impe, will not raise his voice against heretical denials of the true faith. Only one Savior, the Lord Jesus Christ, not Mary who admitted to being a sinner, needing a Savior like all of us, nor was she the 'mother of God.' "God" has/had no mother. Luke 1:47 Mary says, "My spirit hath rejoiced in God my Savior." (Were 'God' to have had a mother as Rome falsely claims, then Mary would indeed be Deity worthy of worshiping and praying to).

AGES-ETERNAL-ETERNITY-EVERLASTING-EVER-FOREVER-EVERMORE

This author (myself) sees a real problem with most of these seven words or /phrases in the English language. It seems quite apparent at least in the English language, that most English speaking people unconsciously equate the above words/phrases with the preconceived false definition of absolute total endlessness, except probably 'ages' (or ages and ages!)

The problem with making all of these English word translations from the original Greek (or the original Aramaic Peshitta) to all of them meaning absolute endlessness is in serious error. They do not all mean the same thing and are not all equal to each other in English meaning/equalivance. The early Greek (and Aramaic) manuscripts prove that. Also it is well to point out that the original Aramaic is even clearer to that end. It is an indisputable truth that our Lord Jesus never used the term 'endless' (in His original language/ tongue) to signify the duration of punishment for the wicked in the coming final judgment, the Lake of Fire (nor in Hell at that). "Long term" yes, "indefinite duration" yes, "ages and ages," yes, but not permanently/endless punishment in Hell or the Lake of Fire! Notice the following verse in Matthew. 25:45

MATTHEW 25:46

And these shall go away into everlasting punishment, but the righteous into life eternal.

Going to Strongs exhaustive concordance, the reference to eternal is as pertaining to the underlying Greek, '166 (aionios) defined by Strong as "...world, perpetual, Messianic period present or future, age, course, eternal, (for) ever, everlasting, world (began) without end etc. These two English words 'eternal and everlasting' in this verse no doubt are commonly defined as permanent, no end, forever and ever endless by most English speaking people. This author (myself) never had one ounce of idea that the Greek 'Aionios' in this verse meant anything other than endless, permanent absolutely time without end. I do believe that most English speaking people have the same take on the underlying Greek behind eternal/everlasting, as well as the dozens of times in the New Testament it is translated differently (coupled with different English words). The very important point to remember is that the adjective eternal/everlasting underlying the English is the Greek 'Aion' (again see Strong's) which is a time word with a beginning and an ending. I.e. 'Literally 'day and night.' The simple fact is that in itself, it cannot literally mean 'permanent/forever, never ending, unless it is modified to mean such.

Simply said to say differently is to add to the divinely inspired text. Yes, there is punishment in both places, (Hell and the Lake of Fire) but such punishment which is not remedial but rather retribution. Yes retribution or 'payback' for wickedness, but remember that such payback can also be remedial in its end effects. It must be remembered 2 Thess. 1:9 is not referring to Hell or the Lake of Fire but to our Lord's return at the rapture, and His raining fiery judgment down on the wicked lost during the terrible period called 'the great day of His wrath.' (The Lake of fire and the final White Throne judgment is reserved for the unsaved according to their "temporal works." Revelation 20 is very clear that the wicked unsaved dead are resurrected to be judged 'according to their works.') The damnationists sometimes without proof refer to 2 Thess. 1:9 as a proof text that this coming judgment is not temporary but final. Also that its real purpose is not remedial, or meant to be corrective in its end results. The fact is that this verse is not the final judgment. The final judgment is fully retributive or a means to bring full recovery to the lost forcing them to admit to the truth. At the final judgment the scripture is clear, "...Every knee shall bow and every tongue shall confess that Jesus Christ is Lord/God..." The judgment taking place in 2 Thess. take place immediately after the rapture (at the sixth seal) and are fully retributive (payback) but not remedial. The final judgment at the Lake of Fire (Philippians 2:10-11) is remedial and eternally permanent in its effect! What else can the wicked do but bow their knee in humble submission, (with such terrible punishment in the Lake of Fire) and give Jesus the ultimate praise!

This final total (unconditional punishment) surrender by the unsaved at the White Throne Judgment, no doubt happily and gladly precipitates their new birth into the family of God. Romans 10:9-10-13. Eternal Damnationists on the other hand attempt to rewrite God's Word and make Jesus the author of eternal death, which He is not. He is plainly the author of eternal life and the scripture is clear that the last enemy our Lord Jesus destroys is DEATH. NO MORE DEATH... PERIOD... FOR ANYONE! 1 Cor. 15:26-27. Our Lord is not going to be burning the lost with fire and brimstone for eternity! To say the unsaved do choose that fate is a vicious lie and a horrible slanderous accusation against a Savior who loves all men and who would have ALL men to be saved and come to the knowledge of the truth. The damnationists as well reject

Revelation 21:4

"And God shall wipe away all tears from their eyes and there shall be no more death, neither sorrow, neither crying, nor pain anymore, for the former thing are passed away."

Again remember the 'former things' were mentioned which were the old heaven and earth in which included the terrible Lake of Fire.

The word 'retribution' comes from the Latin word 'retribution' which means "Giving back what is due" whether that is reward or punishment. In English it means 'Vengeance or Punishment' for evil deeds done. For those who depend on Augustus Strong for correct translating, it must be remembered that he in his exhaustive concordance, held that the primary focus for his work, was to reveal the English words which were used by the King James translators in their translation of the Greek etc. Of course that approach was no guarantee that the English words used by them (the translators) to represent the underlying Greek would properly and exactly represent the words in the original tongue(s). The curse of Ruckmanism (and King James only isms) rears its ugly head and attempts to give the A.V. 1611 version standing as an infallibly correct translation for us today.(?). No...stop here... yes a wonderful and beautiful translation, but infallibly perfect as a translation (?) not even the King James translators claimed such. The one thing we can be sure of is that the A.V. 1611(when rightly divided) can perfectly gives us 100 % clarity on every Bible doctrine we can study from it

AGE OR AGES

John 17:3, "And this is (Aion) eternal life that they may know You, the only true God and Jesus Christ whom You have sent,"

In this phrase "eternal (Aion) life" it is plain to see the adjective Aion modified as by 'to know' indicating life eternal' being 'in Christ' thus in knowing Jesus is endlessness aions. John 17:3.

We will start with the word 'age' which comes from the Greek word 'aion.' In this verse and many others in the English translation the word 'eternal' here, is from the Greek 'aion' which is a time word, of indefinite or long term duration but which in itself does not mean 'endless.' John 3:16 uses the Greek 'aion' or 'aionios' (translated as eternal) to indicate indefinite long term duration, which when coupled with the salvation in Christ forces it to carry the idea of 'endlessness' in regards to the salvation we have in Jesus. The word must be modified to carry the meaning of endlessness! That is the same throughout the rest of the New Testament wherever it is used as 'forever,' or 'everlasting,' This word must be modified to carry the meaning of endlessness! It's no wonder damnationism has so manyfollowers.

We say again that 'Aion', in the original language is an age, or era (plainly an 'age or time word' not endless or eternity) which signifies a period of indefinite duration, or time viewed in relation to what takes place in that period. It certainly cannot have as foremost meaning 'endless.' So 'Aion' is well established as a 'time word' and not an indication of endlessness! (Again, unless it is plainly modified by a word referring directly to God/Christ etc., or that which plainly is eternal in itself such as our salvation in our Lord.)

This force attaching to the words is not so much that of the actual length of a period, but to that period marked by spiritual or moral characteristics. (Much of this is from Vine's Expository Dictionary of New Testament Words.) Also it must be noted that this phrase in the original must be consistently used with its sense of 'indefinite duration.'

REVELATION 20:10 AND FOREVER AND EVER

Where the beast and the false prophet are and shall be tormented day and night forever and ever…

The damnationists love to use this verse also to teach endless damnation in hell fire and brimstone for all of eternity but the original language does not bow in that direction. Yes, no doubt long term, indefinite duration punishment according to their temporal works in the Lake of Fire, but not endless. We find in Vine's expository of New Testament words that he shows the same underlying Greek uses the terms, '…unto the ages of the ages, …forever and ever…or unto many ages…' The damnationists thus attempt to manufacture a new doctrine of God/Christ meeting out endless punishment for finite sins! Vine shows a few verses along this line, such as Rev. 14:11, Hebrews 1:8, 2 Peter 3:18, Heb. 13:8 etc. (and many others.) These verses were not locked into the damnationists false doctrine of endless punishment. Please see Vines for many more Biblical examples Again, the 'time word' aion must be modified to carry the meaning of endlessness! That is indisputable. So to 'know' in this case Jesus, one has endless life or endless aions or eternities of life!

One very important point most damnationists ignorantly overlook, is the "time" element in this verse, verse 10! Plainly it states "...day and night..." thus the verse points out that the time element in the duration of punishment for the wicked will be "day and night" clearly 'on and on, and on and on' for definite "Time" periods of 24 hours each..." going on and on days and nights of limited duration in punishment. No reference of 'aidios' or endless eternal punishment.

Vine well points out that the two Greek terms, 'aidios' and 'aionios' are two entirely different words and need to be understood as following. He says "Aionios should always be translated as 'eternal' and Aidios as everlasting. He further points out that 'aionios' negatives the end of either a time or space, or of unmeasured time and is used chiefly where something future is spoken of (one day coming to pass), where as aidios excludes interruption and lays stress upon permanence and unchangeableness.' Again, our Lord Jesus never used the description of Hell or the Lake of fire as a place of endless punishment for the lost that go there. For Jesus to reward endless punishment for finite sins would make Him a wicked, vengeful, sadistic God!

Then, lastly there is always the perplexing question of the final fate of the beast, false prophet, and the fallen angels. In the light of the Biblical doctrine of final restoration of all things pertaining to the fall of man. (That all will eventually come to salvation in Christ); It is this author's belief that since our Lord did not die for the fallen angels, that they therefore fall outside the realm of possible salvation. That of course means that just as easily the Lord spoke them into existence that He as well can and no doubt will speak them out of existence in that final day of judgment, when every knee (of mankind) shall bow and every tongue confess unto salvation that Jesus is Lord. In that final day, all things will be made or restored to new for endless eternity.

Detroit Baptist Theological Seminary published an article by a Bill Combs which was called,

THE EMBARRASSING PREFACE TO THE KING JAMES VERSION

Posted by Detroit Baptist Theological Seminary. Mr. Bill Combs. When the King James Version of the Bible came off the press of Robert Barker in 1611, it contained an eleven-page preface titled "The Translators to the Reader." This preface is primarily a defense of the new translation, but it also provides important information about the translators' views on the subject of Bible translation. It is an embarrassment (or should be) to King James-only advocates because it contains statements from the translators that are in direct opposition to the KJV-only position. It is most unfortunate that this preface is no longer included in modern copies of the KJV. This post is the beginning of a series that will examine the actual words of the preface in order to refute the erroneous ideas of KJV-only movement with the words of the translators themselves. But before beginning that examination, I will summarize the contents of the preface.

The preface begins by noting, along with examples, that all new endeavors of whatever kind will commonly face opposition. This is also true for persons who attempt to change and improve anything, even if they are important people like kings. However, the greatest opposition and severest vilification is reserved for those who modify or change the current translation of the Bible, even if that translation is known to have defects.

Next there follows a long section praising Scripture, noting its great value and divine origin. But the perfections of Scripture can never be appreciated unless it is understood, and it cannot be understood until it is translated into the common tongue. Translation is therefore a good thing. Thus, God in his providence raised up individuals to translate the Old Testament into Greek. The Septuagint, though far from perfect, was still sufficient as the Word of God, such that the apostles quoted it in the NT. And even thought the Septuagint was the Word of God, scholars believed it could be improved, which led to the Greek versions of Aquila, Theodotion, and Symmachus, as well as the Hexapla of Origen. Both testaments were then translated into Latin, culminating in Jerome's Vulgate. Finally, the Scriptures were translated into many tongues, in-cluding English. However, the preface observes, the Roman Catholic Church has generally not allowed the Scriptures to be rendered into the common tongues. Recently, they have produced their own translation of the Bible into English though they seem to have been forced to do it against their better judgment due to the number of Protestant English Bibles available.

The preface then returns to the problem of opposition to the new translation, and translations in general, by answering several objections. The main argument against the new translation questions the need for it, that is, since there had already been a number of English translation of the Bible, why is there need for another? If previous translations were good, there should be no need for another; if they were defective, why were they ever offered in the first place? The answer is, of course, that "nothing is begun and perfected at the same time." While the efforts of previous English translators are to be commended, nevertheless, they themselves, if they were alive, would thank the translators of this new translation. The previous English Bibles were basically sound, but this new translation affords an opportunity to make improvements and corrections.

The translators argue that all previous English translations can rightly be called the Word of God, even though they may contain some "imperfections and blemishes." Just as the King's speech which he utters in Parliament is still the King's speech, though it may be imperfectly translated into French, Dutch, Italian, and Latin; so also in the case of the translation of the Word of God. For translations will never be infallible since they are not like the original manuscripts, which were produced by the apostles and their associates under the influence of inspiration. However, even an imperfect translation like the Septuagint can surely be called the Word of God since it was approved and used by the apostles themselves. But since all translations are imperfect, the Church of Rome should not object to the continual process of correcting and improving English translations of the Bible. Even their own Vulgate has gone through many revisions since the day of Jerome.

Finally, the translators state the purpose and plan of the present translation. They have not intended to make a new translation, but to make the best possible translation by improving upon previous ones. To do so they have, of course, carefully examined the original Hebrew and Greek since translation should only be done from the original tongues. Also, they did not work hastily, as did the translators of the Septuagint, who, according to legend, finished their work in only seventy-two days. The translators also availed themselves of commentaries and translations of the Scriptures in other languages. In their work they felt it was essential to include marginal notes, despite the fact that some might feel such notes tend to undermine the authority of the Scriptures. These notes are essential since the translators confess that oftentimes they were unsure how a word or phrase should be translated. This is especially true in Hebrew, where there are a number of words which only occur once in Scripture, and even the Jews themselves are uncertain about their translation. And so, as Augustine notes, a "variety of translations is profitable for finding out of the sense of the Scriptures." Lastly, the translators observe that, in spite of criticism from some quarters, they decided not to always translate the same Hebrew or Greek word with the same English word and have retained, over the objections of the Puritans, the old ecclesiastical words like "baptism" instead of "washings." Mr. Combs continues:

In my first post on this subject, I argued that the KJV-only position believes that only the KJV of the Bible is the Word of God, and I suggested that the somewhat official beginning of this movement should be traced to the publication of the 1881 revision of the KJV, the Revised Version (RV).

In my second post, I argued that Dean Burgon might rightly be considered the father of the KJV-only movement. He contended in his book The Revision Revised that the RV must be rejected because in its use of the eclectic Greek NT of Westcott and Hort, the RV had departed from the Traditional Text of the church, the Textus Receptus (TR). According to Burgon's understanding of the doctrine of preservation, the TR must be closer to the original writings than the "grossly depraved" Greek text behind the RV.

In my third post, I remarked that the reason I tie Dean Burgon so closely to the KJV-only movement is that not only did he reject the eclectic text for the TR, like modern KJV-only advocates, but he strenuously objected to the very idea of revising the English words of the KJV, which were to him almost sacrosanct.

In my last post I continued to note that it was not primarily the appearance of new eclectic or critical texts of the NT that motivates KJV-only proponents. Instead, it is the publication of new English versions based on those Greek New Testaments, rather than the TR, that accounts for the continued existence and growth of the KJV-only movement. And as I pointed out, the arguments of Dean Burgon were retransmitted by individuals like Philip Mauro in his 1924 volume, Which Version? Authorized or Revised? But since the RV never really challenged the KJV for dominance, there was not much to which KJV-only advocates had to object in the early decades of the 20th century. This began to change with the publication of the Revised Standard Version (RSV) in 1946, which was itself a revision of the RV, though more particularly of the the American Standard Version (ASV), the American edition of the RV.

The RSV presented a new challenge to the dominance of the KJV. Moody Bible Institute's magazine Moody Monthly praised the RSV NT in 1946. Even the well-known fundamentalist leader John R. Rice initially promoted the RSV in his widely-read paper, Sword of the Lord. From then on a stream of KJV-only literature began to appear: Jasper James Ray, God Wrote Only One Bible (1955); Edward F. Hills, The King James Version Defended (1956); David Otis Fuller, Which Bible? (1970); Peter S. Ruckman, The Christian's Handbook of Manuscript Evidence (1970); etc. Though the RSV was popular in mainline churches, it was not widely accepted in evangelicalism, and not at all in fundamentalism.

The KJV-only movement really exploded in the the 1970s and 80s. Again, it was the appearance of new English Bibles threatening the privileged position of the KJV that explains the growth of the movement. It began with the publication of the solidly conservative New American Standard Bible (NASB) in 1963 (OT, 1971), which was a revision of the ASV. More influential was the New King James Version (NKJV) in 1979 (OT, 1982). While the NASB used the eclectic Greek NT, the NKJV is based on the TR, the same Greek text as the KJV. But no matter, KJV-only proponents criticize the NKJV just as venomously as they do the NASB. Why? Because the NKJV, though translated from the same Hebrew and Greek texts as the KJV, nevertheless, departs from the sacrosanct words of the KJV But dwarfing the impact of those versions was the 1973 publication of the New International Version (OT, 1978). While there have been many English versions of the Bible published since 1611, no English translation ever came close to challenging the dominance of the KJV—until the New International Version (NIV). In 1986 the NIV did what no other version had been able to do in almost 400 years—outsell the KJV. The NIV now accounts for 40% of English Bibles sold. Though not quite as popular, even newer translations like the English Standard Version and the Holman Christian Standard Bible are also selling well, providing further fuel for KJV-only advocates.

Twenty years ago I thought that the KJV-only movement would begin to die out as these new English versions started to take hold among conservative Christians, and more churches made the switch from the KJV. But now I think I was wrong, or at least much too early in my prediction. The KJV still sells very well (second behind the NIV), and KJV-only advocates seem just as vocal and numerous as ever. Googling "KJV-only" produces more than 10 million hits. It appears they will always be with us—or least for a very long time.

THE KJV-ONLY MOVEMENT COMES TO AMERICA

Posted By Bill Combs

In previous posts (here, here, and here), I have argued that the beginning of the KJV-only movement can be traced to the publication of the 1881 revision of the KJV, the Revised Version (RV), and the opposition to it by Dean Burgon, which was set forth in his 1883 volume, The Revision Revised.

Even with the criticism of Burgon and others, the RV was initially well received in England and America. Two Chicago papers, the Tribune and Times, published the entire NT on May 22, 1881. Three million copies of the RV were sold the first year. But as time went on, it became clear that it would not displace the favored place of the KJV in the hearts of most English-speaking people. As Charles Spurgeon perceptively observed, the RV was "strong in Greek, weak in English."

Though the RV was initiated by the Church of England, a group of 34 American scholars assisted in the project. They disagreed with some of the translation decisions, and these were placed in an appendix to the RV. In 1901 the Americans produced their own edition of the RV incorporating the American preferences, which eventually became known as the American Standard Version (ASV).

The KJV-only movement in America is unfortunately associated with fundamentalism, though early fundamentalism was clearly not KJV-only. The name fundamentalism was not coined until 1920 by Curtis Lee Laws, but the founding documents of the movement can be traced to a series of 12 volumes produced between 1910 and 1915 titled The Fundamentals: A Testimony To The Truth. The 90 essays quote from the KJV but also from the RV (or its American edition). The essay on "The Inspiration of the Bible" by James M. Gray affirms: "Let it be stated further in this definitional connection, that the record for whose inspiration we contend is the original record—the autographs or parchments of Moses, David, Daniel, Matthew, Paul or Peter, as the case may be, and not any particular translation or translations of them whatever.

Mauro correctly observes that by 1924 it had become clear that neither the RV nor the American edition, the ASV, were going to offer any real competition to the popularity of the KJV. So although Mauro's book demonstrates the presence of KJV-only sympathies in the USA in the early part of the 20th century, the dominance of the KJV meant there was not much for the KJV-only advocates to be concerned about. As we will see in a future post, it is the appearance of new English versions of the Bible that provided new energy for the KJV-only movement.

There is absolutely no translation without error, nor could there be" One of the contributors to the Fundamentals was a converted lawyer named Philip Mauro. He wrote three essays, one of which is titled Life in the Word (vol. 5). Like other contributors, Mauro occasionally quotes the RV approvingly. However, by 1924 Mauro had a dramatic shift in his thinking as seen in the publication of his book Which Version? Authorized or Revised? The material in Mauro's book is not particularly original, but simply a rehashing of Dean Burgon's arguments. Whereas Mauro previously quoted the RV approvingly, now he strongly condemns it for making "36,000 changes" in the KJV and asks the question, "On what authority" (p. 5). Here we see the common assumption of all KJV-only proponents: the KJV possesses some sacrosanct authority whose text is immutable.

Mauro correctly observes that by 1924 it had become clear that neither the RV nor the American edition, the ASV, were going to offer any real competition to the popularity of the KJV. So although Mauro's book demonstrates the presence of KJV-only sympathies in the USA in the early part of the 20th century, the dominance of the KJV meant there was not much for the KJV-only advocates to be concerned about. As we will see in a future post, it is the appearance of new English versions of the Bible that provided new energy for the KJV-only movement.

BLATANT CALVINIST LIES COURTESY JOHN CALVIN AND AUGUSTINE

Not all men can be recipients of salvation by God's not choosing them to believe and be saved.

1. God/Christ did not intend for all men to be saved.
2. God did not want all men to be saved.
3. Our Lord Jesus did not shed His blood that all could be saved.
4. The Holy Spirit does not draw all men to be saved.
5. Men go to hell for eternity because God did not choose to make them believe unto salvation.
6. Non elect lost souls cannot be saved or come to Christ for the new birth.
7. Lost souls in Hell/Lake of Fire were forced to go there because they were not elected.

CLOSING THOUGHT

For Damnationists Who Proudly Claim the Unsaved Will Spend Eternity In the Lake of Fire

1. The false statement which damnationists claim the lost will 'spend eternity in the Lake of Fire' is a total crucifixion of English word usage.

2. Simply spoken the two words 'spend' and 'eternity' totally contradict each other.

3. How so? Simple. To 'spend' something is indicative of eventually bringing an end to that something.

4. To 'spend' a hundred dollars is to totally extinguish the money from your possession. In other words the money is gone, and gone forever. You have no more use of it unless of course you 'loan' it with the requirement of a full return (probably with interest). In such a case of a loan to someone, it cannot be said that you spent it.

5. In the case of say spending 5 days of hard work, there is a beginning of the daily work, and then in the end of the five days working, no more.

6. So, many many things can be spent, such as money, time, resources, etc. So to indicate something is 'spent' simply indicates that something has come to an end.

7. So...to attempt to say someone will 'spend' eternity contradicts the truth of eternity since eternity cannot possibly end! ETERNITY CANNOT BE SPENT, THERE IS NO BEGINNING OF ETERNITY AND CAN BE NO ENDING THEREOF.

THE SIMPLE FACT IS, THAT NO ONE CAN SPEND ETERNITY in hell/lake of fire...ETERNITY CANNOT BE SPENT! The scripture is clear that the length of duration the lost will spend in the lake of fire is in direct porportion to his works...Revelation 20:13 tells us the lost will be "...judged according to their works. Our Lord cannot reward infinite punishment for finite sins. Remember the lake of fire is part of the old heaven and earth which will pass away with a fervent heat and there will be a new heaven and new earth where dwells no more pain suffering or death/separation from God! Simply put, the everlasting punishment our Lord referred to actually translates from indefinite duration punishment, but not endless. ("Everlasting, Forever" in the original languages clearly denotes 'indefinite duration.')

-LASTLY-

Hard Relevant Questions for Damnationists Who Teach That Death In This Life Permanently and Irrevocably Seals the Fate of the Wicked/Unsaved

1. So...Could 100% of those who enter the place called Hell and later the Lake of Fire, could they have been saved in this life, before they died? *All damnationists emphatically say "Yes."

2. So...If yes, then did not the church fail in winning them to Christ? Remember who our Savior gave the great commission to; it was not to anyone but to His disciples the church! So...will the churches in this life, successfully reach every lost soul who ever lives, by at least giving them the gospel message of salvation yes or no!? All damnationists emphatically say "No, probably not.

3. Is it true that many millions over the centuries have died having never heard the true gospel message, perhaps being raised in false religions or total ignorance and or heathenism? All damnationists emphatically say "Yes"!

4. So it could be said that the 'church' over the centuries has failed in winning many millions to salvation in Christ. So... these millions and millions of billions of not evangelized ignorant lost souls are going to eternally/endlessly perish, to be tormented/tortured burnt in excruciating fire and brimstone without mercy for all of eternity in the torture chambers of Hell, or the Lake of Fire created

by the Lord Jesus Christ!? Isn't that what you believe? All damnationists emphatically say "Yes."

5. So… Is it true that you damnationists do not believe that Hell or the Lake of Fire has any corrective or restorative value in God's placing lost souls there? Also that you believe our Lord's intention in putting lost souls there (in resurrected eternally indestructible bodies) gives the Triune God Head pleasure in inflicting unmerciful extreme suffering on those billions and billions of souls for eternity with no mercy? Remember Revelation 4:11, "Thou art worthy, O Lord, to receive glory and honor and power; for Thou hast created all things, and for Thy pleasure they are, and were created." All damnationists emphatically say "Yes."

6. So…the LORD Jesus created Hell/Lake of Fire and the conditions therein and as well (according to damnationism) finds pleasure in burning people with fire and brimstone (with no mercy) for eternity! This means the damnationist Savior must needs be called a sadist! (A sadist is one who finds pleasure in inflicting pain and suffering upon others).

All damnationists on this point simply deny God is a sadist, but claim the unsaved made the choice to be eternally damned in hell fire and brimstone. So here it is plain that according to them 1.God rewards infinite punishment for finite sins. (Such is justice?). 2. That God allows man's will to overthrow His will when it plainly says, (2 Peter 3:9) The Lord is not slack concerning his promise, as some men count slackness; but is longsuffering to us-ward, **not willing** that any should perish, but that all should come to repentance. (Of course damnationists are quick to say as the apostate Calvinists say that 'all' means only the 'elect.' Thus they add to the Word of God.) 3. That God comes to the end of his (infinite) attributes and gives up in utter defeat in winning those billions and billions of lost souls to Christ. (So this defeated god, the god of damnationists cannot be the God of the Bible!). The Biblical fact is that all of God's painful judgments no matter how severe are yes, corrective, restorative, and judicially correct (and can be vindictive) to lead men to repent and believe on the Lord Jesus Christ for salvation.

7. So...could it be said that our omnipotent, omniscient, omnipresent All Mighty God totally exhausted His abilities and the abilities of His preachers/teachers, evangelists and pastors to reach/convince and win these damned souls to the new birth into God's family for eternity?

All damnationists on this point now have only one of two choices. First, to say yes the Lord is defeated in winning all and believe God is a sadist who has pleasure in the endless torment scenario, or secondly they must be forced to admit our Lord's intention is to save all (eventually) and that, "God is **not willing** that any should perish, but that **all** should come to repentance!. The Lord is *not* slack concerning His promise, as some *men* count slackness, *but* is longsuffering toward us, *not willing* that *any* should *perish, but* that *all* should come to repentance." 2 Peter 3:9.

THE GOD OF THE DAMNATIONISTS SIMPLY IS A FALSE GOD WHO THANKFULLY DOES NOT EXIST AND SADLY THE DAMNATIONISTS DO NOT REALLY KNOW THE LORD JESUS CHRIST WHO SAVED THEM AND BOUGHT AND PAID FOR THEIR SINS -YESHUA THE GOD OF UNIVERSAL CHRISTIAN SALVATION!

THE END

AN INFALLIBLY PERFECT TRANSLATION? AGES-ETERNAL-ETERNITY-EVERLASTING-EVER-FOREVER-EVERMORE

This author (myself) sees a real problem with most of these seven words or /phrases in the English language. It seems quite apparent at least in the English language, that most English speaking people unconsciously equate the above words/phrases with the preconceived false definition to only mean absolute total endlessness, except perhaps 'ages' (or ages and ages!). The English language of today has fairly well permanently convinced most Bible students that the above 7 or so phrases or words can **only mean** permanently/without end. Therefore the early English versions naturally seem to teach endless punishment for the wicked, and who is brave enough to question the early translators?

The problem with making all of these English word translations from the original Greek (or the original Aramaic Peshitta) to all of them meaning absolute endlessness is in serious error. They do not all mean the same thing and are not all equal to each other in English meaning/ equalivance. The early Greek (and Aramaic) manuscripts prove that. Also it is well to point out that the original Aramaic is even clearer to that end. It is an indisputable truth that our Lord Jesus never used the term 'endless' (in His original language/ tongue) to signify the duration of punishment for the wicked in the coming final judgment, the Lake of Fire (nor in Hell at that). "Long term" yes, "indefinite duration" yes, "ages and ages," yes, but not permanently/endless punishment in Hell or the Lake of Fire! Notice the following verse in Matthew. 25:45

Matthew 25:46
>And these shall go away into everlasting punishment, but the righteous into life eternal.

Going to Strongs exhaustive concordance, the reference to eternal is as pertaining to the underlying Greek, '166 (aionios) defined by Strong as "...world, perpetual, Messianic period present or future, age, course, eternal, (for) ever, everlasting, world (began) without end etc. These two English words 'eternal and everlasting' in this verse no doubt are commonly defined as permanent, no end, forever and ever endless by most English speaking people. This author (myself) never had one ounce of idea that the Greek 'Aionios' in this verse meant anything other than endless, permanent absolutely time without end. I do believe that most English speaking people have the same take on the underlying Greek behind eternal/everlasting, as well as the dozens of times in the New Testament it is translated differently (coupled with different English words). The very important point to remember is that the adjective eternal/everlasting underlying the English is the Greek 'Aion' (again see Strong's) which is a time word with a beginning and an ending. I.e. 'Literally 'day and night.' The simple fact is that in itself, it cannot literally mean 'permanent/forever, never ending, <u>unless</u> it is modified to mean such as "...our aionios God."

Simply said to say differently is to add to the divinely inspired text. Yes, there is punishment in both places, (Hell and the Lake of Fire) but such punishment which is not remedial but rather retribution. Yes retribution or 'payback' for wickedness, but remember that such payback can also be remedial in its end effects. It must be remembered 2 Thess. 1:9 is not referring to Hell or the Lake of Fire but to our Lord's return at the rapture, and His raining fiery judgment down on the wicked lost during the terrible period called 'the great day of His wrath.' (The Lake of fire and the final White Throne judgment is reserved for the unsaved according to their "temporal works." Revelation 20 is very clear that the wicked unsaved dead are resurrected to be judged 'according to their works.') The damnationists sometimes without proof refer to 2 Thess. 1:9 as a proof text that this coming judgment is not temporary but final. Also that its real purpose is not remedial, or meant to be corrective in its end results. The fact is that this verse is not the final judgment. The final judgment is fully retributive or a means to bring full recovery to the lost forcing them to admit to the truth. At the final judgment the scripture is clear, "... Every knee shall bow and every tongue shall confess that Jesus Christ is Lord/God..." The judgment taking place in 2 Thess. take place immediately after the rapture (at the sixth seal) and are fully retributive (payback) but not remedial. The final judgment at the Lake of Fire (Philippians 2:10-11) is remedial and eternally permanent in its effect! What else can the wicked do but (gladly) bow their knee in humble submission, (having just experienced such terrible punishment in the Lake of Fire) and give Jesus the ultimate praise!

This final total (unconditional punishment) surrender by the unsaved at the White Throne Judgment, no doubt happily and gladly precipitates their new birth into the family of God. Romans 10:9-10-13. Eternal Damnationists on the other hand attempt to rewrite God's Word and make Jesus the author of eternal death, which He is not. He is plainly the author of eternal life and the scripture is clear that the last enemy our Lord Jesus destroys is DEATH. NO MORE DEATH... PERIOD... FOR ANYONE! 1 Cor. 15:26-27. Our Lord is not going to be burning the lost with fire and brimstone for eternity! To say the unsaved do choose that fate is a vicious lie and a horrible slanderous accusation against a Savior who loves all men and who would have ALL men to be saved and come to the knowledge of the truth. (1 Tim. 2:4). The damnationists as well reject

Revelation 21:4

"And God shall wipe away all tears from their eyes and there shall be **no more death**, neither sorrow, neither crying, nor pain anymore, for the former thing are passed away."

Again remember the 'former things' were mentioned which were the old heaven and earth in which included the terrible Lake of Fire and the experiences of pain and death.

The word 'retribution' comes from the Latin word 'retribution' which means "Giving back what is due" whether that is reward or punishment. In English it means 'Vengeance or Punishment' for evil deeds done. For those who depend on Augustus Strong for correct translating, it must be remembered that he in his exhaustive concordance, held that the primary focus for his work, was to reveal the English words which were used by the King James translators in their translation of the Greek etc. Of course that approach was no guarantee that the English words used by them (the translators) to represent the underlying Greek would properly and exactly represent the words in the original tongue(s). The curse of Ruckmanism (and King James only isms) rears its ugly head and attempts to give the A.V. 1611 version standing as an infallibly correct translation for us today.(?). No... stop here... yes a wonderful and beautiful translation, but infallibly perfect as a translation (?) which not even the King James translators claimed such. The one thing we can be sure of is that the A.V. 1611(when rightly divided) can perfectly gives us 100 % clarity on every Bible doctrine we can study from it

AGE OR AGES

John 17:3, "And this is *(Aion)* eternal life that they may know you, the only true God and Jesus Christ whom You have sent,"

In this phrase "eternal *(Aion)* life" it is plain to see the adjective Aion modified as by *'to know'* indicating life eternal' being 'in Christ' thus in knowing Jesus is endlessness aions. John 17:3.

We will start with the word 'age' which comes from the Greek word 'aion.' In this verse and many others in the English translation the word 'eternal' here, is from the Greek 'aion' which is a time word, of indefinite or long term duration but which in itself does not mean 'endless.' John

3:16 uses the Greek 'aion' or 'aionios' (translated as eternal) to indicate indefinite long term duration, which when coupled with the salvation in Christ forces it to carry the idea of 'endlessness' in regards to the salvation we have in Jesus. The word must be modified to carry the meaning of endlessness! That is the same throughout the rest of the New Testament wherever it is used as 'forever,' or 'everlasting,' This word must be modified to carry the meaning of endlessness! It's no wonder damnationism has so many followers.

We say again that 'Aion', in the original language is an age, or era (plainly an 'age or time word' not endless or eternity) which signifies a period of indefinite duration, or <u>time</u> viewed in relation to what takes place in that period. It certainly cannot have as foremost meaning 'endless.' So 'Aion' is well established as a 'time word' and not an indication of endlessness! (Again, unless it is plainly modified by a word referring directly to God/Christ etc., or that which plainly is eternal in itself such as our salvation in our Lord.)

This force attaching to the words is not so much that of the actual length of a period, but to that period marked by spiritual or moral characteristics. (Much of this is from Vine's Expository Dictionary of New Testament Words.) Also it must be noted that this phrase in the original must be consistently used with its sense of 'indefinite duration.'

Revelation 20:10 and Forever and Ever

> Where the beast and the false prophet are and shall be tormented day and night forever and ever…

The damnationists love to use this verse also to teach endless damnation in hell fire and brimstone for all of eternity but the original language does not bow in that direction. Yes, no doubt long term, indefinite duration punishment according to their temporal works in the Lake of Fire, but not endless. We find in Vine's expository of New Testament words that he shows the same underlying Greek uses the terms, '…unto the ages of the ages, …forever and ever…or unto many ages…' The damnationists thus attempt to manufacture a new doctrine of God/Christ meeting out endless punishment for finite sins! Vine shows a few verses along this line, such as Rev. 14:11, Hebrews 1:8, 2 Peter3:18, Heb. 13:8 etc. (and many others.) These verses were not locked into the damnationists false doctrine of endless punishment. Please see Vines for many more Biblical examples Again, the 'time word' aion must be modified to carry the meaning of endlessness! That is indisputable. So to 'know' in this case Jesus, one has endless life or endless aions or eternities of life!

One very important point most damnationists ignorantly overlook, is the "time" element in this verse, verse 10! Plainly it states "…day and night…" thus the verse points out that the time element in the duration of punishment for the wicked will be "day and night" clearly 'on and on, and on and on' for definite "Time" periods of 24 hours each…" going on and on days and nights of limited duration in punishment. No reference of 'aidios' or endless eternal punishment.

Vine well points out that the two Greek terms, 'aidios' and 'aionios' are two entirely different words and need to be understood as following. He says "Aionios should always be translated as 'eternal' and Aidios as everlasting. He further points out that 'aionios' negatives the end of either a time or space, or of unmeasured time and is used chiefly where something future is spoken of (one day coming to pass), where as aidios excludes interruption and lays stress upon permanence and unchangeableness.' Again, our Lord Jesus never used the description of Hell or the Lake of fire as a place of endless punishment for the lost that go there. For Jesus to reward endless punishment for finite sins would make Him a wicked, vengeful, sadistic God!

Then, lastly there is always the perplexing question of the final fate of the beast, false prophet, and the fallen angels. In the light of the Biblical doctrine of final restoration of all things pertaining to the fall of man. (That all will eventually come to salvation in Christ); It is this author's belief that since our Lord did not die for the fallen angels, that they therefore fall outside the realm of possible salvation. That of course means that just as easily the Lord spoke them into existence at their creation (by Him) that He as well can and no doubt will speak them out of existence in that final day of judgment, when every knee (of mankind not fallen angels) shall bow and every tongue confess unto salvation that Jesus is Lord. In that final day, all things will be made or restored to new for endless eternity.

Detroit Baptist Theological Seminary published an article by a Bill Combs which was called,

THE EMBARRASSING PREFACE TO THE KING JAMES VERSION

Posted by Detroit Baptist Theological Seminary. Mr. Bill Combs. When the King James Version of the Bible came off the press of Robert Barker in 1611, it contained an eleven-page preface titled "The Translators to the Reader." This preface is primarily a defense of the new translation, but it also provides important information about the translators' views on the subject of Bible translation. It is an embarrassment (or should be) to King James-only advocates because it contains statements from the translators that are in direct opposition to the KJV-only position. It is most unfortunate that this preface is no longer included in modern copies of the KJV. This post is the beginning of a series that will examine the actual words of the preface in order to refute the erroneous ideas of KJV-only movement with the words of the translators themselves. But before beginning that examination, I will summarize the contents of the preface.

The preface begins by noting, along with examples, that all new endeavors of whatever kind will commonly face opposition. This is also true for persons who attempt to change and improve anything, even if they are important people like kings. However, the greatest opposition and severest vilification is reserved for those who modify or change the current translation of the Bible, even if that translation is known to have defects.

Next there follows a long section praising Scripture, noting its great value and divine origin. But the perfections of Scripture can never be appreciated unless it is understood, and it cannot be understood until it is translated into the common tongue. Translation is therefore a good thing. Thus, God in his providence raised up individuals to translate the Old Testament into Greek. The Septuagint, though far from perfect, was still sufficient as the Word of God, such that the apostles quoted it in the NT. And even thought the Septuagint was the Word of God, scholars believed it could be improved, which led to the Greek versions of Aquila, Theodotion, and Symmachus, as well as the Hexapla of Origen. Both testaments were then translated into Latin, culminating in Jerome's Vulgate. Finally, the Scriptures were translated into many tongues, including English. However, the preface observes, the Roman Catholic Church has generally not allowed the Scriptures to be rendered into the common tongues. Recently, they have produced their own translation of the Bible into English though they seem to have been forced to do it against their better judgment due to the number of Protestant English Bibles available.

The preface then returns to the problem of opposition to the new translation, and translations in general, by answering several objections. The main argument against the new translation questions the need for it, that is, since there had already been a number of English translation of the Bible, why is there need for another? If previous translations were good, there should be no need for another; if they were defective, why were they ever offered in the first place? The answer is, of course, that "nothing is begun and perfected at the same time." While the efforts of previous English translators are to be commended, nevertheless, they themselves, if they were alive, would thank the translators of this new translation. The previous English Bibles were basically sound, but this new translation affords an opportunity to make improvements and corrections.

The translators argue that all previous English translations can rightly be called the Word of God, even though they may contain some "imperfections and blemishes." Just as the King's speech which he utters in

Parliament is still the King's speech, though it may be imperfectly translated into French, Dutch, Italian, and Latin; so also in the case of the translation of the Word of God. For translations will never be infallible since they are not like the original manuscripts, which were produced by the apostles and their associates under the influence of inspiration. However, even an imperfect translation like the Septuagint can surely be called the Word of God since it was approved and used by the apostles themselves. But since all translations are imperfect, the Church of Rome should not object to the continual process of correcting and improving English translations of the Bible. Even their own Vulgate has gone through many revisions since the day of Jerome. Combs continues…

Finally, the translators state the purpose and plan of the present translation. They have not intended to make a new translation, but to make the best possible translation by improving upon previous ones. To do so they have, of course, carefully examined the original Hebrew and Greek since translation should only be done from the original tongues. Also, they did not work hastily, as did the translators of the Septuagint, who, according to legend, finished their work in only seventy-two days. The translators also availed themselves of commentaries and translations of the Scriptures in other languages. In their work they felt it was essential to include marginal notes, despite the fact that some might feel such notes tend to undermine the authority of the Scriptures. These notes are essential since the translators confess that oftentimes they were unsure how a word or phrase should be translated. This is especially true in Hebrew, where there are a number of words which only occur once in Scripture, and even the Jews themselves are uncertain about their translation. And so, as Augustine notes, a "variety of translations is profitable for finding out of the sense of the Scriptures." Lastly, the translators observe that, in spite of criticism from some quarters, they decided not to always translate the same Hebrew or Greek word with the same English word and have retained, over the objections of the Puritans, the old ecclesiastical words like "baptism" instead of "washings." Mr. Combs continues:

In my first post on this subject, I argued that the KJV-only position believes that only the KJV of the Bible is the Word of God, and I suggested that the somewhat official beginning of this movement should be traced to the publication of the 1881 revision of the KJV, the Revised Version (RV).

In my second post, I argued that Dean Burgon might rightly be considered the father of the KJV-only movement. He contended in his book The Revision Revised that the RV must be rejected because in its use of the eclectic Greek NT of Westcott and Hort, the RV had departed from the Traditional Text of the church, the Textus Receptus (TR). According to Burgon's understanding of the doctrine of preservation, the TR must be closer to the original writings than the "grossly depraved" Greek text behind the RV.

In my third post, I remarked that the reason I tie Dean Burgon so closely to the KJV-only movement is that not only did he reject the eclectic text for the TR, like modern KJV-only advocates, but he strenuously objected to the very idea of revising the English words of the KJV, which were to him almost sacrosanct.

In my last post I continued to note that it was not primarily the appearance of new eclectic or critical texts of the NT that motivates KJV-only proponents. Instead, it is the publication of new English versions based on those Greek New Testaments, rather than the TR, that accounts for the continued existence and growth of the KJV-only movement. And as I pointed out, the arguments of Dean Burgon were retransmitted by individuals like Philip Mauro in his 1924 volume, Which Version? Authorized or Revised? But since the RV never really challenged the KJV for dominance, there was not much to which KJV-only advocates had to object in the early decades of the 20th century. This began to change with the publication of the Revised Standard Version (RSV) in 1946, which was itself a revision of the RV, though more particularly of the the American Standard Version (ASV), the American edition of the RV.

The RSV presented a new challenge to the dominance of the KJV. Moody Bible Institute's magazine Moody Monthly praised the RSV NT in 1946. Even the well-known fundamentalist leader John R. Rice initially promoted the RSV in his widely-read paper, Sword of the Lord. From then on a stream of KJV-only literature began to appear: Jasper James Ray, *God Wrote Only One Bible* (1955); Edward F. Hills, *The King James Version Defended* (1956); David Otis Fuller, *Which Bible?* (1970); Peter S. Ruckman, *The Christian's Handbook of Manuscript Evidence* (1970); etc. Though the RSV was popular in mainline churches, it was not widely accepted in evangelicalism, and not at all in fundamentalism.

The KJV-only movement really exploded in the the 1970s and 80s. Again, it was the appearance of new English Bibles threatening the privileged position of the KJV that explains the growth of the movement. It began with the publication of the solidly conservative New American Standard Bible (NASB) in 1963 (OT, 1971), which was a revision of the ASV. More influential was the New King James Version (NKJV) in 1979 (OT, 1982). While the NASB used the eclectic Greek NT, the NKJV is based on the TR, the same Greek text as the KJV. But no matter, KJV-only proponents criticize the NKJV just as venomously as they do the NASB. Why? Because the NKJV, though translated from the same Hebrew and Greek texts as the KJV, nevertheless, departs from the sacrosanct words of the KJV But dwarfing the impact of those versions was the 1973 publication of the New International Version (OT, 1978). While there have been many English versions of the Bible published since 1611, no English translation ever came close to challenging the dominance of the KJV—until the New International Version (NIV). In 1986 the NIV did what no other version had been able to do in almost 400 years—outsell the KJV. The NIV now accounts for 40% of English Bibles sold. Though not quite as popular, even newer translations like the English Standard Version and the Holman Christian Standard Bible are also selling well, providing further fuel for KJV-only advocates.

Twenty years ago I thought that the KJV-only movement would begin to die out as these new English versions started to take hold among conservative Christians, and more churches made the switch from the KJV. But now I think I was wrong, or at least much too early in my prediction. The KJV still sells very well (second behind the NIV), and KJV-only advocates seem just as vocal and numerous as ever. Googling "KJV-only" produces more than 10 million hits. It appears they will always be with us—or least for a very long time.

THE KJV-ONLY MOVEMENT COMES TO AMERICA

Further Posted By Bill Combs...

In previous posts (here, here, and here), I have argued that the beginning of the KJV-only movement can be traced to the publication of the 1881 revision of the KJV, the Revised Version (RV), and the opposition to it by Dean Burgon, which was set forth in his 1883 volume, The Revision Revised.

Even with the criticism of Burgon and others, the RV was initially well received in England and America. Two Chicago papers, the Tribune and Times, published the entire NT on May 22, 1881. Three million copies of the RV were sold the first year. But as time went on, it became clear that it would not displace the favored place of the KJV in the hearts of most English-speaking people. As Charles Spurgeon perceptively observed, the RV was "strong in Greek, weak in English."

Though the RV was initiated by the Church of England, a group of 34 American scholars assisted in the project. They disagreed with some of the translation decisions, and these were placed in an appendix to the RV. In 1901 the Americans produced their own edition of the RV incorporating the American preferences, which eventually became known as the American Standard Version (ASV).

The KJV-only movement in America is unfortunately associated with fundamentalism, though early fundamentalism was clearly not KJV-only. The name fundamentalism was not coined until 1920 by Curtis Lee Laws, but the founding documents of the movement can be traced to a series of 12 volumes produced between 1910 and 1915 titled The Fundamentals: A Testimony To The Truth. The 90 essays quote from the KJV but also from the RV (or its American edition). The essay on "The Inspiration of the Bible" by James M. Gray affirms: "Let it be stated further in this definitional connection, that the record for whose inspiration we contend is the original record—the autographs or parchments of Moses, David, Daniel, Matthew, Paul or Peter, as the case may be, and not any particular translation or translations of them whatever.

Mauro correctly observes that by 1924 it had become clear that neither the RV nor the American edition, the ASV, were going to offer any real competition to the popularity of the KJV. So although Mauro's book demonstrates the presence of KJV-only sympathies in the USA in the early part of the 20th century, the dominance of the KJV meant there was not much for the KJV-only advocates to be concerned about. As we will see in a future post, it is the appearance of new English versions of the Bible that provided new energy for the KJV-only movement.

There is absolutely no translation without error, nor could there be" One of the contributors to the Fundamentals was a converted lawyer named Philip Mauro. He wrote three essays, one of which is titled Life in the Word (vol. 5). Like other contributors, Mauro occasionally quotes the RV approvingly. However, by 1924 Mauro had a dramatic shift in his thinking as seen in the publication of his book *Which Version? Authorized or Revised?* The material in Mauro's book is not particularly original, but simply a rehashing of Dean Burgon's arguments. Whereas Mauro previously quoted the RV approvingly, now he strongly condemns it for making "36,000 changes" in the KJV and asks the question, "On what authority" (p. 5). Here we see the common assumption of all KJV-only proponents: the KJV possesses some sacrosanct authority whose text is immutable.

Mauro correctly observes that by 1924 it had become clear that neither the RV nor the American edition, the ASV, were going to offer any real competition to the popularity of the KJV. So although Mauro's book demonstrates the presence of KJV-only sympathies in the USA in the early part of the 20th century, the dominance of the KJV meant there was not much for the KJV-only advocates to be concerned about. As we will see in a future post, it is the appearance of new English versions of the Bible that provided new energy for the KJV-only movement.

Last Serious Question For The Eternal Damnationists Who Say God Is Going To Burn Lost Souls In Hellfire/Lake of Fire For Eternity

Say our Lord Jesus were hired by you to be warden over Rikers Island (saying that He ;was still here in bodily form)…the penitentiary for the worst of the worst, the death row cell block. I ask you just what do you as an eternal damnationist say would be the living conditions there in as allowed by Jesus under His watch? Hmmmmm?

*No or little food and water for days and days at a time??

*Unmerciful whippings and beatings for hours and weeks upon weeks??

*Cell temperatures in to the hundreds of degrees constantly??

*Deprivation of sleep and medical treatment??

*Coals of fire spread over prisoners floors him barefoot with fiery liquid brimstone splashed on him at times??

*Never visitation by loved ones but only surrounded by his kind day and night?? Endless suffering??

The Damnationists paint that kind of Jesus over Hell and the Lake of fire for eternity, what a blasphemous insult to our Lord Jesus Christ who in love lay down His life a ransom for all!

BTW high time for the eternal endless damnationists need to wake up and realize …"Eternity cannot be 'Spent."

Simple to understand…that eternity is only a mental concept of time without end. Something that has no ending in itself cannot be spent! To 'spend' something is to totally end its existence such as' spending 50 dollars, or spending a night or a year say on an island…Thus a factual contradiction of terms in the English language where the term 'spend' cancels/contradicts the term eternity! Thus to warn someone they might 'spend' eternity in Hell or the Lake of Fire, is a contradictory lie to say the least! It's always best to speak the truth! This truth irrefutably proves no one can "spend eternity in Hell/Lake of fire!

> The Lord is not slack concerning His promise, as some count slackness but is longsuffering to us ward, <u>*not willing that*</u> any <u>should perish</u> but that all <u>should come to repentance</u>…2 Peter 3:9.

Here the damnationists contradict God's word saying that God *"…IS WILLING THAT BILLIONS PERISH AND BURN IN THE LAKE OF FIRE FOR ETERNITY…"*

BLIND LEADERS OF THE BLIND

I ask the damnationists a very simple question. "Can anyone force Jesus as God to do that which he plainly is not willing to do? No doubt a theological impossibility, but the eternal damnationist arrogantly violates sacred scripture and ignores 2 Peter 3:9 and other verses thus ignorantly painting Jehovah as a God of lies."

We who know the truth, need to break fellowship with, and demand that all Calvinists/ be put out of our churches pulpits and classrooms, unless they repent

Blatant Calvinist Lies Courtesy John Calvin And Augustine as Follows

Not all men can be recipients of salvation since God/Christ did not choosing them to believe and be saved.

1. God/Christ did not intend for all men to be saved.

2. God did not want all men to be saved.

3. Our Lord Jesus did not shed His blood that all could be saved.

4. The Holy Spirit does not draw all men to be saved.

5. Men go to hell for eternity because God did not choose to make them believe unto salvation.

6. Non elect lost souls cannot be saved or come to Christ for the new birth.

7. Lost souls in Hell/Lake of Fire (for eternity) are forced to go there because they were not elected by our Lord due to some supposed secret and unknown decree from the triune God head.

The damnationists plainly reject many many scriptures showing that God will succeed in the end to bring all men to repentance and the new birth into the family of God…

Lastly…

1 Cor. 15:22 tells us that…"Even as in Adam *all* die, even so also in Christ shall *all* be made alive~" All means **to the exclusion of none**, and our Lord plainly said that in Himself all would be made alive (at the end after the Lake of fire every

knee shall bow), and the Bible is clear on ALL that All would be brought to repentance, salvation and the new birth into the family of God. Truly Jesus gives the victory to the will and plan of God to save every man.!

www.ingramcontent.com/pod-product-compliance
Lightning Source LLC
Chambersburg PA
CBHW031400290426
44110CB00011B/223